LEO THE TENTH.

Photogravure from the original painting by D'Urbino.

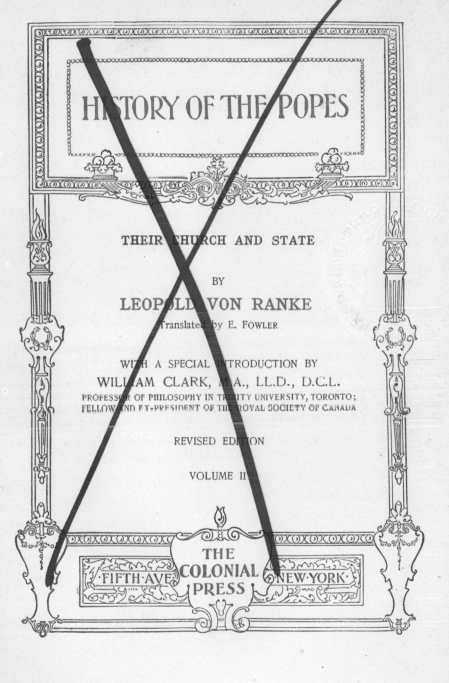

HISTORY OF THE POPES

THEIR CHURCH AND STATE

BY

LEOPOLD VON RANKE

Translated by E. FOWLER

WITH A SPECIAL INTRODUCTION BY

WILLIAM CLARK, M.A., LL.D., D.C.L.

PROFESSOR OF PHILOSOPHY IN TRINITY UNIVERSITY, TORONTO;
FELLOW AND EX-PRESIDENT OF THE ROYAL SOCIETY OF CANADA

REVISED EDITION

VOLUME II

THE
COLONIAL
PRESS

·FIFTH·AVE· ·NEW·YORK·

CONTENTS

BOOK V

BOOK VI

iii

BOOK VII

COUNTER-REFORMATION—SECOND PERIOD, 1590–1630

CHAPTER I

PROGRESS OF THE CATHOLIC RESTORATION, 1590–1617

CHAPTER II

GENERAL WAR—VICTORIES OF CATHOLICISM, 1617–1623

UNIVERSAL EXTENSION OF CATHOLICISM

CHAPTER III

CHAPTER IV

MANTUAN WAR—THIRTY YEARS' WAR—REVOLUTION IN THE STATE OF
AFFAIRS

ILLUSTRATIONS

THE HISTORY OF THE POPES

BOOKS V, VI, AND VII

THE HISTORY OF THE POPES

BOOK V

COUNTER-REFORMATION

FIRST PERIOD, 1563-1589

I N the history of a nation or power, there is no problem
more difficult than that of appreciating correctly the connection of its particular relations with those of the world
in general.

It is true that the individual life of a nation is determined
by causes peculiar to itself, inherent in its nature, and displaying a characteristic consistency through all ages. But each community is subjected to the action of general influences, by which
its progress is powerfully affected.

On this conflict of forces, it is, that the character presented
by modern Europe may be said to have its basis. Nations and
States are separated eternally, on certain points of their existence, but at the same time are knit together in indissoluble
community. There is no national history of which universal
history does not form an important portion. So necessary in
itself, so all-embracing, is the consecutive series of events
through a lapse of ages, that even the most powerful of States
appears but as a member of the universal commonwealth, involved in and ruled by its destinies. Whoever has earnestly
sought to comprehend the history of any people as a whole, to
contemplate its progress without prejudice or illusion, will have
experienced the difficulties arising from this cause. In the several crises of a nation's progressive existence we discern the
different currents that form the sum of human destiny.

3

The difficulty is doubled when, as sometimes occurs, a great movement, agitating the whole world, is originated by an individual power, which then constitutes itself the special representative of the principle actuating that movement. The power thus in action takes then so influential a part in the collective operations of the century, it enters into relations so intimate with all the powers of the world, that its history, in a certain sense, expands into universal history. Such was the epoch upon which the papacy entered at the close of the Council of Trent.

Convulsed to its centre, endangered in the very groundwork of its being, it had not only maintained itself, but found means to gain renewed force. In the two Southern peninsulas, all influences hostile to its ascendancy had been promptly expelled, all the elements of thought and action had been once more gathered to itself, and pervaded by its own spirit. It now conceived the idea of subduing the revolted in all other parts of the world. Rome once more became a conquering power, projects were formed and enterprises engaged in, recalling those proceeding from the Seven Hills in ancient times and during the Middle Ages.

The history of the renovated popedom would be but imperfectly understood, did we limit our attention to its centre only. Its essential importance is best perceived by observing its operations on the world in general.

Let us begin by taking a review of the strength and position of its opponents.

Section I.—State of Protestantism about the Year 1563

On the north of the Alps and Pyrenees the opinions of Protestantism had made vigorous and unceasing progress, up to the time when the Council of Trent closed its last sittings; they extended their dominion far and wide over the Germanic and Sclavonic nations.

Among the Scandinavian races, the tenets of the Protestants had established themselves all the more immutably from the fact that their introduction was coincident with that of new dynasties and with the consequent remodelling of all political institutions. They were received with delight from the very first, as if they bore in their nature some natural affinity with the national disposition. Bugenhagen, the founder of Lutheranism in Denmark, can find no words that suffice to depict the enthusiasm with which his sermons were listened to: " Even on work-a-days " (*Werkeltags*), as he expresses it, " from the first gleam of day the people were eagerly waiting, and on holidays they were in attendance through the whole day." [1] Protestant tenets had now made their way to the most remote countries. It is not known by what agency the Faro Islands were rendered Protestant, so easily was the change effected.[2] In Iceland the last representatives of Catholicism had disappeared by the year 1552, and a Lutheran bishopric was founded at Wyborg in the year 1554. The Swedish governors were accompanied by Lutheran preachers to the most distant shores of Lapland. Gustavus Vasa exhorts his heirs, in his will, made in 1560, to hold fast by the evangelical doctrines, to inculcate the same on their most remote successors, and to admit no false teachers. He makes this almost a condition to the inheritance of the crown.[3]

On the opposite coast of the Baltic also were Lutheran opinions predominant; at least, among such of the inhabitants as used the Germanic tongue. Prussia had given the first example of secularizing church property on a grand scale; this was followed by Livonia, in 1561; the first condition made by the province on its submission to Poland was that it should be at liberty to abide by the Confession of Augsburg. The connection of the Jagellon kings with countries whose adherence to their rule was secured only by the maintenance of Protestant principles, was a check on those princes, which prevented their opposing any determined resistance to the progress of Lutheran tenets. The more important cities of Prussian Poland were confirmed in the exercise of their religion, according to the Lutheran ritual, by express charters granted in the years 1557 and 1558. The smaller towns received privileges yet more explicit some short time after, they being more exposed to attacks from the powerful bishops.[4] A large body of the nobles in Poland proper had been won over to the Protestant confession, which they found more in harmony with that feeling of independence,

---

[1] " Narrative of D. Pomerani," 1539; Sabb. p. visit., in Müller's " Entdecktem Staatscabinet, 4te Eröffn." p. 365.
[2] Münter, " Kirchengeschichte von Dänemark," iii. 529.
[3] " Testamentum religiosum Gustavi I.," in Baaz, " Inventarium Ecclesiæ Sueogoth.," p. 282.
[4] Lengnich, " Account of the religious changes in Prussia," prefixed to the fourth part of the " Geschichte der Preussischen Lande," § 20.

awakened and maintained by the constitution of their States. " A Polish noble is not subject to the king—shall he then be subject to the pope? " was the question they asked. Things went so far in this country that Protestants gained possession of episcopal sees; and, under Sigismund Augustus, they had even obtained the majority in the Senate. That sovereign was undoubtedly Catholic; he heard mass daily and a Catholic sermon every Sunday; he even joined the singers of his choir in the " Benedictus." He confessed regularly, and received the sacrament in one kind; but the creeds that might be prevalent in his court or kingdom seemed but little to disturb his quiet, nor did he show any disposition to embitter the close of his life by a contest with opinions making so vigorous a progress.[5]

An attempt at opposition of this kind had certainly produced no very encouraging results in the neighboring dominions of Hungary. The Diet had constantly refused to pass the resolutions unfavorable to Protestant opinions that were pressed on it from time to time by Ferdinand I. In the year 1554 a Lutheran was elected palatine of the empire, and concessions were soon afterward extorted in favor of the Helvetic Confession in the valley of Erlau. Transylvania was altogether separated from the Catholic Church, the ecclesiastical possessions in that country were confiscated by a formal decree of the Diet, and the princes even appropriated the greater part of the tithes.

We next come to Germany, where the new form of the Church had taken its origin from the peculiar constitution of the national mind, had maintained itself through long and perilous wars, had achieved a legal existence in the empire, and was now in the act of occupying the various territories that divide the country. Already had this process been in great measure accomplished. In North Germany, where the Protestant tenets had taken rise, they were entirely paramount; they had gained permanent ascendancy in those districts of Southern Germany wherein they had been early introduced, and had besides extended their influence far and wide beyond these limits.

The bishops vainly set themselves to oppose their progress in Franconia. In Würzburg and Bamberg, the greater part of

[5] " Relatione di Polonia del Vescovo di Camerino," about 1555. A MS. of the Chigi Library: " Many of these [people of the court] are at liberty to do as they please, for all see that his Majesty is too benignant, and will suffer none to be molested. I could wish that he were more severe in matters of religion."

the nobility, and even the episcopal authorities, had passed over to the reformed Church; the majority of the magistrates and burghers of the towns, with the whole mass of the people, held similar opinions. In the bishopric of Bamberg we find the name of a Lutheran preacher in almost every parish.[6] A Protestant spirit predominated in the government, which was principally in the hands of the estates—bodies corporate, regularly constituted, and possessing the right of imposing taxes—nearly all offices of the law courts were in like manner held by Protestants, and it was observed that their decisions were very commonly adverse to Catholic interests.[7] The bishops retained very little influence, even those who, "with old German and Frankish fidelity," still honored the secular princes in their persons, could no longer endure to see them robed in their clerical ornaments and crowned with the mitre.

No less energetic were the proceedings of Protestantism in Bavaria. Here, too, the new faith had been adopted by a large body of the nobles: a considerable number of the towns was equally inclined toward these doctrines. In the assembly of his States, for example, of the year 1556, the duke was compelled to make concessions which had elsewhere led to the exclusive adoption of the Confession of Augsburg, and which here also promised the same result. The duke himself was not so decidedly opposed to the new doctrines, but that he would occasionally listen to a Protestant sermon.[8]

Far more than this had been gained in Austria. The nobility of that country pursued their studies at Wittenberg, the colleges of the country were filled with Protestants, and it was calculated that not more than a thirtieth part of the population remained Catholic. A national constitution was gradually formed, which was based on the principles of Protestantism.

Enclosed between Bavaria and Austria, the archbishops of Saltzburg had been unable to maintain their territories in obedience to the Catholic rule. They did not as yet endure the presence of Lutheran preachers, but the disposition of the people was none the less explicitly declared. Mass was no longer attended in the capital, nor were fasts solemnized or festivals

[6] Jäck has occupied himself much with this matter in the second and third volumes of his " History of Bamberg."
[7] Gropp, " Dissertatio de Statu Re-ligionis " in " Franconia Lutheranismo infecta," Scriptores Wirceb. i. p. 42.
[8] Sitzinger in Strobel's " Beritäge zur Literatur," i. 313.

observed; those whose dwellings were too far removed from
the preachers of the Austrian localities bordering their country,
remained at home, reading for their edification from the homi-
lies and scriptural commentaries of Spangenberg. This did not
satisfy the people of the hill-country. In Rauris, and the Gas-
tein, in St. Veit, Tamsweg, and Radstadt, the inhabitants loudly
demanded the sacramental cup; this being refused, they abandoned the Lord's Supper altogether. They no longer sent their
children to school; and, on one occasion a peasant rose up in
the church and called aloud to the priest, " Thou liest." The
country people began to preach to each other.[9] We need feel
no surprise if the privation of all worship in accordance with
their newly adopted convictions should give rise to notions the
most visionary and fantastic, among the inhabitants of those
Alpine solitudes.

Advantageously contrasted with this state of things is that
which presents itself as existing in the territories of the ecclesiastical electors on the Rhine. Here the nobles possessed independence, which enabled them to secure a degree of religious
liberty for their vassals beyond what could have been granted
by a spiritual prince. The Rhenish nobles had early received
the Protestant doctrines, and permitted the spiritual sovereign
to make no encroachments, even of a religious character, on their
domains. In all the towns there now existed a Protestant party.
In Cologne its activity was displayed by reiterated petitions.
It became so powerful in Treves as to send for a Protestant
preacher from Geneva, and maintain him in defiance of the
Elector. In Aix-la-Chapelle the Lutheran party made direct
efforts to obtain the supremacy. The citizens of Mayence did
not scruple to send their children to Protestant schools, those
of Nuremberg, for example. Commendone, who was in Germany in 1561, can find no words to describe the servility of the
prelates to the Lutheran princes, and the concessions they made
to Protestantism.[10] He thought he could perceive that there
were Protestants of the most violent opinions even in the privy
councils,[1] and expresses amazement that time should have done
so little in aid of Catholicism.

[9] Extract from a Report of the Canon
Wilh. von Trautmansdorf of the year
1555, in Zauner's " Chronicle of Salzburg," vi. 327.
[10] Gratiani, " Vie de Commendon,"
p. 116.

[1] The most furious heretics are
among them; it appears to me that
time has brought no amelioration—
Commendone, " Relatione dello State
della Religione in Germania," MS. Val-
licelli.

In a similar manner affairs proceeded throughout Westphalia. On St. Peter's day the country people were engaged with the labors of their harvest; the fast-days commanded by the canon were no longer observed. In Paderborn, the town-council watched, with a kind of jealousy, over its Protestant confession. More than one bishop of Münster was disposed to the new creed; and the priests were, for the most part, publicly married. Duke William of Cleves adhered, on the whole, to the Catholic faith, but in his private chapel he received the Lord's Supper in both kinds. The greater part of his council were avowed Protestants; nor did the evengelical form of worship experience any effectual hinderance in his dominions.[2]

We have said enough to show that Protestantism had gained a decided ascendancy through Germany, from the east to the west and from the north to the south. The nobles had from the first enrolled themselves in its ranks; the public functionaries, already numerous and highly respected, were trained up in the new creed; the common people would hear no more of certain articles once insisted on as matters of faith—the fires of purgatory, for example—nor of certain ceremonies, as pilgrimages; no convent could maintain itself, and none dared to exhibit the relics of saints. A Venetian ambassador calculated, in the year 1558, that a tenth part only of the German people still adhered to the ancient religion.

The losses sustained by the Catholic Church in riches and power were no less important than those suffered by her spiritual influence. The canons in nearly all the bishoprics were either attached to the reformed tenets or were but lukewarm and indifferent Catholics. What should prevent them from proposing Protestant bishops, should the doing so appear to them advantageous in other respects? It was without doubt decreed by the Treaty of Augsburg that a spiritual prince should lose both his rank and revenues on departing from the Catholic faith, but this ordinance was not believed capable of restraining a chapter which had become Protestant from electing a Protestant bishop. All that could be insisted on was that the benefice should

[2] Tempesti, " Vita di Sisto V." ; from the " Anonymo di Campidoglio," i. xxiii.: " For many years he communicated in both kinds, but his chaplain had induced him to receive the sacrament in his private chapel, so as not to scandalize his subjects." In a letter given in Niesert's " Müntersche Urkundensammlung," i. xxi., the same thing is said of the Bishop of Münster and the Court of Cleves. W. von Kettler says: " Bishop William imbibed a semi-Lutheran religion in the Court of Cleves."

not be made hereditary. It thus happened that a prince of Brandenburg obtained the archbishopric of Magdeburg, a prince of
Lauenburg that of Bremen, and a prince of Brunswick that of
Halberstadt. The bishopric of Lubeck, also, with those of Verden and Minden, fell into the hands of Protestants, as did the
abbey of Quedlinburg.[3]

The confiscation of church property proceeded with propor-
tionate rapidity. How important were the losses sustained, for
example, in very few years, by the bishopric of Augsburg! All
the convents of Würtemberg were wrested from it in the year
1557. These were followed in 1558 by the convents and parishes
of the county of Oettingen. After the Peace of Augsburg the
Protestants gained an equality with their rivals of the ancient
faith in Dünkelsbühl and Donauwerth; in Nördlingen and
Memmingen they acquired the supremacy. The convents of
these towns,. and among them the rich preceptory of St. An-
thony in Memmingen, with the parochial benefices, were then
irretrievably lost.[4]

In addition to this came the circumstance that the prospects
of Catholicism were by no means encouraging as regarded the
future.

Protestant opinions were predominant in the universities and
other schools: the old champions of Catholicism, who had taken
the field against Luther, and distinguished themselves in religious controversy, were dead or far advanced in years, and no
young men competent to occupy their places had arisen. Twenty
years had elapsed since any student in the University of Vienna
had taken priests' orders. Even in Ingolstadt, which was so
pre-eminently Catholic, no qualified candidates of the faculty
of theology presented themselves for those important offices that
hitherto had always been filled by ecclesiastics.[5] The city of
Cologne established a school with endowments, but when all
the arrangements were completed it appeared that the new
regent was a Protestant.[6] A university was founded by Cardinal Otto Truchsess in his town of Dillingen, for the express
purpose of opposing resistance to the Protestant opinions. It

[3] See also my "History Pol. Zeitschrift," i. ii. 269 et seq.
[4] Placidus Braun, "Geschichte der
Bischöfe von Augsburg," band iii. 533,
535, et seq., on this point from authentic sources.
[5] Agricola, "Historia Provinciæ Societatis Jesu Germaniæ superioris," i.
p. 29.
[6] Orlandinus, "Historia Societatis
Jesu," tom. i. lib. xvi. n. 25: "Hujus
novæ bursæ regens, quem primum præ-
fecerant, Jacobus Lichius, Lutheranus
tandem apparuit."

flourished for some years under the care of certain eminent Spanish theologians, but when these had departed no learned Catholic could be found to take their places, which were at once occupied by Protestants. At this period the teachers in Germany were Protestant with very few exceptions: all the youth of the country sat at their feet, and imbibed hatred of the pope with the first rudiments of learning.

Such was the state of things in the North and East of Europe —Catholicism was utterly banished from many places, it was subdued and despoiled in all; and while endeavoring to defend itself in these regions, still more formidable enemies were pressing forward to assail it in the West and South.

For the Calvinistic modes of belief were without doubt more decidedly opposed to the Roman tenets than were the doctrines of Luther; and it was precisely at the period we are now contemplating that Calvinism took possession of the minds of men with irresistible force.

It had arisen on the borders of Italy, Germany, and France, and had extended in all directions. Toward the east, in Germany, Hungary, and Poland, it constituted a subordinate but very important element of the Protestant movement. In Western Europe it had already raised itself to independent power.

As the Scandinavian kingdoms had become Lutheran, so had the British people become Calvinists; but in Britain the new Church had assumed two distinct forms. In Scotland it had attained power in opposition to the government, and was poor, popular, and democratic, but so much the more irresistible was the fervor which it inspired. In England it had risen to preeminence in alliance with the existing government; there it was rich, monarchical, and magnificent, but was content with mere forbearance from opposition to its ritual. The former naturally approximated more closely to the model of the Genevan Church, and was infinitely more in accordance with the spirit of Calvin.

The French had embraced the tenets of their countryman, Calvin, with all their characteristic vivacity. In defiance of persecution the French churches were soon regulated according to the Protestant forms of Geneva. They held a synod as early as the year 1559. In 1561 the Venetian ambassador Micheli found no province free from Protestantism; three-fourths of the king-

dom were filled with it—Brittany and Normandy, Gascony and
Languedoc, Poitou, Touraine, Provence and Dauphiny. " In
many of these provinces," he remarks, " meetings are held, sermons are preached, and rules of life are adopted entirely according to the example of Geneva, and without any regard to the
royal prohibition. Everyone has embraced these opinions, and
what is most remarkable, even the clerical body, not only priests,
monks, and nuns—very few of the convents have escaped the
infection—but even the bishops and many of the most distinguished prelates." " Your highness," he observes to the doge,
" may be assured that, excepting the common people, who still
zealously frequent the churches, all have fallen away. The
nobles most especially, the men under forty almost without exception; for although many of them still go to mass, that is only
from regard to appearance and through fear; when they are
certain of being unobserved they shun both mass and church."
When Micheli arrived in Geneva he was informed that immediately after the death of Francis II fifty preachers from that
city had proceeded to different towns of France. He was astonished at the respect in which Calvin was held, and the large
amount of money poured in upon him for the benefit of the
thousands who had taken refuge in Geneva.[7] He considered
it indispensable that religious freedom, at least an "interim,"
as he expressed it, should be accorded to the French Protestants, if they would avoid the universal effusion of blood. His
report was, in fact, soon followed by the Edict of 1562. This
granted to Protestantism a legal and acknowledged existence,
and is the basis of the privileges it has since enjoyed in France.
All these changes on every side—in Germany, France, and England—could not fail to affect the Netherlands also. The German influence had first prevailed in that country, and one of
the most powerful motives by which Charles V was induced to
the war of Smalkald was that the sympathy excited by the German Protestants in the Netherlands increased the difficulty of
governing that province, which formed so important a part of

[7] Micheli, " Relatione delle Cose di Francia l'anno 1561 " : " When it was seen that by imprisonment, torture, and burning, no amendment was produced, but rather greater disorders, it was resolved to proceed no more against anyone, excepting those who went about preaching, misleading, and publicly holding assemblies; all others were suffered to live: a great number were liberated from the prisons of Paris and other parts of the kingdom, who then continued in the unrestrained exercise of their religion, talking to all, and boasting that they had gained their cause against the papists — so they called, and still call, their adversaries."

his dominions. By subduing the German princes he prevented, at the same time, an insurrection among his Netherlanders.[8] Yet all his laws, though enforced with excessive rigor (it was calculated at the time that, up to the year 1562, 36,000 Protestants, men and women, had been put to death),[9] were insufficient to impede the progress of the Protestant opinions. The only result was that they gradually took the direction of French Calvinism rather than that of German Lutheranism. Here, too, in defiance of persecution, a formal confession was adopted. In the year 1561, churches were established after the model of Geneva, and by connecting themselves with the local authorities and their adherents, the Protestants obtained a political basis, from which they might hope, not only safety for the future, but a certain importance in the State.

Under these circumstances new energies were awakened in the earlier oppositions to the faith of Rome. In the year 1562 the Moravian brethren were formally acknowledged by Maximilian II, and they availed themselves of this fortunate circumstance to elect a large number of new pastors in their synods—some accounts say 188.[10] In the year 1561 the Duke of Savoy saw himself compelled to accord new privileges even to the poor communities of Waldenses in the mountains.[1] To the most remote and neglected corner of Europe Protestant doctrines had extended their life-inspiring power. How immeasurable an empire had they conquered within the space of forty years! From Iceland even to the Pyrenees—from Finland to the summits of the Italian Alps. Even on the southern side of these last mountains, opinions analogous to Protestantism had, as we have seen, once prevailed—they embraced the whole territory of the Latin Church. A large majority of the upper classes, and of the men most active in public life, were attached to them: whole nations were devoted with enthusiasm to these tenets, which had entirely changed

[8] A view, taken by the Florentine resident, then at the imperial court, and resting as I think on good grounds.
[9] In a report relating to Spain, apparently by Paolo Tiepolo, now in the Venetian Archives, we find "a large portion of those Low Countries is ruined and corrupted by these new opinions; and by all the efforts that have been made, by the many deaths inflicted on many thousands of men (for I am told by eminent persons of those countries that more than 36,000 men and women have suffered death at the hands of justice in little more than seven years), not only is no remedy found for this evil, but on the contrary," etc.
[10] "Regenvolscii Ecclesiæ Slavonicæ," i. p. 63.
[1] Leger, "Histoire des Eglises Vaudoises," ii. p. 38, gives the treaty.

the constitution of States.[2] This is all the more extraordinary
because the Protestant creed was by no means a mere negation
of the papacy—a simple renunciation. It was in the highest
degree positive, a renovation of Christian sentiments and principles, that govern human life even to the most profound re-
cesses of the soul.

Section II.—Resources possessed by the Papacy for active Conflict

The papacy and Catholicism had long maintained themselves
against these advances of their enemy, in an attitude of defence,
it is true, but passive only; upon the whole they were compelled
to endure them.

Affairs now assumed a different aspect.

We have considered that internal development by which
Catholicism began the work of her own restoration. It may
be affirmed generally that a vital and active force was again
manifested, that the Church had regenerated her creed in the
spirit of the age, and had established reforms in accordance
with the demands of the times. The religious tendencies which
had appeared in Southern Europe, were not suffered to become
hostile to herself, she adopted them, and gained the mastery of
their movements; thus she renewed her powers, and infused
fresh vigor into her system. The Protestant spirit alone had
hitherto filled the theatre of the world with results that held
the minds of men enthralled; another spirit, equally deserving
of esteem perhaps, if regarded from an elevated point of view,
though of decidedly opposite character, now entered the lists,
displaying similar power to make the minds of men its own, and
to kindle them into activity.

The influence of the restored Catholic system was first established in the two Southern peninsulas, but this was not

[2] The loss was thus regarded in Rome itself. Tiepolo, " Relatione di Pio IV. e V.": " Speaking only of those nations of Europe which not only used to obey the Pope, but followed in everything the rites and customs of the Roman Church, celebrating public worship in the Latin tongue, it is known that England, Scotland, Denmark, Norway, Sweden, and all the countries of the North are alienated; Germany is almost wholly lost, Bohemia and Poland are deeply infected; the Low Countries of Flanders are so much corrupted that all the Duke of Alva's efforts will scarcely restore them to their original health. Finally, France, by means of these evil humors, is filled with confusion; so that there seems to remain in health, and firm to the Pope, only Spain and Italy, with some few islands, and those countries possessed by your serenity in Dalmatia and Greece."

accomplished without extreme severities. The Spanish Inquisition received the aid of that lately revived in Rome; every movement of Protestantism was violently suppressed. But at the same time those tendencies of the inward life which renovated Catholicism claimed and enchained as her own, were peculiarly powerful in those countries. The sovereigns also attached themselves to the interests of the Church.

It was of the highest importance that Philip II, the most powerful of all, adhered so decidedly to the popedom; with the pride of a Spaniard, by whom unimpeachable Catholicism was regarded as the sign of a purer blood and more noble descent, he rejected every adverse opinion: the character of his policy was, however, not wholly governed by mere personal feeling. From remote times, and more especially since the regulations established by Isabella, the kingly dignity in Spain had assumed an ecclesiastical character; in every province the royal authority was strengthened by the addition of spiritual power; deprived of the Inquisition, it would not have sufficed to govern the kingdom. Even in his American possessions, the King appeared above all in the light of a disseminator of the Christian and Catholic faith. This was the bond by which all his territories were united in obedience to his rule; he could not have abandoned it, without incurring real danger. The extension of Huguenot opinions in the South of France caused the utmost alarm in Spain; the Inquisition believed itself bound to redoubled vigilance. "I assure your highness," observes the Venetian ambassador to his sovereign, on August 25, 1562, "that no great religious movement is to be desired for this country, there are many of the people that long for a change of religion." [1] The papal nuncio considered the result of the council then assembled of equal importance to the royal as to the papal authority. "For the obedience paid to the King," he remarks, "and his whole government, depend on the Inquisition; should this lose its authority, insurrections would immediately follow."

The power possessed by Philip in the Netherlands secured to the southern system an immediate influence over the whole of Europe; but besides this, all was far from being lost in other

[1] "Dispaccio Soranzo, Perpignan, 28 Maggio:" "There are many Huguenots in this province [Spain] who scarcely dare show themselves, because of the severe measures taken against them; but it is suspected that they think of combining, there being many of them throughout Spain."

countries. The Emperor, the Kings of France and Poland, with
the Duke of Bavaria, still adhered to the Catholic Church. On
all sides there were spiritual princes whose expiring zeal might
be reanimated; there were also many places where Protestant
opinions had not yet made their way among the mass of the
people. The majority of the peasantry throughout France,
Poland, and even Hungary [2] still remained Catholic. Paris,
which even in those days exercised a powerful influence over the
other French towns, had not yet been affected by the new doctrines. In England a great part of the nobility and commons
were still Catholic; and in Ireland the whole of the ancient native population remained in the old faith. Protestantism had
gained no admission into the Tyrolese or Swiss Alps, nor had
it made any great progress among the peasantry of Bavaria.
Canisius compared the Tyrolese and Bavarians with the two
tribes of Israel, " who alone remained faithful to the Lord."
The internal causes on which this pertinacity, this immovable
attachment to tradition, among nations so dissimilar, was
founded, might well repay a more minute examination. A similar constancy was exhibited in the Walloon provinces of the
Netherlands.

And now the papacy resumed a position in which it could
once more gain the mastery of all these inclinations, and bind
them indissolubly to itself. Although it had experienced great
changes, it still possessed the inestimable advantage of having
all the externals of the past and the habit of obedience on its
side. In the council so prosperously concluded, the popes had
even gained an accession of that authority which it had been
the purpose of the temporal powers to restrict, and had strengthened their influence over the national churches; they had, moreover, abandoned that temporal policy by which they had formerly involved Italy and all Europe in confusion. They attached
themselves to Spain with perfect confidence and without any
reservations, fully returning the devotion evinced by that kingdom to the Roman Church. The Italian principality, the enlarged dominions of the pontiff, contributed eminently to the
success of his ecclesiastical enterprises; while the interests of

[2] If it were not, in this case, mere
ignorance, as Lazarus Schwendi asserts: " In Hungary all is confusion
and misery; the majority are Huguenots, but the people are in the last
extremity of ignorance."—" Schwendi
au Prince d'Orange," Archives de la
Maison d'Orange-Nassau, i. p. 288.

the universal Catholic Church were for some time essentially promoted by the overplus of its revenues.

Thus strengthened internally, thus supported by powerful adherents, and by the idea of which they were the representatives, the popes exchanged the defensive position, with which they had hitherto been forced to content themselves, for that of assailants. The attack that resulted, its progress and consequences, it is the principal object of this work to consider.

A boundless scene opens before us, the action is proceeding in many places at the same time, and we are called on to direct our attention to the most varying and widely separated quarters of the world.

Religious activity is intimately connected with political impulses; combinations are formed which embrace the whole world, and under whose influence the struggle for mastery succeeds or fails: we shall fix our attention the more earnestly on the great events of general politics, because they often coincide exactly with the results of the religious conflict.

But we must not confine ourselves to generalities; if the conquests of the sword require some native sympathies with the victor on the part of the conquered for their achievement, still more indispensable are these sympathies to the conquest of opinion. We must examine the interests of the several countries to their utmost depths, in order to a full comprehension of those internal movements by which the designs of Rome were facilitated.

There is here presented to us so great an abundance and variety of events and modes of life, that we have to fear the impossibility of comprehending the whole under one view. The state of things before us has its basis fixed on kindred principles, and occasionally exhibits great crises, but it also presents an infinite multiplicity of phenomena.

Let us begin with Germany, where the papacy suffered its first great losses, and where the most important events of the conflict between the two principles again took place. Eminent service was here rendered to the Church of Rome by the Society of Jesuits, which united worldly prudence with religious zeal, and was deeply imbued with the spirit of modern Catholicism. Let us first endeavor to gain a clear perception of the effective power possessed by this order.

Section III.—The First Jesuit Schools in Germany

At the Diet of Augsburg, in the year 1550, Ferdinand I was accompanied by his confessor, Bishop Urban of Laibach. This prelate was one of the few who had never allowed themselves to be shaken in their faith. In his own country he frequently ascended the pulpit, and exhorted the people in the dialect of their province to remain steadfast to the creed of their fathers, preaching to them of the one fold under the one shepherd.[1] The Jesuit Le Jay was at Augsburg on the same occasion, and excited attention by certain conversions. Bishop Urban made his acquaintance, and heard from him for the first time of the colleges established by the Jesuits in different universities. Seeing the decay into which Catholic theology had fallen in Germany, the bishop advised his sovereign to found a similar college in Vienna, and the Emperor received this suggestion very cordially. In a letter that he sent to Ignatius on the subject he declares his conviction that the only means by which the declining tenets of Catholicism could be restored in Germany was to supply the youth of the country with learned and pious Catholic teachers.[2] The preliminaries were easily arranged; in the year 1551 thirteen Jesuits, among whom was Le Jay himself, arrived in Vienna, where Ferdinand immediately granted them a residence, chapel, and pension; he soon after incorporated them with the university, and even intrusted to them the superintendence of that establishment.

It was about this time that they rose into consideration at Cologne, where they had already lived for some years, but with so little success that they had been obliged to dwell apart. In the year 1556 the endowed school, previously mentioned as governed by a Protestant regent, afforded them the opportunity of acquiring a better position; for since there was a party in the city whose most earnest desire it was that the university should remain Catholic, the patrons of the Jesuits finally saw their counsels prevail, and the establishment was committed to the care of that order. Their principal supporters were the prior of the Carthusians, the provincial of the Carmelites, and especially Dr. Johann Gropper, who some-

[1] Valvassor, " Ehre des Herzogthums Krain," Theil ii. buch vii. p. 433.

[2] Printed in Socher, " Historia Provinciæ Austriæ Societatis Jesu," i. 21.

times gave an entertainment, to which he invited the most influential citizens, that he might find opportunity for promoting the cause he had most at heart, after the good old German fashion, over a glass of wine. Fortunately for the Jesuits, one of their order was a native of Cologne, Johann Rhetius, a man of patrician family, to whom the endowed school might more especially be intrusted. But this was not done without strict limitations: the Jesuits were expressly forbidden to establish in the school those monastic habits of life which were usual in their colleges.[3]

They gained firm footing in Ingolstadt also about the same time; their previous efforts had been rendered useless, principally by the opposition of the younger members of the university, who would not permit any privileged school to interfere with the private instruction they were in the habit of giving; but in the year 1556, when the duke, as we have said, had been forced into large concessions in favor of the Protestants, his Catholic counsellers declared it to be imperatively necessary that effectual measures should be taken for upholding the ancient faith. The most active among these were the chancellor Wiguleus Hund, who proceeded as zealously in the maintenance of the ancient Church as he had previously done in the investigation of her primitive history, and the duke's private secretary, Heinrich Schwigger. By their efforts the Jesuits were recalled, and eighteen of them entered Ingolstadt on St. Willibald's day, July 7, 1556, having selected that day because St. Willibald was regarded as the first bishop of the diocese. They found many obstacles opposed to them, both in the city and university, but they gradually overcame them all by favor of the same persons to whom they owed their recall.

From these three metropolitan establishments the Jesuits now extended themselves in all directions.

From Vienna they proceeded to erect colleges of their order throughout the dominions of Austria. In 1556 the Emperor settled them in Prague, where he founded a school, principally for the education of the young nobility. To this he sent his own pages, and the order received countenance and support from the Catholic part of the Bohemian nobles, more espe-

[3] Sacchinus, " Hist. Societatis Jesu," pars ii. lib. i. n. 103.

cially from the houses of Rosenberg and Lobkowitz. One of the most distinguished men in Hungary at that time was Nicolaus Olahus, Archbishop of Gran, of Wallachian extraction, as his name implies. His father Stoia, in an excess of terror at the murder of a Waiwode of his family, had dedicated him to the Church, and his progress in this career had been most auspicious. He had already occupied the important office of private secretary under the last native kings, and had subsequently risen still higher in the service of the Austrian party. Contemplating the general decay of Catholicism in Hungary, he was convinced that the last hope for its restoration was in confirming the hold it retained on the common people, who had not entirely abandoned the anicent creed. Teachers of Catholic principles were required to effect this, and with the purpose of forming such teachers, he established a college of Jesuits at Tyrnau in the year 1561, assigning them a pension from his own revenues to which the Emperor Ferdinand added the grant of an abbey. At the period when the Jesuits arrived, an assembly of the clergy of the diocese had just been convened, their first efforts were devoted to the attempt of reclaiming these Hungarian priests and pastors from the heterodox tenets to which they were inclining. About this time they were summoned into Moravia also. Wilhelm Prussinowski, Bishop of Olmütz, who had become acquainted with the order during his studies in Italy, invited them to his bishopric. Hurtado Perez, a Spaniard, was the first rector in Olmütz; we soon after find them in like manner settled at Brünn.

From Cologne the society spread over the whole of the Rhenish provinces. In Treves, as we have before related, Protestantism had found adherents, and caused some fermentation. Johann von Stein, the archbishop, determined to inflict slight punishments only on the refractory, and to repress innovations chiefly by argument. He invited the two principals of the Jesuit school at Cologne to Coblentz, when he informed them that he desired to have the aid of members of their order "to maintain," as he expresses it, "the flock committed to him in their duty, rather by admonition and friendly instruction than by weapons or menaces." He applied to Rome, also, and very soon came to an arrangement with that court; no long time elapsed before six Jesuits arrived in his diocese from Rome; others were sent from Cologne. On February 3, 1561, they opened their college with great solemnity, and undertook to preach during the fasts of the Lent then approaching.[4]

About the same time Peter Echter and Simon Bagen, two privy counsellors of the elector Daniel of Mayence, were also persuaded that the admission of the Jesuits presented the only means of restoring the decayed university of their city. The canons and feudatories did their best to oppose this idea, but in despite of their efforts a college for the society was established at Mayence, and a preparatory school at Aschaffenburg.

The order continued to advance up the Rhine: they were most especially desirous of obtaining a seat at Spires, not only because many eminent men were included among the assessors of the Supreme Court (*Kammergericht*), over whom it would be of the utmost advantage to obtain influence, but also because they should be there in the immediate neighborhood of the Heidelberg University (which at that time enjoyed a high reputation for its Protestant professors), and could the more effectually oppose its influence. Gradually the establishment they wished for in Spires was effected.[5]

Permitting no loss of time, they also tried their fortune along the Main. Although Frankfort was entirely Protestant, they had yet hope of accomplishing something during the fair. The attempt was not to be made without danger, and, to avoid discovery, they were compelled to change their lodgings every night. At Würzburg they were much more secure, and even received a cordial welcome.[6] The admonition addressed by the Emperor Ferdinand to the bishops at the Diet of 1559, exhorting them at length to exert their utmost power for the maintenance of the Catholic Church, appeared to produce its effect, and contributed largely to this brilliant progress of the society in the ecclesiastical principalities. From Würtzburg they spread throughout Franconia.

The Tyrol had, meanwhile, been opened to them from

---

[4] Browerus, " Annales Trevirenses," tom. ii. lib. xxi. 106-125.
[5] Neuser, for example, in his celebrated letters to the Turkish Emperor, describes himself as a teacher and preacher at Heidelberg, " to which place the most learned men of the whole German nation now resort." Arnold, " Ketzerhist." ii. 1133.
[6] Gropp, " Würzbergische Chronik der letzteren Zeiten," th. i. p. 237.

another quarter. By the desire of the daughters of Ferdinand, they settled themselves at Innspruck, and soon after at Halle, in the same district. In Bavaria they continued to make progress. At Munich, where they arrived in 1559, they were even better satisfied than at Ingolstadt, and declared that city to be the Rome of Germany. Already the order had planted a new and large colony at no great distance from Ingolstadt. Anxious to restore his University of Dillingen to its original destination, Cardinal Truchsess also resolved to dismiss all the professors who still taught there, and intrust that establishment to the care of the Jesuits. A formal agreement was accordingly made at Botzen, between German and Italian commissioners on the part of the cardinal and the order respectively. In 1563 the Jesuits arrived in Dillingen and took possession of the professors' chairs. They relate with much complacency, that the cardinal, on returning from a journey shortly after their arrival, and making a solemn entry into Dillingen, distinguished them above all those who had gone forth to receive him, offered them his hand to kiss, greeted them as his brethren, visited their cells in person, and dined with them: he promoted their wishes to the utmost of his power, and soon established a mission in Augsburg for members of the order.[7]

This was a most remarkable progress to have been made by the society in so short a time. In the year 1551 they had no settled position in Germany: in 1566, their institutions held possession of Bavaria and the Tyrol, Franconia and Swabia, a large part of the Rhenish provinces and Austria. They had penetrated, also, into Hungary, Bohemia, and Moravia. The effect of their exertions soon became perceptible. So early as the year 1561 the papal nuncio declares that "they are winning many souls, and doing great service to the Holy See." This was the first effectual counteraction of Protestant labors, the first enduring impression made against them in Germany.

The efforts of the Jesuits were above all, directed toward the universities. Their ambition was to rival the fame of those of the Protestants. The education of that day was a learned one merely, and was based exclusively on the study of the ancient languages. This the Jesuits prosecuted with earnest zeal, and in certain of their schools they had very

[7] Sacchinus, pars ii. lib. viii. n. 108.

soon professors who might claim a place with the restorers of classical learning. Nor did they neglect the cultivation of the exact sciences. At Cologne, Franz Koster lectured on astronomy in a manner at once agreeable and instructive. But their principal object was still theological discipline, as will be readily comprehended. The Jesuits lectured with the utmost diligence, even during the holidays, reviving the practice of disputations, without which they declared all instruction to be dead. These disputations, which they held in public, were conducted with dignity and decorum, were rich in matter, and altogether the most brilliant that had ever been witnessed. In Ingolstadt they soon persuaded themselves that their progress in theology was such as would enable the university to compete successfully with any other in Germany. Ingolstadt now acquired an influence among Catholics similar to that possessed among Protestants by Wittenberg and Geneva.

With equal industry and care did the society proceed in the conduct of the Latin schools. It was an essential maxim with Lainez that good teachers should be supplied to the lower grammatical classes. He was convinced that first impressions are of the utmost importance to the whole future life of the man, and sought with a discriminating judgment for men who, having once accepted this subordinate office in teaching, would consent to devote themselves to it for their whole lives; since it is only with time that so difficult an occupation can be learned, or the authority proper to a teacher fully acquired. Here also the Jesuits succeeded to admiration. It was found that young people gained more with them in six months than with other teachers in two years; even Protestants removed their children from distant schools, to place them under the care of the Jesuits.

They next established schools for the poor, arranged modes of instruction adapted to children, and enforced the practice of catechising. Canisius prepared his catechism, which satisfied the wants of the learners by its well-connected questions and apposite replies.

This instruction was imparted entirely in the spirit of that fanciful devotion which had characterized the Jesuits from their earliest establishment. The first rector in Vienna was a Spaniard, named Juan Victoria; a man who had signalized his

entrance into the society by walking along the Corso of Rome
during the festivities of the carnival, clothed in sackcloth, and
scourging himself as he walked, till the blood streamed from
him on all sides. The children educated in the Jesuit schools of
Vienna were soon distinguished by their steadfast refusal of
such food as was forbidden on fast-days, while their parents
ate without scruple. In Cologne it was again become an honor
to wear the rosary. Relics were once more held up to public
reverence in Treves, where for many years no one had ventured
to exhibit them. In the year 1560 the youth of Ingolstadt belonging to the Jesuit school walked two and two on a pilgrimage to Eichstadt, in order to be strengthened for their confirmation, " by the dew that dropped from the tomb of Saint
Walpurgis." The modes of thought and feeling thus im-
planted in the schools were propagated by means of preaching
and confession through the whole population.

We have here a case for which the history of the world
could probably not produce a parallel.

When any new intellectual movement has exercised its influence on mankind, this has always been effected by great
and imposing personal qualities, or by the overpowering force
of new ideas; but in this case the effect was accomplished
without any extraordinary display of mental effort. The
Jesuits may have been learned and pious in their way, but
none will assert that their science was the product of a free
exercise of mind, or that their piety arose from the depth and in-
genuousness of a single heart. They had learning enough to
acquire reputation, to awaken confidence, to train and attach
scholars; to more than this they did not aspire. Their piety
not only sufficed to secure them from all reproach on the point
of morals; it was positively conspicuous, and thus was liable to
no question: this was enough for them. Neither their piety
nor their learning disposed them to seek untrodden or undefined paths; but in one respect they were indeed remarkably
distinguished—the severity of their method. With them all
was nicely calculated, every movement and action had its definite
end and aim; such a combination of learning sufficing to its
purpose with unwearying zeal, of studies and persuasion, of
pomp and asceticism, of widely extended influence and unity
in the governing principle and intention, has never been ex-

hibited in the world before or since. At once diligent and visionary, worldly-wise, yet full of enthusiasm; well-bred men and attractive companions; disregarding their personal interests, but laboring for the advancement of each other. We cannot wonder that they were successful.

Another consideration connects itself with this subject in the mind of a German observer. In Germany the papal theology had fallen, as we have said, into almost entire decay. The Jesuits arose to revive it. Who were the Jesuits that first appeared there? They were Spaniards, Italians, and Flemings. The name of their order remained long unknown; they were called the Spanish priests. They took possession of the professors' chairs, and found scholars who attached themselves to their doctrines. From the Germans the society received nothing; its tenets and constitution were completely formed before arriving in Germany. The progress of the order in that country may be generally regarded as a new exertion of influence by the Romance portion of Europe over the Germanic people. The Germans were conquered on their own soil, in their very home; a portion of their country was torn from their hands; and this effect was without doubt produced because the German theologians had never arrived at any clear understanding among themselves, and were not sufficiently magnanimous to endure minor differences in each other. Extreme points of doctrine were insisted on, antagonists assailed each other with reckless violence, so that those who were not wholly fixed in opinion were perplexed and rendered more than ever wavering. A path was thus opened to these foreigners, who gained the mastery of men's minds by a system of belief most carefully constructed, finished in its most minute details, and leaving no shadow of cause for doubt.

Section IV.—Beginning of the Counter-Reformation in Germany

Possessing all the advantages we have described, it is yet obvious that the Jesuits could not have succeeded to so great an extent, had they not been aided by the secular arm and favored by the princes of the empire. For as with political questions, so had it happened with those of a theological nature. No measure had yet been brought into effect by which the constitution of the empire, in its character essentially hierarchical, could be placed in harmony with the new circumstances of religion. The only result of the Peace of Augsburg, as it was at first understood and subsequently expounded, was a new extension of the temporal sovereignty. The different provinces also required a high degree of independence in affairs of religion. The creed adopted by the prince, and the understanding between him and his estates, thenceforth decided the ecclesiastical position to be assumed by the country.

This would seem to be an arrangement expressly devised for the benefit of Protestantism. It nevertheless tended almost exclusively to the promotion of Catholicism. The former was already established before it had come into effect; the latter commenced its restoration only on receiving this support.

This occurred first in Bavaria; and the manner in which it took place there well deserves especial attention, from the immense influence it exercised.

The Bavarian Diet presents us during some time with a series of disputes between the sovereign and his estates. The duke was in perpetual need of money, loaded with debt, obliged to impose new taxes, and frequently compelled to seek assistance from his estates. In return for these subsidies the estates required concessions, principally of a religious kind. A state of affairs, similar to that which had long prevailed in Austria, seemed impending in Bavaria: a legitimate opposition of the estates to the sovereign, based at once on religion and on privileges, unless the latter should himself become a convert to Protestantism.

It was without question this position of things by which, as we have related, the introduction of the Jesuits was chiefly caused. It may, possibly, be true that their doctrines produced an impression on the mind of Duke Albert V, who declared, at a later period, that all he had ever known of God's laws had been imparted to him by Hoffaüs and Canisius, both Jesuits. There was, nevertheless, another cause in operation. Pius IV not only called the attention of Albert to the fact that each religious concession would diminish the obedience of his subjects[1]—which was not to be denied, as German principalities

[1] " Legationes Paparum ad Duces Bavariæ," MS. of the library at Munich,   Prima Legatio, 1563: " But if his illustrious Highness should grant the use of

were then situated—but he enforced the effects of his admonition by marks of favor, abandoning to the duke one-tenth of the property of his clergy. This not only rendered Albert V less dependent on his estates, but also showed him what advantages he might expect from a connection with the Church of Rome.

Then came the question, whether the duke would have power to set aside the religious opposition already organized in his estates?

On this task he entered at a Diet assembled at Ingolstadt in the year 1563. The prelates were already well disposed to his views, and he next tried his influence on the towns. Whether it were that the doctrines of reviving Catholicism and the activity of the Jesuits, who insinuated themselves everywhere, had gained influence in the cities—especially with the leading members of their assemblies—or that other considerations prevailed, suffice it to say that on this occasion the cities did not renew those demands for religious concessions, which they had hitherto always urged with great eagerness; but proceeded to grant supplies without making conditions for new privileges. The only opposition now remaining came from the nobles; that body left the Diet in discontent, nay, much exasperated; menaces, uttered by various noblemen, were repeated to the duke.[2] The most distinguished among them, the Count of Ortenburg, whose claim to hold his county immediately of the empire the duke contested, at length resolved to introduce the evangelical confession into that territory without further delay; but in doing so he placed weapons dangerous to himself and his order in the hands of the duke, the rather, as in one of the castles seized by Albert, a correspondence between the Bavarian nobles was discovered, containing severe and offensive remarks on the sovereign describing him as a hardened Pharaoh, and his Council as sanguinary enemies of the poor Christians.

Other expressions found in these letters were believed to intimate the existence of a conspiracy, and furnished Albert with a pretext for calling his refractory nobles to account.[3] He inflicted a punishment on them that cannot be called rigorous,

the cup without the authority of the Apostolic See, he would himself lose much of his power over his subjects." At the Diet it was asserted that the prince had suffered himself to be dazzled by the tenth (" decimatio ") granted him.

[2] Private notices respecting the violent and unbecoming expressions used in Freiberg, " Geschichte der baierischen Landstände," ii. 352.
[3] Huschberg, " Geschichte des Hauses Ortenburg," s. 390.

but it sufficed to his purpose. Every nobleman compromised
was excluded from the Bavarian Diet; and as these members
had formed the only opposition remaining, the duke was, by
their absence, rendered absolute master of his estates, among
whom there has never since been any question agitated concerning religion.

The importance of this measure was instantly manifest.
Duke Albert had long urged the Pope and Council with great
importunity for a grant of the cup to the laity; he seemed
to consider the whole happiness of his territories to depend on
this concession. In April of the year 1564 he finally received this grant. The result seems scarcely credible. He
did not even suffer the fact of its being sent him to be made
known! The position of his affairs had changed. A privilege departing from the strict tenor of Catholicism now appeared to the duke injurious rather than advantageous. Certain communes of Lower Bavaria, which repeated their former
demands for the cup with clamorous violence, he even compelled to silence by main force.[4]

In a short time there was no prince in Germany more decidedly Catholic than Duke Albert, and he then proceeded
with the most earnest zeal to make his whole territory Catholic
also.

The professors of Ingolstadt were compelled to subscribe
the confession of faith published in pursuance of the decree
issued by the Council of Trent. The officers of the ducal
government were obliged to pledge themselves by oath to a
confession of unquestionable Catholicism; whoever refused
this was dismissed from his employment. Duke Albert would
not endure the Protestant creed even among the common people.
In the first instance he sent certain Jesuits into Lower Bavaria
to convert the inhabitants; and not only the preachers, but
every other person who persisted in retaining the evangelical
faith, were constrained to sell their property and quit the country.[5] The same means were afterward adopted in all other
parts of the dukedom. No magistrate would have ventured to
tolerate Protestants; he who should have done so would have
incurred severe punishment.

[4] Adlzreitter, "Annales Boicæ Gen-
tis," ii. xi. n. 22: "Albert would not
have that indulgence made a matter of
public right."
[5] Agricola, Ps. i. Dec. iii. 116–120.

But with this restoration of Catholicism, all its modern forms were brought from Italy into Germany. An index of prohibited books was prepared; they were sought through the libraries, and burnt in large numbers; those of rigidly Catholic character were, on the contrary, highly favored. The duke left nothing undone to encourage the authors of such books. He caused the " History of the Saints," by Surius, to be translated into German, and printed at his own cost. The utmost veneration was shown toward relics; and St. Benno, of whom in another part of Germany (Meissen) no one would longer hear mention, was solemnly declared the patron saint of Bavaria. Architecture and music, in the taste of the restored Church, were introduced at Munich. Above all, the Jesuit institutions were promoted; for by their agency it was that the youth of Bavaria were to be educated in a spirit of strict orthodoxy.

The Jesuits, on their part, could not sufficiently praise the duke; according to them he was a second Josias, a new Theodosius.

One question only remained to be considered.

As that extension of temporal authority, derived by the Protestant princes from their influence over religious affairs, increased, so much the more oppressive would it have seemed if the Catholic sovereigns had suffered restriction from the restored authority of the ecclesiastical power.

But for this, also a remedy was provided. The popes clearly perceived that they could not succeed in upholding their decaying influence, or in regaining it when lost, without aid from the temporal sovereigns: they cherished no illusion on this subject, and made it their whole policy to preserve a strict alliance with the princes of Europe.

To the first nuncio whom Gregory XIII sent into Bavaria, he gave instructions wherein this conviction is expressed without any circumlocution. " The most ardent wish of his holiness," it declares, " is to restore the decayed discipline of the Church; but he sees that to attain so important an end, he must unite himself with temporal sovereigns: by their piety, religion has been upheld; by their assistance alone, could church discipline and good order be restored." [6]

[6] Legatio Gregorii XIII., 1573: " His holiness is intent upon the consideration of how the discipline of the church, now almost destroyed in Germany, can

The Pope accordingly made over to the duke his authority for stimulating the exertions of the negligent bishops for carrying into effect the decrees of a synod that had been held at Saltzburg, and for constraining the Bishop of Ratisbon and his chapter to erect a seminary: in a word, he confided to him a sort of spiritual supervision, and took counsel with him as to whether it might not be advisable to found seminaries for the conventual clergy, such as were already established for the secular members of the hierarchy. To all this the duke assented very willingly; he stipulated only that the bishops should respect the rights of the sovereign, whether those descending from earlier periods or the privileges but newly acquired, and that the clergy should be kept in discipline and subordination by their superiors. Edicts are extant in which the prince treats the convents as property of the treasury (*Kammergub*), and subjects them to secular administration.

In the course of the Reformation, certain clerical attributes had been appropriated by the Protestant princes; the same thing was now done by the Catholic sovereigns. What occurred in the first case in opposition to the papacy, was here accomplished in concert with it. If Protestant rulers established their younger sons as administrators-extraordinary in the neighboring evangelical bishoprics, so in those that had remained Catholic the sons of Catholic princes received immediate investiture of the episcopal dignity. Gregory had promised Duke Albert, from the very first, to neglect nothing that might be of advantage either to himself or his sons. Two of these sons were very soon installed in the most important benefices, and one of them gradually rose to the highest dignities of the empire.[7]

In addition to all this, Bavaria gained great and real importance in consequence of the position she assumed. Be-

---

by any means be re-established: he perceives that his predecessors have neglected this, or have not sufficiently labored therein, and have not deserved so well of the Christian commonwealth as it was meet they should have done. He has most wisely decided, that for so great a work he must secure the co-operation of the Catholic sovereigns." The ambassador, Bartolomeo, Count of Porzia, distinctly promises: "Suam sanctitatem nihil unaquam prætermissuram esse, quou est e re sua (ducis Bavariæ) aut filiorum." (See text.)

[7] Even Pius V allowed his rigorous principles to bend in favor of the Bavarian duke. Tiepolo, "Relatione di Pio IV. e V.": "Of the other secular princes of Germany, scarcely one seems truly Catholic, excepting the Duke of Bavaria; wherefore, on his account, the Pope has permitted his son to hold the bishopric of Friesingen, though he is still far from the age prescribed by the Council; a thing that he has never conceded to any other person."

coming the champion of a great principle, which was in the act of acquiring new power, she was long regarded by the less powerful German princes of the Catholic faith as their leader.

And the duke now labored zealously for the restoration of the ancient Church in every portion of territory that owned his rule. The Count of Haag had tolerated Protestantism in his domains, but no sooner had this county fallen into the duke's hands than he expelled the Protestants and reinstated the creed and ritual of Catholicism. In the battle of Moncontour the margrave Philibert of Baden-Baden had remained dead on the field; his son Philip, then ten years old, was brought up in Munich under the guardianship of Duke Albert, and, as a matter of course, in the Catholic faith. But the duke would not wait for what the young margrave might decide on when arrived at an age to govern; he instantly despatched his high-steward Count Schwartzenberg, and the Jesuit George Schorich, who had already acted together in the conversion of Lower Bavaria, into the territories of Baden, with commission to restore that country to Catholicism by similar means. It is true that the Protestant inhabitants opposed imperial decrees to these attempts, but those edicts were not regarded; the plenipotentiaries proceeded, as the historian of the Jesuits complacently declares, " to set the minds and ears of the simple multitude free for the reception of the heavenly doctrines "; that is to say, they removed the Protestant preachers, compelled the monks who had not remained strictly orthodox to abjure all dissenting tenets, placed Catholic teachers in all the schools—primary and superior, and banished the laity who would not obey the orders imposed on them. In two years —1570, 1571—the whole territory was again rendered Catholic.[8]

While these things were taking place in the secular principalities, similar events occurred by a necessity still more inevitable in the ecclesiastical sovereignties.

The spiritual princes of Germany were at one time more especially distinguished by their ecclesiastical than by their secular character, and the popes lost not a moment in extend-

---

[8] Sacchinus, pars iii. lib. vi. n. 88, lib. vii. n. 67; Agricola, i. iv. 17, 18. The Pope duly valued the duke on that account. In the relation of the embassy, we are told that he sees with profound joy, that by the labor and industry of your illustrious serenity, the March of Baden is brought back to the Catholic faith, and the margrave educated therein; also that your great care has restored the County of Haag, which had shamefully fallen away from the Church.

ing over the episcopal office in Germany that increase of power accorded to them by the Council of Trent.

First, Canisius was sent to the different ecclesiastical courts with copies of these edicts: he conveyed them to Mayence, Treves, Cologne, Osnaburg, and Würtzburg,[9] and with infinite address he contrived to give meaning and effect to the official respect and courtesy with which he was received. The matter was afterward discussed in the Diet held at Augsburg in the year 1566.

Pope Pius V had feared that Protestantism would then make new demands and obtain new concessions. He had already instructed his nuncio, in case of urgency, to put forward a protest, threatening the Emperor and princes with deprivation of all their rights; he even thought that the moment for this step had arrived;[10] but the nuncio, who had a nearer view of things, did not consider this advisable; he saw that there was nothing more to fear. The Protestants were divided, the Catholics held together. The latter frequently assembled at the house of the nuncio to hold council on the measures to be taken in common. The blameless life of Canisius, his unquestionable orthodoxy, and his prudence procured him great influence in these meetings, wherein it was decided that no concession should be accorded. This Diet was, on the contrary, the first in which the Catholic princes opposed an effectual resistance to the Protestant demands. The Pope's exhortations found attentive listeners; in a special assembly of the ecclesiastical princes, the decrees of the Council of Trent were provisionally accepted.

A new life may be said to have commenced from this moment in the Catholic Church of Germany. These decrees were gradually published in the provincial synods; seminaries were erected in the episcopal sees; the first who complied with the rule to that effect being, so far as I can ascertain, the Bishop of Eichstädt, who founded the Willibald College (*Collegium Willibaldinum*).[1] The *professio fidei* was subscribed by persons of all classes. It is a very important fact that the universities were also compelled to subscribe it; a regulation proposed by Lainez, approved by the Pope, and now carried into effect in

[9] " Maderus de Vita P. Canisii," lib. ii. c. ii.; Sacchinus, iii. ii. 22.
[10] Catena, " Vita di Pio V.": p. 40, gives an extract from the instruction;

Gratiani, " Vita Commendoni," lib. iii. c. ii.
[1] Falkenstein, " Nordgauische Alterthümer," i. 222.

Germany, principally by the zeal of Canisius: not only were no appointments made, but no degree was conferred, even in the faculty of medicine, until the *professio fidei* had first been subscribed. The first university into which this rule was introduced was, so far as I can discover, that of Dillingen; the others gradually followed. The most rigid visitation of the churches commenced, and the bishops, who had hitherto been extremely negligent, now displayed the utmost zeal and devotion.

Among the most zealous of these prelates, Jacob von Eltz, Elector of Treves from 1567 to 1581, more especially distinguished himself. He had been educated in the ancient discipline of Louvain, and had long devoted his literary labors to Catholicism; he had compiled a martyrology and composed a book of prayers. In the time of his predecessor he had taken a very active part in the introduction of the Jesuits into Treves, and on his own accession to the government he had committed the visitation of his diocese to their society. Even schoolmasters were compelled to subscribe the *professio fidei;* strict discipline and subordination were enforced upon the clergy by the severe and methodical system of the Jesuits; parish priests were required to present a monthly report to the dean, who, on his part, was to report every three months to the archbishop; whoever refused obedience to these mandates was instantly removed. Extracts from the edicts of the Council of Trent were printed for the clergy of the diocese, and distributed for the general information and guidance; a new edition of the Missal was also published for the purpose of abolishing all diversities in the ritual. The ecclesiastical tribunal received a new and vigorous organization, principally by the agency of Batholomew Bodeghem, of Delft. The greatest happiness of the archbishop was to find someone desirous of abjuring Protestantism; on such a person he never failed to bestow the blessing of readmission with his own hand.[2]

The prince-bishops were further prompted to the duties of their office by other motives besides those proceeding from their connection with Rome. The spiritual princes were instigated to restore their subjects to the Catholic faith by causes similar to those affecting the secular sovereigns: nay, it was

[2] Browerus, " Annales Trevirenses," ii. xxii. 25, is on these points our principal authority.

even more imperative on them to do so, since a population
inclined to Protestantism would necessarily oppose a more
earnest resistance to their rule on account of their ecclesiastical character.

And precisely in the ecclesiastical city of Treves it is that
this momentous portion of the German history opens to our
view. The archbishops of Treves, like other spiritual princes,
had long been at variance with their capital. In the sixteenth
century, Protestantism added a new element of discord; a stubborn resistance was opposed to the ecclesiastical tribunal in
particular; Jacob von Eltz was at length compelled to a formal
siege of the city, and having subdued it by force of arms he
brought forward an edict of the Emperor in favor of his claims,
and by these means reduced the citizens to obedience, both
spiritual and temporal.

Another measure taken by the archbishop was productive
of very extensive effects; in the year 1572 he decreed the
irrevocable exclusion of all Protestants from his court. This
more particularly affected the provincial nobility, whose hopes
of advancement were generally fixed on the court. The nobles
thus saw their prospects destroyed, and more than one of them
may probably have been induced by this circumstance to return
to the ancient religion.

A neighbor of Jacob von Eltz, Daniel Brendel, Elector of
Mayence, was also a very good Catholic. He revived the
procession of the Corpus Christi, in opposition to the advice of
all about him, and even officiated himself in the ceremony.
He would on no account have neglected vespers, and from the
affairs brought before him he invariably selected those of a
spiritual character for his first attention. The Jesuits bestow
high praise on this prince for the favors they received at his
hands; and he sent several pupils to the *Collegium Germanicum*
in Rome.[3] But he was not prepared to go to the extremities
practised by Jacob von Eltz. His religious zeal was mingled
with a certain character of irony. On establishing the Jesuits
in his electorate he was opposed by remonstrance from some
of his feudal tenants. " How! " said he, " you endure me, who
fall so far short of my duty, and you will not tolerate the Jesuits,

---

[3] Serarius, " Moguntiacarum Rerum   Daniel, especially cap. viii. xi. xxii.
Libri V."; in the section relating to   xxiii.

who perform theirs so perfectly!"[4] The answer he returned
to the Jesuits when they urged him to the complete extirpation
of Protestantism has not been reported to us; but we know
that he continued to suffer Lutherans and Calvinists to retain
a permanent residence both in the city and at court; and in
some places he even tolerated the evangelical ritual.[5] But this
probably may have been only because he did not believe himself
strong enough to suppress it. In a more remote part of his dominions, where no powerful and warlike neighbors, such as
the counts-palatine of the Rhine, were near to hold him in
check, he proceeded to very decisive measures. The restoration of Catholicism in Eichsfeld was his work. There also
the Protestant creed had gained firm hold by favor of the
nobles, and had even made its way into Heiligenstadt, notwithstanding the presence of the chapter which held the
patronage of all the livings; a Lutheran preacher was settled
there, and the communion was administered in both kinds.
On one occasion only twelve citizens of any consideration received the sacrament at Easter according to the Catholic
forms.[6] Things were in this position when in the year 1574
the archbishop appeared personally at Eichsfeld, accompanied
by two Jesuits, for the purpose of holding a visitation of the
churches. He proceeded to no act of violence, but took measures that proved entirely effectual. He removed the Protestant preachers from Heiligenstadt, and founded a college
of Jesuits there. He dismissed no member from the Council,
but he prevented the admission of Protestants for the future
by making a slight addition to the oath taken by the councillors; in virtue of which they bound themselves to obey his
grace the elector, whether in spiritual or temporal matters.
But the most essential change made by Daniel Brendel was
the appointment of Leopold von Stralendorf, a most zealous
Catholic, to the office of high bailiff. This functionary did not
scruple to enforce the milder measures of his master in a spirit
of excessive rigor, adopted on his own responsibility; and in
a consistent administration of twenty-six years, he restored the
Catholic faith to its supremacy in town and country. Disre-

[4] Valerandus Sartorius in Serarius, p. 921.
[5] The complaint of Robert Turner, who looked for a Boniface, and found a "principem politicum" only. In Serarius, p. 947.
[6] Johann Woolf, "Geschichte und Beschreibung von Heiligenstadt," p. 59.

garding the remonstrances of the nobles he expelled the Protestant preachers from the territory, and appointed pupils from
the new Jesuit college in that place.

Another ecclesiastical prince had already given the example
of similar proceedings in that part of the country.

In the diocese of Fulda the evangelical forms of worship
had been tolerated by six abbots in succession; and the young
abbot, Balthazar von Dernbach, surnamed Gravel, had promised, at his election in the year 1570, to allow the continuance
of this practice; but whether it was that the favor shown him
by the Papal Court had inflamed his ambition, or that he considered the restoration of Catholicism likely to increase his
very insignificant authority, or that his convictions had indeed
become decidedly changed, certain it is that he gradually displayed, not only aversion, but even hostility to the Protestant
tenets. He first called in the Jesuits, not that he was acquained
with the order, nor had he ever seen one of its colleges; he knew
them by common report only, and by the accounts he had received from a few students of the College of Treves; but his
purpose may perhaps have been confirmed by the recommendations of Daniel Brendel. The Jesuits accepted his invitation
very cordially; Mayence and Treves combined to establish a
colony in Fulda; the abbot built them a house and school and
granted them a pension. He himself, being still extremely
ignorant, accepted instruction at their hands.[7]

The first result of these proceedings on the part of the abbot
was a dispute with his chapter, which possessed the right to
a voice in such matters, and which entirely disapproved the
introduction of the Jesuits. He soon after attacked the city
also, having found a favorable occasion for doing so.

The parish priest of Fulda, who had hitherto preached evangelical doctrines, returned to Catholicism. He recommenced the
use of Latin in the rite of baptism, and the administration of
the Lord's Supper in one kind only. The inhabitants, long
accustomed to the reformed ritual, did not willingly consent
to abandon it and demanded the removal of the priest. Their
request, as may be supposed, received no attention. Not only

[7] Reiffenberg, "Historia Societatis
Jesu ad Rhenum inferiorem," i. vi. ii.,
who makes an addition in this passage
to the notices of Sacchinus (iii. vii. 68),
from a treatise drawn up for him by the
Jesuit Feurer. On the Protestant side,
complaints of the city of Fulda, and of
the knights of that diocese, in Lehmann,
"De Pace Religionis." ii. ix. 257.

was the Catholic ritual strictly observed in the cathedral, but the Protestant preachers were expelled one after another from the remaining churches also, and Jesuits appointed in their place. The abbot had already dismissed his Protestant councillors and officers, to replace them by others of the Catholic creed.

It was in vain that the nobles remonstrated. The abbot assumed an appearance of surprise, and observed that he hoped they did not mean to dictate the measures which he should pursue for the government of the land committed by God to his rule. Some of the more powerful princes of the empire sent embassies to dissuade him from these innovations, and to request the dismissal of the Jesuits: but he remained immovable; nay, he further proceeded to menaces against the knights of his dominions, who asserted a sort of claim to hold immediately of the Emperor, which was a privilege that would have been much restricted had the ecclesiastical sovereign been able to enforce obedience in matters of religion.

It was thus that Catholicism, which might have been thought conquered, once more arose in Germany with renewed strength. The most varied motives contributed to this result. The revival of church discipline by the edicts of the Council of Trent largely contributed, but motives of internal policy were more active than all others, since it was obvious that a sovereign would be much more powerful if his subjects were attached to his own creed. It is true that the restoration of the Church had at first included separate points only, but these soon presented a boundless prospect to the spirit of reform. That no more effectual resistance was offered to the proceedings of the spiritual princes must in itself have been of infinite moment. At the Peace of Augsburg an attempt had been made to secure the Protestant communities inhabiting ecclesiastical territories, by an express declaration of the Emperor; the spiritual sovereigns now refused to acknowledge this declaration, and would in no case be restricted by it. The imperial power was neither sufficiently strong nor sufficiently resolute to come to any effectual decision regarding it, still less to make it respected. Even in the diets of the empire there was not the energy or the unanimity that would have been required to procure the adoption of measures in its favor. The most important changes occurred without a word of remark, almost without observation; they were not even mentioned by the historians of the period, but passed as things inevitable and that could not be otherwise.

Section V.—Troubles in the Netherlands and in France

While the efforts of Catholicism were producing results so important and extensive in Germany, they were put forth with equal vigor in the Netherlands and in France, though in a manner entirely different.

The principal distinction was that a powerful central authority existed in each of these last-named countries, which took immediate part in every movement, assumed the guidance of all religious enterprises, and was itself directly affected by any opposition offered to a religious undertaking.

There was, consequently, more unity in the different relations of the States, a more perfect combination of means, and more effectual energy of action.

The many and varied measures taken by Philip to enforce obedience in the Netherlands at the beginning of his reign are well known: he was compelled to abandon most of them, one after another, but he clung with stubborn tenacity and inflexible rigor to all that had been framed for the maintenance of Catholicism and religious uniformity.

By the institution of new bishoprics and archbishoprics he completely remodelled the ecclesiastical constitution of the country. In these proceedings he would permit himself to be checked by no remonstrance or appeal to the rights which he was unquestionably invading.

These bishoprics acquired redoubled importance from the increased severity enforced on the discipline of the Church by the Council of Trent. Philip II had adopted the decrees of the Council after a short deliberation, and had then proclaimed them in the Netherlands. The daily life of the people, who had hitherto found means to avoid any violent restraints, was now to be placed under the most rigorous supervision, and subjected to the minute observance of forms from which they had believed themselves about to be entirely emancipated.

In addition to this came the penal laws, of which so many had been issued against the Netherlands under the preceding government; and the zeal of the inquisitors, whom the newly

CHOICE EXAMPLES OF PALEOGRAPHY.

Fac-similes from Rare and Curious Manuscripts of the Middle Ages.

PAGE FROM A PREFACE BY ST. JEROME.

Latin uncial manuscript of the Seventh Century.

The three lines in vermilion which mark the beginning of the page reproduced are said by cenobite savants to be a certain mark of great antiquity. The page is the beginning of St. Jerome's preface to his Latin rendering of the four Evangelists, which was addressed to Pope Damasus, to whom St. Jerome was at one time secretary. The script of the work is a Roman uncial, but is subsequent to the era in which this kind of writing was at its best.

BEATO PAPAE DAMA
SO HIERONIMUS·
NOUUM OPUS FA
CERE ME COGIS EX
UETERI UT POSTEA
EMPLARIA SCRIB
TURARUM TOTO
ORBE DISPERSA
QUASI QUIDAM AR
BITER SEDEAM·ET
QUIA INTER SE UA
RIANT QUAE SINT IL,
LA QUAE CUM CRE
CA CONSENTIANT UE
RITATE DECERNA
PIUS LABOR· SED
PERICULOSA PRE
SUMPTIO· IUDICARE
DE CETERIS IPSU
AB OMNIBUS IU
DICANDUM SENIS
MUTARE LINGUA̅

ET CANESCENTEM
MUNDUM AD INITIA
REI RAHERE PAR
UULORUM QUIS
ENIM DOCTUS PARI
TER UEL INDOCTUS
CUM IN MANUS UO
LUMEN ADSUMSE.
RIT ET A SALIBA QUA
SEMEL INBIBIT UI
DERIT DISCREPARE
QUOD LECTITAT NON
STATIM ERUMPAI
IN UOCEM ME FAL,
SARUM· ME CLA
MANS ESSE SACRI
LECUM QUI AUDE
AM ALIQUID IN UE
TERIBUS LIBRIS AD
DERE MUTARE'
CORRICERE' ADUER
SUS QUAM INUIDIA̅

erected tribunal of Rome was daily stimulating to increased activity.

The people of the Netherlands left no means untried that might induce the King to moderate his rigor; and he did appear at times to be more leniently disposed. Count Egmont thought he had received assurance of this during his sojourn in Spain; it was, nevertheless, scarcely to be hoped for. We have already observed that the authority of Philip throughout his dominions reposed on a religious basis. Had he made concessions to the inhabitants of the Netherlands, they would have been demanded in Spain, where he could not possibly have granted them. He, too, was subjected—a fact we must not refuse to acknowledge—to the pressure of an inevitable necessity. This was, besides, the period when the accession and first measures of Pius V were exciting increased zeal through all Catholic Christendom. Philip II felt an unusual inclination toward this pontiff, and gave an attentive ear to his exhortations. The attack of the Turks on Malta had just been repulsed, and the more bigoted party, enemies to the Protestant Netherlanders, may have availed themselves of the impression produced by this victory, as the Prince of Orange suspected, to lead the King into some violent resolution.[1] Let it suffice to say that toward the end of the year 1565 an edict was promulgated surpassing all preceding ones in severity.

The penal enactments—the decrees of the council, and those of the provincial synods held subsequently—were to be enforced without remission; the inquisitors alone were to take cognizance of religious offences, all civil authorities being enjoined to render them assistance; a commissioner was appointed to watch over the execution of this edict, with orders to give in a report every three months.[2]

The effect of these decrees was manifestly to introduce a spiritual domination, if not exactly similar to that of Spain, yet, at least, resembling the rule of Italy.

Among the first results that ensued was that the people took up arms; the destruction of images began, and the whole country was in the wildest commotion. There was a moment when the authorities seemed about to yield; but, as is usual in such

[1] The prince entertained suspicions of Granvella. See his letters in the " Archives de la Maison d'Orange-Nassau," i. 289.

[2] Strada, after a formula of December 18, 1565, lib. iv. p. 94.

cases, acts of violence defeated the end proposed by them. The moderate and peaceable inhabitants were alarmed, and gave assistance to the government. Victory remained with the Gov-· erness of the Netherlands, and having taken possession of the rebellious towns, she found herself in a position to impose an oath on the public officers, and even on the feudatories of the King, by which they formally pledged themselves to the main-tenance of the Catholic faith and to an armed resistance to heretics.[3]

Even this did not suffice to Philip II. It was that unhappy moment when the catastrophe of his son Don Carlos occurred; he was more than usually severe and unbending. The Pope repeated his exhortations that no concession to the disadvantage of Catholicism should be made; and Philip assured his holiness that he would not suffer a single root of the noxious plant to remain in the Netherlands; either he would uphold the Catholic faith in all its purity, or would consent to lose those provinces altogether.[4] For the better fulfilment of these intentions he sent his best general, the Duke of Alva, with a formidable army, into the Netherlands, even after the troubles had been allayed.

Let us examine the moving principle by which the proceedings of Alva were regulated.

The duke was convinced that all might be arranged in a coun-try disturbed by revolutionary movements, when once the chiefs had been disposed of. That Charles V, after so many important victories, had been very nearly driven from the German Em-pire, he attributed to the forbearance of that monarch, who had spared his enemies when they had fallen into his hands. Frequent reference has been made to the alliance entered into between the French and Spaniards at the Congress of Bayonne, and to the measures concerted there; but of all that has been said of this Convention, thus much only is certain, that the Duke of Alva exhorted the French Queen to disembarrass herself of the Huguenot leaders, by whatever means she could find. What he then advised, he now made no scruple of putting in practice. Philip had intrusted him with some blank warrants bearing the royal signature. The first use he made of them was to arrest

[3] Brandt, " Histoire de la Réformation des Pays-Bas," i. 156.
[4] Cavalli, " Dispaccio di Spagna, 7 Aug. 1567 ": " The King replied that as to matters of religion his holiness might be of good courage; for either he would lose those States, or preserve in them the true Catholic religion; nor would he endure that there should remain one root of that evil plant if all he could do would uproot it."

Egmont and Horn, whom he assumed to have been implicated in the recent insurrections. " May it please your sacred Catholic Majesty," thus begins the letter which he wrote to the King on this occasion, and which seems to imply that he had no express command for the arrest of the counts, " on my arrival in Brussels I procured the necessary information from the proper quarter, and thereupon secured the person of Count Egmont. I have also caused Count Horn and some others to be imprisoned.[5] It will, perhaps, be asked, why he sentenced these prisoners a year afterward to be executed? It was not because he had received proof of their guilt from the trial; the blame attached to them was rather that of not having prevented the disturbances than of having caused them; nor was it by command of the King, who rather left it to Alva to decide on the execution, or not, as he should consider expedient. The cause of their death was as follows: A small body of Protestants had made an incursion into the country. They had effected nothing of moment, but had gained some little advantage at Heiligerlee; and the Duke of Arenberg, a general of high reputation in the royal army, had been left dead on the field. In his letters to the King, Alva said that he had perceived the people to be thrown into a ferment by this mischance; that they were becoming bold; and he considered it expedient to show that he was in no wise afraid of them. He wished also to deprive them of any wish they might have to excite new commotions with a view to rescue the prisoners; and had, therefore, resolved on permitting the execution to proceed immediately. And thus did these noble men lose their lives, though no guilt worthy of death could be found in them; their sole crime consisted in the defence of the ancient liberties of their country. They were sacrificed, not to any principle of justice, but rather to the momentary considerations of a cruel policy. The duke remembered Charles V, whose errors he was determined to avoid.[6]

[5] " Dispaccio di Cavalli, 16 Sett." The late governess complained to the King of the arrests, when Philip replied that he had not commanded them. In proof of this he showed her the letter he had received from Alva. The passage adduced to prove his assertion is before us; it was thus: " Sacra cattolica Maestà, da poi ch' io gionsi in Brusselles, pigliai le information da chi dovea delle cose di qua, onde poi mi son assicurato del conte di Agmon e fatto ritener il conte d'Orno, con alquanti altri." (See text.) " It will be well that your Majesty, for good reasons, should do as much for Montigny [who was then in Spain], and the groom of his chamber." Thereupon followed the arrest of Montigny.

[6] Cavalli, July 3, 1568, gives this despatch also in the extract. It is, if possible, still more remarkable than that before cited: " There has arrived here the account of the execution in Flanders of those poor noblemen who were

We see that Alva was cruel from principle. Who could hope
for mercy from the fearful tribunal that he erected, under the
name of " Council of Disturbances "? He ruled the provinces
by arrests and executions; he razed the houses of the condemned
to the ground, and confiscated their property. He pursued his
ecclesiastical designs together with his political purposes. The
ancient power of the estates was reduced to a mere name, Spanish troops occupied the country, and a citadel was erected in
the most important mercantile city. The duke insisted with
obstinate despotism on the exaction of the most odious taxes;
and in Spain, whence also he drew large sums, people asked,
with surprise, what he could do with all the money. It is, however, true that the country was obedient; no malcontent ventured to move; every trace of Protestantism disappeared; and
those who had been driven into neighboring districts remained
perfectly still.

" Monsignore," said a member of Philip's Council to the papal
nuncio during these events, " are you now satisfied with the
proceedings of the King? " " Perfectly satisfied," replied the
nuncio, with a smile.

Alva himself believed he had performed a master-stroke, and
it was not without contempt that he regarded the French Government, which had not been able to make itself master in its
own territory.

After the rapid progress made by Protestantism in France, a
violent reaction took place in the year 1562, more especially in
the capital.

The close connection of Protestantism with the court faction
had unquestionably been the circumstance most injurious to its
influence. For a certain period the whole population seemed
inclined toward the Protestant confession; but when its adherents, hurried on by their connection with some of the leaders
of faction, took up arms, and committed those acts of violence

prisoners, according to what the Duke
of Alva says (who had authority from
his Majesty to execute them or not, as
he thought best): the people were
somewhat excited, and were exulting in
the defeat of those Spaniards, and the
death of Arenberg; he thought it time
therefore to show that he did not fear
them in any manner; and by this terror
to remove all hope from those who
might have moved for the liberation of
the prisoners, and also to avoid falling
into the error of the Emperor Charles,
who, by sparing the Elector of Saxony
and the landgrave, caused a new conspiracy, by which his Majesty was driv-
en with little dignity from Germany, and
almost from the empire."

that are inseparable from a state of warfare, they lost their advantage in public opinion. " What kind of religion is this? " men asked. " Where has Christ commanded the pillage of our neighbor and the shedding of his blood? " When the city of Paris at length found it needful to assume an attitude of defence against the attacks of Condé, who appeared as the leader of the Huguenots, all public bodies displayed a disposition adverse to Protestantism; the population of the city capable of bearing arms was organized as a military body, and the officers appointed to command this force were required above all things to be Catholics. The members of the university and of the Parliament, with the very numerous class of advocates, were compelled to subscribe a confession of faith, the articles of which were purely Catholic.

It was under the influence of this change in public opinion that the Jesuits established themselves in France. Their commencement was on a very small scale; they had to content themselves with colleges thrown open to them by a few ecclesiastical dignitaries, their partisans, in Billon and Tournon, places remote from the centre of the kingdom, and where nothing effectual could be accomplished. In the larger towns, more particularly in Paris, they at first encountered the most determined opposition; above all from the Sorbonne, the Parliament, and the archbishop, who all believed their own interests liable to be prejudiced by the privileges and character of the order. But they gradually acquired the favor of the more zealous Catholics, and especially of the court, which was unwearied in commending them for " their exemplary lives and pure doctrines, by which many apostates had been brought back to the faith, and East and West induced to acknowledge the presence of the Lord." [7] Thus at length they succeeded in removing all impediments; and in the year 1564 were admitted to the privilege of teaching. In Lyons they had already made their position secure. They had the good-fortune, whether by their merit or mere chance, to include from the first several men of remarkable talents among their members. To the Huguenot preachers

---

[7] In a manuscript in the Berlin Library, MSS. Gall. n. 75, the following document will be found among others: " Délibérations et consultations au parlement de Paris, touchant l'etablissement des Jesuites en France." In this are especially given the messages of the court to the Parliament in favor of the Jesuits; and we are told that . . . they have pierced unyielding and ferocious breasts with the sword of the faith."

they opposed Edmund Augier, who was born in France, but educated in Rome under Ignatius Loyola; and of whom the Protestants themselves are reported to have said that had he not worn Catholic vestments, there would never have existed a more perfect orator. An extraordinary impression was produced both by his preaching and writing. In Lyons, more particularly, the Huguenots were completely defeated, their preachers were exiled, their churches destroyed, and their books burnt. For the Jesuits, on the contrary, in the year 1563, a magnificent college was erected. They had a highly distinguished professor also, Maldonat, whose exposition of the Bible attracted the youth of the country in multitudes, and enchained their attention. From these great cities they extended themselves over the kingdom in all directions; they formed establishments in Toulouse and Bordeaux. Wherever they appeared, the number of Catholic communicants was observed to increase. The catechism of Augier had extraordinary success; within the space of eight years, 38,000 copies of it were sold in Paris alone.[8]

It is possible that the revived popularity of Catholic ideas may have produced an effect on the court, and the rather as it was most decided in the capital. Be this as it may, these ideas acquired a support the more, when in 1568, after long hesitation, the court once again declared itself decidedly Catholic.

This determination proceeded chiefly from the circumstance that Catherine de' Medici felt her power to be more firmly secured since her son had attained his majority. She was no longer compelled to conciliate the Huguenot leaders, as had previously been the case. The example of Alva showed how much could be accomplished by inflexible determination. The Pope continually exhorted her to repress the insolence of the rebels, to arrest their progress, and no longer to endure their existence. At length he accompanied his admonitions by the permission to aleniate church property, by which the treasury gained a million and a half of livres.[9] Accordingly, Catherine de' Medici, following the example given the year before by the Governess of the Netherlands, imposed an oath on the French nobility, by which they bound themselves to abjure every en-

[8] These notices are found in Orlandinus, and the authors who have continued his work, pars i. lib. vi. n. 30; ii. lib. iv. 84; iii. iii. 169 et seq. Juvencius v. 24, 769, gives a biography of Augier.
[9] Catena, " Vita di Pio V.," p. 79.

gagement contracted without the previous knowledge of the King.[10] She demanded the dismissal of all their magistrates from the cities which were suspected of favoring the new doctrines, and assured Philip II in September of the year 1563, that she would tolerate no other religion but the Catholic.

The resolution thus announced was one that could not be enforced in France without the intervention of arms, and war instantly burst forth.

It was entered on with extraordinary zeal by the Catholic party. At the request of the Pope, Philip of Spain sent the French an auxiliary force of practised troops under experienced leaders. Pius V caused collections to be made in the States of the Church, and gathered contributions from the Italian princes; nay, the holy father himself despatched a small body of troops across the Alps; that same army to whose leader he gave the ferocious command to kill every Huguenot that might fall into his hands, and grant quarter to none.

The Huguenots also drew their forces together; they too were full of religious zeal, and looked on the papal soldiers as the army of antichrist arrayed against them. They too gave no quarter, and were equally provided with foreign aid. They were nevertheless entirely defeated at Moncontour.

With what exultation did Pius V receive the Huguenot standards that were sent him after the battle; how joyfully did he place them in the churches of St. Peter and St. John Lateran! He conceived the most daring hopes. It was at this moment that he pronounced the sentence of excommunication against Queen Elizabeth. He even flattered himself with the hope of leading an expedition against England in person.

So far, he was, however, not permitted to proceed.

As had so frequently occurred before, a revulsion of opinion now took place in the Court of France, and this, though occasioned by trifling circumstances of a personal nature only, yet brought about great changes in matters of the highest importance.

The King became envious of the honor gained by his brother the Duke of Anjou, from the defeat of the Huguenots at Moncontour, where he had commanded the troops; and of

[10] The oath is given by Serranus, " Commentarii de Statu Religionis in Regno Galliæ," iii. 153.

the influence acquired by the duke from the repose he had thus procured to the country. He was confirmed in this feeling by those around him, who were equally jealous of Anjou's followers, and who feared lest power should go hand in hand with the honor they had acquired. Not only were the advantages gained followed up with the utmost indifference, and after long delay; but in opposition to the high Catholic party led by Anjou, another and more moderate party appeared at court; which adopted a line of policy altogether different, made peace with the Huguenots, and invited the Protestant leaders to the court. In the year 1569, the French, in alliance with Spain and the Pope, had sought to overthrow the Queen of England; in the summer of 1572, we see them in league with that Queen to wrest the Netherlands from Spain.

Meanwhile, these changes were too sudden and too imperfectly matured, to have consistency or duration. The most violent explosion followed, and affairs resumed their previous direction.

There can be no doubt that Catherine de' Medici, while entering with a certain degree of warmth and earnestness into the policy and plans of the dominant party, which favored her interests, so far as they appeared likely to assist in placing her youngest son Alençon on the English throne, was yet concerting the measures requisite for executing a stroke of policy directly opposed to them. She did her utmost to draw the Huguenots to Paris; numerous as they were, they were there surrounded and held in check by a population far more numerous, in a state of military organization, and easily excited to fanaticism. She had previously given a very significant intimation to the Pope of her purpose in this proceeding, but had she still felt wavering, the occurrences of the moment were such as must at once have determined her. The Huguenots were on the point of gaining over the King himself; they were apparently supplanting the authority of the Queen-mother, and in this danger she hesitated no longer; with the irresistible and magic power that she exercised over her children, she aroused all the latent fanaticism of the King; it cost her but a word to make the people take to arms; that word she spoke. Of the eminent Huguenots, each one was pointed out to his personal enemy, and given over to his vengeance. Catherine had declared herself to wish for the death of six men only; the death of these alone would she take upon her conscience. The number massacred was fifty thousand.[1]

Thus, all that the Spaniards had perpetrated in the Netherlands was exceeded by the French. What the first brought about gradually, with deliberate calculation, and with a certain observance of legal forms, the latter accomplished in the heat of passion, in defiance of all forms of law, and by the aid of a populace roused to a fury of fanaticism. The result appeared to be the same. Not one leader was left whose name might serve as a point round which the scattered Huguenots could gather; many fled, a large number surrendered; place after place returned to attendance on the mass, the preachers were silenced. With pleasure Philip II saw himself imitated and surpassed; he offered Charles IX, who had now for the first time earned a right to be called the most Christian King, to assist the completion of his undertaking by the power of his arms. Pope Gregory XIII celebrated this great event by a solemn procession to the church of San Luigi. The Venetians, who seemed to have no particular interest in the matter, expressed in official despatches to their ambassador, their satisfaction at " this favor of God."

But can it be possible that crimes of a character so sanguinary can ever succeed? Are they not in too flagrant opposition to the more profound mysteries of human events, to the undefined, yet inviolable and ever active principles that govern the order of nature? Men may blind themselves for a time, but they cannot disturb the moral laws on which their existence reposes; these rule with a necessity inevitable as that which regulates the course of the stars.

Section VI.—Resistance of the Protestants in the Netherlands, France, and Germany

Macchiavel advises his prince to execute the cruelties he shall deem necessary in rapid succession, but gradually to permit more lenient measures to follow.

It would almost seem that the Spaniards had sought to follow this advice to the letter, in their government of the Netherlands.

[1] For the sake of brevity, I here refer the reader to my dissertation on the Massacre of St. Bartholomew in the " Histor. Polit. Zeitschrift," ii. iii.

They appeared to be themselves at length of opinion that property enough had been confiscated, heads enough struck off, and that the time for mercy had arrived. In the year 1572 the Venetian ambassador at Madrid declares his conviction that the Prince of Orange would obtain his pardon if he would ask for it. The King received the deputies of the Netherlands very favorably, when they arrived with a petition for the repeal of the impost of the tenth penny, and even thanked them for their pains. He had determined to recall the Duke of Alva, and to replace him by a more clement governor.

But it was now too late. Immediately after the conclusion of that treaty between France and England, which had preceded the Massacre of St. Bartholomew, the insurrection broke out. Alva had believed his work at an end, but the struggle was in fact only then beginning. He defeated the enemy whenever he met them in the open field, but in the towns of Holland and Zealand, where the religious excitement had been most profound, and where Protestantism had attained to a more effectual organization, he encountered a force of resistance that he could not overcome.

In Haarlem, when all means of supporting life were consumed, even to the grass growing between the stones, the inhabitants resolved to cut their way through the besiegers with their wives and children. The dissensions prevailing in their garrison compelled them at last to surrender, but they had shown that the Spaniards might be resisted. The people of Alkmar declared themselves for the Prince of Orange at the moment when the enemy appeared before their gates: their defence was heroic as their resolution, not a man would leave his post, however severely wounded; before the walls of Alkmar the Spaniards received their first effectual repulse. The country breathed again, and new courage entered the hearts of the people.

The men of Leyden declared, that rather than yield they would devour their left arms to enable themselves to continue the defence with their right. They took the bold resolution of breaking down their dams and calling on the waves of the North Sea to expel the besiegers. Their misery had reached its utmost extremity, when a northwest wind, setting in at the critical moment, laid the country under water to the depth of several feet, and drove the enemy from their borders.

The French Protestants had also regained their courage; no sooner did they perceive that their government, notwithstanding the savage massacre it had committed, displayed irresolution, procrastinated and adopted contradictory measures, than they again took arms and soon burst forth anew. La Rochelle and Sancerre defended themselves as Leyden and Alkmar had done—the preachers of peace were heard exhorting men to arms—women shared in the combat with their husbands and brothers. It was the heroic age of Protestantism in Western Europe.

The acts of cruelty, committed or sanctioned by the most powerful princes, were met by a resistance proceeding from various nameless points, but which had its secret origin in the most profound religious convictions, and which no amount of force could overcome.

It is not our purpose at this time to give the details and follow the vicissitudes of the wars in France and the Netherlands—this would lead us too far from our principal object—they are besides to be found in many other books; it must suffice to say that the Protestants maintained their ground.

In the year 1573, and again in the following years, the French Government was repeatedly compelled to enter into negotiations, from which the Huguenots gained a renewal of former concessions.

In the Netherlands the power of the government had fallen to ruin in the year 1576; the Spanish troops not receiving their regular pay, were in open insurrection, and all the provinces had united against them, those which had hitherto maintained their allegiance with those which had revolted, the districts remaining in a great measure Catholic, with those entirely Protestant. The States-General took the government into their own hands, appointed captains-general, governors, and magistrates, and garrisoned the fortified places with their own troops in place of the King's.[1] The Treaty of Ghent was concluded, by which provinces pledged themselves to expel the Spaniards and keep them out of the country. Philip of Spain sent his brother, who might be considered a Netherlander and fellow-countryman, to govern them as Charles V had done: but Don John was not even acknowledged until he had promised to fulfil the prin-

[1] This turn of affairs is made particularly intelligible in Tassis, iii. 15-19.

cipal conditions laid before him; he was compelled to accept
the Treaty of Ghent, and to dismiss the Spanish troops; and
no sooner did he make the first movement to free himself from
the restraint that fettered him, than all parties rose against him.
He was declared an enemy of the country, and the chiefs of
the provinces called another prince of his house to take his
place.

The principle of local government now obtained supremacy
over the monarchical power, the native authority was victorious
over the Spanish rule.

From this state of things various consequences necessarily
arose. The Northern provinces, which had conducted the opposition, and thereby rendered the existing circumstances possible, at once acquired a natural preponderance in all that related to the war and the government; it thus followed that
the reformed religion was propagated through the whole extent
of the Netherlands. It was received in Mechlin, Brussels, and
Ypres. The people of Antwerp divided their churches between
the two confessions, and the Catholics were occasionally compelled to content themselves with the choirs of those churches
which they had so lately held in sole possession. In Ghent the
Protestant tendency was mingled with a civil commotion, and
obtained entire supremacy. The Treaty of Ghent had guaranteed the maintenance of the Catholic Church in its former condition, but the States-General now issued an edict by which
equal liberty was secured to both confessions. Thenceforth
Protestant opinions made rapid advance, even in those provinces
that were principally Catholic, and there seemed good cause for
the expectation that they would eventually become predominant
throughout the country.

How changed was the position now held by the Prince of
Orange. He had but lately been an exile, whose best hope was
to obtain pardon; he was now possessed of a well-established
power in the northern provinces, was sheriff (*Ruwart*) of Brabant, all-powerful in the Assembly of the States, and acknowledged as their chief and leader by a great religious and political party, which was making rapid progress. He was
besides in close alliance with all the Protestants of Europe, and
more especially with his neighbors the Germans.

The aggressions of the Catholics were resisted in Germany

also with a force on the Protestant part which seemed to promise the most important results.

The effects of this resistance were apparent in the general transactions of the empire, in the assemblies of the electors, and in the imperial diets, although there the German system of conducting affairs prevented any adequate results from appearing. They were most sensibly felt, as had been the aggressions that had called forth the resistance, in the several territories and distinct sovereignties into which Germany was divided.

It was in the spiritual principalites, as we have seen, that the question was most earnestly debated. There was scarcely one wherein the prince had not attempted to restore Catholicism to its ancient supremacy. The Protestants, who felt their own strength, retorted with efforts equally comprehensive, and labored with equal energy to bring the ecclesiastical sovereignties themselves to their own opinions.

In the year 1577 Gebhard Truchsess ascended the archiepiscopal chair of Cologne. This was to be ascribed in great measure to the influence possessed by Count Nuenar over the chapter, and perfectly well did that powerful Protestant know who it was that he recommended. It is certain that Gebhard's acquaintance with Agnes von Mansfeld, which is said to have influenced his decision, was not required to determine him against the Catholics. Even at his solemn entry into Cologne, when the clergy met him in procession, he did not alight from his horse, as was the established custom, to kiss the cross. He appeared in the church in a military dress, nor would he consent to perform high mass. He attached himself from the very first to the Prince of Orange, and his principal counsellors were Calvinists.[2] Further, he did not scruple to mortgage land in order to raise troops; was careful to secure the attachment of the nobles, and favored certain of the guilds of Cologne, which had begun to oppose themselves to Catholic usages; all circumstances tending to show the existence of that purpose which he afterward manifested openly—of converting his spiritual sovereignty into a secular electorate.

Gebhard Truchsess still conformed, occasionally at least, and in externals, to the Catholic faith. The adjacent bishoprics of

[2] Maffei, " Annali di Gregorio XIII.," t. i. p. 331.

Westphalia and Lower Saxony, on the contrary, fell, as we have already observed, immediately into the hands of Protestants. The elevation of Duke Henry of Saxe-Lauenburg was most especially important. He had been elected while yet very young, and, though a firm Lutheran, to the archbishopric of Bremen; some time after to the bishopric of Osnaburg, and, in 1577, to that of Paderborn.[3] Even in Münster, a large party, including all the younger members of the chapter, was attached to his interests, and but for the direct intervention of Gregory XIII, who declared a resignation actually made to be null and void, he would have been elevated to that see also, spite of all efforts made to prevent it by the rigidly Catholic party. Indeed, these last were still unable to prevail so far as to secure the election of any other bishop.

It is obvious that a powerful impulse must have been given to Protestant opinions in Rhenish Westphalia—where they had before been widely propagated—by the disposition on the part of the ecclesiastical chiefs. There needed only some fortunate combination of circumstances, some well-directed stroke, to secure the decided predominance of Protestantism in that district.

All Germany would have felt the influence of this event. The same contingencies were probable in regard to the bishoprics of Upper Germany, as those we have seen occurring in the lower part of the empire; and, even in the territories where the restoration had begun, resistance to its efforts was far from being suppressed.

How keenly was this truth experienced by the Abbot Balthasar of Fulda! When it was seen that the intercessions of neighboring princes, and the complaints laid before the diet, produced no effect, but that the abbot persisted, in disregard of all, to complete his restoration of the Catholic faith, and went about enforcing his regulations throughout the abbacy, he was one day encountered at Hamelberg, whither he had gone in the summer of 1576, for the promotion of these very purposes, was assailed by his nobles with arms in their hands, and imprisoned in his own house. Finding that all measures were taken to oppose him, that his neighbors beheld his embarrassment with satisfaction, and that the Bishop of Würzburg was

[3] Hamelmann, "Oldenburgisches Chronikon," s. 436.

even assisting his enemies, he resigned himself, perforce, to the abdication of the government, and was deprived of his dominions.[4]

In Bavaria also, Duke Albert found his purposes still far from being accomplished. He complained to the Pope that his nobility would rather forego the sacrament altogether than receive it in one kind.

But it was of much higher importance that Protestantism was making continual progress in the Austrian provinces, and was gradually acquiring an acknowledged and legalized existence. Under the wisely conducted government of Maximilian II, it not only gained a fixed position in Austria proper, both east and west of the Ens, but had also extended throughout the neighboring districts. That Emperor had scarcely redeemed the County of Glatz from the Dukes of Bavaria, who had held it in mortgage (1567), before the nobles, public officers, towns, and finally the larger part of the people went over to the evangelical confession. Hans von Pubschütz, the captain-general established a Protestant consistory by his own authority; and, upheld by this, he sometimes proceeded further than the Emperor would have desired. Gradually, the estates there also obtained a high degree of power and independence. This was altogether the most prosperous epoch of the county, the mines were thriving, the towns were rich and flourishing, the nobles well educated and orderly, waste lands were reclaimed in all directions, and villages were established among them.[5] The Church of Albendorf, to which, in the present day, thousands of pilgrims annually proceed for the purpose of kissing an old image of the Virgin, was at that time occupied by Protestant preachers during sixty years.[6] Some time later, only nine Catholic burghers were counted in the capital, while there were three hundred of the evangelical faith. We cannot be surprised that Pope Pius V should feel inexpressible aversion to the Emperor Maximilian. On one occasion, when the conversation

[4] Schannat, "Historia Fuldensis," pars iii. p. 268. A letter from the abbot to Pope Gregory, dated August 1, 1576, is particularly remarkable. Schannat gives it from the Archives of the Vatican. "Clamantes," he says of the threats of his enemies, "calling out, that unless I consent to transfer my authority to the bishop, they will destroy me as they would a mad-dog, and then turn the princes of Saxony and Hesse upon my flock."

[5] Joseph Kögler's "Chronik von Glatz," bd. i. heft ii. p. 72. The author was a Catholic parish priest; his work is very sensible and useful.

[6] From 1563 to 1623, "Documentirte Beschreibung von Albendorf" (an earlier printed fragment of the same chronicle), p. 36.

turned on the war that sovereign was engaged in with the Turks, Pius declared outright that he knew not to which side he least wished the victory.[7] Protestantism continued under these circumstances to make progress even in the interior provinces of Austria, over which the Emperor did not exercise immediate control. In the year 1568 twenty-four evangelical pastors were already counted in Carinthia; and in 1571 the capital of Styria had only one Catholic in its Council. Not that the evangelical doctrines found a support in this country from the Archduke Charles, its governor; on the contrary, this prince introduced the Jesuits, and promoted their efforts to the utmost of his power, but Protestant opinions prevailed in the estates.[8] In the diets, where religious affairs were mingled with the administraton of government and the defence of the country, they had the upper hand; for every concession they made in political matters, they demanded religious immunities in return. At the Diet of Bruck on the Muhr, held in 1578, the archduke was compelled to accord the free exercise of the evangelical religion, not only in the domains of the nobles and landed proprietors, where he could not have prevented it, but also in the four important towns of Grätz, Judenburg, Klagenfurt, and Laibach.[9] Thereupon the Protestant institutions were regularly organized in those provinces as in the imperial territories. A Protestant administration of the churches was established; a regular system of preaching and schools arranged, on the model of that prevailing in Würtemburg. In some instances, as at St. Veit, Catholics were excluded from the municipal elections,[10] and were no longer admitted to provincial offices. Under favor of these circumstances, Protestantism first gained the ascendancy in a country so closely neighboring to Italy. The impulse given by the Jesuits was here counteracted by the most steadfast opposition.

In all the provinces of Austria, of the German, Sclavonic, and Hungarian tongues, with the single exception of the Tyrol, Protestantism was in 1578 the predominant religion.

[7] Tiepolo, " Relatione di Pio IV. e V." ; he further adds, " Speaking of the death of the Spanish prince, the Pope said he had heard of it with great regret, because it would grieve him to see the dominions of the Catholic King fall into the hands of the Germans."
[8] Socher, " Historia Societatis Jesu Provinciæ Austriæ," i. iv. 166, 184; v. 33.

[9] Supplication to his imp. Rom. Maj. and intercession of the three principalities and the State, in Lehmann, " De Pace Religionis," p. 461; a document which serves to correct the statement made by Khevenhiller, " Ann. Ferdinandei," i. 6.
[10] Hermann, in the " Kärntnerischen Zeitschrift," v. p. 189.

It thus becomes evident that throughout Germany the progress made by Catholicism was met by successful opposition and equal progress on the part of the Protestants.

Section VII.—Contrasts exhibited in Other Parts of Europe

The epoch we are considering is indeed a most remarkable one; the two great religious tendencies are seen once more in active conflict, with equal hope of obtaining the ascendancy.

As compared with former times, the position of things had materially changed: at an earlier period each party had been willing to treat with the other; reconciliation had been attempted in Germany; a way seemed prepared for it in France; it was demanded in the Netherlands; nor did it appear to be impracticable, since toleration was in some places practised. But the spirit of opposition had now assumed a more hostile and threatening aspect. Throughout Europe the antagonist principles were, so to speak, now provoking each other to the combat. We shall be amply repaid by a slight review of the general state of things as existing in the year 1578-9.

Let us commence in the East, and with Poland.

Here, also, the Jesuits had made their way, under sanction of the bishops, who sought in them for support to their own power. In the year 1569 a college was founded for them in Braunsberg, by Cardinal Hosius, Bishop of Ermeland. They settled themselves in Pultusk and Posen likewise—at each place with the aid of the bishop. The Lutherans of Lithuania proposed to establish a university on their own principles, and the Bishop Valerian of Wilna, considering it highly essential to counteract the effect of this, erected a Jesuit school in his diocese. He was old and failing, and desired to mark his last days by this meritorious action. The first members of the society arrived in his see in the year 1570.[1]

Here, as in other places, the first result of these efforts merely was that Protestants took measures to maintain their influence. In the convocation diet of 1573 they carried a resolution by virtue of which all men were secured from offence or injury on account of religious opinions.[2]

---

[1] Sacchinus, "Historia Societatis Jesu," p. ii. lib. viii. 114; p. iii. lib. i. 112; lib. vi. 103-108.

[2] Fredro, "Henricus I. rex Polonorum," p. 114.

The bishops were compelled to submit: the example of the troubles in the Netherlands was brought forward to prove to them the dangers that might arise from their refusal. The succeeding kings of Poland were also compelled to promise the maintenance of this resolution. In the year 1579 the payment of tithes to the clergy was suspended, and the nuncio declared that 1,200 parish priests were rendered destitute by this regulation. A high court of judicature was established in the same year, composed of laity and clergy in equal numbers, and which took cognizance even of ecclesiastical disputes. The utmost surprise was expressed in Rome that the Polish clergy should endure a tribunal so constituted.

The contest was equally animated in Sweden as in Poland, and was accompanied by very peculiar circumstances—these had immediate reference to the person of the sovereign, who was indeed the object of the struggle.

In all the sons of Gustavus Vasa—" the brood of King Gustavus," as the Swedes called them—there was a very unusual mixture of deep reflection with impetuous wilfulness, of devotional feeling with excessive violence.

The most highly cultivated of these princes was John, the second son of Gustavus. He had married a Catholic princess, Catherine of Poland, who had shared his prison, in the rigorous solitude of which he had received consolation from a Catholic priest; thus these religious disputes awakened his particular interest. The Swedish prince had studied the fathers to gain a clearer comprehension of the state of the Church from the earliest times: he looked favorably on all books treating of a possible reconciliation between the two confessions, and his attention was continually occupied by questions connected with this subject. When he became king he made, in fact, certain approaches toward the Church of Rome; he published a liturgy on the model of that sanctioned by the Council of Trent, and in which the Swedish divines perceived with amazement that not only the usages, but even some of the distinguishing doctrines of the Roman Church, were included.[3] As the intercession of the Pope, as well with the Catholic princes in general, on account of the Russian war, as with the Spanish Court in par-

[3] They are all to be found in the "Judicium Prædicatorum Holmenss. de publicata Liturgia," in Baaz, "Inventarium Ecclesiarum Sueogoth," p. 393.

ticular, with regard to the maternal inheritance of his wife, was likely to be essential to the interests of the Swedish monarch, he did not hesitate to send one of his nobles as ambassador to Rome; he even permitted some few Jesuits from the Netherlands to settle in Stockholm, where he committed an important institution for the education of youth to their charge.

These proceedings naturally excited very sanguine hopes in Rome; and Antonio Possevin, one of the most clever men in the Society of Jesus, was selected to make a strenuous effort for the conversion of King John.

In the year 1578 Possevin arrived in Sweden; the King was not disposed to give way on all points; he demanded that marriage should be conceded to the priests, that the sacramental cup should be granted to the laity, that mass should be performed in the language of the country, that the Church should abandon all its claims to confiscated property, and make other concessions of similar character. Possevin was not authorized to decide on these questions; he promised only to lay the King's demands before the Apostolic See, and then hastened to insist on the dogmatical points of controversy. In regard to these he had much more success. After some few interviews, and a certain time for reflection, the King declared himself resolved to make the *professio fidei* according to the formula of the Council of Trent. This profession of faith he did in fact subscribe, and then confessed. Possevin once more inquired if he submitted to the judgment of the Pope in regard to the sacrament in one kind? John replied that he did so, when the Jesuit solemnly granted him absolution.

It would almost appear that this absolution was the King's most immediate object and principal wish. He had caused his brother to be put to death; it is true that the estates had previously approved that measure, still it was the death of a brother, and was accompanied by circumstances of extreme violence: the absolution he had received seemed to give peace to his mind. Possevin prayed to God that he might be permitted to turn the heart of this prince. John arose and threw himself into the arms of his confessor. "As I embrace thee," he exclaimed, "even so do I embrace the Catholic faith now and forever." He then received the sacrament according to the Catholic ritual.

Having thus successfully accomplished his task, Possevin returned to Rome, and communicated the result to the Pope: he also imparted it, under the seal of secrecy, to the most powerful Catholic sovereigns. There now remained only to take into consideration those demands of the Swedish King on which he made the restoration of Catholicism in his dominions principally to depend. Possevin had great address, was very eloquent, and possessed considerable talent for negotiation, but he had too easily persuaded himself that his end was attained. The account he gave induced Pope Gregory to believe that no concessions were necessary. He therefore demanded, on the contrary, that the King should declare himself freely and unconditionally a Catholic. Charged with letters to that effect, and with indulgences for all who would return to the Roman Church, the Jesuit departed on his second journey.

But the opposite party had meanwhile not remained inactive; Protestant princes had sent warning letters to the King, for intelligence of his proceedings had spread through all Europe. Chytræus had dedicated his work on the Confession of Augsburg to the Swedish sovereign, and had thereby produced a certain impression on that learned prince. The Protestants did not again lose sight of him.

Possevin now arrived, no more as on the previous occasion in the usual dress of civilians, but in the proper costume of his order, and bringing with him a large number of Catholic books. His very appearance seemed instantly to make an unfavorable impression. He hesitated a moment to produce the papal reply, but seeing at length that he must not venture further delay, he laid it before the King in an audience that lasted two hours. Who can penetrate the secret movements of a wavering and unsettled mind? The monarch's self-esteem was perhaps wounded by so positive a refusal of his demands, he was doubtless convinced that nothing was to be accomplished in Sweden without the concessions he had required, and felt no disposition to abdicate his crown for the sake of religion. Enough—the audience was decisive—from that hour the King betrayed coldness and aversion toward the envoy of the pontiff. He required his Jesuit schoolmen to receive the sacrament in both kinds, and to read mass in the Swedish tongue; as they did not obey him, which indeed they could not, he refused to continue the provision he had allowed them. They left Stockholm very soon after, and their departure was doubtless not caused wholly by the plague, as they desired to have it believed. The Protestant nobles, with the King's younger brother, Charles of Sudermania, who was disposed to Calvinism, and the ambassadors of Lubeck, neglected no means that might increase this growing aversion. The sole remaining hope and stay of the Catholics was now the Queen, and after her death the heir to the throne. For that time the sovereign power in Sweden continued essentially Protestant.[4]

In England the government became daily more and more firmly attached to the reformed opinions, under Queen Elizabeth. But in that kingdom there existed assailable points of a different kind; the country was filled with Catholics; not only did the Irish population adhere steadfastly to the ancient faith and ritual, but in England also there was probably one-half of the people, if not—as some have asserted—a larger proportion, still attached to Catholicism. It has always occasioned surprise that the English Catholics should have submitted to the Protestant laws of Elizabeth, which they did at least during the first fifteen years of her reign. They took the oath required from them, although it was in direct opposition to the papal authority; they attended the Protestant churches, and thought they had done quite enough if, in going and returning, they kept together and avoided the society of the Protestants.[5]

A firm conviction was nevertheless maintained in Rome of their secret attachment; all were persuaded that nothing more than opportunity or some slight advantage was required to inflame all the Catholics of the kingdom, and rouse them to resistance. Pius V had already expressed a wish that he could shed his blood in an expedition against England. The hope

[4] In the whole of this account, I confine myself to the reports of the Jesuits (which, so far as I can discover, were never used before), as they may be found at length in Sacchinus, " Hist. Societatis Jesu," etc., pars iv. lib. vi. n. 64-76, and lib. vii. n. 83-111. I am anxious to know whether the continuation of Theiner's " Schweden und seine Stellung zum heiligen Stuhl," will really communicate anything new that may be worthy of notice. This work, filled as it is with coarse invectives, has hitherto excited pity rather than attention; we must hope that " they know not what they do."

[5] " Relatione del presente Stato d'Inghilterra, cavata da una lettera scritta di Londra," etc., Rome, 1590 (printed pamphlet), agrees entirely on this subject with a passage of Ribadaneira, "De Schismate," which Hallam has already quoted (" Constitutional History of England," i. p. 162), and is without doubt the original source: " They have permitted themselves to take impious oaths against the authority of the Apostolic See; and this with little or no scruple of conscience. And then they all go commonly to the synagogues of the heretics, and to their preachings, taking with them their children and families. They consider it distinction enough if they go to church before the heretics, and do not leave it in their company."

and thought of such an enterprise were never abandoned by Gregory XIII, who was much disposed to employ the martial spirit and exalted station of Don John of Austria for its accomplishment. To this effect he despatched his nuncio Sega, who had been with Don John in the Netherlands, into Spain, with the hope of inducing Philip II to concur in his undertaking.

But it happened that, sometimes from the King's disinclination to forward the ambitious views of his brother, sometimes from his objection to being involved in new political embarrassments, and sometimes from other obstacles, the whole affair came to nothing; these vast plans had to be resigned, and their projectors were forced to content themselves with less magnificent enterprises.

Pope Gregory next fixed his attention on Ireland. It was represented to him that there was no people more strictly and steadily Catholic than the Irish, but that the nation was tyrannously maltreated by the English Government; that the people were despoiled, disunited, wilfully kept in a state of barbarism, and oppressed in their religious convictions; that they were thus at every moment prepared for war, and wanted nothing more than the aid of a small body of troops; with 5,000 men Ireland might be conquered, since there was not a fortress in the country that could hold out more than four days.[6] The Pope was easily persuaded to believe these assertions. There was then living in Rome an English refugee, named Thomas Stukely, an adventurer by nature, but possessing in a remarkable degree the art of gaining access to the great, and of winning their confidence. The Pope had appointed him his chamberlain, had created him Marquis of Leinster, and now expended 40,000 scudi to furnish him with ships and men. On the French coast Stukely was to be joined by Geraldine, an Irish exile, commanding a small body of troops which he had got together, also at the Pope's expense. Philip of Spain had no wish to engage in war, but he was glad to give Elizabeth occupation at home, and therefore contributed a sum of money toward

[6] " Discorso sopra il Regno d' Irlanda e della Gente che bisogneria per conquistarlo, fatto a Gregorio XIII.," Library at Vienna, Fugger, MSS." The government of the Queen is declared to be a tyranny: "Leaving the authority to English ministers, who practise every art of tyranny in that Kingdom to enrich themselves; as, for example, transporting all the commodities of the country into England; taxing the people in violation of their ancient laws and privileges; and fomenting wars and factions among the natives of the country; the English not wishing that the inhabitants should learn the difference between living in freedom and in servitude."

this enterprise.[7] Stukely, however, most unexpectedly allowed himself to be persuaded to take part in the expedition of King Sebastian to Africa, with the force destined for Ireland, and he lost his life in that service. Geraldine was thus left to make the attempt alone; he landed in June, 1579, and at first gained some advantages, having seized the fort commanding the harbor of Limerick. The Earl of Desmond was also in arms against the Queen, and the whole island was thrown into commotion. But one misfortune soon followed another, the most serious being the death of Geraldine himself, who was killed in a skirmish. After this the Earl of Desmond could no longer hold out, the supplies sent by the Pope were insufficient, the money expected did not arrive, and the English remained victorious. They punished the insurgents with fearful cruelty: men and women were driven into barns and burnt to death, children were strangled, all Munster was laid waste, and English colonists took possession of the devastated province.

If Catholicism were ever again to raise its head in the dominions of Elizabeth, it was in England itself that the attempt must be made; but this could manifestly not be done until the political relations of Europe should be altered. And if the Pope desired to secure that the English Catholics should continue attached to the faith, if he wished to find them Catholic when the time for active exertion should arrive, it was indispensable that spiritual aid should be supplied to them.

William Allen first conceived the idea of collecting into one body the young English Catholics, who were sent to the Continent for the prosecution of their studies, and, chiefly by the aid of Pope Gregory, he founded a college for them at Douay. But this did not seem sufficient to the Pope; he wished to provide a retreat for these young men beneath his own eye, and where they might be more secure and more tranquil than at Douay, in the turbulent Netherlands; he therefore established an English college in Rome, endowed it with a rich abbey, and placed it, in the year 1579, under the care of the Jesuits.[8]

No student was admitted into this college until he had first

[7] Twenty thousand scudi, according to the nuncio Sega, in his " Relatione compendiosa " (MS. of the Berlin Library): " He also made grants to the Baron d'Acres, to Signor Carlo Buono, and other English noblemen then in Madrid, whom he urged to go on this expedition, together with Bishop Lionese of Ireland."

[8] The accounts of the Jesuits in Sacchinus, part iv. 6; lib. vii. 10–30, may be here compared with Camden's " Statements," " Rerum Britannic," tom. i. p. 315.

pledged himself to return to England on the completion of his studies, and there preach the faith of the Roman Church. They were prepared for that purpose exclusively. Excited to religious enthusiasm by the spiritual exercises of Ignatius, the missionaries sent by Pope Gregory the Great for the conversion of the Anglo-Saxons were placed before them as models for their imitation.

Some of the older students soon entered on this career. In the year 1580 two English Jesuits, Persons and Campian, returned to their native country; constantly pursued, compelled to adopt feigned names, and to assume various disguises, they yet succeeded in reaching the capital, where they separated, the one travelling through the northern, the other through the southern, counties. They usually took up their abode in the dwellings of the Catholic nobles. Their coming was always announced, but the precaution was constantly taken of receiving them as strangers. A chapel had meanwhile been prepared in the most retired part of the house, into which they were conducted, and where the members of the family were assembled to receive their benediction. The missionary rarely prolonged his stay beyond one night. The evening of his arrival was employed in religious preparation and confession; on the following morning, mass was read, the sacrament administered, and a sermon preached. All the Catholics who were in the neighborhood attended, and the number was sometimes very great. The religion that for 900 years had ruled supreme over the island was thus once more inculcated, with the added charm of mystery and novelty. Secret synods were held, a printing-press was set up, first in a village near London, and afterward in a lonely house in a neighboring wood: Catholic books once more appeared, written with all the readiness and ability derived from constant practice in controversy, and sometimes with much elegance; the impression these works produced was strengthened by the impenetrable secrecy of their origin. The immediate result of these proceedings was, that the Catholics ceased to attend the Protestant service, and to observe the ecclesiastical edicts of the Queen; and that the opposite party insisted on their opinions with increased violence, while persecution became more severe and oppressive.[9]

[9] See Campiani, " Vita et Martyrium "; Ingoldstadii, 1584; also Sacchinus.

Wherever the principle of Catholic restoration had not strength enough to acquire the ascendancy, its effect was to exasperate both parties, and to render them more implacable.

An example of this was afforded by Switzerland, although each canton had long possessed the right of self-government in religious affairs, and the dissensions arising from time to time, in regard to the terms of the confederation, and the interpretation of the clauses concerning religion, in the "covenant of public peace" (*Landfriedens*), were very nearly set at rest.[10]

But the Jesuits found their way into that country also; at the instance of a colonel in the Swiss Guard of Rome, they presented themselves in Lucerne in the year 1574, where they met with a cordial reception and zealous support, more especially from the family of Pfyffer.[1] Ludwig Pfyffer alone appeared to have expended 30,000 gulden toward the erection of a Jesuits' college. Philip of Spain and the Guises are also said to have contributed money for that purpose, and the Pope did not fail to display his unwearied generosity toward institutions of this character by furnishing the means for procuring a library. The people of Lucerne were greatly rejoiced at these things; they sent an express memorial to the general of the order, entreating that he would not deprive them of those fathers of the society already in their city. "They were most anxious to see their youth brought up in sound learning, and above all in piety and a Christian life." They promised him, in return, to spare neither pains nor labor, neither life nor means, to serve the society in everything they should desire.[2]

An opportunity was soon presented them of proving their renewed zeal for Catholicism in a matter of some consequence.

The city of Geneva had placed itself under the special protection of Berne, and now endeavored to draw Soleure and Freiburg into the same alliance. These towns had most commonly adhered to Berne in political affairs, though not in religious matters. With respect to Soleure the attempt succeeded—a Catholic city received the very centre of Western Protestantism into its

[10] The most important was doubtless that relating to the fate of the evangelical party settled in Locarno, respecting which F. Meyer made a report in 1836, prepared from original documents. The Protestant cantons assented to that interpretation of the disputed article which favored the Catholics, and allowed that the evangelical party should be compelled to quit their country. They had completely disappeared from the canton in the year 1580.

[1] Agricola, 177.

[2] "Literæ Lucernensium ad Everardum Mercurianum," in Sacchinus, "Historia Societatis Jesu," iv. v. 145.

protection. Gregory XIII was alarmed, and turned his best
efforts to withhold at least Freiburg from the league. Lucerne
then came to his assistance. An embassy from that canton
joined its labors to those of the papal nuncio, and the people of
Freiburg not only declined the proposed alliance, but even invited the Jesuits to their city, where, with the assistance of
Gregory, they established a college.

The effects of Carlo Borromeo's exertions also began to make
themselves apparent. His influence had extended particularly
to the Wald cantons. Melchior Lussi, Landamman of Unterwalden, was esteemed the especial friend of the archbishop.
Borromeo first sent Capuchins into the country, and these friars
produced great impression on the people of the mountain districts, by the rigor and simplicity of their lives; they were followed by the pupils of the Helvetic college, which the archbishop had founded for that express purpose.

Traces of their influence were soon to be discovered in all
public affairs. In the autumn of 1579 the Catholic cantons
concluded a treaty with the Bishop of Basle, in which they engaged, not only to protect him in religious matters, but also
promised to bring back " to the true Catholic faith," if occasion
should serve, whoever among his subjects had gone over to the
Protestant opinions. This engagement was evidently calculated
to arouse the evangelical inhabitants of the cantons, and accordingly dissensions became more decided and bitter than they had
been for a long time. A papal nuncio arrived, who was received in the Catholic cantons with every possible mark of reverence, while in those of the Protestants he was contemned and
insulted.

Section VIII.—Crisis in the Netherlands

The general state of things in Europe was at that time as we
are about to describe. Restored Catholicism, under the form it
had assumed in Italy and Spain, had made an extensive inroad
upon the rest of Europe. It had gained important conquests
in Germany, and had made considerable advances in other countries, but in all it had encountered determined opposition. In
France the Protestants were secured by extensive privileges and
by the strength of their position—military and political. In
the Netherlands they held the supremacy. They were trium-

phant in England, Scotland, and the North. In Poland they had extorted stringent laws in their own favor, and had gained extensive influence in the general affairs of the kingdom. Throughout the territories of Austria they confronted the government, armed with the ancient immunities of the provincial States. In Lower Germany the ecclesiastical institutions seemed to be on the point of suffering material change.

In this position of affairs, vast importance was attached to the issue of the struggle in the Netherlands, where the people were continually resorting to arms.

It was impossible that Philip II could intend to repeat those measures which had already suffered so signal a failure; he was not, indeed, in a condition to do so. It was his good-fortune to receive the assistance of friends who presented themselves spontaneously. Protestantism, also, was arrested in its progress by an obstacle at once unexpected and insurmountable. We shall be well repaid for devoting a short time to the consideration of this important event.

In the first place, it was by no means agreeable to all parties in the provinces, that the Prince of Orange should possess so large an extent of power—least of all was this satisfactory to the Walloon nobility.

Under the government of the King, these nobles had ever been the first to take horse in all wars, most especially in those with France; it thus happened that the leaders of note, whom the people were accustomed to follow, had acquired a certain independence and authority. Under the government of the States, the nobles found themselves, on the contrary, placed in the background; their pay was irregular; the army of the States consisted principally of Dutch, English, and Germans, who, being undoubted Protestants, enjoyed the largest share of confidence.

When the Walloons acceded to the Treaty of Ghent, they had hoped to obtain a leading influence in the general affairs of the country, but the result was altogether contrary—power fell almost exclusively into the hands of the Prince of Orange and his friends of Holland and Zealand.

But the personal disaffection thus occasioned was not all—religious animosities combined with it.

Whatever may have been the cause, the fact is certain, that

in the Walloon provinces but little sympathy was ever excited toward the Protestant movements.

In these districts the new bishops, almost all men of great practical ability, had been peaceably installed. The see of Arras was held by François de Richardot, who had eagerly imbibed the principles of Catholic restoration in the Council of Trent, and who was the subject of incessant praises, for the elegance and learning that he united with force and solidity in his preaching, as well as for the zeal, tempered by acquaintance with the world, evinced in his life.[1] The Bishop of Namur was Antoine Havet, a Dominican, endowed, perhaps, with less worldly prudence, but also a member of the Council, and equally zealous for the promulgation of its edicts and the enforcement of their spirit.[2] The see of St. Omer was occupied by Gerard de Hamericourt, one of the richest prelates in all the provinces, and who was also Abbot of St. Bertin. His ambition was to promote the education of the youth in his diocese: he founded many schools, and was the first who founded a college for the Jesuits in the Netherlands, supported by fixed revenues. Under these and other heads of the Church, Artois, Hainault, and Namur remained in peace, while all the other provinces were exposed to the wild turbulence of the iconoclastic riots,[3] and in consequence, these districts had not been so heavily visited by the reaction under Alva.[4] The decrees of the Council of Trent were discussed with but short delay in the provincial councils and diocesan synods, and their provisions were at once enforced. The influence of the Jesuits extended rapidly from St. Omer, and still more effectually from Douay. Philip II had established a university at Douay in order that such of his subjects as spoke the French language might have opportunity for study without leaving their country. This was in furtherance of that strict ecclesiastical constitution which it was the purpose of Philip to introduce throughout his dominions. Not far from Douay stood the Benedictine abbey of Anchin. At the time when the fury

[1] Gazet, " Histoire Ecclesiastique des Pays-Bas," p. 143, describes him as " subtle and solid in doctrine, forceful in reasoning, rich in matter, polished in language, and grave in manner; but, above all, the excellent piety and virtue that shone in his life gave effectual persuasion to his words."
[2] Havensius, " De Erectione Novorum Episcopatuum in Belgio," p. 50.

[3] Hopper, " Recueil et Mémorial des Troubles des Pays-Bas," 93, 98.
[4] According to " Viglii Commentarius Rerum actarum super impositione Decimi Denarii," in Papendrecht, " Analecta," i. l. 292, the tenth penny was imposed on them with the assurance that it should not be rigidly exacted.

of the iconoclasts was raging in almost every other part of the Netherlands, the abbot, John Lentailleur, was there engaged with his monks in the practice of the spiritual exercises of Ignatius Loyola: inflamed by the enthusiasm excited by these exercises, he determined to institute a college of Jesuits in the new university, and endow it from the revenues of his abbey.   It was opened accordingly in the year 1568, immediately obtained a certain independence of the university authorities, and rapidly acquired unusual prosperity. Eight years afterward, the flourishing state of this university, even as regarded literary study, was principally attributed to the Jesuits.   Not only was their college filled with pious and diligent young men, but the other colleges also had greatly profited by the emulation it excited. Already was the whole university supplied with theologians from this college, and the provinces of Artois and Hainault received numerous priests from the same source.[5]   It gradually became the central point of modern Catholicism for all the surrounding country. In the year 1578 the Walloon provinces were considered among their contemporaries to be, according to their own expression, in the highest degree Catholic.[6]

But this religious organization was endangered no less than the political claims of the provinces by the increasing predominance of Lutheran opinions.

At Ghent the form assumed by Protestantism was such as in the present day we should call revolutionary.   There the ancient liberties which had been crushed by Charles V in 1539, had never been forgotten. The atrocities of Alva had excited peculiar exasperation in that city.   The populace was fierce and ungovernable, much inclined to image-breaking, and violently enraged against the priests. Two daring leaders of the people, Imbize and Ryhove, availed themselves of these tumultuary feelings.   Imbize conceived the idea of establishing a republic, and fancied that Ghent would become a new Rome.   They commenced their proceedings at the moment when their Governor, Arschot, was holding a meeting with certain bishops and Cath-

---

[5] " Testimonium Thomæ Stapletoni " (rector of the university) of the year 1576, in Sacchinus, iv. iv. 124: " Artois and Hainault have had many pastors from that college of the fathers, and our university has received from it many excellent and learned divines." Still higher eulogies follow, but may be omitted, and the rather as Stapleton was himself a Jesuit.

[6] Michiel, " Relatione di Francia ": " The count (the Governor of Hainault) is most Catholic, as is all that region, together with the district of Artois, which is adjacent to it."

olic leaders of the neighboring towns, whom they took prisoners,
together with himself. They next restored the ancient constitution, with modifications, as will be readily supposed, which
secured to themselves the possession of power. They laid hands
on the property of the Church, abolished the bishopric, and confiscated the abbeys. The hospitals and monasteries they converted into barracks, and finally they endeavored to introduce a
similar order of things among their neighbors by force of arms.[7]

Now it happened that some of the leaders taken prisoners with
the Governor, belonged to the Walloon provinces, where the
troops of Ghent were already making incursions. All who were
disposed to the Protestant opinions began to arouse themselves,
and the democratic passions of the people were called in aid of
the religious excitement, as had been done in Ghent. In Arras
a tumult was raised against the Senate. Even from Douay the
Jesuits were expelled in a commotion of the people, spite of the
efforts made by the Council; and although not compelled to
absent themselves more than fourteen days, yet the circumstance
was one of great importance. In St. Omer they maintained
their ground only by the special protection of the Council.

The civic magistracy, the provincial nobility, and the clergy
were all at the same time endangered and oppressed. They
saw themselves menaced by a revolution equally destructive with
that which had just occurred in Ghent; it is therefore not surprising if in this peril they should have recourse to every possible means of defence. They first sent their troops into the
territory of Ghent, which they cruelly devastated, and then
looked around for some alliance from which they might derive
a more certain security than was afforded by their connection
with the general union of the Netherlands.

Don John of Austria was not backward in turning this disposition of mind to his own purposes.

If we consider the conduct and measures of Don John in
the Netherlands from a general point of view only, we are almost inclined to think that they produced no results; that his
existence passed away without leaving a trace, as it had done
without satisfaction to himself. But if we examine more closely
what his position was, what his actions were, and what con-

[7] Van der Vynkt's "Geschichte der Niederlande," bd. ii. buch v. abschnitt 2. This section may perhaps be consid- ered the most important part of the whole work.

sequences resulted from his measures, we shall find that to him above all other persons must be attributed the settlement of the Spanish Netherlands. Don John endeavored for some time to abide by the terms of the Treaty of Ghent, but the independent position assumed by the States, with that held by the Prince of Orange, who was much more powerful than himself —the Viceroy—and the suspicions entertained by each party against the other, made an open rupture inevitable; he therefore resolved to begin the war. This was doubtless in opposition to the will of his brother, but it was unavoidable. There were no other means by which he could hope to secure a single province to the sovereignty of Spain; but by adopting this method he succeeded. He retained possession of Luxembourg, he invested Namur, and the battle of Gemblours made him master of Louvain and Limburg. If the King desired to recover his power in the Netherlands, that was not to be effected by treating with the States-General, which was manifestly impracticable; it could only be done by a gradual subjugation of the separate districts; either by terms of convention or force of arms. This system Don John adopted, and it soon laid open to him the most cheering prospects. He succeeded in reviving the old attachment of the Walloon provinces to the Burgundian race, and had the good-fortune to gain over to his party two men of great power and influence, Pardieu de la Motte, Governor of Gravelines, and Matthieu Moulart, Bishop of Arras.[8]

These were the men who, after the early death of Don John, conducted the negotiations on which everything depended, with great zeal and successful skill.

De la Motte availed himself of the increasing hatred against the Protestants. He effected the removal of many garrisons belonging to the States from the fortresses they occupied, solely on the ground that they might be Protestant, and contrived that a decree should be issued, in the month of November, by the nobles of Artois excluding all who professed the reformed opinions from that province; which decree was at once carried into execution. After this commencement, Matthieu Moulart turned all his efforts to the effecting a reconciliation with Philip.

[8] That they were gained over during the life of Don John appears from the two passages following; 1st, Strada, ii. l. p. 19: " Pardieu de la Motte had not only signified to Don John that he would resume his allegiance to the King, but promised to bring over all he could with him; " 2d, Tassis: " The Bishop of Arras, who was reconciled to the King in the time of Don John."

He began by imploring the assistance of God in a solemn procession, which he conducted through the whole city; and it was, in fact, a very difficult enterprise that he had undertaken; for among other things, he had occasionally to bring about a coalition between men whose claims were directly opposed to each other. He proved himself to be shrewd, conciliating, and indefatigable, and his endeavors were entirely successful.

Alexander Farnese, the successor of Don John, possessed the inestimable gift of persuading, attaching, and inspiring lasting confidence. He was assisted by François de Richardot, nephew of the bishop; "a man," says Cabrera, "of keen penetration and sound judgment in various affairs, and experienced in all; he was capable of conducting every sort of business, be its nature what it might." Sarrazin, Abbot of St. Vaast, was also his zealous supporter. Of him the same Cabrera says, "He was a great politician, with an appearance of tranquil indifference; very ambitious under a show of extreme humility, and was skilled to maintain himself in the good opinion of all." [9]

We do not follow the whole course of the negotiations till they gradually attained their end.

It must suffice to say that on the part of the provinces the interests of self-preservation and of religion pointed to the King; while on the part of Philip II nothing was omitted that priestly influence and dexterous negotiation, combined with the returning favor of the sovereign, could effect. In April, 1579, Emanuel de Montigny—whom the Walloon forces acknowledged as their leader—entered the service of the King. He was followed by Count de Lalaing, without whom Hainault could never have been won. At length, on May 17, 1579, the treaty was concluded in the camp of Maestricht. But to what conditions was the King compelled to submit! It was a restoration of his authority, but was effected only under the strictest limitations. He not only promised to dismiss all foreigners from his army, and to employ troops raised in the Netherlands alone, but he agreed to confirm all those in their places who had acquired office during the troubles. The inhabitants even pledged themselves to receive no garrison of which information had not previously been given to the estates of the country; two-thirds of the Council of State were to consist of men who had been impli-

[9] Cabrera, "Felipe Segundo," p. 1021.

cated in the disturbances. The remaining articles were all in a similar spirit.[10] The provinces acquired a degree of independence exceeding anything that they had ever before possessed.

This event involved a turn of affairs that was of universal importance. Throughout the west of Europe, all attempts hitherto made for the maintenance or restoration of Catholicism had been by open force; and, under this pretext, the sovereign power had labored to complete the destruction of all provincial freedom. But monarchy was now compelled to adopt a different course. If kings desired to reinstate Catholicism, and to uphold their own authority, they must take their measures in firm alliance with constitutional assemblies, and in coalition with public immunities.

We have seen that the royal power was closely restricted; but, spite of all the limits imposed, it had yet obtained important advantages. Those provinces on which the might of the house of Burgundy had been founded, had returned to their allegiance. Alexander Farnese continued the war with the Walloon troops; and, though making slow progress, he still advanced. In 1580 he gained possession of Courtray; in 1581, of Tournay; and in 1582 he took Oudenarde.

But these events did not bring affairs to a complete decision. The union of the Catholic provinces with the King was perhaps the very cause which compelled the northern districts, all exclusively Protestant, not only to form a closer confederation among themselves, but eventually to declare an absolute renunciation of the royal authority.

We will here take a rapid glance at the general history of the Netherlands. A contest of long standing subsisted in all the provinces between the provincial rights and the sovereign prerogative. In the time of Alva, princely power had obtained a preponderance more decided than it had ever before possessed, but which it could not even then long maintain. The Treaty of Ghent demonstrated the complete superiority acquired by the popular bodies over the government. The northern provinces possessed no advantages over those of the south in this respect; had they been of one opinion in religion, they would have constituted one general republic of the Netherlands; but they were

[10] Tassis gives this treaty at full length, lib. v. 394-405.

separated, as we have seen, by a difference of faith. From this circumstance, it followed, first, that the Catholics returned to the protection of the King, with whom they pledged themselves, above all, to the maintenance of the Catholic religion; and a second result was that the Protestants, after long persevering in the struggle, at length cast aside the very name of subjection, and entirely renounced their allegiance to the King. We give the name of the subject provinces to the first of these parties, and designate the last as the republic; but we must not suppose the essential difference between them to have been so great as these names would imply; for the subjected provinces asserted all their rights and the privileges of their estates with the most spirited tenacity, while the republican provinces could not dispense with an institution (the stadtholdership) which was closely analogous to that of royalty. The most important distinction consisted in their religion.

It was by this that the true principles of the contest were brought out, and that events were matured and advanced to their consummation.

Philip II had just at this period completed the conquest of Portugal; and at the moment when he was stimulated by the achievement of this great success to the undertaking of new enterprises, the Walloon States at length agreed to the return of the Spanish troops.

Count de Lalaing was gained over to the Spanish side, and with him his wife, who had been an active opponent of the Spaniards, and to whom their expulsion was principally ascribed. The whole body of the Walloon nobility followed their example. Men persuaded themselves that a renewal of Alva's despotism and violence was no more to be dreaded. The Spanish-Italian army, already withdrawn once, then brought back, and again expelled, returned once more to the country. With the troops of the Netherlands alone, the war must have been indefinitely protracted; the superior force and discipline of the Spanish veterans brought the conflict to a crisis.

As in Germany the colonies of Jesuits, composed of Spaniards, Italians, and some few Netherlanders, had restored Catholicism by the zealous inculcation of its dogmas, and by carefully arranged education, so now in the Netherlands an Italico-Spanish army appeared to unite with the Walloon

Catholics for the reinstatement of the Roman supremacy by force of arms.

At this point of the history we are treating, it is impossible to avoid some slight description of the war; in its course the destinies of religion were also involved.

In July, 1583, the port and town of Dunkirk were taken in six days. They were followed by Nieuport and the whole coast, even to Ostend, Dixmunde, and Furnes.

The character of the war was at once made manifest. In everything relating to politics the Spaniards displayed forbearance; but in all that pertained to religion they were inexorable. It was not to be thought of that the Protestants should be allowed a church; they were refused even the right of private worship; all the preachers taken were instantly hanged. The war was conducted with full consciousness and fixed design, as a war of religion; and, in a certain sense, this was indeed the most prudent system, the existing state of things considered. A complete subjugation of the Protestants could never have been effected but by so decided a mode of proceeding: whatever elements of Catholicism the provinces contained, were aroused to activity, and excited to aid the Spanish cause; and, accordingly, their co-operation was offered spontaneously. The Bailliu Servaes of Steeland delivered the district of Waes to the royalists. Hulst and Axel surrendered; and Alexander Farnese soon found himself sufficiently powerful to prepare for attack on the more important cities. He was already master of the country and the coast; the cities soon followed. In the month of April, Ypres surrendered, immediately afterward Bruges, and finally Ghent, where Imbize himself took part with the reconciliation party. The conditions granted to the communes, in their political character, were very favorable. Their immunities were for the most part respected, but the Protestants were expelled without mercy. The principal condition in every case was that the Catholic clergy should be reinstated and the churches restored to the Catholic worship.

But with all that had been effected, nothing permanent seemed to be gained, no security was possessed while the Prince of Orange survived; his existence gave force and consistency to the opposition, and prevented hope from expiring even in the vanquished.

The Spaniards had set a price of 25,000 scudi on his head, and amidst the fierce excitement of the period there could not fail to be men whose fanaticism and avarice would prompt them to earn this reward. I do not know that the annals of humanity can furnish a more fearful blasphemy than that found in the papers of the Biscayan Jaureguy, who was taken in attempting the life of the prince. He carried about him, as a kind of amulet, prayers in which he besought the merciful Godhead, who appeared to men in the person of Christ, to aid in the completion of the murder, and in which he promised a portion of the reward to the divine persons in the event of his enterprise being accomplished. To the Mother of God at Bayonne he would give a robe, a lamp, and a crown; to the Mother of God at Aranzosu, a crown; and to the Lord Jesus himself, a rich curtain![1] This fanatic was fortunately seized, but another was already preparing to imitate him. At the moment when the outlawry (of the prince) was proclaimed in Maestricht, a Burgundian, named Balthaser Gerard, felt himself inspired by the wish to carry the ban of the empire into execution.[2] The hopes he entertained of earthly happiness and glory if he succeeded, or of the fame of a martyr in the event of failure, were confirmed by a Jesuit of Treves, and thoughts of these things would not suffer him to rest day or night until he set about the accomplishment of the crime. He represented himself to the prince as a refugee, and having thus gained admittance, he found a favorable opportunity in July, 1584, and killed the prince at one shot. He was taken, but all the tortures inflicted on him failed to extort a sigh from his lips, he persisted in declaring that if the deed were not done he would yet do it. Whilst Gerard was expiring at Delft, amidst the execrations of the people, the canons of Herzogenbusch performed a solemn Te Deum in celebration of his act.

[1] Contemporary copy of a vow and of certain prayers, found in the form of an amulet upon Jaureguy, in the Collection of Lord Francis Egerton. " A vos Señor Jesus Christo, redemptor y salvador del mundo, criador del cielo y de la tierra, os offrezco, siendo os servido librarme con vida despues de haver effectuado mi deseo, un belo murico." (See text.) And so it proceeds.

[2] Borgognone, " Inf. Polit." xii., " Account of the death of William of Nassau, Prince of Orange, and of the torments endured by that most generous youth, Balthasar Gerard," contains circumstances differing from the usual accounts: " Gerard, whose mother is from Besançon, was about twenty-eight years old, and was a youth of no less learning than eloquence [he had entertained this design for six years and a half] : The opportunity then offering of taking letters to Nassau from the Duke of Alençon (to whom he was gentleman of the household) on July 7th, an hour and a half after dinner, and the prince just rising from table, he fired an arquebuse loaded with three balls, struck him under the left breast, and made a wound two inches broad, by which he killed him."

The passions of both parties were in fierce commotion, but the impulse communicated to the Catholics was the stronger— it accomplished its purpose and bore off the victory.

Had the prince lived, he would doubtless have found means, as he had promised, to relieve Antwerp, which was already besieged; but no one could now be found to occupy his place.

The measures adopted for the reduction of Antwerp were so comprehensive in their character that all other towns in Brabant were directly menaced by them. The Prince of Parma cut off supplies of provisions from all; Brussels was the first to surrender; that city, accustomed to abundance, was no sooner threatened by want, than discords arose, and soon led to its being surrendered; next fell Mechlin, and at length, on the failure of a last attempt to cut through the dams and procure the means of existence by land, Antwerp also was compelled to yield.

The conditions imposed on the cities of Brabant, as on those of Flanders, were particularly mild; Brussels was exempted from the payment of contributions; Antwerp received a promise that no Spanish garrison should be placed in the city, and that the citadel should not be repaired One condition was indeed permitted to take the place of all others, the restoration namely of all churches and chapels, with the reinstatement of all the exiled clergy, secular and monastic; on this the King insisted with inflexible firmness; he declared that it must be the first and last stipulation of every agreement; the only favor he could be persuaded to grant was that the inhabitants of all towns should be allowed two years either to change their religion or to sell their possessions and quit the Spanish dominions.

How completely had the times changed their aspect! At one period Philip himself had hesitated to grant the Jesuits a fixed establishment in the Netherlands, and they had often since those days, been menaced, attacked, and expelled. The events of this war led to their immediate return, and that under the decided protection of the government. The Farnesi, moreover, were especial patrons of the order. Alexander had a Jesuit for his confessor; he beheld in the society the most efficient instrument for restoring the half Protestant country he had conquered to the Catholic Church, and thus completing the principal purpose of the war.[3] The first city they re-entered was Courtray, the first that had been taken. The parish priest of the town, Jean David, had become acquainted with the Jesuits during his exile at Douay, he now returned to Courtray, but his first step was to join the order. In his farewell sermon to his parishioners, he exhorted them no longer to deprive themselves of the spiritual aid to be derived from that society, and they were readily persuaded into following his advice; instantly afterward the aged John Montagna, who had first established the Jesuits in Tournay, whence he had more than once been compelled to fly, returned to fix their company in that town, where they acquired a permanent residence. On the surrender of Ypres and Bruges, the Jesuits entered those cities also, and the King willingly bestowed on them certain convents which had been deserted during the troubles. In Ghent, the house of the great demagogue Imbize, whence had originated so much mischief to Catholicism, was fitted up for their reception. When the people of Antwerp surrendered, they tried to obtain a promise that those monastic orders only which had existed in the time of Charles V should be reinstated; but this was not conceded to them; they were compelled to admit the Jesuits again, and to restore the buildings before possessed by the order. One of the Jesuit historians relates these facts with infinite complacency, and points it out as a special mark of the divine approval, that the society received back property unencumbered, which they had left loaded with debt; it had passed in the meantime through many different hands, but was nevertheless restored to them without hesitation or inquiry. Brussels did not escape the general destiny; the Town Council declared its assent to their establishment, the Prince of Parma assigned them a pension from the royal treasure, and in that city also the Jesuits assumed an advantageous position. The Prince had already solemnly conferred on them the right to hold real property under ecclesiastical jurisdiction, and freely to avail themselves in those provinces, of the privileges they held from the Apostolic See.

[3] Sacchinus (pars v. lib. iv. n. 58): " It was the opinion of Alexander and his advisers that the society should be instantly settled in every city recovered from the heretics, as a means to secure the public tranquillity, and, at the same time, to promote the piety of individuals." According to the Imago Primi Seculi, this was also the will of the King, "who had recently laid his commands on the general of the order to fill all the chief cities of Belgium with the members." Assertions sufficiently borne out by the facts.

Nor was the patronage of the prince confined to the order of Jesuits; in the year 1585 a small number of Capuchins arrived in the Netherlands, and on addressing a special letter to the Pope, the prince obtained permission for their fixed residence in that country. He then bought them a house in Antwerp; they produced a powerful effect even on the different religious communities, insomuch that the Pope found it needful to restrain the other Franciscans from adopting the reformed rule of the Capuchins.

The most important consequences gradually resulted from all these arrangements; they transformed Belgium, which had previously been half Protestant, into one of the most decidedly Catholic countries in the world. It is also unquestionable that they contributed, at least in the commencement, to the re-establishment of the royal authority.

As one of the results of these changes, the opinion that only one religion ought to be tolerated in a State became more and more firmly established. This is one of the principal maxims in the political system of Justus Lipsius. In affairs of religion, he declares, neither favor nor indulgence is permissible; the true mercy is to be merciless; to save many, we must not scruple to remove one here and there out of the way.

This is a principle that has been received in no country with a more cordial acceptance than in Germany.

Section IX.—Progress of the Counter-Reformation in Germany

The Netherlands being still a circle of the German Empire, it followed of necessity that the events occurring in the former country would be extremely influential on the affairs of Germany. The disputes in Cologne were brought to a decision as one of the first and most immediate consequences of the change in the Netherlands.

The Spaniards had not yet returned, still less had the Catholics achieved their great triumphs, when the Elector Truchsess, of Cologne, determined to adopt the reformed religion, and to marry, without, on that account, resigning his archbishopric. This occurred in November, 1582. He had the greater part of the nobility on his side; the counts of Nuenar, Solms, Wittgenstein, Wied, and Nassau, with the whole duchy of Westphalia, all professing the evangelical opinions. With the Bible in one hand and the sword in the other, the Elector entered Bonn, while Casimir of the Palatinate took the field in considerable force to reduce the city of Cologne, the chapter, and the remaining officers of the archbishopric who were opposed to the Elector Truchsess.

In all the transactions of those times we find this Casimir of the Palatinate always ready to mount his horse or draw his sword, and always followed by martial bands, disposed to Protestantism, but he rarely seemed to effect anything important. He did not carry on the war with the earnest purpose demanded by a contest for religion, because he had always some interest of his own before his eyes; nor did he display the science and energy distinguishing those who appeared against him. In the case we are considering, he did indeed lay waste the plain country of his opponents, but he accomplished nothing in promotion of the general interests;[1] he achieved no conquests, nor did he succeed in obtaining more efficient assistance among the Protestant powers of Germany.

The Catholic powers, on the contrary, gathered all their forces together. Pope Gregory would not permit the business to be subjected to the delays remarked in every proceeding of the Curia; he considered that the urgency of the case made a simple consistory of the cardinals sufficient to decide an affair of so much importance as the despoiling an elector of the empire of his archiepiscopal dignity.[2] His nuncio, Malaspina, had already hurried to Cologne, where, with the special aid of the learned members of the chapter, he not only succeeded in excluding all the less firmly Catholic members from that body, but also in raising to the archiepiscopal throne a prince of the only house still remaining thoroughly Catholic, Duke Ernest of Bavaria, Bishop of Freisingen.[3] Thereupon a German Catholic army appeared in the field, which the Duke of Bavaria had collected, with aid of subsidies from the Pope. The Emperor lost no time in threatening the count palatine Casimir with ban and double ban *(acht und aberacht);* he sent besides admonitory letters to the troops of Casimir, which eventually caused the

[1] Isselt, "Historia Belli Coloniensis," p. 1092: "That whole summer he did nothing worthy of such an army."
[2] Maffei, "Annali di Gregorio XIII.," ii. xii. 8.
[3] Letter from Malaspina to Duke William of Bavaria, in "Adlzreitter," ii. xii. 595: "What we desired," he here remarks, "that we obtained."

army of the palatinate to disperse. When affairs had reached this point, the Spaniards also appeared. They had taken Zutphen in the summer of 1583; they now marched 3,500 Belgian veterans into the archbishopric. To enemies so numerous, Gebhard Truchsess was compelled to yield; his troops would not act in opposition to the imperial mandate; his principal fortress surrendered to the united Spanish and Bavarian forces, and he was himself obliged to seek refuge with the Prince of Orange, at whose side he had hoped to stand forward as a defender of Protestantism.

It will be readily perceived that this event must have contributed largely toward the complete re-establishment of Catholicism in the country. From the first outbreak of the disturbances, the clergy of the diocese had suspended all disputes existing among themselves; the nuncio removed all suspected members, and a Jesuit college was established amidst the very tumult of arms, so that when victory was gained, nothing more was required than to continue the course already entered on. The Catholic clergy had been driven from Westphalia by Gebhard Truchsess—they now returned with other fugitives, and were held in great honor.[4] The Protestant canons continued in exclusion from their prebends, and, contrary to all precedent, they no longer received their revenues. It is true that the papal nuncios were compelled to proceed with great caution and gentleness, even as regarded Catholics, a fact of which Pope Sixtus was well aware, and he commanded the legate by no means to press forward the reforms he might find needful, until he should be certain that all were disposed to receive them. But by this discreet mode of approach, it was that the nuncio imperceptibly reached his end. The canons, however illustrious their birth, at length began again to perform their clerical duties in the cathedral. The Council of Cologne, which was opposed by a Protestant party in the city, supported the Catholic opinions with their utmost power.

The effects of this great revolution could not fail to be felt in all the remaining Ecclesiastical States, and they were further heightened in the neighborhood of Cologne by a particular accident. Henry of Saxe-Lauenburg, Bishop of Paderborn and

[4] "The elector Ernest," says Khevenhiller, "has re-established both the Catholic religion and the temporal government in harmony with ancient usages."

Osnabrück, Archbishop of Bremen, left his palace of Vöhrde one Sunday in April, and proceeded to church; on the way back his horse fell with him, and although still young, in perfect health, and receiving, as it appeared, no serious injury from the fall, he yet died in consequence before the end of the month. It was believed that this prince would have followed the example of Gebhard Truchsess, had the latter been more fortunate. The elections that followed his death were greatly to the advantage of Catholicism. The new bishop of Osnabrück did not refuse to subscribe the *professio fidei*,[5] and the new bishop of Paderborn, Theodore von Fürstenberg, was a most bigoted Catholic; even as canon he had opposed his predecessor, and so early as the year 1580 he effected the passing of a statute to the effect that Catholics only should for the future be received into the chapter.[6] He had also procured the admittance of a few Jesuits, whom he had suffered to preach in the cathedral, and to whom he had confided the upper classes of the gymnasium; the latter with the condition that they should not wear the dress of their order. How much more easily could he now promote the views of his party, being himself in possession of the bishopric! The Jesuits no longer found it needful to conceal their presence, the gymnasium was made over to them without reserve, and they were not only permitted to preach but to catechize. They found abundant occupation. The Town Council was entirely Protestant, and there were very few Catholics among the burghers; in the country around, things were much the same. The Jesuits compared Paderborn to a barren field, demanding infinite labor and yielding no return. We shall, nevertheless, have occasion to show hereafter that in the beginning of the seventeenth century their industry had penetrated this stubborn soil.

In Münster also the death of Henry Saxe-Lauenburg occasioned important changes. No election had hitherto been made in this see, where the younger members supported Prince Henry,

---

[5] According to Strunck, "Annales Paderbornensis," p. 514, Bernard von Waldeck had in earlier times been disposed to Protestantism: during the troubles in Cologne he had remained neuter, and now he adopted the Catholic confession. Chytræus (Saxonia, 812) does not contradict this.

[6] Bessen, "Geschichte von Paderborn," ii. 123. In Reiffenberg, "Historia Provinciæ ad Rhenum Inferiorem,"

lib. viii. c. i. p. 185, may be found a letter from Pope Gregory XIII: " dilectis filiis canonicis et capitulo ecclesiæ Paderbornensis," February 6, 1584, wherein he praises this spirit of opposition: " It is right that it should be thus: the more violently you are attacked, the more vigorous must be your resistance: the Pope himself bears the fathers of the Society of Jesus in his heart."

while the elder opposed him; but Duke Ernest of Bavaria, Elector of Cologne and Bishop of Liège, was now chosen Bishop of Münster also. This election was secured principally by the influence of Dean Raesfeld, the most zealous Catholic in the diocese, who further bequeathed 12,000 rix-dollars from his own revenues for the establishment of a Jesuits' college in Münster, and died soon after making his will. The first members of the order arrived in 1587. They met determined opposition from the canons, the preachers, and the citizens; but were supported by the council and the prince: their schools soon gave proof of their extraordinary merit as instructors; and in the third year of their labors they are said to have counted 1,000 scholars. In that same year, 1590, they acquired complete independence from a voluntary grant of church property conferred on them by the prince.[7]

The Elector Ernest also held the bishopric of Hildesheim. It is true that his power was much more closely restricted in that diocese; he was, nevertheless, able to promote the introduction of the Jesuits; the first who entered Hildesheim was John Hammer, a native of the town, and brought up in the Lutheran faith (his father was still living), but actuated by all the zeal of a new convert. His preaching was remarkable for clearness and force; he effected several brilliant conversions, and eventually made good his position. In the year 1590 the Jesuits obtained a residence and pension in Hildesheim.

We cannot fail to observe that the attachment of the house of Bavaria to the Catholic faith was of the first importance, even as regarded Lower Germany, where in so many dioceses at once, a Bavarian prince appears as its most earnest defender.

We are, nevertheless, not to imagine that this prince was very zealous or very devout in his personal conduct. He had natural children; and it was at one time believed that he would end by adopting a similar course to that taken by Gebhard Truchsess. The caution with which Pope Sixtus treated the Elector Ernest is sufficiently remarkable. He carefully abstained from showing the prince that his irregularities were known to him, perfectly as he was acquainted with them; for otherwise admonitions and exhortations would have been necessary, and

[7] Sacchinus, pars v. lib. viii. n. 83-91. Reiffenberg, "Historia Provinciæ ad Rhenum Inferiorem," i. ix. vi.

these might have driven the self-willed Ernest to resolutions by no means desirable.[8]

It was, indeed, long before affairs in Germany could be treated as those of the Netherlands had been; they required the most delicate regard to various personal feelings and interests.

Duke William of Cleves conformed in externals to the Catholic confession, but his policy was altogether Protestant. He readily accorded protection and shelter to the Protestant exiles, and excluded his son, John William, who was a zealous Catholic, from all participation in public affairs. The Court of Rome might easily have been tempted to display resentment and disapprobation of these proceedings, and to favor the opposition of John William to his father; but Sixtus V was much too prudent to suffer this. He would not even allow the nuncio to hold a conference with the prince, until the latter pressed so earnestly for the interview that it could no longer be avoided without offence. The meeting then took place at Düsseldorf, but the prince was, above all things, exhorted to patience. Sixtus would not permit John William to be invested with the order of the Golden Fleece, for that might awaken suspicion. He further refrained from interceding directly with the father in favor of the son; any connection of the latter with Rome might occasion displeasure; he ventured only so far as to procure the mediation of the Emperor, and thus endeavored to obtain for the prince a position more suitable to his birth. He directed his nuncio to act with regard to certain things as though he did not perceive them; and this considerate forbearance on the part of an authority that had not ceased to be acknowledged, produced its natural effect: the nuncio gradually obtained influence; and when the Protestants applied to the diet for certain concessions, it was principally in consequence of his representations that they were not granted.[9]

Thus, throughout a great part of Lower Germany Catholicism, if not immediately restored, was yet maintained in the hour of danger; confirmed and strengthened, it acquired a degree of preponderance that in the course of time might be matured into absolute supremacy.

[8] Tempesti, " Vita di Sisto V.," tom. i. p. 354.　　[9] Tempesti, " Vita di Sisto V." tom. i. p. 359.

In Upper Germany a similar train of circumstances immediately ensued.

We have alluded to the position of the Franconian bishoprics. A bishop of determined character might easily have conceived the idea of availing himself of this state of things for the attainment of hereditary sovereignty.

It was probably some consideration of this kind by which Julius Echter, of Mespelbronn, was led to hesitate for some time as to the line of policy he should pursue when, in the year 1573, while still very young, and naturally enterprising, he was elected Bishop of Würzburg.

He took an active part in the expulsion of the Abbot of Fulda; and it could not have been any very decided disposition to Catholicism that brought the chapter and States of Fulda into connection with Julius, since it was the determination of their abbot to restore Catholicism that formed their principal complaint against him; and the bishop had a misunderstanding with Rome in consequence of that affair. Gregory XIII imposed his commands on him to restore Fulda, at the time when Gebhard Truchsess proclaimed his revolt. In effect, Julius prepared to make an application to the Elector of Saxony, and to call on the head of the Lutherans for aid against the Pope. He was in the most intimate connection with Truchsess; and the latter, at least, conceived hope that the Bishop of Würzburg would follow his example. The ambassador of Henry Saxe-Lauenburg, Archbishop of Bremen, announced this expectation to his master with great satisfaction.[10]

Under these circumstances it would be difficult to say what the course of Bishop Julius would have been had Truchsess been able to maintain his hold on Cologne; but when the latter failed so completely, Julius Echter not only resigned all thought of imitating him, but was careful to pursue a totally opposite plan.

Is it to be believed that his utmost wish and purpose was to become absolute master in his episcopal domains? or had

[10] Letter of Hermann von der Decken (for Becken must be a false reading), dated December 6, 1582, in Schmidt-Phiseldeck, "Historischen Miscellaischen," i. 25: "On the statements and solicitations of the legate, the bishop of Würzburg required time for consideration; he then ordered his horses and retinue to be prepared, resolving to ride at once to the lord Elector of Saxony, and complain of such unheard-of importunity on the part of the Pope, also to ask advice, aid, and consolation. The lord Elector (of Cologne) has great hope of the most reverend bishops, and believes that their princely graces will revolt from the Pope."

he indeed a profound conviction in his heart that the Catholic faith was the true one? He was a pupil of the Jesuits, had been educated in the Collegium Romanum. Suffice it to say that in the year 1584 he resolved on making a visitation of the churches in a spirit so rigidly Catholic that nothing like it had before been seen in Germany; this he carried into effect in person, and with all the energy of a determined will.

Accompanied by a certain number of Jesuits, Bishop Julius travelled through the whole of his dominions. He began with Gmünden, thence proceeded to Arnstein, Werneck, Hassfurt, and so on from district to district. In each town he summoned the burgomaster and council to his presence, and declared to all his determination that the errors of Protestantism should be rooted from the land. The preachers were removed, and their places filled by the pupils of the Jesuits. If any public officer refused to attend the Catholic worship, he was dismissed without mercy; orthodox candidates were ready to fill the place he vacated. Even private individuals were required to take part in the Catholic service—they had to choose between expatriation and the mass. Whoever regarded the religion of his prince as an abomination, was declared incapable of retaining part or lot in his territory.[1] It was in vain that the neighboring princes remonstrated against these proceedings, Bishop Julius replied to all, that it was not what he was doing that disturbed his conscience, but that he had not begun to do it much earlier. He was most zealously supported by the Jesuits, among whom Father Gerhard Weller was particularly remarked; alone, on foot, and without even a change of clothing, he went about preaching from town to town. In one year (1586) fourteen cities and market-towns, upward of 200 villages, and not less than 62,000 souls, were brought back to Catholicism. The capital of the see was the only town still alienated from the Church, and this the bishop undertook to recover in March, 1587. He caused the Town Council to appear before him, and appointed a commissioner for each quarter and parish, by whom every citizen was to be separately interrogated. This investigation showed that one-half of the inhabitants held Prot-

---

[1] Biography of Bishop Julius in Gropp's "Chronik von Würzburg," p. 335: "They were desired to give up their offices, and seek their living out of the diocese." I have already used this bi- ography, and with it, particularly, "Christophori Mariani Augustani Encænia et Tricennalia Juliana" in Gropp's "Scriptt. Wirceb." tom. 1.

estant opinions, but many were feeble and unsettled in their faith; these readily yielded, and the solemn communion appointed for the celebration of Easter in the cathedral, and at which the bishop himself officiated, was numerously attended. Some held out longer, and a few chose rather to sell their possessions and abandon their country than resign their faith: among these exiles were four members of the Town Council.

The nearest ecclesiastical neighbor of Würzburg, Ernest von Mengersdorf, Bishop of Bamberg, felt himself especially called on to imitate the example thus set by Bishop Julius. There is a well-known hill called Gösweinstein, which rises above the valley of Muggendorf, and to which, even in our own days, pilgrims resort from all the surrounding villages, gaining the summit by steep and lonely paths, conducting through majestic woods and wild ravines. An ancient sanctuary of the Trinity existed in this place, but at the time we are speaking of, it was neglected and decayed. In the year 1587 the Bishop of Bamberg chanced to visit the sanctuary, and took its condition greatly to heart. Incited by the example of his neighbor, he declared that he also would "recover his subjects to the holy Catholic faith—no danger should deter him from performing this his duty." We shall have occasion to observe the zeal with which his successor proceeded on the path he marked out.

While measures were thus but in the first stage of preparation at Bamberg, Bishop Julius was effecting a thorough transformation in the religious affairs of Würzburg. All the old ordinances were revived, devotional exercises in honor of the Mother of God were renewed, brotherhoods of the "Assumption of the Virgin," the "Birth of the Virgin," and many other denominations were again formed. Pilgrimages were undertaken, new modes of devotion were invented, the streets were filled with processions, and the whole country was admonished by church bells at the stated hour for the Ave Maria.[2] Relics were once more collected, and laid with great reverence in pompous shrines. The monasteries were reoccupied, new churches were built in all parts of the diocese. Bishop Julius

[2] "Julii episcopi statuta ruralia," Gropp, "Scriptt." tom. i. His idea is, that the religious movement, which proceeds from the supreme head of the Church of God, communicates itself downward to every member of the body. See p. 444, de capitulis ruralibus.

is said to have laid the foundation of 300, which the traveller may still distinguish by their tall and pointed spires. The change thus wrought in a very few years was observed with astonishment. " What but lately," exclaims one of the bishop's eulogists, " would have been called superstitious—nay, even contemptible—is now considered holy; what was formerly accounted a gospel, is now declared to be mere deceit."

Results so important had not been expected even in Rome. The enterprise of Bishop Julius had been for some time in progress before intelligence of it reached Pope Sixtus V. On the close of the autumn holidays in 1586, Acquaviva, general of the Jesuits, appeared before him, and announced the new conquests achieved by his order. Sixtus was in raptures; he hastened to express his acknowledgments to the bishop, and conferred on him the right of nominating to benefices, even during those months reserved to the Papal See, declaring that Bishop Julius would best know whom to reward by their possession.

But the joy of Pope Sixtus in Acquaviva's report was greatly increased by the receipt of similar intelligence from the Austrian provinces, and more especially from Styria.

Changes were seen to commence in Styria during that very year when the estates of the province acquired so large an extent of privilege from the edicts of the diet held at Bruck, that their position might be compared with that of the Austrian estates, which had also their council for religious affairs, their superintendents, their synods, and a constitution almost republican.

At the very moment when Rudolph II received the oath of allegiance from his subjects, the great difference between himself and his father became apparent to all. He performed the various acts of devotion with the most rigorous exactitude, and his people beheld him with astonishment attending in processions, even during the most severe winter, with uncovered head, and bearing a lighted torch in his hand.

This disposition of the sovereign, and the favor he showed toward the Jesuits, soon caused great anxiety, and in accordance with the spirit of the times occasioned a violent counter-movement. No regular church was allowed to the Protestants in Vienna, but they used the Landhaus for their public worship, and the preacher Joshua Opitz, a follower of Flaccius, there inveighed against the Jesuits with all the vehemence peculiar to his sect. Whilst he systematically "thundered against the priests and all the abominations of popery," he awakened not only conviction, but violent rage in the minds of his hearers, so that on leaving the church they felt, as a contemporary of Opitz declares, "inclined to tear the papists to pieces with their hands."[3] The consequence of this was that the Emperor resolved to prohibit their assemblies in the Landhaus. While this affair was in discussion, and the arguments on both sides were proceeding with passionate eagerness, the nobility, to whom the Landhaus belonged, broke forth into expressions of menace; and while things were thus disturbed the festival of the Corpus Christi arrived. It was the year 1578. The Emperor was resolved to celebrate the feast with the utmost solemnity; after he had heard mass in the cathedral, he walked forth with the procession, which was the first that had been seen for a long time. The host was carried through the streets by a long train of priests, monks, friars, and members of guilds, with the Emperor and princes in the midst of them. It was soon manifest that the city was in excessive commotion; when the procession arrived in the peasants' market, it became necessary to remove a few stalls, in order to make it a passage; nothing more was required to create a general tumult, cries arose on all sides of "To arms! we are betrayed!" The choral followers and priests abandoned the host, the halberdiers and horse-guards dispersed in all directions, Rudolph found himself in the midst of an enraged multitude; he feared an attack upon his person, and laid his hand on his sword; the princes closed round him with drawn weapons, and prepared to defend their sovereign.[4] It will be readily believed that this occurrence produced a very painful impression on a prince of so much gravity, and so firmly attached to the Spanish dignity and stateliness. The papal nuncio profited by the occasion; he pointed out the danger arising to the person of the Emperor from this state of public

[3] Dr. George Eder, who, be it observed, was an adversary: extract from his "Warnungsschrift" in Raupach, "Evangel. Oestreich," ii. 286.

[4] Maffei, "Annali di Gregorio XIII." tom. i. p. 281, 385, written without doubt from the reports of the nuncio.

feeling, and declared that God himself had given him a warning, in that commotion, to delay no longer the fulfilment of the promises he had made to the Pope.   The Spanish ambassador supported the legate; Magius, the provincial of the Jesuits, had frequently counselled Rudolph to adopt decisive measures, and his advice now received attention.   On June 21st the Emperor issued an order to Opitz and his assistants, whether in church or school, to leave the city that very day " while the sun was shining," and to depart, within fourteen days, from the hereditary dominions of Austria.   Rudolph expected an insurrection of the people, and had a body of trustworthy men prepared under arms for a case of emergency.   But how could anyone venture to oppose himself to the sovereign, while he had the letter of the law on his side?   The people contented themselves with conducting the exiles on their way with demonstrations of regret and compassion.[5]

From that day there commenced a Catholic reaction in Austria, which acquired force and efficiency from year to year.

In the first place it was determined to expel Protestantism from the imperial cities.   The towns east of the Ens, which had separated from the estates of the knights and nobles twenty years before, could offer no resistance, the reformed clergy were removed, and their places filled by Catholic priests; private persons were subjected to a close examination.   A formula, according to which the suspected were interrogated, has come into our possession.   " Dost thou believe," inquires one of its articles, " that everything is true which the Church of Rome has laid down as the rule of life and doctrine?"   " Dost thou believe," adds another, " that the Pope is the head of the one sole apostolic Church?"   No doubt was to be endured.[6] The Protestants were expelled from all offices of state; none were admitted to the class of burghers who did not declare themselves Catholic.   In the universities, that of Vienna not excepted, all who applied for a doctor's degree were first required to subscribe the *professio fidei*.   A new regulation for schools was promulgated, which prescribed Catholic formularies, fasts, worship according to the Catholic ritual, and the

[5] Sacchinus, pars iv. lib. vi. n. 78: " It shames me to declare the numbers that escorted the departing exiles, sacrilegious as they were and worthy of all execration, and what marks of kindness were bestowed on them; this very fact showing the magnitude of the evil."

[6] Papal, Austrian, and Bavarian articles of Confession of Faith in Raupach.

exclusive use of the catechism arranged by Canisius. In Vienna, all Protestant books were taken away from the booksellers' shops, and were carried in heaps to the episcopal court. Search was made at the custom-houses along the river, all packages were examined, and books or pictures not considered purely Catholic were confiscated.[7]

With all these severities, the object of the rulers was not yet attained. It is true that in Lower Austria thirteen cities and markets were in a short time restored to the Catholic ritual, and the crown lands and mortgaged property were again in Catholic hands; but the nobility still offered effectual opposition, the towns on the west of the Ens were in close alliance with them, and were too strong to be successfully assailed.[8]

Many of these measures had nevertheless, as will be readily understood, a general effect from which none could wholly withdraw himself; in Styria they were especially influential, and produced an immediate return to Catholic opinions.

The Archduke Charles had been compelled to make concessions to his Protestant subjects, at the very moment when in other places the Catholic reaction was proceeding so prosperously. The members of his house found it difficult to pardon him for this. His brother-in-law, Duke Albert of Bavaria, exhorted him to remember that the terms of the Treaty of Augsburg empowered him to enforce upon his subjects the adoption of the religion professed by himself. He advised the archduke to take three measures: first, to appoint Catholics only to every office about the court, and above all, to the Privy Council; secondly, to separate the different estates at the diet, since he could more easily deal with each singly; and thirdly, to establish a good understanding with the Pope, and to request that a nuncio might reside at his court. Gregory XIII was indeed ready of his own accord to offer assistance. He knew that want of money had been the principal inducement to the archduke's compliance with the demands of his Protestant subjects; he therefore took the best means for rendering him independent of them by transmitting him funds, to the amount, a very large one for those times, of 40,000 scudi. He further deposited a still more important sum in Venice,

---

[7] Khevenhiller, "Ferd. Jahrb." i. 90.   [8] Raupach, "Kleine Nachlese Evang.
Hansitz, "Germania Sacra," i. 632.   Oestreich," iv. p. 17.

which was to be at the disposal of the archduke, in the event of disorders arising in the Austrian territories as a consequence of his efforts for the restoration of Catholicism.

Thus encouraged by example, exhortation, and substantial aid, the Archduke Charles assumed from the year 1580 a much more resolved and imposing attitude.

In that year he affixed an explanation to the concessions he had previously granted, which was in fact tantamount to their revocation. The estates presented the most humble prayers at the footstool of their sovereign, and it seemed for a moment that the urgency of their entreaties was about to prevail,[9] but upon the whole he remained firm; the measures announced were persisted in, and the expulsion of the reformed preachers commenced in the archducal territories.

The year 1584 brought affairs to a decision. In that year the papal nuncio Malaspina made his appearance in the diet. He had succeeded in separating the prelates from the secular estates with which they had always before taken part, and in forming between them, the ministers of the duke, and the leading Catholics in the country, a strict alliance, of which he was himself the centre. The whole dukedom had hitherto seemed to be Protestant, but Malaspina found means to gather a strong Catholic party round the prince, and, supported by this, the resolutions of the archduke became immutable. He persisted in his determination to root the Protestant opinions from his territories, declaring that the treaty of Augsburg accorded him rights, even over the nobles, beyond any that he had hitherto exercised, and a more obstinate resistance would but induce him to put those rights in force; he should then see who would venture to show himself rebellious. Menacing as was the tenor of these declarations against the Protestants, yet such was the state of affairs, that they produced him results equally favorable with those he had formerly derived from his concessions. There were various considerations which made it impossible for the estates to refuse the supplies he demanded; they were therefore all conceded.[10]

[9] " According to his inborn, benevolent, patriotic, and princely German disposition," says the supplication of the three States.

[10] Valvassor, " Ehre des Herzogthums Krain," contains authentic and detailed information on all these affairs. But Maffei, " Annali di Gregorio XIII." lib. ix. c. xx., lib. xiii. c. i. gives an extremely valuable account He had, without doubt, the report of the nuncio before him.

Thenceforward the counter-reformation made progress throughout the archducal territories. The parishes and town councils were filled with Catholics. No citizen ventured to attend any but a Catholic church, or to send his children to any but the Catholic schools.

The change was not effected peaceably in every instance. The Catholic pastors and the commissioners of the archduke were sometimes met with insult and driven from the place. The archduke himself was once in some danger when hunting, in consequence of a rumor having spread in the neighborhood that a pastor of that district had been taken prisoner. The peasants rushed to their arms, and the poor persecuted preacher was himself obliged to step forward among them for the purpose of protecting his ungracious sovereign from their rage.[1] In defiance of these indications of popular feeling, the changes nevertheless proceeded. The most coercive measures were adopted. A papal historian recapitulates them in few words: " Exile," he says, " confiscation, and severe chastisement for all who proved refractory." The ecclesiastical princes who had possessions in those districts lent their aid to the temporal authorities. The Archbishop of Cologne, who was also Bishop of Freisingen, changed the council of his town of Lack, and subjected the Protestant burghers to fines and imprisonment. The Bishop of Brixen determined to make a direct transfer of the lands in his lordship of Veldes. Similar dispositions were evident in all the Austrian possessions. Although the Tyrol had remained Catholic, the Archduke Ferdinand thought proper to enforce the most rigid subordination on his clergy, and the regular attendance of all classes at the sacrament. Sunday schools were established for the common people, and Cardinal Andreas, the son of Ferdinand, caused catechisms to be printed, which he distributed to the youth of the schools and to the uneducated classes of all ages.[2] Nor were these mild measures permitted to suffice in such districts as had received the Protestant doctrines. In the margraviate of Burgau, although but a recent acquisition, and in the bailiwick of Schwaben, although the jurisdiction was matter of dispute, the same coercive measures were adopted as had been pursued by the Archduke Charles in Styria.

[1] Khevenhiller, " Annales Ferdinandei II." p. 523.

[2] Puteo in Tempesti, " Vita di Sisto V." tom. i. p. 375.

For all these things Pope Sixtus could find no eulogies that seemed to him sufficient. He extolled the Austrian princes as the firmest pillars of Christendom. To the Archduke Charles more particularly he sent the most obliging letters.[3] The acquisition of a countship, which just then lapsed to the archduke as feudal lord, was considered by the court at Grätz to be a recompense sent directly by heaven for all the service he had rendered to Christendom.

The Catholic confession owed its return to supremacy in the Netherlands principally to the fact that it had accommodated itself to existing privileges; but in Germany that was by no means the case. On the contrary, the respective sovereigns of that country extended their power and importance in proportion with their success in promoting Catholic restoration. The intimacy of this connection between the ecclesiastical and political interests, and the extent to which it proceeded, are most remarkably exemplified by Wolf Dietrich von Raittenau, Archbishop of Saltzburg.

The archbishops of former days, who had lived amid the tumults of the Reformation, contented themselves with an occasional edict, promulgated to oppose innovations; with the menace of a punishment or an attempt at conversion; but all; as Archbishop Jacob says, by mild, paternal, and truthful means.[4]

Very different was the disposition of the young Archbishop Wolf Dietrich von Raittenau, when he ascended to the archiepiscopal throne of Saltzburg in 1587. He had been educated in the *Collegium Germanicum* in Rome, and was thoroughly imbued with the principles of Catholic restoration. He had seen the brilliant commencement of the administration of Sixtus V, and had conceived extreme admiration for that pontiff. His zeal was further stimulated by the elevation of his uncle Cardinal Altemps, in whose house in Rome he had been brought up, to the purple. In the year 1588, on returning from a journey which had taken him back to the Papal Court, he proceeded to the execution of the designs formed under the

[3] Extract from the Briefs, in Tempesti, i. 203.
[4] It is true that a more severe edict was issued in the name of Jacob, but not until he had been obliged to commit the administration to a coadjutor.

impressions received there. All the citizens of his capital were instantly called on to make public profession of the Catholic faith. Many evinced great reluctance, and he allowed them a few weeks for reflection. Then, on September 3, 1588, he commanded them to depart within one month from the city and diocese. That one month only, and, after pressing entreaties the delay of a month longer, was allowed these recusants for the purpose of selling their property. Of this they were required to present an inventory to the archbishop, who would then permit them to sell it to such persons only as were approved by himself.[5] Very few could resolve on deserting their faith, and those who did so were compelled to do public penace in the church with lighted tapers in their hands. The greater number, including many of the most wealthy burghers, preferred to leave their country. The loss of these citizens occasioned no regret to the prince, who believed he had discovered various means of maintaining the splendor of the archbishopric. He had already much increased the taxes, had raised the tolls and duties, imposed new burdens on the salt of Hallein and Schellenberg, converted the contributions in aid of the Turkish war into a regular land tax, and introduced duties on wine, with an income tax and legacy duty. He was entirely regardless of established immunities and vested rights. The dean of the diocese was said to have committed suicide in a fit of despair, at seeing the chapter deprived of its privileges. The principal object of the archbishop's enactments respecting the preparation of salt, and the whole business of mining, was the destruction of the independence enjoyed by the works before his time, and their subjection to the absolute control of his treasury. Throughout Germany no similar example of a regularly organized fiscal system was presented during that century. The young archbishop had brought the ideas of an Italian principality with him across the Alps. The art of raising money appeared to him the most important talent of a statesman, the highest problem of political economy. He had taken Sixtus V as his model; like him he desired to have an obedient, thoroughly Catholic, tribute-paying State in his hands. The expatriation of the principal citizens from Saltzburg was even

[5] Edict relative to the Reformation in Göckingk, " Vollkommene Emigrationsgeschichte von denen aus dem Erzbist-hum Salzburg vertriebenen Lutheranern," i. p. 88.

a source of satisfaction to the archbishop, because he considered
them rebels. He ordered their deserted houses to be taken
down, and palaces in the Roman style to be erected on their
sites.[6]

Wolf Dietrich was above all things delighted with splendor.
He never refused knightly entertainment to any foreigner, and
on one occasion appeared at the diet with a train of 400 persons.
In the year 1588 he was but twenty-nine years of age; buoyant
of spirit and full of ambition, he had already fixed his eyes and
hopes on the highest ecclesiastical dignities.

The process adopted in the spiritual and secular principalities
was repeated, wherever circumstances rendered it practicable,
in the cities also. The Lutheran burghers of Gmünden made
bitter complaints because they had been struck off the roll of
candidates for the Town Council. In Biberach the council appointed by the commissary of Charles V, on the occasion of
the Interim, still maintained its ground; the whole town was
Protestant, the council alone was Catholic, and carefully excluded every Protestant.[7] Heavy oppressions were endured by
those of the reformed faith in Cologne and Aix-la-Chapelle.
The members of the Council of Cologne declared that they had
promised the Emperor and the Elector to tolerate no other religion than the Catholic, and they sometimes punished the attendance on a Protestant sermon with fines and imprisonment.[8]
In Augsburg, also, the Catholics gained the upper hand; disturbances occurred on the introduction of the new calendar,
and in the year 1586 the evangelical superintendent was expelled the city, eleven clergymen at one time, and a large number
of the more determined citizens were also driven forth soon
after. Something very similar occurred from similar causes in
Ratisbon during the year 1587. Many other towns began to
claim the right of reforming their religious institutions: nay,
certain counts, nobles, and knights of the empire who had
been converted by some Jesuit, believed themselves entitled to

[6] Zauner's " Saltzburger Chronik," sie-
benter Theil, is our most important authority on this subject. This part of the
chronicle was itself constructed after a
contemporary biography of the archbishop.
[7] Lehmann, " De Pace Religionis, ii.
pp. 268, 480.
[8] Lehmann, 436, 270.

assert a similar right, and each resolved to restore Catholicism in his small domain.

It was an immeasurable reaction. The Protestant doctrines were now repulsed with an energy equal to that with which they had formerly advanced. Preaching and the inculcation of Catholic doctrines contributed their share to the production of this result, but much more was accomplished by political measures, especial ordinances, and open force.

As the Italian Protestants had formerly fled across the Alps, and sought refuge in Switzerland and Germany, so now were seen far more numerous bodies of German fugitives seeking refuge in the northern and eastern districts, from the oppressions that assailed them in the west and south. The Belgians in like manner retreated to Holland. It was a mighty triumph of Catholicism, which now extended its victories from land to land.

The progress and extension of this triumph were most especially promoted by the nuncios, who at that time began to reside regularly in Germany.

A memoir of the nuncio Minuccio Minucci, dated 1588, is still extant, and we gain from it a clear perception of the views entertained and acted upon in those times.[9]

A particular attention was given to the subject of education; it was greatly regretted that the Catholic universities were not better endowed, to the end that they might attract distinguished teachers. Ingolstadt was the only one possessed of means sufficiently ample; as things were, everything depended on the Jesuit seminaries. It was the wish of Minuccio Minucci, that in these schools there should not be so much attention given to producing great scholars, or profound theologians, as good and effective preachers; a man of moderate acquirements, who did not aspire to the summit of learning, or seek to become renowned, was in his opinion the most extensively useful teacher and most profitable servant of the Church. He recommended that this principle should be acted on in the different institutions for German Catholics in Italy. In the *Collegium Germanicum,* there had originally been a distinction made in the treatment of young men from noble families and

[9] "Discorso del molto illustre e revmo. Monsignor Minuccio Minucci, sopra il modo di restituire la Cattolica religione in Alemagna, 1588," MS. Barb.

those of the middle classes. Minucci disapproved of the departure from this custom, which not only made the nobles averse to go thither, but had also the effect of awakening an ambition in the middle class, which could never afterward be satisfied, and of causing an eagerness for high places, prejudicial to the careful performance of duty in the more humble offices. An attempt was moreover then made to attract a third or intermediate class to the colleges, the sons of superior public officers namely, to whom, according to the common course of things, the principal share in the administration of their native provinces would at some future period be confided. Arrangements had already been made in Perugia and Bologna by Gregory XIII, for the reception of these students. We may here perceive that the distinctions of rank still prevailing in German society were already well defined, even in those days.

The principal dependence of the Church was always on the nobles, and to them the nuncio particularly attributed the maintenance of Catholicism in Germany; for to this class the most valuable ecclesiastical appointments and benefices belonged as their exclusive right: they defended it in consequence as their hereditary property. It was for this reason that they now opposed the introduction of religious freedom into the dioceses; [10] they feared the great number of Protestant princes, who would in that case engross all the benefices. These nobles must be carefully protected and conciliated; they were by no means to be annoyed by the laws against plurality of benefices: in their favor it was decided that there was a certain utility in the change from one residence to another, which tended to unite the nobility of different provinces for the defence of the Church. No attempt ought to be made for the appointment of men from the burgher class to the higher ecclesiastical benefices; a few learned men in a chapter were very useful, as was seen in Cologne; but to carry this practice further would ultimately ruin the German Church.

The question next arose of how far it might be possible to reclaim to the Catholic faith such districts as had become entirely Protestant.

[10] Especially in Upper Germany: "The example of the suppression of the others [of Lower Germany] warned the nobles to be more careful in defence of these, and in this the heretics agreed with the Catholics, both parties perceiving that by the occupation of the princes, themselves and their posterity are deprived of the hope of extracting that profit from the benefices which they may expect from them so long as the canons retain the right of free election."

The nuncio was far from recommending open violence; he considered the Protestant princes much too powerful to be coerced, but he suggested other means by which he thought the end desired might eventually be attained.

He maintained that it was above all things essential to preserve a good understanding between the Catholic sovereigns, particularly between Bavaria and Austria. The Treaty of Landsberg was still in existence; he advised that this should be renewed and extended; Philip of Spain he thought might also be advantageously included in that league.

And might it not be possible to win back some of the Protestant princes? The Elector Augustus of Saxony had long been thought to evince a disposition friendly to Catholicism; an attempt had from time to time been made on this sovereign, principally by the intervention of Bavaria; but the utmost caution had been required in these proceedings (the wife of the Elector, Anne of Denmark, being firmly attached to the Lutheran doctrines), and they had never produced any useful effect. Anne died in the year 1585, and the day of her death was not only one of deliverance for the oppressed Calvinists, but also afforded to the Catholics an opportunity of again approaching the Elector. It would seem that Bavaria, which had before labored in this cause, was now making arrangements for a further effort, and Pope Sixtus V held himself ready to forward absolution for the Elector to Germany.[1] But before anything could be effected, Augustus himself expired. The Catholics

---

[1] As early as 1574, Duke Albert of Bavaria was encouraged by Gregory XIII to attempt the renewal of the negotiations once opened with the Elector of Saxony, for the introduction of the Catholic faith into his dominions, seeing that he was harassing and driving out the Calvinists. The Pope thought it advisable to send an agent to the Court of Saxony; but this Duke Albert opposed, saying the matter would then become known to the Elector's councilors: "And what could then be expected, but the ruin of the project?" He goes on to say: "Here it is judged that art will be required; so that, while seemingly occupied with some other business, the erring [prince] may be piously circumvented; if his wife learn the attempt, she, the more vehement from her weaker sex, will beset him with importunate counsels."—" Legationes Paparum ad Duces Bavariæ," MS. in the Library of Munich. Minucci informs us that the first overtures were made to Augustus in the days of Pius V.

The whole passage is remarkable: "Even from the times of Pope Pius V, of blessed memory, Duke Albert of Bavaria, who lives in heaven, labored hard with Duke Augustus of Saxony, now dead, and brought things so far that there was good hope of success. But it pleased God to call him away, and no one remained to think or speak of so great a work till the days of Gregory, of glorious memory, when Father Possevin set himself to work upon those foundations; and, finally, in the present most fortunate pontificate of Sixtus, the wife of the said Duke Augustus being dead, there were those who thought the occasion favorable for again attempting the conversion of that prince. But divine providence did not grant him time to await the benediction which his holiness was preparing to bestow upon him, sending it by means of Duke William of Bavaria, even to his own house." We hence discover how early that line [of the Saxon princes] was practised upon.

had, however, other princes in view. It was thought that Louis, count-palatine of Neuburg, displayed indifference to all proposals of hostility to Catholicism, and was particularly forbearing toward the Catholic priests who were occasionally found in his dominions. William IV of Hesse, also a pacific and learned prince, was observed to accept occasionally the dedication of Catholic books; to these sovereigns particular attention was directed, nor were the higher members of the German nobility in the northern districts left out of consideration; hopes were especially entertained of Heinrich Ranzau.

The results of these purposes and endeavors were indeed remote, and could perhaps not be safely calculated on; but there were other projects, the execution of which depended more on their own determination and force of will.

The nuncio affirmed that the greater number of the assessors in the supreme court of the empire (*Kammergericht*) were even yet disposed to Protestantism. There still survived men of that earlier period, when Protestants, either concealed or openly professed, sat in the councils of most sovereigns, even in those of Catholic countries. The nuncio thought this circumstance well calculated to " drive the Catholics to despair," and was urgent in his entreaties for a remedy. He believed that it would not be difficult to compel the assessors of Catholic countries to make a profession of faith, while all newly appointed members might be required to take an oath that they would either not change their religion, or would resign their offices. He maintained that the preponderance in the *Kammergericht* belonged of right to the Catholics.

The nuncio did not yet abandon the hope of retrieving the lost bishoprics—he believed this might be done without using violence, if existing rights were efficiently asserted. These bishoprics had not yet wholly broken off all connection with Rome; the ancient right of the Curia to fill up the benefices which became vacant during the reserved months was not absolutely denied. The Protestant bishops themselves still believed that their nomination required to be confirmed by the sanction of the Pope, and Henry of Saxe-Lauenburg had an agent at Rome to procure this confirmation in his case. If the Papal See had not yet derived all the advantage from this deferential feeling that might have been drawn from it, that was the consequence of a practice on the part of the Emperor, who supplied the place of the papal sanction by a dispensation (*Indulto*) from himself. The appointments to the vacant benefices made in Rome always came too late, or some error of form was discovered in them, so that the chapters were always legally free to make their own choice. Minucci now earnestly pressed the Emperor to abstain from granting dispensations; and in the state of feeling then prevalent at the imperial court, he readily obtained a promise to that effect. Duke William of Bavaria had already proposed confiding the nomination to benefices, either to the nuncio or to some trustworthy German bishop. Minucci was of opinion that a *dataria* should be established in Rome expressly for Germany; that a list of noble Catholics, properly qualified, should be kept there; which list could easily be prepared and duly rectified, as changes should occur, by means of the nuncio or the Jesuits; all vacancies could then be filled without delay, in accordance with the guide and standard thus obtained. No chapter would venture to reject the candidates legally nominated by Rome, and the Curia would acquire great consideration and a large extent of influence from this measure.

We cannot fail to perceive that the complete restoration of the Church to its former authority was sought for with constancy of will and great energy. To conciliate the nobles, to allure the higher classes of the citizens into the Roman interest, to educate the youth under the influence of Rome, to regain the ancient power over the bishoprics, even over those that had become Protestant, to recover supremacy in the *Kammergericht,* to convert powerful princes of the empire, and to secure to the leading Catholic sovereigns a voice in the affairs of the German confederation; such, and so numerous, were the projects to be undertaken at one and the same time.

And we are not to believe that these suggestions and counsels were treated with neglect; at the moment when they were laid before the authorities in Rome, preparations were made in Germany for carrying them into effect.

The efficiency and good order of the *Kammergericht* depended in a great measure on the yearly visitations which were made during the sittings of the diet by seven estates of the empire in rotation. In these visitations the majority had

for the most part been Catholic; but in the year 1588, it was
Protestant—the Protestant archbishop of Magdeburg, among
others, was to take share in it. The Catholic party resolved
that this should not be permitted; and when the Elector of
Mayence proceeded to summon the estates, the Emperor, of
his own authority, commanded him to postpone the visitation
for that year. But the omission of one year availed nothing—
the order of succession remained as before. A Protestant Archbishop of Magdeburg was long to be feared: it thus happened
that the prorogation was repeated from year to year, the ultimate consequence being that no regular visitation was ever
held again; an omission from which that noble institution of
the highest tribunal in the empire suffered irreparable injury.[2]
Complaints soon arose that unlearned Catholics were preferred
in that body to learned Protestants. The Emperor also desisted
from granting the *Indulto*. In the year 1588 Minucci advised
that attempts should be made for the conversion of Protestant
princes; and in the year 1590 one had already been gained over;
this was Jacob of Baden, who takes the first place in a long
series.

Section X.—The League

The great movement thus engrossing Germany and the
Netherlands extended its influence over France also, with
irresistible force. The affairs of the Netherlands had, for a
long period of time, been intimately connected with those of
France. The French Protestants had frequently given assistance to those of the Netherlands, and the latter were equally
ready to lend their aid to the Protestants of France. The ruin
of Protestantism in the Belgic provinces was an immediate injury to the French Huguenots.

But in addition to this came the fact that in France, as well
as other countries, the tendency toward a restoration of Catholicism was constantly gaining extension of influence and increase of power.

The first appearance of the Jesuits has been already noticed,

[2] Minucci had besides written to Rome especially on the subject of the Kam-mergericht; and there is cause for be-lieving that his representations occa-sioned the inhibition. He regarded the Protestant majority with detestation, as we have said, " that the heretics should have the superior power and the larger number of votes in that Senate, is no other than a reduction of the German Catholics to despair."

and from that time they had continued to make progress: they were more especially patronized, as will be readily supposed, by the house of Lorraine. Cardinal Guise established a school for them in 1574 at Pont-à-Mousson, which was frequented by the princes of his house. The duke erected a college at Eu in Normandy, which was at the same time intended for the reception of fugitives from England.

They had besides many other patrons—sometimes it was a cardinal, a bishop, or an abbot—sometimes a prince or high officer of the State, who took upon himself the cost of a new establishment. In a short time they had settled themselves at Rouen, Verdun, Dijon, Bourges, and Nevers, while their missionaries traversed the kingdom in all directions.

But they found auxiliaries in France, with whose aid they had been obliged to dispense in Germany.

The cardinal of Lorraine had brought a few Capuchin friars with him from the Council of Trent, and had assigned them an abode in his palace at Meudon; but on his death they departed, the order being at that time restricted to Italy by its statutes. In the year 1573, the chapter-general sent a few of the brethren across the mountains for the purpose of first trying the ground. They were so well received that on their return they promised "the richest harvest," and the Pope did not hesitate to remove the restriction confining them to Italy. The first colony of Capuchins took their way across the Alps in the year 1574; they were conducted by Fra Pacifico di San Gervaso, who had been permitted to select his associates according to his own judgment.

These Capuchins were all Italians, and they naturally attached themselves in the first instance to their own country-people.

They were joyfully received by Queen Catherine, who instantly founded a monastery for them in Paris. So early as the year 1575 they had gained a settlement in Lyons also, where they received the support of certain Italian money-changers, at the recommendation of the Queen.

From these central points they soon extended themselves into the country, from Paris to Caen and Rouen, from Lyons to Marseilles, where Queen Catherine bought them ground for building. In 1582 they formed a new colony in Toulouse,

and in 1585 another in Verdun: they very soon succeeded in
making the most brilliant conversions, as for example in 1587,
that of Henry Joyeuse, one of the first men of his day in
France.[1]

These religious movements produced a more powerful effect
in France, at least in one respect, than they had even done in
Germany, since they gave rise to institutions, imitated, it is
true, from existing ones, but with forms entirely peculiar.
Jean de la Barriere, who had obtained the Cistercian abbey
of the Fenillans, near Toulouse, at the age of nineteen, by
favor of the strange abuses that had become prevalent in the
Church of France, now caused himself to be consecrated regular abbot (in 1577), and received novices, with whom he endeavored, not only to renew, but even to exceed, the austerities
practised by the original institution of Citeaux.   Solitude, silence, and abstemiousness were carried to the utmost extremity.
These monks never left their convent except for the purpose of
preaching in the neighboring districts: within their walls they
wore no shoes, and no covering for the head; they abstained,
not only from meat and wine, but even from eggs and fish,
living on bread and water, the utmost addition being a few
vegetables.[2]   These severities did not fail to excite reverence
and call forth imitation.   Don Jean de la Barriere was in a
short time invited to the court at Vincennes.   He traversed a
large part of France with sixty-two companions, never permitting the slightest interruption to the ascetic practices of the convent.   His institute was shortly afterward confirmed by the
Pope, and extended its influence throughout the kingdom.

The whole body of the secular clergy seemed also to be inspired by a new zeal, and although holding their appointments
in perfect freedom from all responsibility, the parish priests
once more applied themselves sedulously to the care of souls.
In the year 1570 the bishops not only demanded the adoption
of the decrees promulgated by the Council of Trent, but even
required the abrogation of the concordat to which they owed
their own existence.   These propositions they renewed from
time to time with increased urgency.[3]

[1] Boverno, " Annali dei frati Cápucci-
ni," i: 546; ii. 45, f.
[2] Felibien, " Histoire de Paris," tom.
ii. p. 1158.
[3] "Remontrance de l'Assemblée gén-
érale du Clergé de France, convoquée en
la Ville de Melun, faite au Roi Henri
III. le 3 Juillet, 1579, Recueil des Actes
du Clergé," tom. xiv.   Thuanus also
gives an extract.

Who shall attempt accurately to define all the causes by which the religious feelings of the period were induced to take this direction? We can be certain of the facts only, and these show that a very important change became manifest about the year 1580. A Venetian writer asserts that the number of Protestants had diminished by seventy per cent., and that the mass of the people had again become decidedly Catholic. Novelty and the energy of impulse were now acting on the side of Catholicism.[4]

But under these circumstances the Catholic spirit assumed a new position in regard to the regal authority.

The court was living in a state of continual self-contradiction; Henry III was unquestionably a good Catholic; no one could expect favor at his hands who did not attend the mass; he would not suffer Protestants to hold the magistracy in any town of his kingdom; but notwithstanding all this, he continued now as in former times to dispose of ecclesiastical appointments in accordance with the exigencies of court favor, and without the slightest regard either to worth or talent; neither did he cease to appropriate and squander the property of the Church. He delighted in processions, practised various devotional exercises, and spared himself no penance; but this did not prevent him from leading the most disgraceful life, or from permitting others to lead it also—an abandoned licentiousness was the fixed habit of the court; the profligate excesses committed during the carnival provoked the anger of the preachers, some of the courtiers were refused Christian burial on account of the circumstances attending their death, and the expressions uttered by them in their last moments: this happened even in the case of the King's especial favorites.

Thus, the rigid spirit of Catholicism prevailing, though favored in many ways by the court, was yet in effect and essentially in direct opposition to it.

The King, moreover, persevered in the old system of politics, which was manifested principally in his hostility to Spain. At any other time this would have signified nothing; but at the

[4] Lorenzo Priuli, " Relatione di Franza, 5 Giugno, 1582 " :. " We have cause for surprise, humanly speaking, that things are not in a worse condition than they are; for, by the grace of God, in despite of the little regard that has been and is paid to the matter, the number of the Huguenots has diminished by seventy per cent., while the Catholics show the utmost zeal and fervor in all affairs of religion."

moment we are treating of, the religious principle, even in France, was more powerful than regard for national interests; as the Huguenots felt bound to the Protestants of the Netherlands, so did the Catholics consider themselves the natural allies of Philip II and Farnese. The Jesuits, who had performed so many services for the Spanish power in the Netherlands, could not look on without alarm, when it became obvious to them that the enemies they had combated there were receiving aid and support in France.

To this cause of uneasiness was added the death of the Duke of Alençon, which took place in 1584, and as the King had no heir, nor any hope of one, Henry of Navarre became the next expectant of the crown.

The fear of future evil has perhaps more influence over the minds of men than a misfortune actually present; the prospect of Henry's accession caused the utmost agitation among the French Catholics,[5] and above all, as was natural, in the Guises, the old antagonists of Navarre, who feared the influence he must acquire even as heir to the throne—how much more then the power he would exercise as king. We cannot be surprised that they should look to Philip of Spain for support.

And nothing could be more welcome to that monarch in the general state of his policy at that moment. He was not withheld by any scruple from entering into a formal treaty with the subjects of a foreign prince.

The principal question remaining was, whether Rome, where the union of princes with the Church had been so much talked of, would sanction the insurrection of powerful vassals against their sovereign.

And it cannot be denied that this sanction was accorded. There were some of the Guise party whose consciences were uneasy at the step about to be taken; the Jesuit Matthieu therefore proceeded to Rome for the purpose of obtaining a declaration from the Pope, by which their scruples might be set at rest. On hearing the representations of Matthieu, Gregory declared that he fully approved the intention of the French princes

[5] A document was at that time published in Rome, showing how desirable it was that a Guise should succeed to the throne: " Of the inclination of the Catholics toward the house of Guise, and of the benefit to be derived by Christianity and the Catholic King from the succession of one of those princes." This paper was sent to Spain: it was ascribed to Cardinal Este. " Dispaccio Veneto, 1584, 1mo Dcbr."

to take up arms against heretics, and that he removed every scruple they might entertain on the subject. He had no doubt but that the King would himself approve their purpose; but even if he should not do so, they must nevertheless proceed with their plans, and pursue them till they achieved the grand object of exterminating the heretics.[6] The process against Henry of Navarre had been already commenced; before its conclusion Sixtus V had ascended the papal throne, and he pronounced sentence of excommunication against Navarre and Condé. By this act he gave a more effectual assistance to the purposes of the League than he could have afforded by any other mode of co-operation.[7]

The Guises had already taken arms, and labored to get as many provinces and fortified towns as they possibly could into their own hands.

At the first movement they made themselves masters of many important places, as Verdun, Toul, Lyons, Bourges, Orleans, and Mezieres, without drawing a sword. To avoid the appearance of being vanquished by force, the King then recurred to a method he had already adopted, and declared their cause his own. But in order to be admitted to their alliance, he was obliged to ratify and extend the conquest of the League by formal treaty, and saw himself obliged to surrender Burgundy, Champagne, a great part of Picardy, and many fortified places in other parts of the kingdom, to the possession of the Guise party.[8]

These things being arranged, the King and the Guises proceeded to prosecute the war against the Protestants in common. But with how great a difference! The King took half-measures only, and all were utterly ineffectual. The Catholics even suspected him of wishing success to the Protestant arms, that so he might seem to be compelled by the menacing aspect of their force to conclude a peace disadvantageous to the Catholic interest. Guise on the contrary took an oath, that should God grant him victory, he would not dismount from his

[6] " Claude Matthieu au duc de Nevers, 11 Févr. 1585." This is perhaps the most important piece of information given in the whole fourth volume of Capefigue, " Réforme," etc. p. 173.
[7] Maffei, " Historiarum ab Excessu Gregorii XIII." lib. i. p. 10: " He allowed himself to be induced by the repeated prayers of the Leaguers, and by the advice and entreaty of King Philip, to assail the Huguenots and their chiefs with divine arms."
[8] Reflections of Cardinal Ossat on the effects of the League in France: " Life of Cardinal Ossat," i. 44.

horse until he had established the Catholic religion in France forever. With his own troops, and not those of the King, he surprised the Germans at Auneau, when they were marching to the assistance of the Huguenots, whose best hopes were placed on their aid, and annihilated them completely.

The Pope compared him with Judas Maccabeus. He was indeed a man whose grandeur of character commanded the passionate homage of the people, and he became the idol of all Catholics.

The King was on the contrary in a position of the utmost difficulty; he did not know what to do, nor even what to desire. The papal ambassador, Morosini, declared that he seemed to consist as it were of two persons: he wished for the downfall of the Huguenots, and dreaded it quite as much; he feared the defeat of the Catholics, and yet desired it: such was the effect of this mental discord, that he no longer dared to follow his own inclinations, and could not even trust his own thoughts.[9]

This was a state of mind which inevitably deprived him of the confidence of all, and could not but tend to utter ruin.

The Catholics firmly believed that the very man who had placed himself at their head was secretly opposed to them. Every transient occasion of intercourse with the adherents of Navarre, every mark of favor, however trifling, bestowed on a Protestant was counted against him; all maintained that the most Christian King himself was the principal hindrance to a complete restoration of Catholicism, and they detested the King's favorites, and above all the Duke d'Epernon, with hatred all the more bitter, because Henry set him up in opposition to the Guises, and intrusted to him the most important governments of the realm.

Under these circumstances there was formed by the side of the league of the princes an alliance, whose members were of the burgher class, but whose object was equally the support of Catholicism. In every town the populace was acted on by preachers, who combined a furious opposition to the government with a vehement zeal for religion. In Paris things were carried still further; the project of a popular union for the

[9] " Dispaccio Morosini," in Tempesti, " Vita di Sisto V." p. 346: " The King, though he is so great a monarch, is as poor as great; and in proportion as he is poor is he prodigal. He displays extraordinary piety, and yet he abominates the sacred league: he is in arms against the heretics, and is yet jealous of the Catholic triumphs."

defence of the Catholic faith was there formed, the first movers being three preachers and an influential citizen.[10] They bound themselves by oath in the first instance, to shed the last drop of their blood in this cause. Each then named a few trusty friends, and the first meeting was held at the cell of a monk in the Sorbonne. They soon perceived the possibility of comprising the whole city in their union; a small number was selected to form a committee, and conduct the movement; these men were empowered to levy money in any case demanding it. A member was appointed as superintendent for each of the sixteen quarters of the city; the enrolling of members proceeded rapidly, and with the utmost secrecy. On those newly entered a discussion was first held in the committee, and if they were not approved, no further communication was made to them. They had agents in all the colleges, one for the audit-office, one for the procurators of the court, one for the clerks, one for the greffiers, etc. In a short time the whole city, which had before received a Catholic military organization, was comprehended in this more secret and more effective league; but not satisfied with Paris, its branches were sent forth to Orleans, Lyons, Toulouse, Bordeaux, and Rouen, where associations were also formed, which despatched their delegates to the confederates in Paris. All then solemnly pledged themselves to labor for the removal of government abuses, and above all, to endure the presence of no Huguenot in France.

This is the compact known as the League of the Sixteen. When its members found themselves arrived at a certain degree of strength, they gave notice to the Guises; and Mayenne, the brother of the duke, came with the most profound secrecy to Paris, when the union between the princes and the citizens was completed.[1]

Henry III already felt the ground trembling beneath his feet.

[10] The Anonymo Capitolino, on the " Life of Sixtus V," has some original notices on this subject. He calls the founder, Carlo Ottomani, " an honorable citizen," who first communicated his plans to the preachers. At their very first assembly, Ottomani proposed an alliance with the princes; in the second meeting, it was resolved to nominate sixteen persons, one for each quarter, " to whom should be reported by trusty persons, whatever was said or done in them relating to public affairs." In the third meeting, which took place on Candlemas day, a council of ten persons was named, with the right of raising contributions, and a deputation to the Duke de Guise was at once agreed on. This account makes important additions to all we find regarding this matter in Cayet, from Manaut and Maheutre, and in Poulain, De Thou, and Davila.

[1] In the palace of Rens, behind the Church of St. Augustine, they all swore to maintain their league, which was not only defensive, but absolute.—Anon. Capit.

The proceedings of his enemies were reported to him from day to day. In the Sorbonne they had become so bold as to propose the question whether it were permitted to withdraw allegiance from a prince who neglects to perform his duty; and to this question a reply was returned in the affirmative by a council of from thirty to forty doctors. The King was excessively irritated; he threatened to do as Pope Sixtus had done, and chain the refractory preachers to the galleys; but he did not possess the energy of the pontiff, and contented himself with ordering the advance of the Swiss who were in his service to the neighborhood of the capital.

Alarmed by the menace implied in this movement, the citizens sent to Guise entreating him to come and protect them. The King caused it to be intimated to him that a compliance with this request would be viewed unfavorably; but the duke appeared in Paris nevertheless.

Everything now seemed ready for a great explosion.

The King commanded the Swiss to enter Paris, when it instantly burst forth. The city was immediately barricaded, the Swiss were driven back, and the Louvre was menaced. The King had no alternative but flight.[2]

The Duke of Guise had before been master of a large portion of France; he was now in possession of Paris. The Bastille, the Arsenal, the Hôtel de Ville, and all the surrounding places fell into his hands. The King was completely overpowered. He was very soon compelled to pronounce an interdict against the Protestant religion, and to resign various fortified places to the Guises, in addition to those they already held. The Duke of Guise might now be considered as lord of half France, and Henry III gave him legal authority over the other half, by conferring on him the dignity of lieutenant-general of the kingdom. The States were convoked, and there could be no doubt but that Catholic opinions would predominate in that assembly. The most decisive measures were to be expected from it, ruinous for the Huguenots, and entirely to the advantage of the Catholic party.

[2] Maffei blames Guise for having suffered this: " Satisfied with the mere show of empty popularity and ill- omened power, he permitted Henry to depart in safety."

Section XI.—Savoy and Switzerland

It will be readily perceived that the preponderance of Catholicism in the mighty realm of France would inevitably produce a corresponding effect on the neighboring kingdoms and communities.

The Catholic cantons of Switzerland attached themselves more closely than ever to the ecclesiastical principle and to the Spanish alliance.

The establishment of a permanent "nunciature" was productive of the most remarkable effects in Switzerland as well as in Germany.

In the year 1586, and immediately after the adoption of this measure, the Catholic cantons united to form the Golden or Borromean League, in which they bound themselves and their descendants forever, "to live and die in the true, undoubted, ancient, apostolic Roman Catholic faith."[1] Thereupon they received the host from the hand of the nuncio.

If the party by which the administrative power was seized at Mühlhausen in the year 1587 had gone over to the Catholic creed, as they seemed on the point of doing, and if they had done so at the right moment, they would have been supported without doubt by the Catholics: conferences had already been held on the subject at the house of the nuncio in Lucerne; but the people of Mühlhausen deliberated too long. The Protestants, on the contrary, pressed forward their expedition with the utmost promptitude, and re-established the old government, which was upon the whole favorable to themselves.[2]

It was, however, at this moment that the three forest cantons, in concert with Zug, Lucerne, and Freiburg, took a new and most important step. After long negotiations, they concluded a treaty with Spain on May 12, 1587, in which they promised to maintain perpetual friendship with the King, conceded to him the right of raising recruits in their territories, and of marching his troops through their mountains; Philip, on his side, making corresponding concessions to them. But

[1] "Their eternal posterity." This is the expression used in the records of the League.—Lauffer, "Beschreibung Helvetischer Geschichte," bd. x. s. 331.
[2] The importance of the Mühlhausen affair, as regarded religion, is made very evident by the narrative of the Anonymo Capitol., founded on the reports of the nuncio, to which we shall again refer in examining Tempesti.

the most important part of their mutual engagement was that
each promised to aid the other with the utmost extent of his
powers, in the event of either being involved in war on account
of the holy apostolic religion.[3]   And in this treaty the six cantons
made no exception; not even in favor of the confederated cantons; on the contrary, it was against them in particular that
this part of the treaty must have been arranged, seeing that
there was no other power with which there was any probability
of their being involved in a war from motives of religion.

Here also then, how much more powerful was the influence
of religious feeling than that of national attachment! A community of faith now united the ancient Switzer with the house
of Austria! The Confederation became for the moment a
secondary consideration.

It was most fortunate that no cause for immediate hostilities
arose. The influence of this league was therefore confined in
the first instance to Geneva.

Charles Emanuel, Duke of Savoy, a prince whose whole life
had been marked by restless ambition, had often evinced a desire
to seize the first favorable occasion for regaining possession of
Geneva, regarding himself as the legitimate sovereign of that
city; but his purposes had hitherto been always defeated by
opposition from the Swiss and French, from both of whom the
Genevese received protection.

But circumstances were now altered; under the influence of
Guise, Henry III promised in the summer of 1588 that he
would no longer impede any enterprise undertaken against
Geneva.

Receiving this intimation, the duke prepared himself for
the attack. The Genevese did not lose their courage, and made
occasional incursions on the ducal territories. But, on this
occasion, Berne afforded them but very insufficient aid. The
Catholic party had insinuated their partisans into the very midst
of this city, closely interwoven as it was with Protestant interests; there was a faction there which would not have been
unwilling to see Geneva fall into the hands of the duke.[4] It

[3] "Traité d'alliance faite entre Philippe
II." etc. Dumont, "Corps Diplo-
matique," vol. i. p. 459.
  [4] The fifth article of the treaty leaves
no doubt on the subject, even though
the judicial evidence of guilt on the
part of Wattenwyl is involved to a certain extent in obscurity. Extracts from
contemporary pamphlets, and from the
acts of the Council of Berne, are to be
found in Gelzer, "Die drei letzen Jahr-
hunderte der Schweizergeschichte," bd.
i. p. 128, 137.

thus happened that he very soon gained the advantage. He had hitherto held the countships bordering on Geneva under closely limited conditions, imposed on him by former treaties of peace with Berne; he now seized the occasion, and made himself for the first time master in those districts. He expelled the Protestants, whom he had previously been obliged to tolerate, and made the whole country exclusively Catholic. Charles Emanuel had till that time been prohibited from erecting fortresses in that portion of his territories; he then built them in places where he could not only make them serve for defence, but also for harassing Geneva.

But before these affairs had proceeded further, other enterprises had been undertaken, from which consequences of much, more extensive importance might be expected, and which seemed not unlikely to produce a complete revolution in all the relations of Europe.

Section XII.—Attack on England

The Netherlands were in great part subdued, and negotiations had already commenced for the voluntary submission of the remainder. In Germany the efforts of Catholicism had prevailed in many districts, and a project was conceived, by which those yet wanting to their triumph might be overcome. In France, the Champion of Catholicism was proceeding on a path that by victories, investment of fortresses, attachment of the people, and legitimate authority seemed inevitably leading him to the possession of exclusive sovereignty. The ancient metropolis of the Protestant faith, the city of Geneva, was no longer protected by her former allies. At this moment the plan was formed of laying the axe to the root of the tree by an attack on England.

The central point of the Protestant power and policy was without doubt in England; the provinces of the Netherlands yet remaining unsubdued, as well as the Huguenots of France, found their principal support in Queen Elizabeth.

But the internal struggle had, as we have seen, already commenced even in England. Swarms of Jesuits and pupils from the seminaries, impelled by religious enthusiasm, sedulously cultivated for this very purpose, and by the desire to revisit their

native country, were constantly pouring into the kingdom;
Elizabeth opposing them by the utmost severity of laws enacted
to that end. In the year 1582 it was declared high treason to
attempt the perversion of one of her subjects from the established religion of the realm to that of Rome.[1] In 1585 she
commanded all Jesuits and priests of the seminaries to depart
from England within forty days, under pain of being punished
as traitors, much in the same manner as so many Catholic princes
had dealt with the Protestants in driving them from their several territories.[2] To this effect she then brought the high court
of commission into operation; a tribunal expressly appointed
to take cognizance of all offences against the acts of Supremacy
and Uniformity, not only in accordance with the usual forms
of law, but by all means that could be devised, even to the
exaction of a solemn oath; a kind of Protestant Inquisition.[3]
Elizabeth was nevertheless extremely anxious to avoid the appearance of attacking liberty of conscience. She affirmed that
the Jesuits were not seeking the restoration of their religion,
but that their purpose was to lead the people to an insurrection
against the government, and thus prepare the way for foreign
enemies. The missionaries protested " before God and the
saints," " before heaven and earth " (as they expressed themselves), that their object was entirely and solely religious, and
in nowise regarded the Queen's majesty.[4] But what understanding could discriminate between these motives? The Queen's
inquisitors were not to be satisfied with a simple affirmation.
They demanded an explicit declaration, as to whether or not
the anathema pronounced against Elizabeth by Pius V were
lawful and binding on Englishmen. The prisoners were also
required to say what they would do, and to which side they
would attach themselves, in the event of the Pope's absolving
them from their allegiance, and making an attack on England.
The harassed and frightened men saw no means of extricating
themselves from such a dilemma. They made an attempt by declaring that they would render unto Cæsar the things which

[1] Camden, " Rerum Anglicarum Annales regnante Elizabetha," i. p. 349.
[2] Ibid. p. 396.
[3] " As well by the oaths of twelve
good and lawful men, as also by witnesses, and all other means and ways
you can devise."—Neal, " History of the
Puritans," vol. i. p. 414. It might at
least have been " lawful means and
ways."

[4] Campiani, " Vita et Martyrium,"
p. 159: " I affirm before God and his
angels, before heaven and earth, before
the world and this tribunal, that I am
not guilty of lese-majesty, nor of sedi-
tion, nor of any conspiracy against my
country."

were Cæsar's, and unto God the things which were God's; but
their judges interpreted this subterfuge itself as a confession.
The prisons were accordingly crowded; execution was followed
by execution; and Catholicism also had its martyrs. Their
number in the reign of Elizabeth has been calculated at 200.
The zeal of the missionaries was not subdued by this oppression,
as will be readily comprehended. The number of the refractory,
the recusants, as they were called, increased with the increasing
severity of the laws, and their exasperation increased in like
proportion. Pamphlets were circulated even about the court,
in which the act of Judith in destroying Holofernes was held
up as an example of piety and heroic courage worthy of imitation. The eyes of the greater number were still turned toward
the imprisoned Queen of Scotland, who according to the papal
decision was the legitimate queen of England. They cherished
a constant hope that a general revolution would be brought
about by an attack from the Catholic sovereigns. In Italy and
Spain the most fearful representations were circulated of cruelties practised on the true believers in England; accounts that
could not fail to excite abhorrence in every Catholic heart.[5]

No man took more earnest part in this feeling than Pope
Sixtus V. It is doubtless true that he felt a sort of esteem
for the personal qualities of Queen Elizabeth: her high and
dauntless spirit awakened his admiration, and he even sent
her an invitation to return into the bosom of the Catholic
Church. How extraordinary a proposition was this! As if the
power to choose remained with her: as if all her previous life,
all that gave importance to her existence, her position in the
world, had not bound her irrevocably to the interests of Protestantism; even though her convictions had not been entirely
sincere. Elizabeth replied not a word; but she laughed. When
the Pope heard this, he declared that he must then think of
means for depriving her of her dominions by force.

Before that time he had but intimated such a design, but in
the spring of 1586 he openly proceeded to active measures, and
boasted that he would support Philip of Spain in his enterprise

[5] " Theatre of the cruelties perpetrated
by the heretics of our day." It begins
with a " special description of the cruelties and atrocities of the English schis-
matics in the reign of Henry VIII.,"
and concludes with " a description of
the English Inquisition, and of the
Machiavellian acts of cruelty committed
by the Calvinistic Protestants in England and Ireland during the reign of
Elizabeth." Plates are added, depict-
ing unheard-of tortures, a most horrible
sight.

against England with assistance of a very different character
from that furnished to Charles V by earlier popes.[6]

In January, 1587, he made loud complaints of the dilatory
proceedings of Spain, and insisted on the numerous advantages
the King would derive from a victory over England in relation
to his future efforts for the perfect subjugation of the Netherlands.[7]

He soon became much irritated by the delays of Spain.
When Philip II published a *pragmatica,* imposing restrictions
on all ecclesiastical dignitaries, and consequently affecting those
claimed by the Roman Curia in his dominions, the Pope burst
into a flaming passion. " What," he exclaimed, " can Don
Philip conduct himself thus violently against us, while he permits himself to be maltreated by a woman? "[8]

And the King was certainly not spared by Elizabeth; she
openly took part with the people of the Netherlands, and her
admirals, Drake in particular, made every coast of Europe
and America insecure. What Pope Sixtus had uttered, was
in fact the question secretly asked by all Catholics—they were
astonished at the long endurance of that mighty sovereign, and
the many injuries he had suffered without avenging them. The
Cortes of Castile exhorted him no longer to defer the exaction
of vengeance.

Philip received even personal insults. He was made the subject of mockery in masks and comedies. This was on one
occasion reported to him, when the aged monarch, who had
always been accustomed to reverence, sprang up from his chair
in a state of irritation, such as had never before been seen in
him.

In these dispositions were the Pope and King, when they
received intelligence that Elizabeth had caused the imprisoned
Queen of Scotland to be put to death. This is not the place
to inquire into the legal right she may have had for commanding this execution: it must, upon the whole, be regarded as an
act of political justice. The first thought of it arose, so far
as I can discover, at the time of the massacre of St. Bartholo-

[6] " Dispaccio Gritti, 31 Maggio, 1586":
" The Pope will send him four times as
much; he desires that a feint should
be made of going to encounter Drake,
but that the expedition should then turn
toward England."

[7] " Dispaccio Gritti, 10 Genn., 1587."
[8] Complaining that the King should
let himself be roughly handled by a
woman, and yet should brave him (his
holiness).

mew. The then Bishop of London, in one of his letters to Lord Burleigh, expressed his fear lest so treacherous a beginning should have its continuation in England. He thinks the ground of this peril to be principally in the Scottish Queen. " The security of the kingdom," he declares, " demands that her head should be cut off." [9] But how much more powerful had the Catholic party now become in Europe! How much more violent were the excitement and commotion it was now causing in England itself! Mary Stuart maintained at all times a secret correspondence with her cousins the Guises, with the King of Spain, and the Pope; she was in alliance with all the disaffected in England. The Catholic principle, in so far as it was from its nature opposed to the existing government, was represented by Mary Stuart. On the first success of the Catholic party, she would indubitably have been proclaimed Queen of England. This was her position: it resulted from the state of things; but it is also certain that she made no attempt to withdraw from it, and it cost her the forfeit of her life.

But this execution brought the plans of Philip and the Pope to maturity. This was beyond what they could endure. Sixtus filled the consistory with his vociferations against the English Jezebel, who had laid hands on the anointed head of a princess subject to none but Jesus Christ, and, as she had herself acknowledged, to his vicegerent. To show how cordially he approved of the activity displayed by the Catholic opposition in England, he raised William Allen, the first founder of the seminaries, to the dignity of cardinal; an elevation which was regarded, at least in Rome, as a declaration of war against England. A formal treaty was also now concluded between Philip and the Pope [10]—Sixtus promising the King 1,000,000 of scudi in aid of the enterprise; but as he was always on his guard, especially where money was the question, he pledged himself to pay it when Philip should have taken possession of an English sea-port. " Let your Majesty no longer delay," he wrote to the King, " for all delay will tend to change a good intention into a bad performance!" Philip called every resource of his

[9] Edwin Sandys to Lord Burghley, Fulham, September 5, 1572: " The saftie of our quene and realme, yf God wil: furtwith to cutte of the Scotish quenes heade; ipsa est nostri fundi calamitas."—Ellis's " Letters," second series, vol. iii. p. 25.

[10] The original views of the Pope, " Dispaccio Gritti, 27 Guigno, 1587:" " The Pope made a large offer to the King for the expedition, but he wishes to have the nomination of the King, and that the kingdom shall be a fief of the Church."

kingdom into action, and fitted out the Armada called the " Invincible."

And thus the powers of Italy and Spain, from which influence so mighty had gone forth over the whole world, aroused themselves for an attack upon England. The King had caused a collection to be made from the archives of Simancas, of all the claims he possessed to the English throne on the extinction of the line of Stuart. The expedition was associated in his mind with the most brilliant prospects, especially that of universal dominion over the seas.

All things seemed now combining toward one result—the ascendancy of Catholicism in Germany, the renewed attack on the Huguenots in France, the attempt upon Geneva, the enterprise against England. At the same moment a decidedly Catholic sovereign, Sigismund III, succeeded to the crown of Poland (an event of which we shall speak further hereafter), with the prospect of future accession to the throne of Sweden.

But whenever any principle, be it what it may, tends to the establishment of absolute dominion in Europe, there is invariably opposed to it a vigorous resistance, having its origin in the deepest springs of human nature.

Philip found himself confronted in England by the national energies in all the force of their youth, and elevated by the full consciousness of their destiny. The bold corsairs, who had rendered every sea unsafe, gathered around the coasts of their native land. The whole body of the Protestants, even the Puritans, although they had been oppressed as heavily as the Catholics, rallied around the Queen, who now maintained to an admirable degree that masculine courage with which she was endowed, and gave proof of her princely talent of winning, retaining, and controlling the minds of men. The insular position of the country, and even the elements, co-operated to the defence of England. The invincible Armada was annihilated even before the assault had been made: the expedition failed completely.

It is nevertheless evident that the plan, the great purpose itself, was not immediately abandoned.

The Catholics were reminded by the writers of their party that Julius Cæsar, as well as Henry VII, the grandfather of Elizabeth, had both been unfortunate in their first attempts on

England, but had at last become masters of the country—that God often delayed the victory of the faithful. The children of Israel, in the war that they had undertaken by express command of God, with the tribe of Benjamin, were twice beaten with great loss. It was not until the third attack that they gained the victory: " Then, the devouring flames made desolate all the towns and villages of Benjamin—men and cattle were slain by the edge of the sword." " Therefore," they exclaimed, " let the English ponder on these things, and not be too much elated because their chastisement is delayed." [1]

Neither had Philip of Spain by any means lost his courage. He proposed to fit out smaller and more easily managed vessels, and with these at once to attempt a landing on the English coast, without waiting in the Channel to be joined by the force of the Netherlands. In the arsenal at Lisbon preparations proceeded with the utmost activity. The King was resolved to stake everything upon the undertaking, even should he be obliged, as he once said at table, to sell the silver candlesticks that stood before him. [2]

But while this project was occupying his thoughts, other prospects were opened to his view— a new theatre presented itself for the activity of the powers wielded by Roman Catholicism as now represented by Spain and Italy.

Section XIII.—Assassination of Henry III

In a short time after the calamitous dispersion of the Spanish fleet, a reaction took place in France, unlooked for, and, as so frequently has been the case, violent and sanguinary.

At the moment when the Duke of Guise, who ruled the States of Blois at his will, seemed, by virtue of his office of constable, to be on the point of gathering the whole power of the kingdom

---

[1] " Andreæ Philopatri (Parsoni) ad Elizabethæ reginæ Angliæ edictum responsio," §§ 146, 147: " No force [he adds] has been repelled by their own courage; but rather by those casualties so common to warfare; the inclemency of weather namely, an insufficient acquaintance with the seas, and perhaps negligence and unskilfulness in some of those engaged; and, finally, by the will of God, who may have been pleased in his mercy to spare the unfruitful tree to the third gospel year."

[2] " Dispacci Gradenigo, 29 Sett., 1588 ": " Although the King has greatly felt this turn of evil fortune, he yet shows himself more than ever resolved to continue the enterprise with all his forces." " 11 Ott.: " " His Majesty is most earnest in thinking of this matter, and is eagerly making preparation for next year." " 1 Nov.: " " These candlesticks shall be sold (the King exclaimed), if there be no other means of raising money."

into his hands, Henry III caused him to be assassinated. That King, perceiving himself beset and enchained by the Spanish and Catholic party, tore himself at once from their trammels, and placed himself in direct opposition to them.

But the death of Guise did not extinguish his party nor annihilate the League. This latter assumed for the first time a position of undisguised hostility, and allied itself more closely than ever with Spain.

Pope Sixtus was entirely on the side of this party.

The assassination of the duke, whom he loved and admired, and in whom he beheld a pillar of the Church, had already caused him extreme regret and indignation;[1] he found it an insufferable addition when Cardinal Guise was also murdered. "A cardinal-priest!" he exclaimed in the consistory, "a noble member of the Holy See, without process or judgment, by the secular arm, as if there were no Pope in the world, as if there were no longer any God!" He reproached his legate Morosini for not having instantly excommunicated the King. He ought to have done it even though it had cost him a hundred times his life.[2]

The King was but slightly disturbed by the Pope's indignation, and could not be induced to give liberty to Cardinal Bourbon, or the Archbishop of Lyons, whom he had also imprisoned. He was continually urged by the Roman Court to declare Henry of Navarre incapable of succeeding to the throne, but instead of doing so he entered into alliance with him.

The Pope then resolved to adopt measures of the uttermost severity; he cited the King to appear in person at the Court of Rome, there to render an account for having murdered a cardinal, and threatened him with excommunication if he failed to release his prisoners within a specified time.

Sixtus declared that he was bound to act thus; should he do otherwise he must answer for it to God as the most useless of pontiffs; but since he had thus fulfilled his duty, he need not

[1] The Pope also complained very particularly that Henry III had contrived to obtain a brief from him which "conceded to him the power of being absolved from any sin whatsoever, if still reserved to the Apostolic See, and with which he now desires to cover the heavy offence that he has committed." —"Dispaccio Veneto."

[2] Tempesti, ii. 137, has given the speech of the Pope at full length, with his letter to Morosini: "The cardinal being assassinated [it says] in the very face of your illustrious lordship, you, the legate à latere, how does it happen that you did not instantly publish the interdict? This you should have done, even had it cost you a hundred lives!"

fear the whole world; he made no doubt that Henry III would perish as King Saul had done.[3]

By the zealous Catholics and the adherents of the League the King was abhorred as a reprobate and outcast, the demonstrations of the Pope confirmed them in their violent opposition, and before it could have been expected, his prediction was fulfilled. On June 23d the *Monitorium* was published in France. On August 1st the King was assassinated by Clement.

The Pope himself was amazed: " In the midst of his army," he exclaimed, " on the point of conquering Paris, in his own Cabinet, he has been struck down by a poor monk, and at one blow." He attributed this to the immediate intervention of God, who thereby testified that he would not abandon France.[4]

How is it that an opinion so erroneous can possibly have gained possession of the minds of men? This conviction prevailed among innumerable Catholics; " It is to the hand of the Almighty alone," wrote Mendoza to Philip, " that we must ascribe this happy event." [5] In the distant University of Ingolstadt the young Maximilian of Bavaria was then pursuing his studies, and in one of the first letters from his hands remaining to our days he expresses to his mother the joy which he had received from the intelligence that " the King of France had been killed." [6]

This occurrence had nevertheless another and less auspicious aspect; Henry of Navarre, whom the Pope had excommunicated, and whom the Guises so rancorously persecuted, now succeeded to his legitimate rights—a Protestant assumed the title of King of France.

The League, Philip II, and the Pope were resolved that they would not suffer him on any condition to attain to the enjoyment of his kingdom. The Pope sent a new legate to France in the place of Morosini, who appeared to be much too lukewarm. This was Gaetano, who was believed to be disposed to the Spanish party, and the pontiff gave him a sum of money, a thing he had never done before, to be applied as might be most ad-

[3] " Dispaccio Veneto, 20 Maggio, 1589: " " The Pope accuses himself of negligence for not having made any remonstrance, or taken other steps, during five months that have elapsed since one cardinal has been assassinated, and another, with an archbishop, kept prisoner; he fears the wrath of God, etc."
[4] " Dispaccio Veneto, 1 Sett.: " " The Pope in the consistory declared that the occurrence of the French King's death must be considered to have been at the express will of God, and ought to make all men confident that he would continue to have France in his especial guard."
[5] " Capefigue," v. 290.
[6] Wolf, " Maximilian I." th. i. s. 107.

vantageous for the purposes of the League. He was commanded
above all things to take care that no other than a Catholic should
be King of France. The crown ought without doubt to belong to a prince of the blood, but that was not the only condition to be insisted on; the strict order of hereditary succession
had more than once been departed from, but never had a heretic
been suffered to succeed; the first essential was that the King
should be a good Catholic.[7]

In this disposition of mind the Pope considered it even praiseworthy in the Duke of Savoy that he had taken advantage of
the disorders prevailing in France to gain possession of Saluzzo,
which then belonged to the French. It was better, Sixtus declared, that the duke should take it than that it should fall into
the hands of the heretics.[8]

And now everything depended on securing that the League
should be victorious in the conflict with Henry IV.

To this effect a new treaty was concluded between Spain and
the Pope. The most zealous of the inquisitors, Cardinal Sanseverina, was intrusted, under the seal of confession, with the
arrangement of the terms. The Pope promised to send without fail an army of 15,000 foot and 800 horse into France, and
further declared himself ready to furnish subsidies when the
King should have penetrated with a powerful army into that
kingdom; the papal forces were to be commanded by the Duke
of Urbino, a subject of the Pope and an adherent of the King
of Spain.[9]

And thus were these Spanish and Italian powers, combined
with their adherents in France, prepared in arms to secure
the throne of that country to their party forever.

A more attractive prospect could not have been laid open,
either to the Spanish sovereign or the Pope. Philip would
render himself and his successors forever free from that ancient
rivalry by which the efforts of Spain had so long been restricted; the sequel showed how much he had it at heart. For

---

[7] " Dispaccio Veneto, 30 Sett." The
Pope declares that it does not require
that he should be elected of the blood-
royal, more than any other family, being what had often happened before;
but never a heretic to our holy religion;
that Savoy, Lorraine, or even Mayenne,
pretended to the crown; but his holiness did not wish to favor one more
than another.—Extract from the Instruction in Tempesti, ii. 233.

[8] The Pope was reproached on that
account, but " he justified himself with
many reasons, as to the taking of Saluzzo by the said duke, with his participation."—" Dispaccio Veneto."
[9] Authentic notice in the autobiography of the cardinal, and which has
been adopted by Tempesti, ii. 236.

the papal power also it would have been an immense advance to have exercised an active influence in placing a sovereign on the throne of France. Gaetano was accordingly directed to demand the introduction of the Inquisition, and the abolition of the privileges claimed by the Gallican Church; but the most significant of all triumphs would have been the exclusion of a legitimate prince from the throne, on considerations purely religious; the ecclesiastical impulse then pervading the world in all directions, would thereby have achieved complete supremacy.

BOOK VI

INTERNAL CONFLICTS, DOCTRINAL AND POLIT-
ICAL.—A.D. 1589–1607

THE course now taken by the moral and intellectual development of the century was in a direction totally
opposed to that which might have been expected from
the characteristics of its commencement.

At that time the restraints of ecclesiastical authority were
cast aside, the nations labored to separate themselves from their
common spiritual chief; in the Court of Rome itself, those principles on which the hierarchy was founded were treated with
ridicule and contumely; profane tastes predominated in literature and the arts, while the maxims of a pagan morality were
acted on without reserve or concealment.

How entirely was all this now changed! In the name of
religion it now was that wars were undertaken, conquests
achieved, and States revolutionized. There has been no period
in which theologians were more influential than at the close of
the sixteenth century. They sat in the councils of kings, and
discussed political affairs from the pulpit in the presence of the
whole people—they directed schools, controlled the efforts of
learning, and governed the whole range of literature. From
the confessional they gained opportunity for surprising the secret struggles of the soul with itself, and for giving the decisive
bias to all the doubtful questions arising in private life. It may
perhaps be affirmed that the eager violence with which they
opposed each other, the fact that each of the two great divisions
found its antagonist in its own body, was precisely the cause
of that comprehensive and pervading influence.

And if this might be said of both parties, it was more particularly true of the Catholics. Among them the ideas and
institutions by which the minds of men are more immediately
and effectually disciplined and guided were arranged with the

123

most perfect adaptation to the end proposed; no man could now exist without a father confessor. Among Catholics, moreover, the clergy, either as associates of some order, or in any case as members of the general hierarchy, constituted a corporation, combined in the strictest subordination, and acting in the most perfect unity of spirit. The head of this hierarchical body, the Pope of Rome, again acquired an influence but little inferior to that which he had possessed in the eleventh and twelfth centuries; by means of the enterprises which he was continually undertaking for the furtherance of his religious purposes, the Roman pontiff kept the world in perpetual movement.

Under these circumstances the boldest pretensions of the days of Hildebrand were revived—axioms that had hitherto been preserved in the arsenals of the canon law, rather as antiquities than for use, were now brought forth into full effect and activity.

Our European commonwealth has, however, at no time been subjected to the dominion of pure force; at all periods it has been imbued by the effect of thought and opinion: no enterprise of importance can succeed, no power can rise into universal influence, without immediately suggesting to the minds of men the ideal of a forthcoming advancement of society. From this point proceed theories: these reproduce the moral import and significance of facts, which are then presented in the light of a universal and effectual truth, as deduced from reason or religion, and as a result arrived at by reflection. They thus anticipate, as it were, the completion of the event, which at the same time they most effectually promote.

Let us consider in what manner this took place at the period of which we are treating.

Section I.—Theory of Ecclesiastical Policy

The principle of the Catholic religion is not unfrequently declared to have an especial connection with, and natural inclination toward, the monarchical or aristocratic forms of government. A century like the sixteenth, in which this principle displayed itself in vigorous action and full self-consciousness, is particularly competent to instruct us on this point. As the result of our examination we shall find that the Catholic religion did in fact adhere to the existing order of things in Italy and Spain; that it further assisted the sovereign power in Germany to establish a new preponderance over the estates of the respective territories; in the Netherlands it promoted the subjugation of the country, and in Upper Germany, as well as in the Walloon provinces, it was upheld by the nobles with peculiar attachment. But if we inquire further, we shall perceive that these were not the only sympathies awakened by the Catholic religion. If we find it maintained by the patricians in Cologne, we see it supported with equal ardor by the populace in the neighboring city of Treves. In the large towns of France it was in every case associated with the claims and struggles of the people. The principal consideration of Catholicism indeed was, where the best support, the most effectual resources were to be found. If the existing authorities were adverse to its influence, Catholicism was very far from sparing them, or even from acknowledging their power: it maintained the Irish nation in its hereditary opposition to the English government. In England itself, Catholicism labored with its utmost force to undermine the allegiance demanded by the Queen, and frequently broke out into active rebellion; finally, its adherents in France were confirmed by their religious advisers in their insurrection against their legitimate sovereigns. The religious principle in general has in fact no inherent predilection for one form of government more than another. During the short period of its renovation, Catholicism evinced the most diversified preferences: first, toward monarchy, for example, in Italy and Spain, and for the confirmation of territorial sovereignty in Germany; next, it lent itself in the Netherlands to the maintenance of the legally constituted aristocratic bodies, and at the close of the century it formed a decided alliance with the democratical tendency. This was the more important, because it now stood forth in the utmost plenitude of its activity, and the movements in which it took part represent the most influential political occurrences of the day. If the popes had succeeded at this juncture, they would have secured a perpetual predominance over the State. They advanced claims, and their adherents propounded opinions and principles, by which kingdoms and states were threatened at once with internal convulsions, and with the loss of their independence.

It was the Jesuits principally who appeared on the arena for the purpose of announcing and defending opinions of this character.

They first laid claim to an unlimited supremacy for the Church over the State.

They were compelled by a sort of necessity to the discussion of this point in England, where the Queen was declared head of the Church by the laws of the land. This declaration was met by the chiefs of the Catholic opposition with the most arrogant pretensions from the other side. William Allen maintained that it was not only the right, but the duty of a people, to refuse allegiance to a prince who had departed from the Catholic Church, more especially when their refusal was further sanctioned by the commands of the Pope.[1] Parsons declares it to be the primary condition of all power in a sovereign, that he should defend and cherish the Roman Catholic faith: he is bound to this by his baptismal vows, and by his coronation-oath; if he refuse to fulfil these conditions, it is blindness to consider him as capable of reigning; it becomes, on the contrary, the duty of his subjects, in such a case, to expel him.[2] Such opinions are perfectly natural in these authors. They considered the exercise of religion to be the grand purpose and duty of life; they believed the Roman Catholic religion to be the only true one; they concluded that no authority, opposing itself to that religion, could be legitimate, and by consequence they make the existence of a government, and the allegiance accorded it, to depend on the application of its power for the benefit of the Roman Catholic Church.

This was the general tenor of the doctrines now rising into acceptance. The assertions put forward in England during the heat of dispute, were repeated by Cardinal Bellarmine from the solitude of his study, whence he sent them forth in ample treatises, and formed into an elaborate and well-connected system.

[1] In the letter, "Ad persecutores Anglos pro Christianis responsio (1582)," I remark the following passage: "If kings have violated the faith given to God and the people of God, the people on their part are not only permitted but enjoined, at the command of God's vicar, who is certainly the supreme pastor of all nations, to desist, on their side, from keeping faith with such 'kings.'"

[2] "Andreæ Philopatri (Personi) ad Elizabethæ reginæ edictum responsio,"

No. 162: "It is not only lawful, but it is even incumbent on all Christians, by the precepts of the divine law, and at the utmost jeopardy of their souls, if they can bring it about." No. 163: "But it is even more imperative—when the matter has been decided by the Church and its supreme director, the Pope of Rome, for it appertains to him, by virtue of his office, to guard the safety of religion and divine worship, and to separate the leprous from the pure, lest the latter be infected."

He grounded his reasonings on the proposition that the Pope is placed over the whole Church as its guardian and chief, by the immediate agency of God himself.[3]   He is thus endowed with the fulness of spiritual power; to him it is granted that he cannot err; he judges all, and may be judged by no man; there accrues to him accordingly a large amount of secular authority. Bellarmine does not go so far as to attribute a secular power to the Pope as of divine right,[4] although Sixtus V held this opinion, and was displeased to find it abandoned; but so much the more unhesitatingly does the cardinal invest him indirectly with this power.   He compares the secular power to the body, and the spiritual to the soul of man; attributing to the Church a dominion over the State, similar to that which the soul exercises over the body.   It is the right and the duty of the spiritual power to impose a curb on the temporal authority whenever the latter opposes an obstacle to the purposes of religion.   It is not to be affirmed that the Pope has claim to an immediate influence on the legislation of a State;[5] but if a law were required for the safety of souls, and the sovereign refused to proclaim it, or should a law be found injurious to the welfare of souls, and the sovereign persisted obstinately in maintaining it, then the Pope has indubitably the right to enact the first and annul the second.   With this principle he was enabled to proceed to great lengths; for does not the soul command even the death of the body when this becomes needful?   As a general rule, the Pope certainly cannot depose a prince, but should it become needful to the safety of souls, he then possesses the right of changing the government, and of transferring it from one person to another.[6]

<hr/>

[3] "Bellarminus de conciliorum autoritate," c. 17: The supreme pontiff is simply and absolutely above the universal Church, and superior to general councils; he is thus subjected to no jurisdiction on earth.
[4] "Bellarminus de Romano pontifice," v. vi.: "We assert that the pope, as pope, though possessing no mere temporal authority, yet, for the purposes of spiritual good, has supreme power to dispose of the temporal matters of all Christians."
[5] "Bellarminus de Romano pontifice," v. vi.: "As regards persons, the pope cannot, as pope, ordinarily depose temporal princes, even for a just cause, in the same way that he deposes bishops, that is, as ordinary judge; yet, as supreme spiritual prince, he can

change kingdoms, taking them from one ruler to bestow them on another; if that be needful to the welfare of souls, etc."
[6] These doctrines are, in fact, nothing more than a revival of those held in the thirteenth century.   Thomas Aquinas had already employed that comparison of the soul and body which here performs so conspicuous a part: "The secular power is subordinate to the spiritual, as the body is to the soul." In the "Tractatus de potestate summi pontificis in rebus temporalibus adversus G. Barclajum," Bellarmine brings forward more than seventy writers of different countries, who regard the power of the pope in nearly the same light as himself.

But to these assertions there lay the manifest objection, that
the sovereign authority was also based on divine right.

Or if not, then what was its origin, and wherein consisted
its inherent import and sanction?

The Jesuits made no scruple of deriving the power of the
prince from the people; they blended into one system their doctrine of the papal omnipotence with their theory of the sovereignty of the people. This opinion had already been expressed
more or less explicitly by Allen and Parsons, and it lay at the
foundation of their tenets. Bellarmine labored to establish it
in its utmost extent. He considers that God has not bestowed
the temporal power on any one man in particular. It follows,
consequently, that he has confided it to the many. Hence the
temporal authority resides with the people, and the people confide it sometimes to one, sometimes to many, but always retaining the power of altering the forms of government, of resuming
the sovereignty, and of confiding it to new hands. Nor is it to
be supposed that these views were peculiar to Bellarmine; they
were, in fact, the doctrines prevalent in the Jesuit schools of
that period. In a manual for confessors, which was dissemi-
nated throughout the Catholic world, and which had been revised by the Master of the Sacred Palace (*Magister Sacri
Palatii*), the regal power is considered to be subject to the Pope,
not merely as regards the welfare of souls,[7] but also—and the
assertion is made without ceremony—it is declared therein that
a sovereign may be deposed by the people for tyranny or neglect
of his duties; and that another may be selected by the majority
of the nation to fill his place.[8] Franciscus Suarez, primarius
professor of theology at Coimbra, has made it his especial object, in his defence of the Catholic against the Anglican Church,
to expound and confirm the doctrines of Bellarmine.[9] But it
is by Mariana that this idea of the sovereignty of the people is
most fully elaborated. He has a manifest predilection for the

[7] Aphorismi confessariorum ex doc-
torum sententiis collecti, autore Eman-
uele Sa, nuper accurate expurgati a
Revmo. P. M. sacri palatii, ed. Antv."
p. 480. But the author adds, as though
he had said too little: "Some able
jurists have, nevertheless, thought that
the pontiff is endowed with supreme
civil power."

[8] Ibid. p. 508 (ed. Colon. p. 313):
"Rex potest per rempublicam privari
ob tyrannidem, et si non faciat officium
suum et cum est aliqua causa justa, et
eligi potest alius a majore parte populi
(see text): quidam tamen solum tyrannidem causam putant." Some, however,
consider that tyranny is the only cause.

[9] R. P. Franc. Saurez Granatensis,
etc., " defensio fidei Catholicæ et Apos-
tolicæ adversus Anglicanæ sectæ er-
rores, lib. iii., de summi pontificis supra
temporales reges excellentia et potestate." It is very evident that Bellarmine's doctrine, of the right of the people to resume the power they have dele-
gated, had excited especial opposition.

subject, and setting forth all the questions that can arise on its different bearings, he decides them without reserve to the advantage of the people, and the prejudice of the princely authority. He has no doubt that a prince may be deposed, nay, put to death, in the event of his actions becoming prejudicial to religion. He pronounces on Jacques Clement, who first took counsel of divines, and then proceeded to assassinate his King, a eulogium replete with pathetic declamation.[10] In this he is at least entirely consistent. The fanaticism of the murderer had without doubt been inflamed by these very doctrines.

For they had, indeed, been propounded in no place with such furious vehemence as in France. Anything more anti-royalist than the diatribes thundered from the pulpit by Jean Boucher it would be impossible to find. It is in the Estates that this preacher considers the public might and majesty to be deposited: to them he attributes the power to bind and to loose; the inalienable sovereignty; the right of jurisdiction over sceptre and realm—for in them is the origin and source of all power; the prince proceeds from the people—not of necessity, or by compulsion, but by free choice. He adopts the views of Bellarmine as to the connection between Church and State, and repeats the illustrative comparison of the body and soul. He declares the free choice of the people to be limited by one condition only—one thing alone is forbidden—to select a heretic sovereign; by doing this, the people would draw down the curse of God on their heads.[1]

How extraordinary a combination of spiritual pretensions and democratical ideas; of absolute freedom and complete subjection, contradictory in itself, and utterly anti-national; but which, nevertheless, enchained the minds of men as by an inexplicable spell!

The Sorbonne had, hitherto, defended the royal and national

[10] " Mariana de rege et regis institutione." The following expressions are found among others: " Jacques Clement, having ascertained from divines, whom he had consulted, that a tyrant might be lawfully destroyed, made to himself a mighty name by slaying the King."

[1] Jean Boucher, " Sermons," Paris, 1594, in various places. The following words are found, p. 194: " The Church holds dominion over the kingdoms and States of Christendom; not to usurp direct power, as over its own temporalities; but, without doubt, indirectly to prevent anything occurring in temporal matters that might be to the prejudice of Christ's kingdom, as was heretofore declared by the similitude of the body and soul." And further: " The difference between the priest and the king renders this matter clear to us, the priest being of God alone, which cannot be said of the king; for, if all kings were dead, the people could easily make themselves others; but if there were no more priests, it would be needful that Jesus Christ should come in person to create new ones."

privileges with the utmost constancy against the pretensions of
the ultramontane priesthood. But when, after the assassination of the Guises, these tenets were preached from all the pulpits; when it was proclaimed through the streets, and represented by symbols on the altars and in processions, that
Henry III had rendered himself unfit to wear the crown; "the
good burghers and inhabitants of the city," as they called themselves, sought for aid, "in the scruples of their conscience,"
from the theological faculty of the University of Paris, desiring
to receive from this body a valid decision in regard to the legitimacy of their opposition to their sovereign. The Sorbonne
assembled accordingly on January 7, 1589. Their decision is
expressed as follows: "After having heard the mature and
unbiased opinions of all the *magistri;* after having examined
many and various arguments, taken verbally, for the most part,
from the Sacred Scriptures, the canon law, and papal ordinances, it has been declared by the dean of the faculty, without
one dissenting voice: first, that the people of this realm are absolved from the oath of allegiance and fidelity given by them
to King Henry; further, that this people may combine together
without scruple of conscience—may gather forces, arm themselves, and collect money for the defence of the Roman Catholic
and apostolic religion against the abominable enterprises of the
aforesaid King."[2] Seventy members of the faculty were assembled on this occasion; of these, the younger more particularly supported the resolutions with the most eager enthusiasm.[3]

The general assent with which these theories were greeted,
is, without doubt, principally attributable to their being at that
moment the real expression of the facts—of the phenomena
then passing before the eyes of the people. In the French
troubles, an alliance had even been entered into between the
ecclesiastical and popular oppositions; each advancing from its
own side to a junction with the other. The citizens of Paris
were confirmed and kept steady in their resistance to their lawful sovereign, by a legate from the Pope. Bellarmine himself
was, for a certain period, in the train of the legate. The doc-

[2] "Responsum facultatis theologicæ
Parisiensis," printed in the "Addition
au Journal de Henry III," vol. i. p.
317.
[3] Thuanus declares the number of
those present to have been sixty only;
and will not affirm their unanimity, although the document alluded to expressly says: "The opinion of all and
singular of the masters being heard,
who were of the number of seventy, it
was concluded, none dissenting."

trines which he had elaborated in his learned solitude, and which he had so successfully, and with so logical a consistency, promulgated, were now embodied and expressed in the event which he witnessed, and which, in some measure, he had contributed to produce.

The state of things here described was further promoted and favored by the fact that Spain assented to these doctrines, and that they were tolerated by a prince so jealous of his power and prerogatives as was Philip II. The Spanish monarchy was, indeed, essentially based on a combination of ecclesiastical attributes. It may be gathered from many passages of Lope de Vega, that it was so understood by the nation, that, in their sovereign, the people loved the majesty of religion, and desired to see it represented in his person; but, in addition to this, comes the circumstance, that Philip was allied, for the furtherance of Catholic restoration, not with the priests only, but also with the revolted people. Tht inhabitants of Paris reposed a more entire confidence in him than in the French princes, who were chiefs of the League. The Spanish King had, besides, a new support in the doctrines of the Jesuits. At some future time he might have something to tear from this society; but they now upheld his policy by a justification at once religious and legitimate, from which even his consideration and dignity in Spain itself derived important advantages, and which eminently promoted the opening of his path to foreign enterprises. It was to this momentary utility of the Jesuit doctrines, rather than to their general purport and tendency that Philip of Spain gave his attention.[4]

And is not this usually the case with regard to political tenets? Do these tenets arise out of the facts, or are they the originators and creators of events? Are they cherished for their own sakes, or for the utility to which men believe they may be turned?

[4] Pedro Ribadeneira, in his book against Machiavelli, which was completed and presented to the prince of Spain as early as 1595, repeated them, in a moderated form it is true, still he did repeat them: "Tratado de la religion y virtudes que deve tener el principe Christiano para governar y conservar sus estados, contra lo que Nicolo Machiavello y los politicos d'este tiempo enseñan." Anveres, 1597. He considers princes as servants of the Church, and not her judges; they are armed to punish heretics and other enemies and rebels to the Church, but not to give her laws, or to expound the will of God. He repeats the comparison of body and soul. The kingdom of the earth, as St. Gregory declares, must remain subjected to the kingdom of heaven.

Section II.—Conflict of Opinions

At no time, however, has either a power or a doctrine, least of all a political doctrine, gained pre-eminence in Europe to the extent of obtaining an absolute and undivided sovereignty.

We cannot indeed conceive of any which, when compared with the ideal, and with the highest demands of the human mind, shall not appear contracted, partial, and insufficient.

A firm resistance has at all times arisen against every opinion that has labored to obtain exclusive domination, and this antagonism proceeding from the inexhaustible depths of human life in its congregated masses, has invariably called new and vigorous energies into action.

Perceiving and acknowledging that no power will rise into effectual existence which does not repose on the basis of opinion, we may further assert that in opinion it also finds its limits; that conflict of ideas by which great social results are elaborated, have invariably their completion also in the regions of thought and of conviction.

Thus it now happened, that the idea of a sacerdotal religion, supreme over all other authority, was encountered by a mighty opposition from that national independence which is the proper expression of the secular element in society.

The Germanic institution of monarchy, widely diffused among the nations of Romanic or Latin origin, and deeply rooted among them, has never been disturbed either by the pretensions of the priesthood or by the fiction of the sovereignty of the people, which last has in all cases been eventually proved untenable.

The extraordinary connection into which these two principles had entered at the period we are considering, was opposed by the doctrine of the divine right of monarchy.

It was next assailed by the Protestants, who appear to have been for some time wavering, with all the zealous eagerness of an adversary who sees his opponent venture on a dangerous game, and attempting a path that must lead him to ruin.

God alone, as the Protestants maintained, appoints princes over the human race; he reserves to himself the office of exalting and abasing them; of apportioning and moderating the powers they are called on to exercise. It is true that he no

longer descends from heaven to point out with a visible finger
the individual to whom authority shall belong, but by his eternal
providence, laws and a settled order of things have been introduced into every kingdom, in accordance with which the ruler
is chosen.   If a prince attain the command by virtue of these
appointed regulations, his right is unquestionable, as though
God's voice had said, " This shall be your king." God did indeed
of old point out to his people, Moses, the Judges, and the first
Kings; but when a fixed order had once been established, those
who afterward succeeded to the throne were equally with them
the anointed of God.[1]

From these principles the Protestants deduced the consequence, that obedience is due even to unjust and culpable
princes.   They argued that, no man being perfect, so, if it were
once permitted to depart from the ordinance of God, men would
avail themselves of the slightest defects as a pretext for their
deposition of a sovereign.   They maintain that even heresy in
the monarch did not suffice to absolve his subjects entirely from
their allegiance.   An impious father was not indeed entitled
to obedience from his son, when his commands were in contravention of God's law; but, on all other occasions, the son remains bound to pay him reverence and to continue in subjection.

The effect would have been of much importance had the
Protestants alone devised and firmly upheld these opinions; but
they became of infinitely greater moment, from the fact that
they gained acceptance with a part of the French Catholics, or,
rather, that these last arrived at similar conclusions by their
own unbiassed reflections.

In despite of the papal excommunication, a band of good
Catholics, of no inconsiderable numbers, maintained their allegiance to Henry III, and on his death transferred it to Henry
IV.   The Jesuits failed to influence this party, which was at
no loss for arguments to defend the position it had taken up,
without, on that account, departing from Catholicism.

In the first instance, its members labored to define the authority of the clergy and its relation to the secular power, from an
opposite point of view to that adopted by the other side.   They

---

[1] " Explicatio controversiarum quæ a
nonnullis moventur ex Henrici Bor-
bonii regis in regnum Franciæ consti-
tutione . . . opus . . . a Tossano Ber-
cheto Lingonensi e Gallico in Latinum
sermonem conversum." Sedani, 1590,
cap. 2.

maintained that the spiritual kingdom is not of this world, and
that the power of the clergy relates to spiritual things only; it
followed that excommunication, by its very nature, affected the
participation in spiritual benefits only, and could in no case deprive a man of his temporal rights.   In the case of a king of
France, they further declared that he could not even be excluded from the communion of the Church, for this was among the
rights that were inalienable from " the banner of the lilies ";
how much less allowable, then, is the attempt to deprive him of
his inheritance!   And where does it stand clearly written that
subjects may rebel against their king and resort to arms against
him?   God has appointed him; therefore it is that he calls himself king by the grace of God.   There is but one case in which
a subject may lawfully refuse him obedience; namely, if he
should command anything running counter to the laws of God.[2]
From this doctrine of divine right, they then concluded that it
was not only lawful for them to acknowledge a Protestant king,
but even their duty to do so.   Such as God has given the king,
so must the subject accept him; to obey him is the command
of God; no ground can exist that should justify the depriving
a sovereign of his right.[3].   They further declared that their
decision was that most advantageous to the Catholic cause:
they maintained that Henry IV was judicious, mild, and just;
that nothing but good was to be expected from him.   Should
he be rejected, inferior pretenders to power would rise on every
side, and, in the universal discord that would ensue, the Protestant party would find means to acquire complete predominance.[4]

Thus, there arose within the bosom of Catholicism itself
an opposition to those pretensions which the papacy had been
emboldened, by the Restoration, to put forth; and from the
very first it was doubtful whether power would be found in
Rome for its suppression.   The tenets maintained by this party
were not, perhaps, entirely matured; their defenders were less
practised than those of the Jesuit pretensions, but they were
firmly rooted in the convictions of the European world; the

[2] I here follow an extract from an anonymous writing which appeared at Paris, in 1588, and which I find in Cayet, " Collection universelle des mémoires," tom. lvi. p. 44.
[3] Etienne Pasquier, " Recherches de France," pp. 341-344.

[4] Exposition in Thuanus, lib. xcvii. p. 316: " That the sectaries, on the dissolution of the empire, and on the several parts of the kingdom being divided from the general body, would attain the greater power."

position assumed by those upholding them was in itself entirely just and blameless, and they derived an important advantage from the fact, that the papal doctrines were in close alliance with the Spanish power.

The sovereignty of Philip II seemed daily to become more perilous to the general freedom; it awakened throughout Europe that jealous aversion, which proceeds less from the acts of violence committed, than from the apprehension of such violence, and from that sense of danger to freedom which seizes on the minds of men, although they cannot clearly account to themselves for its presence.

So intimate a connection now subsisted between Rome and Spain, that the opponents of the papal claims were also antagonists to the progress of the Spanish power: they hereby performed an office now become needful to the safety of Europe, and could thus not fail of obtaining approbation and support. A secret sympathy united the nations; determined allies arose unsolicited and from unexpected quarters in aid of that national party of French Roman Catholics; they appeared in Italy itself before the eyes of the Pope, and first of all in Venice.

Some few years previously, in 1582, a change had taken place in Venice, which was effected silently, and was almost overlooked in the history of the republic, but which was nevertheless of powerful influence. Up to that period, all affairs of moment had been confided to a few patricians—men advanced in years, who had been chosen from a small circle of families; but, at the time we are contemplating, a discontented majority in the Senate, consisting principally of the younger members, had instituted a successful struggle for a share in the administration, to which they were beyond doubt entitled by the letter of the constitution.

It is true that even the previous government had ever maintained a zealous guard over the Venetian independence, and had sedulously asserted it on all occasions; but it had always coalesced, so far as was by any means practicable, in the views of the Church and of Spain. The new administration no longer adhered to this policy; they rather evinced an inclination, from the mere spirit of opposition, to throw difficulties in the path of those powers.

In this mode of proceeding, the interests of the Venetians were moreover nearly engaged.

For they remarked with displeasure, on the one hand, that the doctrine of papal omnipotence, and of the blind obedience due to the pontiff, was preached among them also; while, on the other, they anticipated the total destruction of the balance of power in Europe, should the Spaniards succeed in organizing a predominant influence in France. The liberties of Europe seemed hitherto secured by the hostility subsisting between those two countries.

It thus happened, that the course and results of events in France were observed with redoubled strength of interest; and writings in defence of the royal prerogative were seized on with avidity. An extraordinary influence was exercised by a society of statesmen and men of letters, which assembled at the house of Andrea Morosini. Leonardo Donato and Nicolo Contarini, each of whom held afterward the office of doge, were among its members, as was Domenico Molino, subsequently a leading ruler in the republic, with Fra Paolo Sarpi and other distinguished men: all these persons were then of an age at which men are best fitted, not only to assimilate new ideas, but also to retain them with tenacity, and carry them out to their consequences. They were all decided opponents of ecclesiastical pretensions, and of the Spanish ascendancy.[5] It must always be highly important to the construction and the efficiency of a political system, even when it is based on facts, that men of talent should be found to stand forward as representing it in their own persons, and that they should agree among each other to disseminate its principles, each in his own immediate circle. This is of increased importance in a republic.

Under these circumstances, men did not content themselves with mere thoughts and inclinations. The Venetians had felt confidence in Henry IV from the very commencement of his career; they had believed him capable of reviving the fortunes of France, and restoring the lost balance of power. They were bound by manifold obligations to the Pope, who

[5] In the "Vita di Fra Paolo Sarpi" (by Fra Fulgentio, but called the "Anonimo,") p. 104, in Griselini's "Memoirs of Fra Paolo," pp. 40, 78, and in various passages of Foscarini, we find notices of this "ridotte Mauroceno." In addition to those before mentioned, Pietro and Giacopo Contarini, Giacopo Morosini, and Leonardo Mocenigo also belonged to it, though not attending so regularly as the first-named; as did likewise Antonio Quirini, Giacopo Marcello, Marino Zane, and Alessandro Malipiero, who, old as he was, constantly accompanied Fra Paolo home.

had excommunicated Henry, and were encompassed both on land and sea by the Spaniards, who desired to destroy that prince. The extent of their power was not such as to command great influence in the world, yet the Venetians were the first of all the Catholics who had courage to acknowledge Henry of Navarre as King of France. When his accession was notified to them by their ambassador Mocenigo, they at once empowered that functionary to congratulate Henry on the occasion.[6] Their example did not fail to influence others. Although the grand duke Ferdinand of Tuscany had not courage for a public acknowledgment of the new sovereign, he nevertheless entered into relations of personal friendship with him.[7] The Protestant prince suddenly beheld himself surrounded by Catholic allies—nay, received into their protection and shielded by them from the supreme head of their own church.

At all times when an important decision is to be made, the public opinion of Europe is invariably declared in a manner that admits of no doubt. Fortunate is he on whose side it takes its stand. Thenceforth his undertakings are accomplished with greatly increased facility. This power now favored the cause of Henry IV. The ideas connected with his name had scarcely found expression; they were nevertheless already so influential as to make it not altogether impossible that the papacy itself might be won over to their side.

Section III.—Latter Times of Sixtus V

We return once again to Sixtus V. His internal administration, with the part he took in the restoration of the Church, has already been considered: we will now give some few words to the description of his policy in general.

In doing this we cannot fail to remark the extraordinary fact that the inexorable justice exercised by this pontiff, the rigid system of finance that he established, and the close exactitude of his domestic economy, were accompanied by the most inexplicable disposition to political plans of fantastic extravagance.

[6] Andreæ Mauroceni " Historiarum Venetarum," lib. xiii. p. 548.

[7] Galluzzio, " Istoria del Granducato di Toscana," lib. v. (tom. v. p. 78).

What strange ideas were permitted to enter his head!

He flattered himself for a long time that his power would suffice to put an end to the Turkish empire. He formed relations in the East—with the Persians, with certain Arab chiefs, and with the Druses. He fitted out galleys and hoped to obtain others from Spain and Tuscany. He fancied he should thus be enabled to co-operate by sea with Stephen Bathory, King of Poland, who was appointed to make the principal attack by land. For this undertaking Sixtus hoped to combine all the forces of the Northeast and Southwest. He even persuaded himself that Russia would not only enter into alliance with the King of Poland, but would consent to subject herself to his command.

Another time he amused himself with the notion that he could make the conquest of Egypt, either by his own resources or with the aid of Tuscany alone. On this hope he founded the most extensive designs: the formation of a passage to connect the Red Sea with the Mediterranean;[1] the restoration of commerce as pursued by the ancients, and the conquest of the Holy Sepulchre. But supposing these plans should be found not immediately practicable, might not an incursion at least be made into Syria, in order to have the tomb of the Saviour hewn out of the rock by skilful masters in their craft, and brought, carefully wrapped and protected, to Italy? He already entertained the hope of seeing this sanctuary, the most sacred in the world, erected in Montalto. Then would his native province, the March of Ancona, where the Holy House of Loretto was already placed, comprise within its limits both the birth-place and tomb of the Redeemer.

There is yet another idea which I find attributed to Sixtus V, and which exceeds in eccentricity all those we have enumerated. A proposal is declared to have been forwarded to Henry III, after the assassination of the Guises, to the effect that he should acknowledge a nephew of the Pope as his successor to the crown of France. This suggestion is said to have been made by the legate, with the knowledge of the pon-

[1] " Dispaccio Gritti, 23 Agosto, 1587: " " The Pope began to talk of the canal that the Kings of Egypt had made to pass from the Red Sea into the Mediterranean." Sometimes he formed the project of attacking Egypt with his own troops alone. He made known his want of money, which was to be employed in an armament with which he designed to fall on Egypt, and to pay the galleys that should effect this enterprise.

tiff. His holiness had persuaded himself that if this nomination were made with all due solemnity, the King of Spain would bestow the infanta in marriage on the successor so declared; all would be ready to acknowledge a succession thus constituted, and the disturbances would be brought to an end. It has been affirmed that Henry was attracted for a moment by these propositions, and might have yielded his assent, had it not been represented to him how deplorable a reputation for cowardice and want of forethought he would leave behind him by doing so.[2]

These were plans, or rather—for that word has too definite a meaning—these were fantasies, castles in the air, of the most extraordinary character. How flagrantly are these visions in disaccord with the stern reality, the rigid practical activity, earnestly pressing forward to its end, by which this pontiff was usually distinguished!

We may nevertheless be permitted to declare that even these had their origin in the exuberance of thoughts too mighty for accomplishment.

The elevation of Rome into the acknowledged metropolis of Christendom, to which, after a certain lapse of years, all nations, even those of America, were to resort—the conversion of ancient monuments into memorials of the subjugation of heathenism by the Christian faith—the accumulation of a treasure, formed of money borrowed and paying interest, as a basis for the secular power of the Papal States—all these are purposes surpassing the limits of the practicable, which found their origin in the ardor of religious enthusiasm, but

[2] This notice is contained in a " Mémoire du Seigneur de Schomberg, Maréchal de France sous Henri III.," among the Hohendorf MSS. in the Imperial Library of Vienna, No. 114: " Some time after the death of M. de Guise, which happened at Blois, the cardinal-legate, Morosino, proposed on the part of his holiness, that his Majesty should declare the Marquis de Pom [the name is probably misspelt], his nephew, heir to the crown, and cause him to be received as such with the due solemnities. In that case, his holiness was assured that the King of Spain would confer the infanta in marriage on the said marquis; and, this being done, all the troubles of France would find an end. Whereat the King being on the point of letting himself be persuaded, and that by some who were then about his Majesty, M. de Schomberg parried this blow (rompit ce coup) by such reasons as that it would be the overturning of all order in France; would abolish the fundamental laws of the kingdom, and leave to posterity a certain proof of the cowardice and narrow-mindedness of his Majesty." It is perfectly true, that Schomberg claims the merit of having baffled these projects; but I am not on that account disposed to consider it a mere castle in the air. The Mémoire, which advocates the rights of Henry IV, has all the more appearance of being genuine, from the fact that it lies obscurely mingled up with other papers. It is, however, remarkable that nothing further should have been said on the subject.

which were yet highly influential in determining the restless activity of this pontiff's charatcer.

From youth upward, the life of man, active or passive, is but the reflection of his hopes and wishes. The present, if we may so speak, is compassed round by the future, and the soul resigns itself with unwearied constancy to anticipations of personal happiness. But as life advances, these desires and expectations become attached to more extensive interests; they aspire to the completion of some great object in science, in politics, in the more important general concerns of life; they expand, in a word, into cares for the universal interest. In the case of our Franciscan, the fascination and stimulus of personal hopes had been ever all the more powerful, because he had found himself engaged in a career which opened to him the most exalted prospects: they had accompanied him from step to step, and had sustained his spirit in the extremity of his obscure penury. He had eagerly seized on every word foreboding prosperity, had treasured it in the depths of his heart, and, in the anticipation of success, had connected with each some magnificent design suggested by monkish enthusiasm. At length his utmost hopes were realized; from a beginning the least auspicious, the most hopeless, he had risen to the highest dignity in Christendom—a dignity of which, eminent as it was, he yet entertained a conception exaggerated beyond the reality. He believed himself immediately selected by a special providence for the realization of those ideas that floated before his imagination.

Even when arrived at the possession of supreme power, he retained the habit and faculty of discerning, amid all the complexities of general politics, whatever opportunity might present itself for magnificent enterprises, and employed himself in projects for their execution. But to the charms of power and lasting renown he was profoundly sensible; hence in all his acts we descry an element of a strictly personal character predominant. The lustre surrounding himself he desired to see diffused over all immediately belonging to or connected with him, his family, his birth-place, his native province. This wish was nevertheless invariably subordinate to his interest in the general welfare of Catholic Christendom: his mind was ever accessible to the influence of grand and elevated ideas. A certain difference is, however, to be remarked. To one portion of his plans he could himself give effectual accomplishment; for the execution of the other, he was compelled to depend on external aid. As a consequence, we perceive that he applied himself to the first with that inexhaustible activity which results from conviction, enthusiasm, and ambition. With regard to the last, on the contrary, he was by no means so earnest, whether because he was by nature distrustful or because the chief part in the execution, and consequently in the gain and glory, had to be resigned to others. If we inquire what he really accomplished, toward the completion of his oriental projects, for example, we perceive that he did no more than form alliances, make exchange of letters, issue admonitions, and take similar steps—all preliminary only. That any measures, effectively adapted to the end he proposed, were ever taken, we cannot perceive. He would form the plan with all the eagerness of an excitable imagination, but since he could not immediately proceed to action, and the accomplishment of the work lay in remote distance, his will was not efficiently exerted, the project by which he had perhaps been considerably occupied was suffered to fall into oblivion, while some other succeeded to its place.

At the moment now in question, the Pope was absorbed by the grandest views connected with the undertaking against Henry IV. He anticipated a decisive victory for strict Catholicism, and hoped to see the universal supremacy of the pontificate fully restored—his whole life for the moment was engrossed by these prospects. He was persuaded that all the Catholic States were entirely agreed on this point, and would turn the whole force of their united powers against the Protestant who laid claim to become king of France.

In this direction of his thoughts, and while thus ardently zealous, he was made acquainted with the fact that a Catholic power—one too with which he had believed himself in particularly good intelligence — Venice, namely — had offered congratulations to that very Protestant. He was profoundly afflicted by this proceeding. For a moment he attempted to restrain the republic from taking further steps; he entreated the Venetians to wait. Time, he assured them, brought forth marvellous fruits; he had himself learned from the good and venerable Senators to permit their arrival at maturity.[3]

Notwithstanding this request, the republic persisted, and acknowledged De Maisse, the former ambassador of France, after he had received his new credentials as plenipotentiary of Henry IV. Hereupon the Pope proceeded from exhortations to menaces. He declared that he should well know what it behooved him to do, and commanded that the old *monitoria* proclaimed against the Venetians in the time of Julius II should be sought out, and the formula of a new one prepared.

It was yet not without pain and deep regret that he did this; let us listen for a moment to the words of the pontiff, as uttered in conference with the ambassador, whom the Venetians sent to him on this occasion.

"To fall at variance with those whom we do not love," said the Pope, "that is no such great misfortune; but with those whom one loves, that is indeed a sorrow. Yes! it will cause us much grief"—he laid his hand on his breast—"to break with Venice.

"But Venice has offended us. Navarre! [it was thus he called Henry IV] Navarre is a heretic, excommunicated by the Holy See: and yet Venice, in defiance of all our remonstrances, has acknowledged him.

"Does the Signory make pretension to be the most sovereign power of the earth? Does it belong to Venice to give example to all the rest of the world? There is still a King of Spain—there is still an Emperor.

"Has the republic any fear of Navarre? We will defend her, if it be necessary, with all our force—we have nerve enough.

"Or does the republic propose to inflict some injury on us? God himself would be our defender.

"The republic should prize our friendship beyond that of Navarre; we can do more for her welfare.

"I beseech you to recall at least one step. The Catholic King has recalled many because we desired it, not from fear of us, for our strength, as compared with his, is but as a fly compared with an elephant; but he has done it from love, and be-

---

[3] "9th Sett. 1589: " "That for the love of God they should not proceed so fast with this Navarre; that they should hold back to see, etc."

cause it was the Pope who had spoken, the vicegerent of Christ, who prescribes the rule of faith to him, and to all others. Let the Signory do as much: they can easily find some expedient that shall serve as the pretext; that cannot be difficult for them, they have wise and aged men enough, every one of whom would be capable of governing a world." [4]

But so much was not said without eliciting a reply. The envoy-extraordinary of the Venetians was Leonardo Donato, a member of the society we have described as assembled by Andrea Morosini. He was deeply imbued with the spirit of the ecclesiastical and political opposition, was a man of what would now be called the most consummate skill in diplomacy and had already successfully conducted many difficult and delicate negotiations.

The various motives by which the Venetians were influenced could not well be set forth in Rome; Donato, therefore, gave prominence to those which the Pope had in common with the republic, and which were consequently assured of finding acceptance with his holiness.

Was it not manifest, for example, that the Spanish predominance in the south of Europe became more decided, and more perilous from year to year? The Pope felt this as deeply as any other Italian prince. He could take no step in Italy even at this time, without first obtaining the consent of Spain; what then would be the state of things when the Spaniards should have gained the mastery in France? On this consideration, then, on the necessity for maintaining the balance of power in Europe, and on the means by which it might be restored, Donato principally insisted. He labored to prove that the republic, far from seeking to offend the Pope, had rather arranged her policy with a view to defending and promoting the most important interests of the Papal See.

The Pope listened to his words, but appeared to be utterly immovable—by no means to be convinced. Donato resigned

[4] The Pope spake for so long a time that the ambassadors said it would have taken them an hour and a half to read it before the Senate, had they written it all down. Among other matters, he continually insisted on the effects of excommunication: "Three have been excommunicated; the late King, the Prince of Condé, and the King of Navarre. Two of them have met with an evil death, the third still vexes us; and God upholds him for the exercise of our faith; but he also will finish, and will come to a bad end: we need have no doubt concerning him.—December 2d. The Pope published a most solemn jubilee, inviting all to supplicate the Divine Majesty for the peace and extension of the Catholic faith." During this jubilee, Sixtus would see no one, to the end that he "might live to himself and to his devotions."

all hope of accomplishing anything, and requested an audience of leave. This he obtained on December 16, 1589, when the pontiff assumed an appearance of intending to refuse him his blessing.[5] Yet Sixtus was not so perfectly enslaved but that arguments of sound reason produced their effect. He was self-willed, imperious, and obstinate; yet his convictions were not altogether incapable of change: it was not impossible to lead him into new views of things, and he was in the main good-natured—even while continuing the dispute, and stubbornly defending his position, he felt himself moved in his heart, and even convinced. In the midst of that audience he became suddenly mild and compliant.[6] "He who has a colleague," he exclaimed, "has a master. I will speak to the congregation; I will tell them that I have been angry with you, but that you have overcome my resentment." They waited some days longer, when the Pope declared that he could not approve what the republic had done, but he would refrain from adopting the measures he had contemplated against her. He gave Donato his blessing and embraced him.

This may be called an almost insensible change of mere personal feeling. The most important results were, nevertheless, involved in it. The Pope himself permitted the rigor with which he had persecuted the Protestant King to relax. Neither would he absolutely condemn the Catholic party attached to Henry, and by which his former policy had been opposed. A first step is always important; because the whole tendency of the course pursued is involved in and determined by it. This was instantly perceived on the part of the opposition: it had originally sought only to exculpate itself; it now proceeded to attempt convincing and gaining over the Pope himself.

Monseigneur de Luxembourg soon after appeared in Italy, bearing a charge from the princes of the blood and Catholic peers attached to Henry IV. He was permitted to enter Rome, in January, 1590; and, in spite of the warning representations of the Spaniards, Sixtus granted him an audience. The envoy expatiated particularly on the personal qualities of Henry,

---

[5] "Dispaccio Donato:" "Dopo si lungo negotio restando privo d'ogni speranza."
[6] Ibid.: "At length, inspired by God, * * * said he would consent, and that he had permitted himself to be conquered by us."

placing his courage, magnanimity, and kindness of heart in
the most brilliant light. The Pope was quite enchanted with
this description. " In good truth," he exclaimed, " it repents
me that I have excommunicated him." Luxembourg declared
that his lord and King would now render himself worthy of
absolution; and, at the feet of his holiness, would return into
the bosom of the Catholic Church. " In that case," replied
the Pope, " I will embrace and console him."

For already his imagination was powerfully excited, and
he at once conceived the boldest hopes from these advances.
He suffered himself to believe that the Protestants were pre--
vented from returning to the Catholic Church by political
aversion to Spain, rather than by religious convictions in hostility with those of the Roman See; and thought he ought not
to repel them.[7] There was already an English ambassador in
Rome—one from Saxony was announced. The pontiff was
perfectly ready to hear them. " Would to God," he exclaimed,
" they would all come to our feet ! "

The extent of the change that had taken place in the convictions of Sixtus V was made manifest by the mode of his
proceeding toward Cardinal Morosini, his legate in France.
The forbearance of this minister toward Henry III had in
earlier days been reproved as a crime; and he had returned
to Italy, laboring under his sovereign's displeasure. He was
now brought into the Consistory by Cardinal Montalto, and
Sixtus received him with the declaration that he rejoiced to
see a cardinal of his own creation, as was Morosini, obtaining
universal approbation.[8] He was invited to the table of Donna
Camilla.

How greatly must this total change have astonished the
strict Catholic world! The Pope evinced a favorable disposition toward a Protestant whom he had himself excommuni-

[7] " Dispaccio Donato, Genn. 13, 1590:"
" The Pope is dissatisfied with the
opinions of the cardinals and other prelates, who pressed him to dismiss this
Monseigneur de Luxembourg, and accuses them of desiring to become his
pedants [his teachers, as we should
say] in a matter that he had been study-
ing all his life. He added that he would
rejoice to see the Queen of England,
the Duke of Saxony, and all the others
presenting themselves at his feet with
good dispositions. That it would displease his holiness were they to go to
other princes [Catholics must here be
understood] and hold communication
with them; but it consoled him to see
them approaching his feet to seek for
pardon." These sentiments he repeated in various forms at each audience.

[8] " He declared himself particularly
satisfied that a cardinal created by himself should be so highly appreciated by
all. The illustrious cardinal Morosini
acquired great credit and renown by the
relations he gave as to affairs in
France."

cated; and who, according to the ancient ordinances of the Church, had rendered himself incapable even of receiving absolution, by the commission of a double apostasy.

That from all this there should result a reaction, was in the nature of things. The party holding rigid Catholic opinions was not so entirely dependent on the Pope as to make their opposing him out of the question; and the Spanish power supplied them with a support of which they eagerly availed themselves.

The adherents of the League in France accused the Pope of avarice. They asserted that he would not open his purse; but desired to retain all the money he had heaped up in the Castle of St. Angelo for his nephews and other connections. A Jesuit in Spain preached publicly on the deplorable condition of the Church. " It was not the republic of Venice only that favored the heretics; but—hush, hush," he said, placing his finger on his lips, "but even the Pope himself." These words resounded through Italy. Sixtus V had become so sensitive on these subjects that when the general of the Capuchins proclaimed an exhortation to general prayers, "to invoke the favor of God for the affairs of the Church," he considered this as a personal affront, and suspended the Capuchin.

Nor was the effect confined to mere hints and private complaints. On March 22, 1590, the Spanish ambassador appeared in the papal apartments to make a formal protest in the name of his sovereign against the proceedings of the Pope.[9] There was an opinion, as these things show us, more orthodox, more Catholic, than that of the Pope himself. The Spanish ambassador now appeared in the palace to give this opinion effect and expression before the very face of the pontiff. It was an extraordinary incident: the ambassador knelt on one knee and entreated his holiness for permission to execute the commands of his lord. The Pope requested him to rise, saying it would be heresy to pursue the course he was contem-

[9] The following questions were laid before the pontiff by the Spanish envoy so early as March 10: " He demanded a reply as to three things; that is, the dismissal of Luxembourg, the excommunication of the cardinals and other prelates adhering to Navarre; and the assurance that he would never render this Navarre eligible to the crown of France." He had besides given notice of a protest, whereupon the Pope menaced him with excommunication: " He threatens to excommunicate and inflict capital punishment on all who shall dare to attempt what he had intimated, driving him forth, and closing the door in his face."

plating against the vicar of Christ. The ambassador would not suffer himself to be disconcerted. "His holiness," he began, "ought to proclaim the excommunication of all adherents to the King of Navarre without distinction. His holiness should declare that Navarre was incapable of ascending the French throne under every circumstance and for all time. If this were not done, the Catholic King would abandon his allegiance to his holiness, for the majesty of Spain could not permit the cause of Christ to be brought to ruin." [10] Scarcely would the Pope allow him to utter his protest to this extent; he exclaimed that this was not the business of the King. The ambassador rose, then knelt down again, resolved to continue. The Pope called him a stone of offence, and went away. But Olivarez was not yet content and would not permit himself to be baffled; he declared that he would and must complete his protest, should the Pope condemn him to the loss of his head; he knew well that the King would avenge him and bestow the recompense of his fidelity on his children. Sixtus V on the other hand was violently enraged. He maintained that no prince on earth was empowered to dictate to the Pope, who is appointed by God as the superior of every other sovereign; that the proceedings of the ambassador were positively sacrilegious; his instructions authorized him to make protestation only in the event of the pontiff's evincing indifference toward the cause of the League. How did he know that this was the case? Did the ambassador pretend to direct the steps of his holiness?

Catholicism in its genuine forms appeared now to have but one aim—one undivided opinion. It seemed in the road to victory, and on the very point of success; but there were formed unexpectedly within itself two parties—two systems of opinion opposing each other politically and ecclesiastically; the one disposed to make aggressions, the other prepared for resistance. The struggle was commenced by each party exerting its utmost power in the effort to win over the head of the Church to its own side. The one already held possession

---

[10] " Che S. Sa. dichiari iscommunicati tutti quei che seguitano in Francia il Navarra e tutti gli altri che quovis modo li dessero ajuto, e che dichiari esso Navarra incapace perpetuamente alla corona di Francia: altramente che il re suo si leverà della obedienza della chiesa, e procurerà che non sia fatta ingiuria alla causa di Christo e che la pietà e la religione sua sia conosciuta." (See text.) But would make his piety and religion known.

of the Pope, and now labored to retain him by menaces, bitterness, and almost by force. Toward the other a secret feeling had disposed him at a very critical moment, and this now sought to secure him entirely for itself: attempts were made to allure him by promises; the most attractive prospects were displayed before him. For the decision of the contest, the question to which party the pontiff should attach himself, was one of the utmost importance.

The demeanor of this Pope, so renowned for active energy and decision of character, was at that moment such as to fill us with amazement.

When letters arrived from Philip II, expressing the determination of that sovereign to uphold the rightful cause and support the League with all the force of his kingdom—nay, with his own blood—the Pope was instantly full of zeal. Never would he expose himself, as he then declared, to the disgrace of not having opposed a heretic like Navarre.[1]

He was none the less soon afterward perceived to incline toward the opposite side. When the difficulties in which the affairs of France involved him were represented to the pontiff, he exclaimed, that if Navarre were present, he would entreat him on his knees to become Catholic.

No prince was ever placed in a more extraordinary position with regard to his plenipotentiary than that occupied by Sixtus V in relation to his legate Gaetano, whom he had sent to France during the time of his most intimate alliance with the Spaniards. The pontiff had certainly not yet gone over to the side of the French, but his mind had been rendered irresolute, and he had been brought into a state of neutrality. Without the slightest regard to this change, the legate pursued his original instructions. When Henry IV besieged Paris after the victory of Ivry, it was from the papal legate that he experienced the most effectual resistance. In his presence it was that the magistrates and leaders of the people took an oath never to capitulate or make terms with Navarre. By the dignity attached to his spiritual office, and by a deport-

[1] He declared, even in the Consistory, he had written to the King with his own hand to the effect that he would constantly labor with all his power, spiritual and temporal, to prevent anyone from becoming king of France, who was not to the entire satisfaction of his Catholic majesty. So early as January, 1590, the ambassadors say: " in his negotiations, the Pope speaks of his designs to one in one sense, and to another in a sense totally different."

ment remarkable for address and firmness, Gaetano succeeded in holding them to their engagements.[2]

It was, in fact, by the party attached to rigidly orthodox Catholicism that the superiority in strength was finally manifested.

Olivarez compelled the Pope to dismiss Luxembourg, although under the pretext of a pilgrimage to Loretto. Sixtus had intended to select Monsignore Serafino, who was believed to hold French opinions, for a mission to France. Olivarez uttered loud complaints and threatened to appear no more at the audience; the Pope replied that he might depart in God's name. Olivarez, nevertheless, eventually prevailed, and the mission of Serafino was laid aside. There is an invincible force in an orthodox opinion, adhered to with unflinching steadfastness, and more especially when it is advocated by a man of vigorous mind. Olivarez had the congregation which managed affairs connected with France, and which had been constituted in earlier times, in his favor. In July, 1590, negotiations were entered into for a new alliance between Spain and the Pope,[3] and his holiness declared that he must do something in favor of the Spaniards.

But it must not be supposed that he had meanwhile abandoned the other party. There was at the papal court, at this very moment, an agent from Lesdiguieres, one of the leaders of the Huguenots, an envoy from the Landgrave, and an emissary from England. The imperial ambassador was further alarmed by the approach of the Saxon envoy, whose arrival was expected, and against whose suggestions, which he greatly dreaded, he was already seeking means of defence. The intrigues of Chancellor Crell extended their effect even to Rome.[4]

Thus did the powerful prince of the Church, the sovereign

---

[2] " Discours véritable et notable du siège de la ville de Paris en l'an 1590," in Villeroy, " Mémoires d'Estat," tom. ii. p. 417.

[3] The King was to furnish 20,000 foot soldiers and 3,000 cavalry; the Pope 15,000 infantry and 2,000 horse. The ambassadors pressed the cardinals for the conclusion and signing of the treaty. (" Disp. 14 July.") The Pope proposed in the congregation the question: " Whether it belong to the pontiff to elect a king of France, failing the princes of the blood." Being exhorted to remain neutral, he commended that advice; but declared that he could not

refrain from doing something. (" Disp. 28 July.") The despatch of July 21st says, in the meantime, " Lesdiguieres had sent one of his creatures to treat with his holiness, who talked with the same at great length."

[4] The fact that the imperial ambassador warned the Pope against Saxon insinuation cannot otherwise be explained. The ambassador of the Emperor prays the Pope to give no ear to the man who is said to have been sent by the Duke of Saxony, in matters likely to be prejudicial to his master and the house of Austria; and this has been promised to him.

who lived in the persuasion that he was invested with a direct authority over the whole earth, and who had amassed a treasure that might well have enabled him to perform some mighty deed, remain undecided and incapable of action when the moment for decision had arrived.

Are we permitted to reproach him with this as a fault? I fear that we should do him injustice. He had seen through the condition of things, he perceived the dangers on both sides, he suffered himself to be subjected to the influence of conflicting opinions. No crisis presented itself by which he might have been compelled to a final decision. The elements that were dividing the world had filled his very soul with the confusion of their conflict, and neither could there obtain the decisive mastery.

It is certain that by this irresolute state of his own spirit, he placed himself in a position wherein it was impossible that he should effectually influence the world. On the contrary; he was himself re-acted on by the forces then agitating society, and this effect was produced in a manner highly peculiar.

Sixtus had succeeded in suppressing the banditti, principally by establishing friendly relations with his neighbors. But since these were now interrupted—since opinions prevailed in Tuscany and Venice which were altogether different from those held in Naples and Milan, and the Pope would declare himself decidedly for neither, he became the object of suspicion, first to one and then to the other of these neighbors, and under favor of this state of things, the banditti once more aroused themselves to activity.

In was in April, 1590, that they appeared again—in the Maremma under Sacripanti; in Romagna they were led by Piccolomini, and Battistella was their chief in the Campagna of Rome. They were amply provided with money, and it is said that they were observed to disburse large numbers of Spanish doubloons. They found adherents principally among the Guelfs, and were already once more traversing the country in regularly organized bands, with banners flying and military music. Nor were the papal troops by any means disposed to offer them battle.[5] This state of things produced an imme-

[5] " Disp. 21 July: " " The outlaws commit their ravages up to the very gates of Rome." The despatches of March 17th, April 7th and 28th, May 12th, and June 2d contain details of these disorders.

diate effect on all the relations of the country. The people of Bologna opposed themselves to the Pope's intention of adding to the Senators of their city with a boldness and independence of action long unthought of.

In this condition, surrounded by so many pressing disquietudes, and without having even attempted to announce a decision, or to adopt a resolution concerning the most important affairs, Pope Sixtus V died, on August 27, 1590.

A storm burst over the Quirinal at the moment when he breathed his last. The ill-taught multitude persuaded themselves that Fra Felice had made a compact with the evil spirit, by whose aid he had risen from step to step, and that the stipulated period having now expired, his soul had been carried away in the tempest. It was in this manner that they signified their discontent at the number of new taxes he had imposed, and expressed those doubts of his perfect orthodoxy which had for some years been frequently agitated. With impetuous fury they tore down the statues that had been erected in his earlier days, and even came to a resolution in the Capitol that no statue should ever again be erected to a pontiff during his lifetime.

Section IV.—Urban VII, Gregory XIV, Innocent IX, and their Conclaves, 1590–1591

The new election was now of redoubled importance. To which of the two principles just commencing their contest the pontiff about to be chosen should attach himself, must principally depend on the personal dispositions of the man selected; and it could not be doubted that his decision would involve consequences which must influence the whole world. The tumult and intriguing strife of the conclave hence assume peculiar importance, and require us to devote a few words to their consideration.

During the first half of the sixteenth century the College of Cardinals was powerfully influenced either by the imperial faction or by that of France. It was even remarked by one of the popes that the cardinals no longer possessed any freedom of election. But from the middle of the century the influence thus exerted by foreign powers had materially declined,

The Curia was left much more to its own decisions; and there arose, from the ferment of its internal agitations, a principle or custom of very singular character.

It was the habit of each pontiff to nominate a number of cardinals, who gathered round his nephews and kinsmen in the next conclave, maintained the family interests of the Pope just deceased, formed a new power, and usually sought to raise one of their own party to the papal throne. It is a remarkable fact that they never succeeded, that the opposition was victorious on every occasion, and in most cases put forward an adversary of the last pope.

I will not attempt any close investigation of this matter. We have testimonies relating to these elections that are not altogether unworthy of credit; but it would be impossible to gain correct and clear views of the personal relations and motives really in action on these occasions: our best efforts could but result in the production of mere shadows.

It must suffice that we direct attention to the principle. At the period in question, the pontiff elected was invariably the antagonist, and never the adherent, of the pope preceding, he was the creature—that is to say, of the last but one. Paul IV was thus advanced to the Papal See by the creatures of Paul III, while Pius IV was elected by the enemies of Paul IV, and the Caraffa family. Borromeo, the nephew of Pius IV, was sufficiently disinterested to give his support to a man of the party opposed to his own, because he considered him to be the most pious and best fitted; but he did this in the face of earnest remonstrance from the creatures of his uncle, who, as the report informs us, " could scarcely believe that they said what they said, or were doing what they did ";[1] and accordingly they sought to turn their compliance to account on the next occasion. They endeavored to make this custom a fixed precedent, to give it the force of an established rule; and the successor of Pius V was in fact selected from the creatures of Pius IV. A similar practice prevailed at the election of Sixtus V, who was elevated from among the adversaries of his predecessor, Gregory XIII.

We are therefore not to be surprised at constantly finding men of opposite characters successively occupying the papal

[1] See Appendix, No. 63.

throne. Each faction was alternately driven from its place by the other.

In virtue of this mode of succession, the opponents of Sixtus V, especially those of his later policy, found a cheering prospect opened before them. Sixtus had raised his nephew to great power, and Montalto now entered the conclave with a train of cardinals devoted to his interests, as numerous as any that had appeared on previous occasions. He was nevertheless compelled to give way. The creatures of Gregory succeeded in electing an opponent of the late pontiff, one who had indeed been especially offended by Sixtus, and was unequivocally attached to the Spanish interests; this was Giovanni Battista Castagna, Urban VII.[2]

But they were not fortunate in their choice. Urban VII died before he had been crowned, before he had nominated a single prelate, and when he had worn the tiara twelve days only; the contest of election had consequently to be opened anew.

It was decided by the fact that the Spaniards again took the most earnest part in its proceedings. They saw clearly the great importance of the result as regarded the affairs of France, and King Philip resolved on a step for which he was reproached in Rome as for a dangerous innovation, and which his own partisans could excuse only by alleging the difficult circumstances in which he was placed.[3] He nominated seven cardinals, from all of whom he hoped to obtain good service, and declared that he would acknowledge no candidate but these. At the head of these nominees stood the name of Madruzzi, and the Spanish cardinals instantly put forth their utmost efforts to carry the election of this their chief. But they were met by an obstinate resistance. The college refused Madruzzi because he was a German, and because it was not to be suffered that the papacy should again fall into the hands of barbarians.[4]   Neither would Montalto permit any one of

[2] " Conclave di papa Urbano VII.," MS.: " The proceedings of this election were directed by Cardinal Sforza (head of the creatures of Gregory XIII) and the Genoese cardinals." In a despatch from De Maisse, ambassador of France in Venice, and which is given in F. Von Raumer's " Histor. Briefen," i. p. 360, we are told that Colonna, having already placed himself in the pontifical seat, was dragged from it by Cardinal Sforza; but this should scarcely be understood literally.

[3] " The great interest that this Catholic King has in this election, and the heavy expenses that he has borne without assistance for the benefit of Christianity, make it incumbent on us to excuse him."

[4] Cardinal Morosini said: " Italy would fall a prey to barbarians, which would be a shame to all."—" Conclave della sede vacante di Urbano VII."

the remaining nominees to be chosen. He would have vainly
attempted to raise one of his own adherents to the papal chair,
but he had at least the power of excluding the candidates
whom he opposed. The sittings of the conclave were unusu-
ally protracted: the banditti were masters of the country; intelligence of property plundered and villages burnt was daily
brought to the city; there was even fear of commotions in
Rome itself.

There remained but one method of arriving at a conclusion;
this was to select from the candidates, the one least objectionable to the kinsmen of Sixtus V. In the Florentine accounts[8]
we are told that the Grand Duke of Tuscany contributed largely
to this result; those written by the Romans ascribe it to Cardinal Sforza, the leader of the Gregorian cardinals. Retired
within his cell, perhaps because he had been told that it would
be for his advantage to remain silent, and suffering at the
moment from fever, lived Cardinal Sfondrato, one of the seven.
In his favor the different parties agreed, and a family alliance between the houses of Montalto and Sfondrato was at
once brought into discussion. Montalto then visited the cardinal in his cell; he found him in prayer before the crucifix,
still not entirely free from fever, and informed him that he
would be elected on the following morning. When the time
arrived, Sfondrato was led to the chapel where the votes were
taken, by the cardinals Montalto and Sforza. He was duly
elected, and assumed the name of Gregory XIV.[9]

The new pontiff was a man who fasted twice every week,
said mass daily, repeated the prescribed number of prayers
on his knees, and then devoted an hour to his favorite author,
St. Bernard; carefully noting down such passages in the work
before him as he found more particularly striking—a man of
a spirit most pure and blameless. It was however remarked,
half jestingly, that as he had come into the world too early—
at seven months—and had not been reared without difficulty,
so there was upon the whole too little of the earthly element
in his composition. Of the practices and intrigues of the
Curia he had never been able to comprehend anything. He
took it for granted that the cause upheld by the Spaniards

[8] Galluzzi, " Storia del Granducato di
Toscana," v. 99.
[9] Tasso has celebrated this accession
to the throne in an admirable canzone,
" Da gran lode immortal."

was the cause of the Church; he was a born subject of Philip II, and a man after his own heart. Without any delay he declared himself decidedly in favor of the League.[5]

" Do you," he wrote to the Parisians, " you, who have made so praiseworthy a beginning, continue to persevere; make no halt until you have attained the end of your course. Inspired by God, we have resolved to come to your assistance. First, we send you a subsidy in money, and that indeed beyond our means; next, we despatch our nuncio, Landriano, to France, that by his efforts he may bring back all who have deserted from your banners; and finally we send you, though not without heavily burdening the Church, our dear son and nephew Ercole Sfondrato, Duke of Montemarciano, with cavalry and infantry to defend you by force of arms. Should you require yet more, we will provide you with that also.[6]

In this letter the whole policy of Gregory XIV is expressed. It was, however, extremely effective. The explicit declaration of his intentions, the renewal of excommunication against Henry IV, by which it was accompanied, and lastly the exhortation with which Landriano was charged to all the clergy, nobles, judicial functionaries, and the third estate, to separate themselves, under pain of heavy penalties, from Henry of Bourbon, produced a deep impression.[7] Many of the followers of Henry, who held rigidly Catholic opinions, were at length perplexed and shaken by this decisive step of the head of their Church; they declared that the Church had a regular succession as well as the kingdom, and that it was no more permitted to change the religion than the dynasty. It was at this time that what was called the third party arose among the adherents of the King. This continually exhorted him to return to the Catholic faith. It remained firm in its allegiance to him on this condition, and with this expectation only, and possessed the more importance because it included the most powerful men among those immediately surrounding the King.

But results of still higher moment were to be expected from

[5] " Cicarella de Vita Gregorio XIV.," to be found in all the later editions of Platina.
[6] Gregory XIV: " To my well-beloved sons the councillors of the sixteen quarters of the city of Paris." In Cayet, " Chronologie novenaire," " Mémoires coll. univ." tom. lvii. p. 62.

[7] Even Cayet remarks this: " The party of the King was free from division until Gregory XIV issued his monitorial bulls; then some wished to form a third party, to consist of the rigid Catholics belonging to the royal party.

the further measures announced by Gregory in the letter just quoted, and which he carried into effect without delay. He sent the Parisians 15,000 scudi every month; he despatched Colonel Lusi into Switzerland to raise troops, and having solemnly committed the standard of the Church to Ercole Sfondrato, as their general, in Santa Maria Maggiore, he sent him to Milan, where his forces were to assemble. The commissary who accompanied him, the Archbishop Matteucci, was largely provided with money.

Under these auspices, Philip II no longer hesitated to take earnest part in the affairs of France. His troops advanced into Brittany, and at the same time possessed themselves of Toulouse and Montpellier. On some provinces he thought he had peculiar claims, in others he was in close confederacy with the leading chiefs; these alliances had been gradually formed by certain Capuchin friars and were kept up by their agency. He was considered in many provinces as " the sole protector of the orthodox faithful against the Huguenots," and was invited in the most pressing terms even to Paris. Meanwhile the Piedmontese attacked Provence, and the papal army united with that of the League at Verdun. It was a general movement of the Spanish and Italian powers for the purpose of drawing France by force into those rigidly Catholic opinions prevailing in Spain and Italy. The treasures accumulated with so much effort by Pope Sixtus, and which he had so jealously guarded, were now converted to the profit of Spain. After Gregory XIV had taken from the castle of St. Angelo those sums to the expenditure of which the late pontiff had not attached conditions, he seized those which had been most strictly tied up. He was of opinion that a more pressing necessity than now assailed the Church could never occur.

The decision with which these measures were entered on, the prudence of the King, the wealth of the pontiff, and the influence exerted on France by their united dignity and authority, made it impossible to calculate the extent to which this twofold ambition, temporal and spiritual, might have proceeded, and the results that might have ensued; but in the midst of the undertaking Gregory XIV expired. He had possessed the papal chair only ten months and ten days, and yet had effected alterations of such vast importance. What might not have been the consequence had he retained this power during a course of years? The loss of the pontiff was the heaviest affliction that could possibly have befallen the party of Spain and the League.

It is true that the Spaniards once more carried their measures through the conclave. They had again appointed seven candidates[10] and one of these cardinals, Giovanni Antonio Fachinetto, Innocent IX, was elected. He also appears to have been disposed toward the interests of Spain, so far as can be judged; it is certain that he afforded supplies to the League, and there is a letter still extant, in which he urges Alessandro Farnese to hasten the preparation of his forces, to move forward into France and relieve the city of Rouen—movements which that general then executed with so much ability and success.[1] But the misfortune was that Innocent IX was already very old and failing; he scarcely ever left his couch; even his audiences were given there. From the death-bed of an aged man, who was himself incapable of moving, proceeded exhortations to war, by which France—nay, all Europe—was set in commotion. Two months had scarcely elapsed from the elevation of Innocent IX to the pontifical seat, when he also died.

And thus were the conflicts of election renewed in the conclave for the fourth time. They were now the more important, because these continual changes had enforced the conviction that it was most essential to choose a man of vigorous powers and with a fair chance for length of life. The decision now to be arrived at was one that must influence a considerable period of time. Thus, the proceedings of this conclave were of high and important interest for the history of the whole world.

[10] In the " Histoire des Conclaves," i. 251, it is said that the Spaniards wished to re-establish their reputation; but this is only a mistranslation. In the MS. which forms the groundwork of this book, " Conclave di Innocenzio IX." (Inff. Politt.), we find that they might not lose the authority they had regained, which is in strict accordance with the state of affairs.

[1] According to Davila " Historia delle guerre civili di Francia," Innocent does not appear to have been so decidedly favorable to the League; but the letter just cited (it is in Cayet, p. 356) removes all doubt.

Section V.—Election and Character of Clement VIII

The prosperous course of Spanish interests in Rome during the last year, had enabled them finally to gain over Montalto himself to their party. His house had acquired possessions in the Neapolitan territory, and while Montalto pledged himself to oppose no further resistance to the will of the King, Philip promised in return that he would not absolutely exclude all the adherents of Sixtus V. They were thus to be henceforward in alliance, and the Spaniards no longer delayed to put forward the man from whose active co-operation they might hope the most effectual aid in the French war.

Among all the cardinals, Santorio, holding the title of Sanseverina, was considered the most zealous. He had sustained many conflicts with the Protestants, even when living at Naples in his youth; and in his autobiography, still extant in MS., he describes the massacre of the Huguenots at Paris as " the renowned day of St. Bartholomew, in the highest degree cheering to Catholics." [1] He had invariably advocated the most violent opinions, was the leading member in the congregation for the management of French affairs, and had long been the soul of the Inquisition. He was in good health, and of tolerably vigorous years.

On this man the Spaniards desired to confer the supreme spiritual dignity—one more devoted to them they could not have found. Olivarez had already arranged all preliminaries,[2] no doubt of success seemed to remain. Of fifty-two votes he had secured thirty-six—exactly sufficient to decide the choice, for which two-thirds of the whole number were always required. On the first morning after the close of the conclave, the cardinals accordingly proceeded to the formal act of election. Montalto and Madruzzi, the chiefs of the united factions, led Sanseverina from his cell, which was instantly stripped of all it contained by the servants, according to the custom always practised in regard to the cells of the pontiffs elect. Thirty-six cardinals accompanied him to the Pauline chapel. He had

[1] He speaks of a just anger of King Charles IX, of glorious memory, in that celebrated day of St. Bartholomew, most joyful to Catholics. Appendix, No. 64.
[2] " Conclave di Clemente VIII.,"

MS.: " The Count of Olivarez, the faithful and inseparable friend of Sanseverina, had arranged everything before leaving Rome for the government of Sicily."

already been entreated to forgive his opponents, and had declared that he would pardon all, and would adopt the name of
Clement, as a first intimation of his placable intentions. Empires and nations were then commended to his protection.

But in the selection of this prelate, one circumstance had been
left out of view. Sanseverina was reputed to be so rigidly austere that everyone feared him.

It thus happened that many voters had steadily refused to
take part with him—as, for example, the younger cardinals:
these joined themselves to his ancient personal adversaries, and
this party now assembled in the Sistine chapel. There were,
it is true, but sixteen persons when all were met together, and
they wanted one more vote to secure them the power of exclusion: some of those present then evinced a disposition to submit
to their destiny and acknowledge Sanseverina, but the experienced Altemps had sufficient influence to make them still hold
out. They relied on his judgment, and believed him to understand the matter better than themselves.

And a similar disinclination was in fact prevailing even among
those who had given their word to Sanseverina, but many of
whom rejected him in their hearts; they had resigned themselves to the wishes of the King and Montalto, but were only
waiting an opportunity to recall their assent. On assembling
in the chapel of election, there were symptoms of disquietude and
agitation, altogether unusual when the choice had been previously decided. The counting of the votes was commenced, but
there was an evident reluctance to bring it to a conclusion. Sanseverina's own countrymen threw obstacles in his way.[3] There
wanted only some one who would open a way for the expression
of the feeling by which so many present were actuated. Ascanio Colonna at length found courage to do this. He belonged
to the Roman barons, by whom the inquisitorial severity of
Sanseverina was more especially dreaded. He exclaimed, " I
see that God will not have Sanseverina, neither will Ascanio
Colonna!" He then left the Pauline chapel, and passed over
to the opposite party in the Sistine.

By this act the latter gained the victory. A secret scrutiny
was accorded. There were many who would never have dared

[3] In regard to this matter, we have
the accounts contained in printed and
MS. conclaves, as also that left us by
Severina himself, and which I will give
in the appendix. (See No. 64, §§ 1 and
4.)

openly to retract their promised votes, but who were glad to
do so in secret, and when assured that their names would be
concealed. When the balloting lists were opened, thirty votes
only were found for the proposed candidate.

Sanseverina had come to the Vatican assured of his election.
He believed himself already in possession of that plenitude of
spiritual authority to which he attributed so exalted a significance, and in defence of which he had so earnestly battled : between the prospect of attaining to the fulfilment of his highest
wishes, and that of a future perpetually burdened by the sense
of rejection : between the condition of ruler and that of servant,
he had passed seven hours as between life and death. The decision was at length made known. Bereaved of his hopes, he was
sent back to his dismantled cell. " The next night," he tells
us in his autobiography, " was, of all the unhappy moments I
had ever experienced, the most unhappy ; the heavy sorrow of
my soul, and my inward anguish, forced from me, incredible
to relate, a bloody sweat."

He was sufficiently acquainted with the nature of a conclave
to know that he must entertain no further hopes. His friends
did indeed once more propose him, but the attempt was utterly
vain.

By this event the Spaniards themselves also lost ground.
The King had named five candidates, not one of whom could
carry his election. They were now compelled to attempt the
elevation of a sixth, whom the Spaniards had also nominated,
but only as a supernumerary.

This was Cardinal Aldobrandino, an adherent of Sixtus V,
whom Philip had rejected the year before, and had now named,
rather to oblige his confederate Montalto, than of his own accord. To him they now recurred, as to the only candidate
whose election was possible. He was entirely agreeable to Montalto, as may be imagined ; and the Spaniards could say nothing in opposition, because he had been nominated by themselves.
He was not unwelcome to the rest of the electors, and was indeed generally beloved. Thus Aldobrandino was elected with
but little opposition, on January 20, 1592. He assumed the
name of Clement VIII.

The conclusion of these conflicts, as regarded the Spaniards,
was sufficiently curious. They had labored to win Montalto

to their side, in the hope of thereby securing the election of their own partisan; and now it was in consequence of this very alliance that they were compelled to aid in the elevation of a friend of Montalto, and a creature of Sixtus V, to the papal seat.

It is to be observed, that on this occasion a change in the course of the papal elections was originated, which we cannot consider unimportant. Men of opposite factions had for a long time invariably succeeded each other. Even now the same thing had occurred, the adherents of Sixtus V had been driven three times from the contest, but the victors had possessed only a transitory enjoyment of power, and had not been able to form any new or powerful faction. Deaths, funerals, and new conclaves had rapidly followed each other. The first who once more attained the papal throne, in the full vigor of life, was Clement VIII. The government of which he was the head, was that of the same party by whom the most enduring tenure of power had of late years been held.

Attention was now universally directed to the inquiry of who the new ruler was, and what might be expected from him.

Clement VIII was born in exile.[4] His father, Salvestro Aldobrandino, of a distinguished Florentine family, but a determined and active antagonist of the Medici, was banished on the ultimate triumph obtained by that house in the year 1531, and compelled to seek his fortune in other lands.[5] He was a doctor of law, and had previously given lectures at Pisa. We find him, soon after his banishment, in Venice, where he took part in the amelioration of the Venetian statutes, and in an edition of the institutes. We next meet him in Ferrara or Urbino, forming part of the council or tribunal of the duke; but more permanently in the service, first of one and then of another among the cardinals, as whose deputy he was charged with the administration of justice or of the government in one or other of the ecclesiastical cities. He is perhaps most clearly distinguished by the fact, that in this uncertain mode of life he found

[4] See Appendix, No. 65.
[5] Varchi, " Storia Fiorentina," iii. 42–61. Mazzuchelli, " Scrittori d'Italia," I. i. 392, gives as usual a most elaborate and instructive article under this name, but it is not complete. Among other omissions, is that of the activity he displayed in Venice, with the description of which Giovanni Delfino begins his relation, in a manner that leaves no doubt of the fact: " Silvestro Aldobrandino came to this city when driven from Florence in the rebellion; he reformed our statutes and revised the laws and ordinances of the republic." See Appendix, No. 70.

means to educate five excellent sons. The most highly gifted among them was perhaps Giovanni, the eldest, whom they called the charioteer of the family. It was by him that their path was cleared. Entering on the judicial career, he rose from its dignities to that of cardinal in the year 1570. Had longer life been granted to him, it is believed that he might have had well-founded hopes of the tiara. Bernardo gained renown in the possession of arms. Tommaso was an eminent philologist; his translation of Diogenes Laertius has been frequently reprinted. Pietro was reputed to be an excellent practical jurist. The youngest, Ippolito, born at Fano in the year 1536,[6] was at first the cause of some anxiety to his father, who feared that he should be unable to provide him with an education worthy of his talents; but in the first instance Cardinal Alessandro Farnese took the boy under his protection, and settled on him a yearly allowance from the revenues of his bishopric of Spoleto; the rising fortunes of his brothers were afterward sufficient of themselves to bring him forward. He soon obtained the prelacy, and next succeeded to the office of his eldest brother in the court of the Rota. He was nominated cardinal by Sixtus V, who despatched him on an embassy to Poland. This it was that first brought him into a sort of connection with the house of Austria. All the members of that family considered themselves his debtors, for the address with which he had liberated the Archduke Maximilian from the captivity he had been held in by the Poles—a service, in the performance of which he had used his authority with a prudence and foresight that could not but insure admiration as well as success. When Philip II resolved on naming a cardinal, created by Sixtus, as a supernumerary, it was this circumstance that induced him to prefer Aldobrandino to others. And thus did the son of a homeless fugitive, of whom it was at one moment feared that he must pass his life in the labors of the desk, attain to the highest dignity in Christendom.

There is a monument in the church of Santa Maria alla Minerva in Rome, the inscription on which it is impossible to read without a certain feeling of satisfaction. It is that erected

---

[6] In the baptismal register of the cathedral parish of Fano we find the following entry: " On the 4th of March, 1536, a male child of Master Salvestro's, who was lieutenant here, was baptized; he received the name of Ippolito."

by Salvestro Aldobrandino to the mother of so noble a band of sons, and is inscribed as follows: "To his dear wife Lesa, of the house of Deti, with whom he lived in harmony for seven and thirty years."

The new pontiff brought to his office all that activity peculiar to a family which has contended with difficulties. He held his sittings in the early hours of morning, his audiences in the afternoon;[7] all reports were received and investigated, all despatches were read and discussed, legal arguments were sought out, early precedents compared. It was no unusual thing for the Pope to display more knowledge of the subject in question than was possessed by the referendaries who laid it before him. He labored with equal assiduity when pope, as when he was auditor of the Rota; his attention was given to the details of internal policy as to those of Europe in general, or to the great interests of the ecclesiastical authority. The question "In what he took pleasure?" was asked: "In everything or nothing," was the reply.[8]

Nor would he permit himself to incur the blame of the slightest negligence in his spiritual duties. Baronius received his confession every evening; he celebrated mass himself every morning at noon. Twelve poor men dined daily in the same room with himself, at least during the early years of his pontificate, and the pleasures of the table were in his case altogether out of the question. On Fridays and Saturdays, moreover, he fasted. When he had labored earnestly through the week, his recreation on the Sunday was to send for certain pious monks, or for the fathers of the Vallicella, and hold discourse with them on the more profound questions of divinity. The reputation for virtue, piety, and an exemplary life that he had always enjoyed, was raised to an extraordinary degree by such modes of proceeding. He knew this, and desired it; for by this reputation his efficiency as sovereign pastor of the Church was increased.

Clement VIII conducted himself on all occasions with en-

[7] Bentivoglio, "Memorie," i. p. 54, sets before us the whole order of the week.
[8] "Relatione al card. d'Este," 1599. MS. Fosc. He carried on war like Julius II, he built like Sixtus V, he reformed like Pius V, his conversation, moreover, was seasoned with wit. Then comes the following description: "Of phlegmatic and sanguine complexion, but withal somewhat choleric; fat, and large in person, of grave and retired habits, and mild, affable manner, slow in movement, circumspect in action, deliberate in execution; he is tenacious of secrets, profound in his designs, and diligent in carrying them to their end." See Appendix, No. 69.

lightened deliberation. He labored willingly, being endowed with one of those natures that derive fresh strength from their toils: but he was careful to regulate the ardor of his pursuits, and to mitigate the severity of his efforts by due exercise.[9] He would sometimes display great irritation, would become violent, and use bitter words; but if he perceived that the persons before him were rendered silent by the majesty of the papacy, but yet perhaps betrayed dissent and resentment by their looks, he would command himself and seek to remove the painful impression. He desired that nothing should be perceived in him but what was becoming in itself and consonant with the idea of a good, pious, and wise man.[10]

Former popes had believed themselves raised above all law, and had endeavored to turn the administration of their high office into a means of mere personal enjoyment; but the spirit of the age would at that time no longer permit this to be done. Personal inclinations must now be kept in subjection. The man was merged in his office; no one could then have either obtained or administered that office without making his conduct conform to the idea entertained of its character.

It is manifest that the strength of the papacy itself was immeasurably increased by this change. Human institutions are strong only so long as their spirit has vital existence, and exhibits its efficacy in those who wield the powers they create.

Section VI.—Absolution of Henry IV

And now the most interesting subject of inquiry to all was, how this pontiff, so remarkable for talent, activity, and force, and withal so blameless in character, would consider and treat the most momentous question of Europe—that of affairs in France.

Would he attach himself unconditionally to Spain, as his immediate predecessors had done? There was nothing in his previous life that imposed on him the necessity for this, neither

[9] Venier, " Relatione di Roma," 1601: " The gout disturbs him less than formerly, because of his prudent regimen, in which he is very strict, and closely abstains from drinking: this prevents his becoming too fat, to which his complexion inclines him: and, on that account, he takes long walks whenever the pressure of affairs permits him, making up for the time thus spent by his great capacity." See Appendix, No. 71.

[10] Delfino: " It is well ascertained that his holiness acts on all occasions with great zeal for the honor of God, and with a great desire for the public good."

was he led to it by personal inclination. He did not fail to perceive that the predominance of Spain was becoming oppressive even to the papacy, and would despoil it more especially of its political independence.

Or would he decide for the party of Henry IV? It is true that this prince gave intimations of a disposition to become Catholic, but such a promise was more readily given than fulfilled: he was still a Protestant. Clement VIII feared to be deceived.

We have seen how Sixtus V stood wavering between these two possibilities, and the serious perplexities arising from that cause. The party of the zealots still retained its strength in Rome, and the new Pope durst not expose himself to their animosity and opposition.

He was surrounded by difficulties on every side, and was constantly on his guard, that no word might lay him open to attack, or awaken slumbering enmities. It is only from his acts, from the general tenor of his conduct, that we are enabled gradually to infer his opinions and feelings.

At his accession to power, the Papal See had a legate in France, who was believed to be in the Spanish interests, and an army which had been sent to oppose Henry IV. Rome also paid subsidies to the League. The new Pope could make no change in all these things. Had he withheld his subsidies, withdrawn his troops, or recalled his legate, his reputation for orthodoxy would have been endangered, and he would have exposed himself to more rancorous animosities than Pope Sixtus had experienced. He was, however, far from increasing the efforts made by the papacy for the League, or from giving them a new impulse; on the contrary, he took ever favorable opportunity for their gradual diminution and restriction.

But no long time had elapsed before he found himself compelled to a step of a less ambiguous character.

In the year 1592, Cardinal Gondi was despatched into Italy by Henry IV, with instructions to proceed also to Rome. The King was daily becoming more disposed to Catholicism, but his idea on the subject seems rather to have been that of reuniting himself to the Catholic Church by a sort of treaty arranged under the mediation of Venice and Tuscany, than a positive submission. And was not even this very desirable for the Pope? Was not the return of the King to Catholicism a palpable advantage, under whatever form it might take place? But Clement did not consider it expedient to go into the affair, nor did he consent to receive Cardinal Gondi. The presence of Luxembourg had produced many vexatious consequences to Sixtus V, while no useful result had followed. Remembering this, Clement sent a monk, Fra Franceschi, to Florence, where Gondi had already arrived, to inform the cardinal that he could not be received in Rome. It was perfectly satisfactory to the Pope that the cardinal, and even the grand duke, complained; he desired that his refusal should excite attention, and cause a discussion. This, however, was only one side of the affair; to irritate the King, or to reject all advances toward a reconciliation, could not possibly be the Pope's intention. We find from the Venetian reports, that Fra Franceschi had affixed a remark to his official communication, purporting that he had reason to believe the cardinal might be granted an audience privately, or that he would be received in secret.[1] It would seem, indeed, that Gondi did really proceed to Rome, where the Pope is reported to have told him that he must knock at his door more than once. It is at least certain that an agent of Gondi's appeared in Rome, and after he had been admitted to several conferences, he declared to the Venetian ambassador that " by the blessing of God he had ample reason for hope, and to be satisfied,[2] but was not permitted to say more." In a word, the open repulse was accompanied by secret advances and encouragement. Clement VIII did not wish to offend the Spaniards, nor yet to repel the King of France. His conduct was calculated to secure that neither should be done.

A new question, and one of much higher moment, had meanwhile arisen.

In January, 1583, that part of the states of France which adhered to the League, assembled to elect a new King. As the ground for excluding Henry IV lay entirely in the religion he professed, the papal legate exercised an unusual degree of au-

---

[1] " Dispaccio Donato, 23 Oct. 1592," from a relation made to the Florentine ambassador, Nicolini. The explanation of Fra Franceschi was that he believed the Pope would admit him; but that his holiness wished to put the Catholics out of all doubt, and would not suffer the shadow of an appearance that he [the pontiff] was receiving an embassy from Navarre.

[2] Ibid. After having allowed the first heat of the pontiff's displeasure to pass away.

thority over the discussions. The legate was still Sega, bishop of Placentia, who had been chosen by Gregory XIV, a man imbued with the opinions prevailing under that pontiff, both as to Spanish and ecclesiastical affairs. Clement considered it expedient to send him particular instructions, and admonished him to be careful that neither violence nor bribery should influence the votes; he also entreated him to be on his guard against all precipitation in so weighty a matter.[3]

An exhortation of this kind would have been sufficiently significant, if addressed to an ambassador, who considered himself bound to govern his conduct by the slightest intimation from his sovereign, but which was conceived in terms too general to cause this churchman, whose hopes of promotion were rather in the Spanish sovereign than the Pope, to withdraw from a party with which he had always acted, and which he believed to be orthodox. Thus Cardinal Sega made not the slightest change in his line of proceeding on that account. On June 13, 1593, he published a declaration, wherein he called on the estates to elect a king, who should not only be truly Catholic, but also resolved to render useless all the efforts of the heretics and capable of carrying his resolution into effect. He added, that this was what his holiness desired more than any other earthly event.[4]

The general measures of the Pope were of a similar character with this instruction. He adhered for the most part to the rigidly orthodox ecclesiastical party attached to Spain; not, it is true, with the fervor and devotion by which other popes had been distinguished; if he possessed these qualities, they were effectual in secret only; it was enough for him to proceed quietly and without reproach, as the order of public affairs demanded, in adherence to that party which had already been adopted, and which seemed to have the closest analogy with the character of his office. We may, nevertheless, clearly perceive that he had no wish for the perfect estrangement of the opposite party; he was careful, on the contrary, to avoid provoking it to hostilities, and by secret advances and indirect expressions inspired it with the hope of reconciliation, to take

[3] Davila has given an extract from this instruction, xiii., p. 810.
[4] He [the king to be selected] sought to have the courage and other virtues required for successfully repressing and annihilating all the efforts and evil designs of the heretics. This is what in all the world his holiness most exhorts and desires." (In Cayet, 58, 350.)

place at some future day. He contented the Spaniards, but
their rivals were suffered to believe that his actions were not
altogether uncontrolled; that their character was indeed determined by deference to the wishes of Spain, and not by any
harsher feeling. The indecision of Sixtus arose from the strife
of opposite opinions contending within himself, and by which
he was prevented from adopting decided measures. Clement
respected both sides, and chose his line of policy with the purpose of conciliating both: his proceedings were governed by
prudence and circumspection; they resulted from extensive
experience and the wish to avoid exciting enmities. But it followed necessarily that he too failed to exercise any decisive
influence.

The affairs of France, thus left to themselves, proceeded all
the more freely toward the development of their natural impulses.

A circumstance of primary importance was, that the chiefs
of the League fell into discord among themselves. The sixteen
attached themselves closely to Spain. Mayenne pursued the
aims of his personal ambition. The zeal of the sixteen became
all the more fiery; they proceeded to the most atrocious crimes
against all who were either known or suspected to be deserters
from their party; as for example, to the assassination of the
president Brisson. For these things, Mayenne thought it
requisite to punish them, and caused the most violent of their
leaders to be executed. Favored by these dissensions, a mode
of thinking of greatly moderated character, both in politics
and religion, was observed to prevail in Paris, even so early as
the year 1592: it was still Catholic, but was opposed to the
course hitherto pursued by the League, and above all, to the
sixteen and the Spaniards. A combination was formed, not
greatly differing from that of the League itself, but with the
purpose of placing all the offices of the city in the hands of
moderate men holding its own opinions: this they found
means to effect in great measure during the course of that
year.[5] Similar tendencies evinced themselves throughout the
kingdom, and powerfully affected the results of the elections
for the states; thence it was that all the proposals made by the
Spaniards were encountered by so effectual an opposition from

    [5] Cayet (lib. iv. tom. lviii. p. 5) gives the propositions that were made in the
first assembly.

that assembly. While bigoted preachers still declared every man excommunicated who did but speak of peace with the "heretic," even though he should attend the mass, the parliament was reminding its members of those essential laws of the realm which excluded foreign princes from the crown; it was manifest that this whole party, which was called the political party, was only waiting the conversion of Henry IV to subject itself to his rule.

Wherein did the difference then consist between them and the Catholic royalists in the camp of Henry? It consisted in this only, that the first, before professing their allegiance, desired to see a step really taken which the last believed they might venture to await; for the Catholic royalists were also of opinion that the King must return to their Church, although they did not consider his right or legitimacy to depend on his doing so. Their antipathy to the Protestants in the immediate circle of the King may also have caused them to insist the more earnestly on this point. The princes of the blood, the most distinguished statesmen, and the principal part of the court, were attached to that "tiers-parti," whose distinctive characteristic was in this demand.[6]

When affairs had assumed this appearance, it became evident to all, and the Protestants themselves did not deny it, that if Henry desired to be king he must become Catholic. We need not investigate the claim of those who assert that they gave the final impulse to that determination. The principal part was effected by the grand combination of circumstances, the necessity of things.[7] In the completion of the act by which he passed over to Catholicism, Henry associated himself with that national sentiment of the French Catholics, which was represented by the "tiers-parti," and the party called the "political," and which had now the prospect of maintaining the ascendancy in France.

This was in fact merely that "Catholic opposition," which had gathered round the banners of legitimacy and national independence, for the purpose of resisting the ecclesiastical and Spanish interests. But how greatly had it now increased in power and importance! It had without question predominance

[6] It is thus described by Sully, v. 249.
[7] That Henry had resolved on this in April, 1593, is proved by his letter to the Grand Duke of Tuscany, dated the 26th of that month.—Gulluzzi, "Istoria del Granducato," tom. v. p. 160.

in the public opinion of the country; the people throughout
France declared for it, if not openly, at least in private. It now
attained a firm internal support from the change of religion
in the King, that prince moreover so warlike, so generous, and
so successful. Thus enforced and extended, this party once
more appeared before the Pope, and implored his recognition
and blessing. What glory would he obtain, and how effectual
an influence, if he would now at least declare himself without circumlocution in its favor! And there was still so much
depending on it. The prelates who had received the King into
the bosom of the Church had indeed done so only with the express condition that he should prevail on the Pope to accord
him absolution.[8] This was also earnestly enforced by the most
powerful members of the League, with whom Henry had commenced negotiations.[9] Although promises are not always performed, it is yet unquestionable that the papal absolution, had
it been granted at this moment, would have produced important
effects on the course of events. Henry IV sent one of the
great nobles of his kingdom, the Duke of Nevers, to solicit this
from the Pope, and a truce was agreed on while awaiting the
reply.

But Clement was distrustful and wary. As the hopes of a
religious ambition had influenced Sixtus V, so did the fear of
being deceived and involved in vexatious consequences restrain
Clement VIII. He still felt apprehensive lest Henry should,
after all, return to Protestantism, as he had done once before,
and declared that he should not believe the King sincerely attached to the Catholic Church, until an angel from heaven
should come and whisper it in his ear. He looked around him
and found the greater part of the Curia still adverse to the
French. A pamphlet still appeared from time to time, in which
the assertion was reiterated, that Henry IV, being, as he was,
" hæreticus relapsus," could not receive absolution, even from
the Pope himself. Clement did not feel courage to offer a defiance to the Spaniards, by whom this opinion was put forward
and maintained.[10] And was not the party, thus entreating his

[8] " The clergy had given him absolution, on condition that he should send
to beg the approval of the Pope for
what they had done."—Cayet, 58, 390.
[9] Villeroy, " Mémoires," Coll. Univ.,
62, 186.
[10] " Les intimidations qui furent faites
au Pape Clement VIII. par le duc de
Sessa;" not very authentic, however,
and printed long since in the
" Mémoires de M. le Duc de Nevers,"
ii. 716, although given by Capefigue,
" Histoire de la Réforme," tom. viii., as
something new.

forgiveness, still employed in resisting the claims of the Romish Church? " Rebels to the crown and the Church," as he expressed himself—" bastards, the children of the bondwoman and not of the wife, while the Leaguers have proved themselves the true sons." [1] Considered from this point of view, it would without doubt have required some resolution to grant their request, and Clement could not man himself to the effort.[2] The Duke of Nevers entered Rome with a full consciousness of his high rank, as well as of the weight attached to his mission. He expected to be received with joy, and expressed himself to that effect. The King's letter, which he had brought with him, was conceived in a similar tone. The Pope thought it sounded as if Henry had not only been long a Catholic, but as though he had come like a second Charlemagne, from a victory over the enemies of the Church. Nevers was quite amazed to find himself so coldly received, and to see how indifferent an ear was turned to his proposals. When he found all his efforts fruitless, he asked the Pope at length what the King should do to merit favor from his holiness. The Pope replied, that there were theologians enough to France to instruct him on that head. " But will your holiness be satisfied with what the theologians shall decide?" To this the Pope refused a reply. He would not even consider the duke as ambassador from Henry, but only as Louis Gonzaga, Duke of Nevers. He did not wish their conversations to be considered as official communications, but simply as private discourses, and was not to be prevailed on to give any written decision. " Nothing remains to me," remarked Nevers to Cardinal Toledo, by whom he was informed of the Pope's determination, " but to lament the misfortunes that France will have to endure from the rage of the soldiery, when the war breaks forth anew." The cardinal said not a word, but he smiled. Nevers left Rome, and gave expression to his displeasure in bitter reports.[3]

[1] " Disp. 20 Ag. 1593." Relation of Henry's conversion: " The Pope was but little moved by these advices, and altogether continued with his mind involved in the usual doubts and perplexities." He told the Venetian ambassador that Henry was and would remain " hæreticus relapsus," and that his conversion was not to be relied on.
[2] " Relatio dictorum a Clemente VIII. papa, die 28 Dec. 1593, in consistorio."— " Mém. de Nevers," ii. 638.

[3] Two writings, but almost entirely to the same purport: " Discours de ce que fit M. de Nevers à son voyage de Rome en l'année 1539," and " Discours de la légation de M. le duc de Nevers," both in the second volume of the " Mémoires de Nevers," before mentioned, the first almost verbatim in Cayet; extracts in Thuanus and Davila, and lately, as if from unknown sources, in Capefigue.

Men have rarely much feeling except for their own personal situation. The Roman Curia understood only what was of advantage to itself. We can find no true sympathy for the fate of France in its proceedings.

It is true that we know enough of this pontiff to believe that he did not mean absolutely to repulse the adherents of Henry IV; least of all would he do that now, when their strength was so much greater than formerly. On the contrary, he assured a secret agent, that the King had only to show himself completely Catholic, and absolution should not be wanting. It is characteristic of Clement, that while in public he so stubbornly refrained from taking any part in the return of Henry to the Catholic faith, yet, in private, he caused it to be intimated to the Grand Duke of Tuscany, that he would yet make no objection to anything the clergy of France might decide on doing.[4] The grand duke was also empowered to communicate favorable expressions on the part of the Pope to the chiefs of the Catholic royalists.[5] But, in all this, he thought only of securing himself; and thus the affairs of France were left to do as they could.

The truce was at an end. The sword was once more drawn —all was again depending on the fortune of war.

But here the superiority of Henry became at once and decidedly manifest. To the commanders opposing him, that firmness of conviction, which had formerly secured them so strong a position, was now wholly wanting. The doctrines of the political party, the conversion of the King, and the successful progress of his fortunes, had shaken the opposition of all. One after another went over to his side, without regarding the want of the papal absolution. Vitri, the commandant of Meaux, who no longer received the pay of his troops from the Spaniards, was the first; and he was followed by Orleans, Bourges, and Rouen. The most important consideration now was, the turn affairs would take in Paris. The political or national party had there obtained a decided preponderance. After many vicissitudes, it had gained over the first families, and had filled the most important places from its own members. The armed citizens were already commanded by men of the prevalent opinions. The Hôtel de Ville was directed by the

[4] See Appendix, No. 65; "Vita et Gestis Clementis VIII."
[5] Davila, lib. xiv. p. 939.

same party. The prévôt des marchands and the echevins belonged to it with only one exception. Under these circumstances, no further impediment could now exist to the return of the King, which took place on March 22, 1594. Henry IV was amazed to find himself received with acclamation so joyful, by a people from whom he had so long experienced the most obstinate resistance, and thought he might justly infer that they had been previously acting under the force of a tyrannous government; but this was not altogether true. The spirit of the League really had been predominant over the minds of men, although another had now taken its place. The King's return was principally to be attributed to the triumph of a political opinion. The Leaguers now endured persecutions similar to those they had so often inflicted. Their most influential founders and chiefs—the formidable Boucher, for example— left the city with the Spanish troops. More than a hundred, who were considered the most dangerous, were formally banished. All the authorities, with the whole population, took the oath of allegiance. Even the Sorbonne—whose most obstinate members, and among them the rector of the university himself, were banished—gave in its adhesion to the ruling opinions. How different were its present decisions from those of the year 1589. The Sorbonne now acknowledged that all power comes from God, according to the thirteenth chapter of Romans; that whoever opposes the king, withstands God also, and subjects himself to damnation. This assembly reprobated the opinion that obedience might be lawfully refused to a king, because he was not acknowledged by the Pope, as the suggestion of wicked and ill-advised men. The members of the university now took the oath of fidelity to Henry IV in a body. Rector, dean, theologians, decretists, physicians, artists, monks, and conventuals, students and officers, all pledged themselves to shed their blood for his defence. Nay, more than that, the university instituted a campaign against the Jesuits, on the ground of this its new orthodoxy, accusing them of seditious principles; which principles they had, in fact, but lately shared; and reproaching them with their attachment to Spanish interests. The Jesuits defended themselves for some time with good effect; but in that same year, a man named Jean Chastel,[6]

[6] Juvencius, partis v. lib. xii. n. 13, gives the following description of the criminal: " The disposition of the youth was gloomy and morose, his

who had attended their schools, made an attempt to assassinate the King, and admitted, in the course of his examination, that he had often heard the Jesuits declare that a man might lawfully slay a king who was not reconciled to the church. This event made it impossible for the order to oppose itself any longer to the ascendancy of the party against which they had hitherto so constantly labored. The populace was with difficulty restrained from storming their college; and all the members of the society were at length condemned, as seducers of youth, disturbers of the public peace, and enemies of the King and State to quit the kingdom within fourteen days.[7] Thus did those opinions, which had first appeared as opposition, and had confirmed their hold, from a small and feeble commencement, gradually gain possession of Paris and the kingdom, while they drove their antagonists from the field. Changes of similar character took place in all parts of the French dominions. New submissions were daily made to the King's authority. He had been crowned and anointed at Chartres; prayers were put up for him in all the pulpits; the monastic orders acknowledged him; he exercised those ecclesiastical prerogatives of the crown, which are of such high significance, without opposition; and herein found occasion to show himself a good Catholic. Wherever the ritual of the Church had been departed from during the late troubles, he took care to re-establish it; and where it had maintained itself in exclusive possession, he solemnly confirmed to it the right of doing so. All this he did without having yet been reconciled with the Pope.

It had, however, now become urgently necessary to the pontiff himself, that the means of a reconciliation should be considered.[8] If he had delayed longer, a schism might have been occasioned. An entirely separate church might have been established.

It is true that the Spaniards still opposed themselves to this reconciliation. They maintained that Henry was by no means

morals were depraved, his mind was disquieted by the remembrance of crime, and of one in particular, that of having ill-treated his mother. . . . Conscience, the avenger of crimes, continued to torture his mind, bewildered by dread fears; to mitigate these [quem ut leniret], either deprived of reason, or urged on by hellish fury, he formed the design of a monstrous parricide, by which, having done service to religion and the realm, he might the better, as

he madly imagined, obtain forgiveness of his sins."

[7] "Annuæ Literæ Societatis Jesu," 1596, p. 350. Such is the commotion remaining after our late shipwreck, that we have not yet collected all our scattered goods and muniments.

[8] On November 5, 1594, the Venetian ambasador first mentions finding the Pope "more favorably inclined than of old" toward the affairs of France.

a true convert; that the time when a schism was most to be apprehended, was when he should have received absolution:[9] they even particularized the occasions on which it was likely to break out.[10] The Pope had still to exercise considerable resolution before he could place himself in opposition to those whose power encompassed him, and who had a large party in the Curia. It was no light thing to separate himself from opinions that were considered orthodox; for which his predecessors had so often employed their weapons, spiritual and temporal, and to which he had himself for many years given his sanction. He perceived, nevertheless, that all delay must now be injurious, and that he must expect nothing more from the opposite party. He was convinced that the party now predominant in France, though in spiritual affairs opposing the rigid doctrines to a certain extent, yet displayed an obvious sympathy with the interests of Rome in temporal matters. The adverse feeling might, perhaps, be removed, when the favorable sentiment would become more available. Suffice it to say, that Clement now showed himself disposed to concession at the first word addressed to him. We have reports of the negotiations by the French plenipotentiary D'Ossat; they are agreeable, instructive, and worth reading; but I do not find that he had any great difficulties to overcome. It would be useless to follow the proceedings in detail; the general state of affairs had already determined the Pope. The only question remaining was, whether Henry would, on his part, agree to certain demands to be made by the pontiff. Those who were unfavorable to the proposed reconciliation would willingly have raised these demands to the utmost, maintaining that, on this occasion, the Church required the most effectual securities; but Clement remained firm to the more moderate conditions. He required, particularly, the restoration of Catholicism in Bearn; the introduction of the decrees issued by the Council of Trent, so far as they were compatible with the laws of the kingdom; an exact allowance of the concordat, and the education of the heir-presumptive to the crown, the Prince of Condé, in the Catholic faith. It was still very desirable for Henry that he should be reconciled with the Papal See. His power was based on his conversion to Catholicism; and this act would receive its full authenticity only from the accordance of

[9] "Ossat à M. de Villeroy, Rome, 6 Dec. 1594."—"Lettres d'Ossat," i. 53.
[10] See Appendix, No. 70, § 3.

absolution by the Pope; for though by far the greater number
gave in their adhesion, yet there were still some who made the
want of this a pretext for their continued opposition.[1]   Henry
assented to these conditions with little difficulty: he had already
prepared their fulfilment in some degree of his own accord, and
had it much at heart to prove himself a good Catholic.   However greatly increased his power had become since the mission
of Nevers, yet the letter in which he now entreated absolution
from the pontiff sounds much more humble and submissive than
the former.   " The King," it declares,[2] " returns to the feet of
your holiness, and beseeches you in all humility, by the bowels
of our Lord Jesus Christ, that you deign to confer upon him
your holy blessing and your supreme absolution."   The Pope
was entirely satisfied.[3]

Nothing further now remained but that the College of Cardinals should declare its assent.   But Clement would not permit
the question to be laid before a regularly assembled consistory,
where a recurrence to resolutions adopted under a different class
of circumstances might easily have occasioned undesirable results.   The cardinals were invited to give their opinions to the
pontiff, each in a special audience; an expedient that had frequently been adopted before on similar occasions.   Having received them all, he declared that two-thirds of the votes were
favorable to the absolution.

Preparations were accordingly made for the completion of the
ceremony, which took place on the seventeenth of December,
1595.   The pontiff's throne was erected before the Church of
St. Peter, the cardinals and Curia reverently surrounding their
sovereign.   The petition of Henry, with the conditions to which
he had assented, were read aloud.   The representative of the

---

[1] " Du Perron au Roi, 6 Nov. 1595: "
" It would be a superfluous discourse
here to insist on the advantage you may
derive from the favor and authority of
this Holy See, for, being in your hands,
it may serve you as a useful instrument
not only to replace and to preserve your
subjects in peace and obedience, but
also to prepare for you all sorts of greatness beyond your kingdom; or at the
least to keep your enemies in some fear
and order, by the dread of that same
authority of which they have availed
themselves to trouble your states and
people."—" Les Ambassades du Cardinal du Perron," i. 27.
[2] " Requête du Roi," among the remarks of Amelot in Ossat, i. 160.
[3] The Court of Rome still considered
the resolution imprudent and hazardous.
Dolfino, " Relatione ": " The Pope has
found means to expedite the most
serious affairs, not only well, but with
the utmost celerity.   For in spite of the
many well-known obstacles raised before him, he bestowed his benediction
on the French King, received him into
the bosom of the Church, and sent him
a legate, when every one discouraged
his doing so, under the pretext that it
was not for his dignity to send one before the King had sent his ambassador
to Rome; and in this affair the authority of your signory availed no little,
for so his holiness told me in regard to
certain services that I performed at that
time in your name."

most Christian king thereupon threw himself at the feet of the Pope, who, touching him lightly with a wand, thus imparted the absolution.   The Papal See once more appeared on this occasion in all the splendor of its ancient authority.[4]

And this ceremony was, in fact, the manifestation of a great result effectually secured.   The ruling power in France, now strong in itself and firmly seated, was again become Catholic. Its interest consequently was to keep on good terms with the Pope.   A new central point for Catholicism was formed in that country, and from this a most efficient influence must inevitably proceed.

When more nearly contemplated, this event is seen to offer two distinct aspects.

It was not by the immediate influence of the Pope, nor by victory obtained by the rigidly Catholic party, that France had been recovered; it was rather by the union of opinions taking a medium between the two extremes of party.   This result was indeed brought about by the superior force of that body which had at first constituted the opposition.   It followed that the French Church assumed a position entirely different from that accorded to those of Italy, the Netherlands, or the newly established Church of Germany.   It submitted to the Pope, but this was done with a freedom and essential independence proceeding from its origin, and the consciousness of which was never again resigned.   Thus the Papal See was far from having the right to consider France as a complete conquest.

But the second aspect, the political side, presented the most important advantages.   The lost balance of power was restored. Two great sovereignties, each jealous of the other, and both involved in continual strife and conflict, kept each other within due limits; both were Catholic, and might eventually be guided into the same direction; but in any case, the Pope assumed between them a position of far more perfect independence than his predecessors had for a long time found it possible to attain. From those fetters, hitherto thrown about him by the Spanish preponderance, he was now, to a great extent, freed.

This political result was indeed brought into view only by the progress of events.   It was on the lapse of Ferrara to the Papal

[4] Ossat, who is generally very circumstantial, passes rapidly over this ceremony.   "All was done," he says, "in a manner suited to the dignity of the most Christian crown."   But this was not the general opinion.

See that French influence first became again manifest in the affairs of Italy; and this was an event which in many respects was of so great an importance to the progress of political power in the States of the Church, that we may for a moment allow it to divert our attention, as it did that of contemporaries, from the affairs of religion. We will begin with a retrospective glance at the duchy under the last of its princes.

Section VII.—Ferrara Under Alfonso II

It has been frequently assumed that Ferrara was in a peculiarly prosperous condition under the last prince of the family of Este. This is nevertheless merely an illusion, and has originated, like so many others, from antipathy to the secular dominion of Rome.

Montaigne visited Ferrara under Alfonso II. He admired the broad streets of the city and its handsome palaces, but he remarked that it looked desolate and depopulated, as travellers have so frequently done in our own days.[1] The prosperity of the country depended on the maintenance of the dams and the regulation of the waters, but neither the dams nor the streams and canals were kept in good order. Inundations were not infrequent. The Volana and Primero were suffered to become choked with sand, so that their navigation was totally suspended.[2]

It would be even more erroneous to believe the subjects of this house either free or happy. Alfonso II enforced the claims of his exchequer with extreme severity. On the conclusion of every contract, were it only for a loan, one-tenth of the amount fell to the duke, and he levied a tenth on every article that entered the city. He had the monopoly of salt, and burdened the trade in oil with a new tax. By the advice of Christofano da Fiume, his commissioner of customs, he finally took the trade in flour and bread into his own hands. None might venture to procure these first necessaries of life except from the ducal officers, nor did any man dare even to lend a bowl of flour to his

[1] Montaigne, " Voyage," i. 226-231.
[2] An account of the States of the Church, about the beginning of the seventeenth century, declares that the duke had transferred the peasants, whose duty it was to labor on the Po, to his own property of Mesola, so that the necessary works on the river had fallen into decay, and could not be restored.—Inff. Politt. tom. ix.

neighbor.[3]   The nobles themselves were not permitted to hunt for more than a few days, and then were never allowed to use more than three dogs.   One day six men were seen hanging in the market-place; dead pheasants were tied to their feet, and this was said to be in token of their having been shot while poaching on the ducal preserves.

It is obvious, then, that the writers who insist on the prosperity and activity of Ferrara cannot mean to speak of the country or the city, but simply of the court.

In those storms that convulsed the first ten years of the sixteenth century, in which so many prosperous families and mighty principalities were totally ruined, and when all Italy was shaken to its centre, the house of Este succeeded in maintaining its ground, and by the union of political address with stout-hearted self-defence, had managed to weather all danger.   Other qualities were also united to these.   Who has not read of that race which, as Bojardo expresses himself, was destined to maintain all bravery, virtue, courtesy, and social gayety alive in the world;[4] or of its dwelling-place, which, as Ariosto says, was adorned, not only with ample royal palaces, but with fair studies also and excellent manners.[5]   But if the house of Este had the merit of bestowing patronage on science and poetry, it has been richly rewarded.   The memory of that splendor and power which so rapidly pass away has been perpetuated by great authors in works that must live forever.

As matters had stood under the earlier dukes of Ferrara, so Alfonso II sought to maintain them.   His views and objects of pursuit were similar to those of his predecessors.

He had not indeed to sustain the violence of conflict by which they were assailed, but being continually involved in dissensions

[3] Frizzi, " Memorie per la Storia di Ferrara," tom. iv. p. 364; and more particularly Manolesso, " Relatione di Ferrara ": " The duke is less beloved than his predecessors, and that because of the tyranny and exactions of Christofano da Fiume, called Il Frisato, ' the scarred ' (Sfregiato), his comptroller of taxes.   Il Frisato offered to sell goods, for the benefit of the people, at much lower prices than others, and yet to derive large profits for his excellency. The affair pleased Alfonso well; but though Il Frisato satisfies the duke by giving him the sums he expected, he does not please the people, to whom he sells things very bad in quality, and very dear as to price."

[4] Bojardo, " Orlando Innamorato," ii. 22:
" Da questa   (stirpe) fia servato ogni valore,
Ogni bontade et ogni cortesia,
Amore, leggiadria, stato giocundo
Tra quella gente fiorita nel mundo."
[Be still transmitted by that favored race
Which in the world's respect doth foremost shine,
Love, honor, valor, courtesy, and grace,
Each gentle virtue and each art divine.—
C. F.]
[5] Ariosto, " Orlando Furioso," xxxv. 6.
" Nor for its walls alone and royal towers,
But eke for learning fair and for the Graces' bowers.—C. F."

with Florence, and not feeling very secure of the Pope, who was his feudal lord, he held himself constantly in an attitude of defence. Next to Padua, Ferrara was reputed the strongest fortress in Italy. Twenty-seven thousand men were enrolled in the militia,[6] and Alfonso labored to encourage a military spirit in his people. Desiring to strengthen himself by a friendship sufficiently important to counterbalance the favor enjoyed by Tuscany at the Court of Rome, he attached himself to the German Emperor's. He not infrequently traversed the Alps with a splendid train, received the hand of an Austrian princess in marriage, and is reported to have used the German language. In 1566 he marched into Hungary, to the aid of the Emperor against the Turks, with a body of troops 14,000 strong.

The prosperity of literature increased greatly under his patronage. I do not indeed know of any country where its connection with the State has been more closely intimate. Two professors of the university, Pigna and Montecatino, were successively prime ministers of the duchy, and this without relinquishing their literary labors. It is at least certain that Pigna, while conducting the government, still delivered his lectures, and even published a book from time to time.[7] Battista Guarini, the author of the " Pastor Fido," was sent as ambassador to Venice, and afterward to Poland. Even Francesco Patrizi, though engaged in the most abstruse subjects, yet speaks in high terms of the sympathy he experienced from the court. All these were of one mind; scientific discussions were followed by propositions, touching various disputed questions of love, such for example as were once handled by Tasso, who was at one period a member of the university. Sometimes the court gave theatrical representations, at others a similar entertainment was offered by the university; but this theatre possessed also literary attractions, since attempts were continually made for the production of new forms, and it is to these that the perfec-

---

[6] " Relatione sopra la Romagna di Ferrara:" " All subjects capable of bearing arms were inscribed in the lists of the militia by the military commissioner deputed for that purpose. They were compelled to hold themselves contsantly ready to serve on foot or horseback, according to their means, and in return they enjoyed certain exemptions."

[7] Manolesso: " Signor Giovambattista Pigna is the private secretary, and through his hands all business affairs must pass. He lectures publicly on moral philosophy, and is writing the history of the house of Este; he is a philosopher, an orator, and an excellent poet; is well acquainted with Greek, and though laboring for his prince, transacting affairs, and writing whatever is needed, he does not neglect his studies, but so fulfils each of his employments, that it might be thought he was occupied with that alone."

tion of the pastoral drama must be ascribed, as also the foundation of the opera. Ferrara was sometimes visited by foreign
ambassadors, cardinals, and princes, more especially by those of
the neighborhood, as Mantua, Guastalla, and Urbino—occasionally too an archduke would appear. Then the court displayed
its utmost splendor; tournaments were given, in which the nobility of the land spared no cost; a hundred knights sometimes
assembled and tilted in the court of the palace. There were also
representations from some fabulous work, or legend of poetry,
as the names given to them sufficiently show—" The Temple of
Love," " The Island of Happiness," for example.[8] Enchanted
castles were attacked, defended, and conquered.

It was the most extraordinary union of poetry, learning, politics, and chivalry. The pomp of display became ennobled by
the spirit which inspired it, and which offered ample amends for
the defects of the means employed.

In the " rime," as well as in the epic, of Tasso, this court is
presented in very lively colors, together with that prince (" in
whom force and elevation of character shone so nobly forth,
and of whom it is difficult to decide whether he is a better knight
or general "), his wife, and above all, his sisters. The elder
was Lucretia, who passed but little of her time with her husband
in Urbino, and for the most part resided in Ferrara, exercising
no slight influence over public affairs, though still more earnestly occupied in the promotion of literary interests, to which, and
to the musical genius of the day, her patronage gave impulse
and encouragement. It was this princess who secured the advancement of Tasso at the Court of Ferrara. The younger,
Leonora, held a less conspicuous position; she was gentle and
retiring of manner, and delicate in health, but was endowed like
her sister with a mind of great force.[9] During an earthquake,
both refused to quit the palace. Leonora more particularly displayed a stoical indifference; when, at length, they yielded, it
had almost been too late, the roof falling in on the instant of
their departure. Leonora was considered almost a saint; the
deliverance of the city from an inundation was attributed to her

[8] Extracts from descriptions which appeared at the time—from the " Tempio
d' Amore," for example—may be found
in Muratori, Serassi, and Frizzi.
[9] In the year 1566 she conducted the
regency in the absence of the duke, according to Manolesso, " to the infinite
satisfaction of the subjects. She has
not married [he continues] nor will she
marry, because of the delicacy of her
health; she has nevertheless a very
high spirit."

prayers.[10] The homage offered to them by Tasso was in accordance with their respective characters: toward the younger, restrained and subdued, and as one who controls the expression of his thoughts; his admiration of the elder was more unreserved; he compared her to the full-blown fragrant rose, which maturity has deprived of no charm, etc. Other ladies adorned the courtly circle; among them were Barbara Sanseverina and her daughter Leonora Sanvitale. Tasso has described, with incomparable grace, the serene self-possession of the mother, and the radiant charm of youthful beauty in the daughter; no portrait could place them more clearly before us. Then follow descriptions of visits to the rural palaces of the duke; of the hunting parties and other amusements entered into on those occasions; in short, of the whole course and proceeding of that brilliant life, few there are who can resist the impression which those descriptions, in their rich and musical flow, are so well calculated to produce.

Yet it is not to such impressions that we must entirely surrender ourselves. The same power by which the country was maintained in so implicit an obedience did not fail to make itself felt at the court also.

These scenes of poetry and enjoyment were occasionally interrupted by others of a very different character: events in which the most exalted were as little spared as those of lower station.

One of the house of Gonzaga had been murdered, and all believed the young Ercole Contrario to be guilty of the crime: it was at least known that the murderers had found refuge on one of his estates. The duke commanded that they should be given up, and Contrario, to avoid being accused by them, caused them to be put to death himself, and sent their dead bodies only to the duke. Hereupon he was himself one day summoned to the court, and received audience on second of August, 1575. The house of Contrario was the most ancient and wealthy of Ferrara. Ercole was its last remaining scion; yet he had not long entered the palace before he was carried out of it a corpse. The duke said that the young man had been suddenly struck with apoplexy while in discourse with him; but no one believed the assertion; traces of violence were perceived on the body; it was indeed acknowledged by the friends of the duke, that their lord

[10] Serassi, " Vita di Torquato Tasso," p. 150.

had caused him to be put to death, but they excused this act, on the ground that he had not chosen to sully a name so illustrious by a more disgraceful death.[1]

This was a sort of justice that kept everyone in terror—the rather, as the possessions of the family had by this event fallen to the duke.

But it would not on the whole have been advisable for anyone to have opposed himself in the slightest degree to the sovereign will.[2] This court was indeed very dangerous and slippery ground. All the subtlety of Montecatino could not enable him to retain his footing to the last. The most distinguished preacher in Italy was at that time Panigarola, and he had been induced to settle at Ferrara, but not without difficulty. He was suddenly banished with injurious violence; and when it was asked for what crime he thus suffered, the only one adduced was, that he had negotiated respecting promotion with some other court. Neither could the changeful, susceptible, and melancholy Tasso at length keep his ground there; the duke seemed attached to him, felt pleasure in listening to him, and often took him to the ducal palaces in the country; nor did he disdain to correct the descriptions of military proceedings that appear in the "Gerusalemme." But after Tasso had shown some inclination to enter the service of the Medici, they were never cordially friends. The hapless poet left Ferrara; but impelled by an irresistible longing, he returned, and a few reproachful words, uttered in an excess of melancholy, sufficed to determine the duke to hold the unfortunate man imprisoned during seven long years.[3]

We here see the whole character of the Italian principality, as it existed in the fifteenth century: based on judiciously calculated political relations, it was absolute and unlimited in the power of its internal administration; surrounded by splendor, closely connected with literature, and jealous even of the very appearance of power. Extraordinary aspect of human affairs! The whole power and all the resources of a country produce a

---

[1] Frizzi, "Memorie," iv. 382.

[2] When Tasso was not in good humor, he expressed himself in different terms from those quoted above. In a letter to the Duke of Urbino he says, "Because I knew that the duke was naturally much disposed to malignity, and full of a certain overweening arrogance, which he derives from the nobility of his blood, and from the consciousness that he has of his own importance, which is in some respects certainly real." "Lettere," n. 284. "Opere," tom. ix. 188.

[3] Serassi, "Vita del Tasso," p. 282.

court—the centre of the court is the prince; finally, then, the ultimate product of all this gathered life is the self-sufficiency of the sovereign. From his position in the world, the obedience he receives, the respect accorded to him, there results only the sense of his own value, the conviction of his own importance.

Alfonso II was childless, although he had been three times married. His whole feeling is expressed in the peculiar mode of his conduct under these circumstances.

He had two purposes to secure; the one was, to prevent his subjects from thinking it possible that they could fall off from his house; the other, to retain the nomination of a successor in his own hands, and to avoid raising up a rival against himself.

In September, 1589, he repaired to Loretto, where the sister of Sixtus V, Donna Camilla, then was; he spared neither gifts nor promises to gain her over. He hoped that she would procure him permission from the pontiff to name any one of his connections, whom he might prefer to be his successor; but the negotiations had but just been effectually commenced when Sixtus V expired.

By a similar expedient—presents to the sister-in-law of the Pope, and alacrity in the service of his nephew—Alfonso gained access to Gregory XIV in the year 1591. When he perceived hope of success, he proceeded to Rome himself, for the more effectual conduct of the negotiations. The first question was, whether that bull of Pius V, which forbade all new investiture of papal fiefs that had lapsed to the feudal lord, were applicable to Ferrara. Alfonso maintained that it was not, because Ferrara never had lapsed. But the words were too precise, and the congregation decided that the bull applied beyond all doubt to Ferrara. All that yet remained to be inquired was, whether a pope had not the power to give a special determination in a special case. This the congregation did not venture to say he could not do; but they added this condition, that the necessity must be urgent, and the utility clearly obvious.[4] An important step was hereby made. It is not improbable that, if expedition had been used, and a new investiture at once prepared in favor of

[4] " Dispaccio Donato:" " When the utility and urgent necessity were most evident, which was done to facilitate the way to the Signor Duke's wishes." Cardinal Sanseverina now assures us that it was he who principally contributed to frustrate this design, though with great difficulty, and amid violent opposition; the Pope is also declared to have repented in the end of that qualification of the bull.

some one person then named, the affair might have been brought to the end desired; but Alfonso would not name his heir; neither was he entirely agreed on this point with the Sfrondrati, who wished him to choose the Marquis Filippo d'Este, while he preferred his nearer kinsman, Cesare. Time passed while these things were in discussion, and Gregory also died before anything had been concluded.[5]

Negotiations had, meanwhile, been opened with the imperial court likewise; for though Ferrara was a papal fief, Modena and Reggio were fiefs of the empire. The previous policy of the duke here did him good service: he was on the best terms with the Emperor's most influential minister, Wolf Rumpf. Rudolph II accorded him the renewal of his investiture; and even granted him a certain period of time within which he was permitted to choose whomsoever he might wish to appoint, as his successor.

But all the more inflexible was Clement VIII, who had now become pope. It seemed to him more for the Catholic and ecclesiastical interests to retake possession of a lapsed fief than to grant it anew: it was thus too that the holy pontiff Pius V had decided for such cases. In the year 1592, Clement proposed in a secret consistory, that the bull of Pius should be ratified according to its original tenor, and without the addition made by Gregory XIV. In that form it was accordingly confirmed.[6]

The term granted by the Emperor had also elapsed; and the duke was compelled to resolve on pointing out his successor. Alfonso I had married Laura Eustachia, when he was advanced in years, and after she had borne him a son. From this son descended Don Cesare d'Este, whom, after long delay, the duke appointed his successor. But he still proceeded with the most cautious secrecy. Without the knowledge of any one person, and in a letter written with his own hand to the Emperor, he completed the nomination; but, at the same time, he entreated his Majesty pressingly to let no one know what he had done; not even the ambassador from Ferrara to the imperial court. He requested the Emperor to express his approval in no other

[5] " Cronica di Ferrara," MS. of the Albani Library, also affirms that there was no doubt of Gregory's intention to do something for Ferrara. He left the congregation in a fit of anger, and became ill in consequence. Alfonso went to a villa of Cardinal Farnese's, " waiting the event, whether the life or 'death of the Pope—death ensued—then the duke returned." See Appendix, No. 63, § 3.

[6] " Dispaccio Donato, 27 Dec. 1592."

manner than by returning the letter with the imperial signature affixed.[7]

Alfonso desired to hold the supreme authority in his small territories undivided to his last breath. He was resolved not to see his court turn toward the rising sun. Cesare himself received no intimation of the favor prepared for him. He was held, on the contrary, under a more rigid rule than before; was even restricted, in a certain sense, as to the splendor of his appearance (being forbidden to have more than three nobles in his train); and it was only when the duke's life was at the lowest ebb, when the physicians had resigned their last hope, that Alfonso permitted him to be summoned, and informed him of his good fortune. The testament was opened in presence of the principal inhabitants of the duchy. These persons were admonished by the minister to be true to the house of Este. The duke told Cesare that he left him the fairest dominion in the world; strong by its military force, its population, and its allies, both in Italy and beyond her limits; from whom he might promise himself help on all occasions. This being done, Alfonso II expired on the same day, twenty-seventh of October, 1597.

Section VIII.—Conquest of Ferrara

Cesare took possession of the imperial fiefs without opposition, and received homage even from that of the Pope. In Ferrara he was robed by the magistrate in the ducal mantle, and greeted by the people as their sovereign with joyful acclamations.

His predecessor had assured him of foreign aid, as well as of the native strength he would find in his new dominions. Cesare was very soon placed in a position to put these promises to the test.

Clement remained immovable in his determination to resume possession of Ferrara. So many pontiffs had already made the attempt, that he believed he should secure himself eternal re-

[7] " Relatione di quello che è successo in Ferrara dopo la morte del Duca Alfonso" (MS. Barber.): "The duke, within the year allowed for his decision, wrote a letter with his own hand to the Emperor, and named Don Cesare, praying his imperial Majesty earnestly that in confirmation he would merely place his signature; that he would then seal and restore the document by means of Count Ercole Rondinelli, but not confide its import either to him or to any other person; all which his highness the duke did, that Don Cesare might not be inflated, and that he might not be honored or courted as their prince by the nobility."

nown by its accomplishment. When intelligence was brought him of Alfonso's death, he declared that he was sorry the duke had left no son; but that the Church must have her own again. He would not listen to the ambassadors of Cesare, and called his taking possession, usurpation. He threatened to place him under the ban of the Church, if he did not resign the duchy within fourteen days; and to give the greater effect to his words, the pontiff at once prepared to take arms. A new loan was raised, and a new *monte* founded, that the money in the castle of St. Angelo might remain untouched.[1] He also despatched his nephew, Cardinal Pietro Aldobrandino, to Ancona, with a staff of experienced military commanders, for the purpose of gathering troops. Recruiting parties were sent in all directions, and the provinces were burdened with heavy contributions.

Cesare also seemed at first to be full of spirit.[2] He declared that he would defend his good right to the last drop of his blood, without fear that either his religion or salvation would be endangered by his doing so. Accordingly, the fortifications of his strongholds were repaired, the militia of the country were put under arms, a body of his troops advanced to the frontiers of the Papal States; and we find an invitation to him to appear in Romagna, where the inhabitants were dissatisfied with the papal government, and only wanted some fair occasion to overturn it. He had also the good fortune to see the neighboring Italian States taking part with him. His brother-in-law, the Grand Duke of Tuscany, declared that he would never abandon his cause. The Republic of Venice prevented the Pope from recruiting in Dalmatia, and refused him the arms and other munitions of war that he desired to obtain from Brescia. The aggrandizement of the Papal States was a project abhorrent to the hearts of all its neighbors.

Had the position of Italy been similar to that which she had held a hundred years earlier—independent, upon the whole, of foreign influences, and left to her own efforts—Clement VIII

[1] Many affirm, nevertheless, that this did not happen, but Delfino declares, "though suffering great dearth of money, he got together an army of 22,000 foot and 3,000 horse in little more than a month, and without touching the treasure in the castle, for he desired to preserve the reputation of the Church." See Appendix, No. 70.

[2] Nicolò Contarini "delle Historie Venetiane," MS., tom. i. lib i.: "Cesare in the beginning showed himself very courageous, and wished to defend his rights, either because he did not foresee the violence of the struggle, or because the inexperienced, as they show terror in dangers present, so are they valiant in regard to those that are remote." The narrative of Contarini supplies much exact and impressive intelligence respecting this occurrence.

would probably not have effected more than Sixtus IV had then done; but those times were gone by; everything now depended on the general state of European relations, and on the great powers of that period, France and Spain.

The inclinations of the Spaniards did not admit of doubt. Cesare d'Este relied so implicitly on Philip II that he proposed him to the Pope as umpire. The King's governor of Milan declared for Cesare without reserve, and offered him Spanish garrisons for his fortresses; but it could not be denied that Philip himself, who had all his life striven to repress commotions in Italy, was reluctant to give occasion for war at his advanced age, and governed all his proceedings with infinite caution, as did also his ambassador at Rome.[3]

So much the more important, under these circumstances, was the decision given by Henry IV. The restoration of France to Catholicism, as well as to power, was immediately followed by the most important consequences to Italy. It was with the assent and aid of the Italian princes that Henry IV had secured his fortunes; and they did not doubt but that he would now prove himself grateful, and take part with them in their differ-ence with the Holy See. The crown of France was, besides, under great obligation to the house of Este. That family had advanced more than 1,000,000 of scudi to the royal house of France during the civil wars; this sum had never yet been repaid; and would have now sufficed to raise an army such as no pope could have hoped to withstand.

These, however, were not the considerations by which Henry IV was influenced. He knew that, notwithstanding his conversion to Catholicism, he should still be often obliged to do many things that could not fail to displease the Roman Court. In the affair of Ferrara, he saw nothing more than an opportunity for causing these things to be forgotten, and for once more raising the lilies, as his statesmen expressed it, at the Court of Rome. Without hesitation or delay, therefore, he sent assurances to the Holy Father of assistance from France. He declared himself not only ready to lead an army across the Alps

---

[3] Delfino describes the fear that was felt in Rome regarding him: "There is a well-founded idea firmly rooted among the people there, that the benediction bestowed on the King of France has been so great an offence to the "Catholic" and the Spaniards, that they will never forget it; and his holiness thinks this has been clearly shown in the affair of Ferrara." See Appendix, No. 70.

whenever the Pope should desire it, but, even if need were, to appear in person, with all his force, for the defence of the pontiff.

It was by this declaration that the matter was decided. The Roman Court, already sensible to the many embarrassments preparing for it, by the unfriendly dispositions of its neighbors, and the open resistance of Ferrara, now breathed again. " I cannot express," writes Ossat to the King, " what good-will, praise, and blessing your Majesty has obtained for your offer." He assures his master that, if his promise be fulfilled, he will assume a position similar to that held in the Church by Pepin and Charlemagne. On his part, the Pope now made immediate preparation for the formal excommunication of his opponent.

So much the more were the princes alarmed and surprised; they complained of black ingratitude, and lost all courage for supporting Cesare d'Este, which they would otherwise doubtless have done, either openly or in secret, with their whole powers.

These things produced an immediate effect on Ferrara. The rigid government of Alfonso had of necessity caused many to feel dissatisfied. Cesare was new to the duties of sovereignty, without effectual talent, and wholly inexperienced. He had formed no personal acquaintance even with the members of his council, until holding his first sitting as their sovereign.[4] His older friends, those who knew him, and in whom he felt confidence, were despatched to different courts, so that he had no one near him on whom he could firmly rely, or with whom he could hold confidential communication. He could not fail to make false steps. From the highest class downward there prevailed a feeling of insecurity; such as frequently precedes approaching ruin. The more important personages, those who possessed a share in the power of the country, already began to calculate the advantages that might accrue from a change, and made advances toward the conclusion of a secret compact with the pontiff. An-

[4] Niccolò Contarini: " Cesare retired to consult his ministers, of whom many, because of the retirement in which he had lived (for so did he enjoin, who held command), were unknown to him except by sight; he was incapable of arriving at any resolution of himself, and was much unsettled in his thoughts, because those who advised him were full of their own private purposes and of their hopes from Rome, toward which court they looked, and by whose prom- ises their loyalty had been previously infected." Ossat also (" Lettres," i. 495) asserts the main source of his misfortunes to have been " the little fidelity found even among his counsellors, who in part because of his irresolution, and partly to gain pensions and other benefits from the Church, hoped and feared more from the Holy See than from him, and so turned toward the Pope."

tonio Montecatino proceeded to Rome for that purpose; but the
most grievous and most unfortunate circumstance was, that dissensions arose in the house of Este itself.   Lucrezia had detested
the father of Cesare; she hated himself no less, and would not
consent to be his subject.   She herself, the sister of the duke
just departed, made no difficulty of entering into an alliance
with Clement VIII and Cardinal Aldobrandino.

The Pope had meanwhile completed the act of excommunication.   On December 22, 1597, he went in all the pomp of a
solemn procession to St. Peter's, and ascended with his immediate attendants to the loggia of the Church; a cardinal read
the bull before the people.   Don Cesare d'Este was therein declared an enemy to the Church, guilty of treason, fallen under
the greater censures and under the sentence of malediction:
his subjects were freed from their oath of allegiance, and his
officers were admonished to quit his service.   After the bull
had been read, the Pope, assuming a look of anger, threw a
large burning taper on the ground in the piazza beneath him.
Trumpets and drums pealed forth, cannon were fired, and the
roar of the populace rose above all.

Circumstances were so arranged, that this excommunication
necessarily produced its full effect.   A copy of the bull was
carried into Ferrara by one of her own inhabitants,[5] who had
it sewed into his clothes and delivered it to the bishop.   On the
following day, December 31, 1597, a canon of the cathedral was
to be interred.   The church was hung with black, and the people
had assembled to hear the funeral sermon.   The bishop ascended the pulpit and began to speak of death.   " But much
worse," he suddenly exclaimed, " than the death of the body,
is the perdition of the soul which now threatens us all."   He
ceased speaking and commanded the bull to be read aloud.
In this document, all who would not separate themselves from
Don Cesare were menaced with being " cut off like withered
branches from the tree of spiritual life."   This being done, the
bull was fixed on the church door, the people filled the place
with sighs and lamentations, and dismay seized the whole city.

[5] A certain Coralta. At his first attempt to enter he was driven back by
the soldiers; he made his way by declaring that he lived there, and had
not yet set off for Bologna (though he
had indeed just arrived from that city,
and had dismounted from his horse
at a short distance from the gate).   Dis-
coursing with the soldiers, he seated
himself among them; at last feeling secure, he bade the guard farewell, entered the city, and gave the bishop the
bull with the letter from the Archbishop
of Bologna.—" Relatione di quello che,"
etc.

Don Cesare was not the man to appease a commotion of this character. He had been advised to enlist Swiss and Germans for his defence, but could not summon resolution to do so. He would not have Catholics, because they were adherents of the Pope; still less would he take Protestants, because they were heretics. " Just as if he had anything to do," says Nicolò Contarini, " with exercising the office of an inquisitor." He now asked his confessor what he was to do. This was a Jesuit, Benedetto Palma. He recommended Don Cesare to submit.

He [6] was now in so difficult a position that, in order to present this submission under favorable conditions, he was obliged to have recourse to the person whom he knew to be his most violent enemy. To secure a tolerable retreat, he was compelled to avail himself of the secret, and in a certain sense treasonable connection, into which Lucrezia had entered with Rome. Commissioned by the duke, Lucrezia therefore betook herself, abating nothing of her accustomed splendor, to the enemy's camp.

The adherents of Cesare constantly affirmed that she might have obtained better conditions for him; but won over by the promise of Bertinoro, which she was to hold for life with the title of its duchess, and personally attracted by the young and clever cardinal, she agreed to all that was required from her. On January 12, 1598, the treaty was drawn up, by virtue of which Don Cæsar resigned his rights to Ferrara, Comacchio, and his portion of Romagna, in return for which he was to be released fom the ban of the Church. He had flattered himself that he should at least save something, and felt that to be so completely despoiled was indeed very hard. He once more called together the principal magistrates of the city, the council of elders (Giudice de' Savj), with some few nobles and men of the law (doctoren), to hear their advice. They gave him no consolation; each was already thinking only of the means by which he might best secure his own position with the new

[6] Contarini: " As he who abandons all hope will often commit himself rather to the guidance of his enemy than to the direction of a friend, so Cesare now went to seek the Duchess of Urbino, and to her, whom he well knew to be of good intelligence with Cardinal Aldobrandino, he remitted all his fortunes. She accepted the office gladly; having arrived at the point that from the first she had desired: with a great train, as if in triumph, and accompanied by the Marchese Bentivoglio, commandent of the duke's forces, she performed her voyage." He considers Lucrezia ' a woman of dark and evil thoughts, she was long the most bitter enemy of Don Cesare, though she pretended the contrary.' "

power that was expected. In all quarters men were already emulating each other in eagerness to tear down the arms of the house of Este, and to drive out their officers. For the prince nothing further remained but to sign the deed of his expulsion, and depart from the inheritance of his fathers.

And thus did the house of Este lose Ferrara. The archives, museum, library, and a part of the artillery, which Alfonso I had cast with his own hand, were removed to Modena; all besides was lost. The widow of Alfonso carried away her property in fifty wagons. The sister of the latter, married in France, assumed to herself the claims of her family to that crown; but the most unexpected result was that witnessed in the case of Lucrezia. No time was allowed her for taking possession of her duchy. On February 12th, exactly one month after she had concluded the treaty just described, she expired. When her testament was opened, it was found that the very man who had driven her family from their ancient possessions, Cardinal Aldobrandino, was constituted heir to her wealth—universal legatee. She had even made over to him her claims, which were now to be contested with Cesare himself. It would seem that she had desired to bequeath to her ancient enemy an opponent who might embitter his whole life. There is something fiend-like in this woman, who appears to have found pleasure and satisfaction in securing the destruction of her house.

And now the ducal sovereignty was superseded by that of the Ecclesiastical States. On May 8th the Pope himself entered Ferrara. He desired immediately to enjoy the sight of his new conquest, and to bind it by suitable institutions to the Church.

He began with clemency and acts of grace. Ecclesiastical dignities were conferred on several among the leading men of Ferrara.[7] Cardinals' hats, bishoprics, and auditorships were liberally distributed. Among those promoted was the young Bentivoglio, who was made private chamberlain to the Pope. The power of the dukes had been founded on their possession of municipal privileges; the Pope now resolved to restore to

[7] Contarini: "To Bevilacqua, who had great power, the Latin patriarchate of Constantinople was given, Saciato was created auditor of the Rota, and abbacies were bestowed on others."

the citizens their ancient rights. He formed a council (conseglio) from the three classes, giving twenty-seven seats in it to the greater nobles, fifty-five to the inferior nobility and principal citizens, and eighteen to the guilds of the trades. These rights were carefully distinguished. Those of the first class were most important; but to balance this advantage came the fact, that their nomination depended for the most part on the will of the Pope. To this " conseglio " Clement now intrusted the duty of providing for the due supply of the means of life to the city, the regulation of the rivers, the appointment of judges and mayors (podestas), and even the nomination to chairs in the university. All these were rights that the duke had jealously reserved to himself, and these changes were the commencement, as will be obvious, of a new order of things. Attention was also given to the welfare of the lower classes. The severity of the fiscal arrangements was materially modified and relaxed.[8]

But these advantageous measures were not applicable in all cases. Even the papal government was not wholly formed of clemency and mildness. The nobles were soon dissatisfied with the judicial administration of ecclesiastical officers. The principal " Giudice de' Savj," Montecatino, found the restrictions imposed on the rights of his office insufferable, and sent in his resignation. Universal discontent was excited by the circumstance that Pope Clement thought it requisite to secure himself in his new conquest by the erection of a fortress. The representations made by the inhabitants for the prevention of this purpose, though most earnest and imploring, were unavailing. It was precisely one of the most populous parts of the city that was selected for the citadel;[9] whole streets were removed, together with churches, oratories, hospitals, the summer residences of the duke and his court, and the beautiful Belvedere, celebrated by so many poets.

It had, perhaps, been expected, that by these devastations the memory of the ducal house would be completely obliterated; but they served, on the contrary, to restore it to life; the half-

[8] Frizzi, " Memorie," v. p. 25.
[9] " Dispaccio Delfino, 7 June, 1598: " " The Pope thinks of building a citadel on the side next Bologna, because of the discontent displayed by the nobles at the want of respect shown them by the ministers of justice, and because the ancient dues of the municipality were not restored to them, complaining that they have been deceived." See Appendix, No. 70.

forgotten attachment to the hereditary line of princes returned. All those who had belonged to the court retired to Modena; and Ferrara, which had never been particularly animated, became more than ever desolate.

But it was not possible that all who wished to follow the court should do so. There is yet remaining a MS. chronicle by an old servant of the ducal house, in which he sets forth the proceedings of Alfonso's court with great complacency. Its pleasures, its concerts, its sermons—all are enumerated. " But now," he says in conclusion, " all this has passed by; now there is no longer a duke in Ferrara; there are no more princesses, no concerts, and no concert-givers; so passes the glory of this world; for others, the world may be rendered pleasant by changes, but not for me, who am left behind, alone, aged, frail, and poor. Nevertheless, God be praised." [10]

Section IX.—Commotions Among the Jesuits

The great and fortunate results obtained by Clement VIII from acting in harmony with the policy of France were manifestly calculated to bind him more and more closely to its interests. He now found the advantage of having conducted himself with so much caution in the affairs of the League; of his having opposed no obstacle to the development of events in France, and of having resolved, though it were but at the last moment, to grant the desired absolution. The war now proceeding on the frontiers of France and the Netherlands awakened as lively an interest in Rome as though the cause had been their own, and all were decidedly on the French side. When the Spaniards succeeded in the conquest of Calais and Amiens, a dissatisfaction was produced at the Court of Rome, such as, according to Ossat, " could not be described; an extremity of sorrow, shame, and indignation." [1] Delfino tells us, that the Pope and his nephews feared, lest the Spaniards should

[10] " Cronica di Ferrara: " " ' Sic transit gloria mundi.' For some to change their plans is agreeable, but not for me, who have remained without a master; old, deprived of all my teeth, and poor, yet let God be praised. [Laudetur Deus]."

[1] " Ossat à Villeroy," May 14, 1596; 20 April, 1597: " The dangers of Marseilles caused great alarm to the Pope and his nephews; the losses of Calais and Amiens grieved him sorely, and the rather because worse things were reported; they dreaded lest, on the decline of the French importance, the Spaniards should avenge themselves for the absolution; therefore it is that Rome rejoices in the prosperity of France."

avenge on them the disappointment which Philip of Spain had endured in regard to the absolution.[2]   Fortunately, Henry IV soon retrieved his endangered reputation by the reconquest of Amiens.

Not that people at Rome had begun to feel any affection for those whom they had formerly combated. The measures taken by those chiefs of the clergy, who had been the first to attach themselves to Henry, and had founded the opposition party previously described, had never been forgotten; promotion was much more readily accorded to the adherents of the League, when they returned voluntarily—that is, when they were precisely in the same condition as the Curia itself. But there soon arose a Catholic party, even among the adherents of the King (for the opinions of men, however nearly they may approximate, yet manifest varieties of disposition); whose determination it was to evince the most rigid Catholicism, because they desired above all things to maintain a good understanding with the Court of Rome. To this party the pontiff especially attached himself, hoping to reconcile all the differences still existing between the French and Roman interests; he desired and endeavored above all to accomplish the restoration of the Jesuits, who, as we have related, had been driven out of France, and thus to secure a wider field for the extension of the Romish doctrines, notwithstanding the adverse disposition manifested in France, and in defiance of its influence.

In this design Clement was aided by a commotion in the Society of Jesus itself, and which, though taking its rise within the order, had yet close analogy with the change of the general tendencies in the Roman Court.

So strangely are the affairs of this world sometimes complicated, that at the moment when the connection of the Jesuits with Spain was charged against them by the university of Paris, as their heaviest crime; when it was asserted and believed in France that every Jesuit was bound by a fifth vow to devote himself to Spain and to pray daily for King Philip;[3] at that very moment the company was enduring the most violent assaults in Spain itself; first from discontented members of its own body, then from the Inquisition, next from another ecclesiastical order, and finally from the King himself.

[2] See Appendix, No. 70.   [3] " Pro nostro rege Philippo."

196 RANKE

This was a turn of affairs that had its origin in more than one cause, but of which the immediate occasion was as follows.

At the first establishment of the order, the elder and already educated men, who had just entered it, were for the most part Spaniards; the members joining it from other nations were chiefly young men, whose characters had yet to be formed. It followed naturally that the government of the society was, for the first ten years, almost entirely in Spanish hands. The first general congregation was composed of twenty-five members, eighteen of whom were Spaniards.[4] The first three generals belonged to the same nation. After the death of the third, Borgia, in the year 1573, it was once more a Spaniard, Polanco, who had the best prospect of election.

It was, however, manifest that his elevation would not have been regarded favorably, even in Spain itself. There were many new converts in the society, who were Christianized Jews. Polanco also belonged to this class, and it was not thought desirable that the supreme authority in a body so powerful, and so monarchically constituted, should be confided to such hands.[5] Pope Gregory XIV, who had received certain intimations on this subject, considered a change to be expedient on other grounds also. When a deputation presented itself before him from the congregation assembled to elect their general, Gregory inquired how many votes were possessed by each nation; the reply showed that Spain held more than all the others put together. He then asked from which nation the generals of the order had hitherto been taken. He was told that there had been three, all Spaniards. "It will be just, then," replied Gregory, "that for once you should choose one from among the other nations." He even proposed a candidate for their election.

The Jesuits opposed themselves for a moment to this suggestion, as a violation of their privileges, but concluded by electing the very man proposed by the pontiff. This was Eberhard Mercurianus.

A material change was at once perceived, as the consequence of this choice. Mercurianus, a weak and irresolute man, re-

---

[4] Sacchinus, vii. 99. In the second general congregation the disproportion was decreased, though not to any great extent. Of thirty-nine members, twenty-four were Spaniards. See Appendix, No. 93.

[5] Sacchinus, "Historia Societatis Jesu," pars iv.; sive Everardus, lib. i.: "The origin of these movements was twofold: national rivalries, and the hatred of new converts felt by the Spaniards." See Appendix, No. 93.

signed the government of affairs, first indeed to a Spaniard
again, but afterward to a Frenchman, his official admonitor; factions were formed, one expelling the other from the offices of
importance, and the ruling powers of the order now began to
meet occasional resistance from its subordinate members.

But a circumstance of much higher moment was, that on the
next vacancy—in the year 1581—this office was conferred on
Claudius Acquaviva, a Neapolitan, belonging to a house previously attached to the French party, a man of great energy, and
only thirty-eight years old.

The Spaniards then thought they perceived that their nation,
by which the society had been founded and guided on its early
path, was now to be forever excluded from the generalship.
Thereupon they became discontented and refractory,[6] and conceived the design of making themselves less dependent on Rome,
either by the appointment of a commissary-general for the
Spanish provinces, or by whatever other expedient might secure
the desired result. Acquaviva, on the other hand, was not disposed to concede the smallest portion of that authority accorded
to him by the letter of the constitution For the purpose of
restraining the disaffected, he set over them superiors on whose
devotion to himself he could rely; young men, whose opinions
as well as age were more in harmony with his own,[7] and also,
perhaps, as was affirmed, certain members of inferior merit—
coadjutors, who were not invested with all the privileges of
the order, and who therefore depended, one and all, on the
protection of the general—they were, besides, Neapolitans[8] and
his countrymen.

The aged, learned, and experienced fathers (*patres*) thus
saw themselves excluded, not from the supreme dignity only,

[6] Mariana, " Discurso de las Enfer-
medades de la Compañia": " The Spanish nation is persuaded that it is to be
forever deprived of the generalship;
and this belief, whether true or false,
cannot but occasion displeasure and
disunion; and all the more, because this
nation founded the company, upheld it,
directed it, and even sustained it for a
long time from its own substance."
See Appendix, No. 93.
[7] Mariana, c. xii.: " They place mere
boys in the government, because they
are more enterprising, and are more
easily bent to the necessities of the
times."
[8] We have here, in addition to Mari-

ana, the memorials presented to
Clement VIII, which are also of moment. They are printed in the " Tuba
magnum clangens sonum ad Clementem
XI.," p. 583: "We see how the general,
to the great detriment of our religion,
and the scandal of the world, has no
regard to age, merit, or service, but
appoints whom he pleases as superiors;
for the most part, young men and
novices, who, without any merit or experience, preside with great arrogance
over their seniors; . . . and, lastly,
the general, being a man, has also his
private affections; and, because he is a
Neapolitan, the Neapolitans are in the
best condition."

but also from the official appointments of the provinces. Acquaviva declared that their own defects were to blame for this; one was choleric, another melancholy. Naturally, says Mariana, distinguished men are like others—liable to be afflicted with some defect. But the true cause was, that Acquaviva feared these fathers, and desired more pliant tools for the execution of his commands. Men have generally a particular satisfaction in the active part accorded to them in public affairs, and will at least not quietly suffer themselves to be forcibly expelled from their possession. Jealousies and disputes arose in all the colleges; the new superiors were received with silent animosity; they could carry out no measure of essential importance, and were but too happy when they could make their way without troubles and commotions. They had, nevertheless, the power of avenging themselves, and they in their turn conferred the subordinate offices exclusively on their personal adherents (for they could not long fail to secure adherents, the monarchical constitution of the order, and the ambition of its members considered). Of the more unmanageable among their opponents they freed themselves by transferring them to other provinces; and this they took care to do, precisely when some deliberation of importance was impending. Thus a system of personal offences and retaliations was established; every member had the right of pointing out whatever defects he perceived in another—nay, it was imposed on him as a duty to do so—a regulation that might not be without some utility in the comparative innocence of a small association, but which had now become a system of the most abominable espionage and tale-bearing. It was made the instrument of concealed ambition, and of hatred wearing the appearance of friendship. " Were anyone to read over the records of Rome," says Mariana, " he would perhaps not find a single upright man, at least, among us who are at a distance : " universal distrust prevailed; there was none that would have uttered his thoughts without reserve, even to his own brother.

These disorders were increased by the fact that Acquaviva could not be induced to leave Rome for the purpose of visiting the provinces, as Lainez and Borgia had done. This was excused by the declaration, that it was advantageous to have the statement of affairs in writing, and in an unbroken series, without the interruption proceeding from the contingencies of a journey. But the immediate consequence certainly was, that the " provincials," through whose hands passed the whole of the correspondence, acquired a still further increase of independence. It was useless to complain of them, since they could easily foresee and provide against all complaints in such a manner as to render them nugatory, and this the more certainly, because Acquaviva was always disposed to favor their side. Their places might be fairly considered secured to them for life.

Under these circumstances, the older Jesuits in Spain became convinced that a state of things, which they felt to be a tyranny, would never be changed or amended by efforts confined within the limits of the society; they consequently resolved to look around for help from those beyond its influence.

They first had recourse to the national spiritual authority of their own country—the Inquisition. A great number of offences were reserved, as is well known, to the jurisdiction of the Inquisition. One of the discontented Jesuits, impelled, as he affirmed, by a scruple of conscience, accused his order of concealing, and even remitting, transgressions of the kind so reserved, when the criminal was one of their society. The Inquisition immediately caused the Provincial implicated, together with his most active associates, to be arrested.[9] Other accusations being made in consequence of these arrests, the Inquisition commanded that the statutes of the order should be placed before it, and proceeded to make further seizures of parties accused. The excitement occasioned by these things among the orthodox Spaniards was all the more violent, from their being unacquainted with the cause of these arrests, and from the prevalence of an opinion, that the Jesuits were seized on account of some heresy.

The Inquisition was, however, competent to inflict a punishment on the criminal only: it could not prescribe changes in the regulations of the society. When the affair, therefore, had proceeded thus far, the discontented members applied to the King also, assailing him with long memorials, wherein they complained of the defects in their constitution. The character of this constitution had never been agreeable to Philip II. He used

[9] Sachinus, pars v. lib. vi. n. 85: " Quidam e confessariis, seu vere seu falso, delatus ad provincialem tum Castellæ, Antonium Marcenium; erat de tentata peullæ per sacras confessiones pudicitia, quod crimen in Hispania sacrorum quæsitorum judicio reservabatur."

to say that he could see through all the other orders, but that the order of Jesuits he could not understand. He seemed to be startled and struck by the representations laid before him of the abuses resulting from absolute power, and the disorders attendant on secret accusations. Amid all the demands made on his time by that great European conflict in which he was engaged, Philip yet found means to bestow attention on this affair also. He at once commanded Manrique, bishop of Cartagena, to subject the order to a visitation, with particular reference to these points.

It will be remarked that this was an attack affecting the character of the institution, and that of its chief himself; it received increased importance from the fact of its originating in that country whence the society had drawn its existence, and where it had first taken a firm position.

Acquaviva did not suffer himself to quail before it. He was a man who concealed an inflexible intrepidity of character beneath extreme gentleness and amenity of manner; of a disposition similar to that of Clement VIII, and, indeed, of many eminent men of that day; above all things deliberate, moderate, patient, and taciturn. He would never permit himself to pronounce a positive judgment; he would not even suffer one to be pronounced in his presence; least of all, when it concerned an entire nation. His secretaries were expressly commanded to avoid every offensive or bitter word. He loved piety, even in its external forms. At the altar his deportment expressed profound enjoyment of the service; yet he was averse to everything that tended toward enthusiasm or fanaticism. He refused to allow an exposition of the Song of Solomon to be printed, because he found offence in the expressions which appeared to hover on the confines separating spiritual from material love. Even when uttering censures he won affection; rendering manifest the superiority of calmness: he reconducted the erring into the paths of right by pure reason and clear argument. Youth clung to him with enthusiastic attachment. " One must needs love him," writes Maximilian of Bavaria, from Rome, to his father, " if one do but look at him." These qualities; his unwearied activity, distinguished birth, and the constantly increasing importance of his order, secured him a very eminent position in Rome. If his antagonists had gained over the national au-

thorities in Spain, he had the Court of Rome on his side.   With
that court he had been familiar from his youth up.   He was
chamberlain when he entered the order ; and he had the power of
managing it with that mastery, which is derived from native
talent, and perfected by long practice.[10]

The character of Sixtus V [1] made it particularly easy for
Acquaviva to excite the antipathies of that pontiff against the
proceedings of the Spaniards.   Pope Sixtus had formed the
hope, as we know, of rendering Rome, more decidedly than it
ever yet was, the metropolis of Christendom.   Acquaviva assured him, that the object really labored for in Spain was no
other than increased independence of Rome.   Pope Sixtus hated
nothing so much as illegitimate birth; and Acquaviva caused
him to be informed that Manrique, the bishop selected as " Visitator " of the Jesuits, was illegitimate.   These were reasons sufficient to make Sixtus recall the assent he had already given to
the visitation.   He even summoned the case of the provincial
before the tribunals of Rome.   From his successor, Gregory
XIV, the general succeeded in obtaining a formal confirmation
of the rule of the order.

But his antagonists also were unyielding and crafty.   They
perceived that the general must be attacked in the Court of
Rome itself.   They availed themselves of his momentary absence.   Acquaviva had been charged with the arrangement of a
difference between Mantua and Parma, to win Clement VIII
to their wishes.   In the summer of 1592, at the request of the
Spanish Jesuits and Philip II, but without the knowledge of
Acquaviva, the pontiff commanded that a general congregation
should be held.

Astonished and alarmed, Acquaviva hastened back.   To the
generals of the Jesuits these " Congregations " were no less
inconvenient than were the Convocations of the Church to the
popes; and if his predecessors were anxious to avoid them,
how much more cause had Acquaviva, against whom there prevailed so active an enmity!   But he was soon convinced that
the arrangement was irrevocable; [2] he therefore resumed his

---

[10] Sacchinus, and still more particularly Juvencius, " Hist. Soc. Jesu," partis quintæ tomus posterior, xi. 21, and
xxv. 33-41.

[1] See Appendix, § 4, Nos. 49 to 56.

[2] In a " Consulta del Padre Cl. Acquaviva coi suoi Padri assistenti," MS. of
the Corsini Library, n. 1055, which gives,
upon the whole, a faithful relation of
these internal dissensions, and is, in
general, strictly in accord with Mariana,
Acquaviva is presented as rendering the

composure and said, "We are obedient sons; let the will of the holy father be done." He then hastened to take his measures.

He contrived to obtain extensive influence over the elections, and was so fortunate as to see many of his most formidable adversaries, Mariana, for example, rejected, even in Spain.

When the congregation was assembled, he did not wait to be attacked. In the very first sitting he declared that he had had the misfortune to displease some of his brethren; and, therefore, begged that his conduct might be investigated before any other business was entered on. A commission was thereupon appointed, and charges were formally made; but it was impossible to convict him of violating any positive law: he was much too prudent to expose himself to such an accusation, and was triumphantly acquitted.

Having thus secured himself personally, he joined the assembly in its investigation of the proposals regarding the general affairs of the institute.

Philip of Spain had demanded some changes, and had recommended others for consideration. On two things he insisted: the resignation of certain papal privileges; those of reading forbidden books, for example, and of granting absolution for the crime of heresy; and a law, by virtue of which every novice who entered the order should surrender whatever patrimonial rights he might possess, and should even resign all his benefices. These were matters in regard to which the order came into collision with the Inquisition and the civil government. After some hesitation, the demands of the King were complied with, and principally through the influence of Acquaviva himself.

But the points recommended by Philip for consideration were of much higher moment. First of all came the questions, whether the authority of the superiors should not be limited to a certain period; and whether a general congregation should not be held at certain fixed intervals? The very essence and being of the institute, the rights of absolute sover-

following account of a conversation held by himself with the Pope: "His holiness said, that I was not sufficiently well informed on subjects of religion; that I had been deceived by false accusers and had proved myself too credulous." Among the causes by which a congregation was rendered necessary, the following were specified: "Because many excellent and able men, being but slightly known to the generals, have never any share in the government; but, by coming to Rome, to attend the congregations, they would become better known, and might thus more easily acquire a part in the said government; so that this should not continue to be almost entirely restricted to a few persons."

eignty, were here brought into question. Acquaviva was not on this occasion disposed to comply. After an animated discussion, the congregation rejected these propositions of Philip; but the Pope, also, was convinced of their necessity. What had been refused to the King was now commanded by the Pope. By the plenitude of his apostolic power, he determined and ordained that the superiors and rectors should be changed every third year; and that, at the expiration of every sixth year, a general congregation should be assembled.[3]

It is, indeed, true that the execution of these ordinances did not effect so much as had been hoped from them. The congregation could be won over, and, though the rectors were changed, yet they were selected out of so narrow a circle, that the same men were soon returned to their appointments. It was, nevertheless, a very serious blow to the society, that it had been compelled, by internal revolt and interference from without, to a change in its statutes.

And there was already a new storm arising from the same quarter.

At their first establishment, the Jesuits had assented to the doctrinal system of the Thomists. Ignatius himself had expressly enforced on his disciples the tenets propounded by the angelic doctor (Doctor Angelicus).

But they very soon became persuaded that with these doctrines they could not perfectly attain their end in their contest with the Protestants. They wished to be independent in their tenets as well as in their lives. It was mortifying to the Jesuits to follow in the train of the Dominicans, to whom St. Thomas had belonged, and who were regarded as the natural expositors of his opinions. After they had already given so many intimations of these views and feelings, that allusion had occasionally been made in the Inquisition to the free mode of thinking perceptible among the Jesuit fathers,[4] Acquaviva came forward in the year 1584, proclaiming them openly in his " Order of Studies." He affirmed that St. Thomas was, indeed, an author deserving the highest approbation; but that it would be an insufferable yoke to be compelled to follow his footsteps in

[3] Juvencius furnishes a circumstantial notice as to these things in his first book, which he calls the eleventh, " Societatis domesticis motibus agitata," and it is from them that I derive the account given in the text.

[4] Lainez himself was suspected by the Spanish Inquisition.—Llorente, iii. 83.

all things, and on no point to be allowed a free opinion; that many ancient doctrines had been more firmly established by recent theologians, who had brought forward many new arguments, which served admirably in the conflict with heretics; and that in all such it was permitted to follow these doctors.

This was amply sufficient to occasion powerful excitement in Spain, where the chairs of theology were occupied, for the most part, by Dominicans. The "Order of Studies" was declared to be the boldest, most presumptuous, and dangerous book of the kind; both the King and the Pope were applied to on the subject.[5]

But how greatly must the commotion have increased when the system of the Thomists was soon afterward positively abandoned in one of the most important doctrinal works of the Jesuits!

In the whole domain of theology, Catholic and Protestant, the disputes respecting grace and merits, free-will and pre-destination, were still the most important and exciting; they continually occupied the minds and employed the learning and speculative powers of clergy and laity alike. On the Protestant side, a majority was secured to that severe doctrine of Calvin, of the particular decree of God, according to which " some were predestined to eternal blessedness, and others to everlasting damnation." The Lutherans, with their milder views, were here at disadvantage, and lost ground, now in one place and now in another. A different tendency of opinions was mani-fested on the Catholic side. Whenever there was the slightest disposition shown to the very mildest form of Protestant belief, or even to a more rigid construction of St. Augustine's Ex-positions, as, for example, in the case of Bajus at Louvain, it was instantly attacked and suppressed. On this occasion the Jesuits displayed particular zeal. The system of doctrine pro-pounded by the Council of Trent, and which would never have been established but for the influence of their brethren, Lainez and Salmeron, was defended by them against every symptom

[5] Pegna, in Serry, " Historia Congre-gationum de auxiliis divinæ gratiæ," p 8: " This book being given over to the censorship, it was declared by those censors (Mariana and Serry speak of the Inquisition) that it was the most dangerous, rash and arrogant book that had ever appeared on a similar subject; and that, if its precepts were put in practice, great injury and many dis-turbances would be occasioned to the Christian republic."

of deviation toward the tenets that had then been abjured and abandoned; nor did even that system always suffice to content their polemical zeal. In the year 1588, Luis Molina of Evora came forward with a book, in which he examined these disputed points anew, and labored to explain the difficulties still remaining, in new arguments.[6] His especial object in this work was to vindicate a yet wider sphere of action for the free-will of man than was asserted by the doctrines of St. Thomas or of Trent. In Trent the work of salvation had been declared to be chiefly founded on the inherent righteousness of Christ, which, being infused into us, calls forth or gives birth to love, conducts to all virtues and to good works, and finally produces justification. Molina proceeds an important step further. He maintained that free-will, even without the help of grace, can produce morally good works; that it can resist temptation; and can elevate itself to various acts of hope, faith, love, and repentance.[7] When man has advanced to this point, then God, for the sake of Christ's merits, grants him grace,[8] and by means of this he experiences the supernatural operations of sanctification; but even in the reception of this grace, and in the furtherance of its growth, free-will is continually in action: everything, in fact, depends on this will; it rests with us to make the help of God effectual or ineffectual. On the union of the will and of grace it is that justification depends; they are combined, as are two men who are rowing in a boat. It is obvious that Molina could not here admit the doctrine of predestination as announced by Augustine or by Thomas Aquinas. He considers it too stern—too cruel: he will not hear of any other predestination than that which is simply and purely foreknowledge. Now God, from his supreme insight into the nature of each man's will, has previous knowledge of what each will do in given cases, although he was left free to do the con-

[6] " Liberi arbitrii cum gratiæ donis concordia." In these controversies it has always been considered needful to distinguish carefully between the editions of Lisbon, 1588, of Antwerp, 1595, and of Venice, because they all differ from each other.

[7] Herein the general co-operation of God (" concursus generalis Dei ") is always presupposed; but in this nothing more is meant than the natural state of free-will, which certainly could not, without God, be what it is: God is ever present by general co-operation with the free-will, so that it naturally wills, or does not will, as he shall please. It is much in the same manner that Bellarmine identifies natural and divine law, because God is the author of nature.

[8] This grace also he apprehends and explains very naturally, Disput. 54: " When a man is pondering on matters of belief gathered from the statements of the preachers, or elsewhere, God's influence flows in some special manner into those statements, whereby he aids the perception of them."

trary; yet an event does not occur because God foreknew it, but God foresaw it because it would happen. This was a doctrine that certainly went into an extreme directly opposed to that of Calvin, and was also the first which attempted to rationalize this mystery, if we may so speak. It is intelligible, acute, and superficial, and could therefore not fail to produce a certain effect; it may be compared with the doctrine of the sovereignty of the people, which the Jesuits promulgated about that time.[9] That these opinions should provoke opposition in their own church was an inevitable consequence, had it been only that they departed from the Doctor Angelicus, whose " Summa " was still the principal text-book of Catholic theologians; they were even censured, and that openly, by certain members of their own society, as Henriquez and Mariana. But much more eagerly did the Dominicans engage in the defence of their patriarch. Not content with writing and preaching against Molina, they attacked him in their lectures also. It was at length agreed that a disputation should be held between the two parties, and this took place at Valladolid on March 4, 1594. The Dominicans, who believed themselves in exclusive possession of the orthodox creed, became vehement. " Are the keys of wisdom, then," exclaimed a Jesuit, " confided to your hands? " The Dominicans burst into loud outcries—they considered this to be an attack on St. Thomas himself.

Thenceforth a complete estrangement existed between these two orders; the Dominicans would have nothing more to do with the Jesuits. Of these last the greater number, if not all, took part with Molina. Acquaviva himself, with his " assistants," were on his side.

But here also the Inquisition prepared to interfere. The grand inquisitor—it was that same Geronimo Manrique who had been selected as " visitator of the order "—showed a disposition to condemn Molina; he gave him notice that his book

[9] This disposition toward rationalism had shown itself in other places also; as, for example, in the tenets maintained by Less and Hamel at Louvain, in 1585. As for what we are to consider sacred Scripture, it is not necessary that every word should have been inspired by the Holy Spirit." From the words they proceed at once to the truths of Scripture: " It is not necessary that each separate truth and opinion should have been communicated to the writer himself by the Holy Spirit." In these declarations we already find a part, at least, of the essential propositions of Molina. Here, too, attention is drawn to their entire disagreement with the views of the Protestants. " How widely do these opinions differ from those of Luther, Calvin, and other writers of these times, from whose doctrine and arguments it is difficult to vindicate the other [St. Augustine and Thomist] tenets! "

was not likely to escape with a mere reprobation or prohibition, but would be condemned to the flames. Of the complaints that Molina made against the Dominicans in return, the grand inquisitor refused to take cognizance.

This was a controversy by which the whole world of Catholicism was set in commotion, as well for the doctrines themselves as on account of their champions; it also greatly increased the violence of that enmity to the Jesuits which had arisen in Spain.

And from this state of things there resulted the extraordinary phenomenon, that while the Jesuits were driven out of France for their attachment to Spain, they were in that country made the objects of the most perilous assaults. In either country, political and religious motives combined to produce this result; the political was in both of the same character—it was a national opposition to the privileges and immunities of the order. In France it was more impetuous and fiercer, but in Spain it was more definite and better founded. In regard to doctrine, it was by their new tenets that the Jesuits had provoked hatred and persecution. Their doctrine of the sovereignty of the people, and the opinions they held as to regicide, were the causes of their ruin in France, their tenets respecting free-will had produced the injury they suffered in Spain.

This was a moment in the history of the society which was of infinite importance to its future direction.

Against the assaults of the national authorities, the Parliament and the Inquisition, Acquaviva sought aid from the central point and general referee of the whole Church—from the pontiff himself.

He availed himself of the favorable moment when the grand inquisitor, Manrique, had just died and his place had not yet been filled up, and prevailed on the Pope to summon the dispute concerning doctrine to Rome for examination. If the decision were only deferred, it would be an important point gained, for in Rome a variety of influences were at that time readily to be found, of which, at any critical moment, good and efficient use might be made. On October 9, 1596, the documents relating to the proceedings were sent to Rome, and the most learned theologians of both sides appeared to fight out their battle under the eyes of the sovereign-pontiff.[10]

[10] Pegna, " Pegna, Dean of the Rota, and a most sufficing witness of these things," as Serry calls him. " Molina, discerning what might result from his

In the French affair Clement took part with the Jesuits: he considered it unjustifiable that an entire order should be condemned on account of one single person who might have deserved punishment, more especially that order by whose efforts the restoration of Catholicism had been most effectually promoted, and which was so powerful a support to the Church. Was not the order suffering for its devotion to the Papal See and for the ardor with which it asserted the claims of the papacy to the highest power on earth? It was above all essential that the Pope should succeed in extinguishing the opposition still continued against him in France. The more intimate his connection became with Henry IV, the more perfect their harmony in regard to politics, so much the more effectual would his representations be; and the declarations of Henry were now constantly becoming more and more conciliatory.[1]

And herein the efforts of the Pope were greatly aided and facilitated by the well-considered conduct of the order.

The Jesuits carefully abstained from all evidence of irritation or aversion against the King of France, and they were also no longer inclined to plunge themselves into further danger for the lost cause of the League. When they became aware of the turn which the papal policy had taken, they at once adopted a similar direction. Father Commolet, who, even after the conversion of Henry IV, had exclaimed from the pulpit that an Ehud was needed to rise against him, and who, when the King became victor, was obliged to take flight; even he changed his opinion after arriving in Rome, and declared himself for the absolution of the King. Among all the cardinals there was none who contributed so largely to this absolution, whether by his readiness of concession, his conciliatory measures, or his personal influence with the Pope, as the Jesuit Toledo.[2] And these things the Jesuits did while the Parliament was continually passing new resolutions against them; decrees of which Acquaviva complained, but without

book being prohibited and burnt, as the inquisitor-general had warned him, instantly sent notice to Rome, where, by the labor of his general, his holiness summoned the cause before himself, ordering the Inquisition not to conclude on or give sentence in it."
[1] The Jesuits wished to deny that their affairs had become connected with politics; but we see from Bentivoglio, "Memorie," ii. 6, p. 395, how much re-

gard was paid to their interests by Cardinal Aldobrandini during the negotiations at Lyons; and it was precisely then that the King declared himself in their favor ("Le Roy au Cardinal Ossat, 20 Janv. 1601.")
[2] Du Perron à Villeroy, "Ambassades," i. 23: "I will only tell you that Cardinal Tolet has done wonders, and has shown himself a good Frenchman."

permitting himself to be hurried into violence or intemperate zeal on that account. It had not been found possible to expel all the members of the order, and those who remained in France now declared for the King, exhorting the people to be faithful to him and to love him. Many were already hastening to return to the places they had left, but Acquaviva did not approve this, and directed them to wait the permission of the King. They took care to secure that Henry should be made aware of both these circumstances, and he was highly pleased, thanking the general in special letters. The Jesuits did not neglect to use all the means they possessed for confirming him in these dispositions. Father Rocheome, who was called the French Cicero, prepared a popular apology for the order, which the King found particularly convincing.[3]

To these efforts on the part of the Pope and the order combined, there were now added certain political considerations of Henry IV himself. He saw, as he says in one of his despatches, that by the persecution of an order which counted so many members remarkable for talent and learning, which had so much power, and so large a body of adherents; he should raise up implacable enemies to himself, and might give occasion to conspiracies among the more rigid Catholics—a class still very numerous. He perceived that he could not expel the Jesuits from the places wherein they still maintained themselves—the attempt might even occasion the outbreak of popular commotions.[4] Henry had, besides, made such important concessions to the Huguenots, by the edict of Nantes, that he owed some new guarantee to Catholicism. In Rome people already began to murmur, and the Pope himself gave occasional intimations that he feared he had been deceived.[5] Finally, however, the King attained a position high enough to permit his taking a more comprehensive survey of the general state of things than his parliament had done, and had no longer cause to fear the connection of the Jesuits with Spain. Father Lorenzo Maggio hastened to France, in the name of the general, to assure the King with the most solemn oaths of the order's true allegiance. " Should it prove otherwise, then might all account himself and

[3] Gretser has translated it into Latin for the convenience of those who do not understand French.—Gretseri " Opera," tom. xi. p. 280.
[4] " Dispaccio del Re de 15 Agosto,

1603, al re Jacopo d' Inghilterra;" abridged in Siri, " Memorie recondite," i. p. 247.
[5] " Ossat à Villeroy," i. 503.

his brethren the very blackest of traitors." [6]   The King thought
it more advisable to make trial of their friendship than their
enmity. He saw that he could use them for his own advantage
against Spain.[7]

Influenced by so many motives of external policy and internal necessity, Henry declared himself, as early as 1600, and
during the negotiations of Lyons, ready to admit the order
again. He chose the Jesuit Cotton for his confessor, and, after
many previous indications of favor, an edict was published in
September, 1603, by which the Jesuits were re-established in
France. Certain conditions were imposed on them; the most
important being, that, for the future, all members of the order
in France, whether superior or subordinates, must be Frenchmen.[8] Henry doubted not that he had arranged all in a manner
that might justify his feeling perfect confidence.

He bestowed his favor on them without hesitation or reserve, giving them his assistance even in their own affairs, and
more particularly in their contentions with the Dominicans.

In this controversy, Clement VIII showed a lively theological interest. Sixty-five meetings and thirty-seven disputations
were held in his own presence on all the points that could be
brought into question as regarded the tenets under examination.
He wrote much on the subject himself; and, so far as we can
judge, was inclined toward the old established doctrines, and
to a decision in favor of the Dominicans. Bellarmine himself
said, that he did not deny the pontiff's inclination to declare
himself against the Jesuits, but that he also knew of a certainty
that his holiness would not do so. It would indeed have been
too dangerous, at a time when the Jesuits were the most distinguished apostles of the faith throughout the world, to break
with them about one article of their creed. They did, in fact,
once make a show of intending to demand a council, when the
Pope is said to have exclaimed, " They dare everything—everything!" [9] The French also took too decided a part to be safely

[5] Sully, liv. xvii. p. 307.
[7] He saw clearly that he might derive
service and facilities from them on many
occasions for his own advantage and
that of his friends against the Spaniards
themselves.—" Dispaccio in Siri."
[8] " Edictum Regium," in Juvencius,
p. v. lib. xii. n. 59. In Juvencius we find
all that was said at the time in favor of
the Jesuits; and in Ludovicus Lucius,

" Historia Jesuitica," Basileæ, 1627, lib.
ii. c. ii., whatever was said against them.
Neither clearly informs us of the points
on which the decision turned; they are,
nevertheless, to be more readily gathered from the defender than the accuser.
[9] Serry, 271. Contarini also affirms that
they uttered menaces: The dispute being removed to Rome, and discussed
among theologians, the Pope, and the

opposed. Henry IV was on the Jesuit side; either because he found their expositions convincing, which was certainly possible, or that he gave a particular support to that order which most earnestly opposed itself to Protestantism, as a means of placing his own orthodoxy beyond doubt. Cardinal du Perron took part in the congregations and supported the Jesuit disputants with well-directed zeal. He told Clement VIII that a Protestant might subscribe the creed of the Dominicans; and it is very probable that by this remark he may have produced an impression on the pontiff's mind.

The active rivalry between Spain and France, by which the whole world was set in commotion, became mingled with these disputes also. The Dominicans found as zealous a support from the Spaniards as did the Jesuits from the French.[10]

From all this it resulted that Clement VIII did not, in fact, pronounce any decision: it would have involved him in new perplexities had he offended either one or the other of those influential orders, or of those powerful sovereigns.

Section X.—Political Situation of Clement VIII

It was now generally made one of the most essential objects of the Papal See, to estrange from itself neither one nor the other of those two powers, with whom the balance of the Catholic world then rested. The Pope now sought to appease their mutual animosities; or, at least, to prevent them from breaking out into open war, and to maintain the Roman influence over both.

majority of those consulted, inclined to the opinion of the Dominicans; but the Jesuits, seeing themselves in danger of falling from that credit by which they pretended to hold the first place in the Catholic Church, as regarded doctrine, were resolved to use every means for warding off that blow. The tenet which they threatened to adopt, according to Contarini, was, that the Pope was certainly infallible; but that it was no article of faith to hold one man or another as the true Pope: The power of the Jesuits, and the authority of those who protected them, was so great, that all this was looked over, and a show made of not perceiving it: thus, instead of deciding on the controverted questions, they ended by temporizing, that they might not bring worse consequences on their shoulders.

[10] Principal passages in Du Perron:

"Ambassades et Negociations," liv. iii. tom. ii. p. 839. "Lettre du 23 Janvier, 1606": "The Spaniards openly profess to support the Jacobins (Dominicans), from hatred, as I think, to the friendship displayed toward your Majesty by the father-general of the Jesuits, and by almost all his order, excepting those who depend on the fathers Mendozze and Personius, particularly the English Jesuits; so that they seemed to intend changing a religious dispute into a quarrel of state." It is manifest from this that the Jesuits, a small fraction excepted, were now accounted to be on the French side. Serry tells us, p. 440, that the Dominicans were at that time excluded from the French Court: The preachers were less acceptable in France at that time, and had lately been removed from public offices about the court.

The papacy here appears to us in its most praiseworthy vocation, mediating and making peace.

It was to Clement VIII that the world was principally indebted for the peace concluded at Vervins on May 2, 1598. He seized the favorable moment when the King of France was compelled by the disordered state of his finances, and the King of Spain by the increasing feebleness of his advanced age, to think of some accommodation. He took the initiative, and it was from him that the first overture proceeded. The general of the Franciscans, Fra Bonaventura Calatagirona, whom he had happily selected and sent to France for this affair, removed the first and greatest difficulties. The Spaniards held a large number of fortresses in France, and were prepared to restore them all with the exception of Calais, but the French insisted on the restitution of Calais also; and it was by Fra Calatagirona that the Spaniards were prevailed on to resign it.

This being accomplished, the negotiations at Vervins were formally opened; a legate and a nuncio presided over them. The general of the Franciscans continued to mediate with the utmost ability; his secretary, Soto, also gained no slight credit in these affairs. The most important result was, that the King of France resolved to separate himself from his allies—England and Holland. This was instantly considered to be an advantage to Catholicism; because the secession of Henry from the Protestant system appeared hereby to be completed. Henry consented after long hesitations, and the Spaniards then made an effectual restitution of all their conquests; the right of possessorship was restored to its condition of the year 1559. The legate declared that his holiness would have more pleasure in this consummation than in the acquisition of Ferrara; that a peace, comprehending and tranquillizing all Christendom, would be of much higher importance in his estimation than the mere temporal conquest.[1]

Only one point was left unsettled by this peace—the dispute between Savoy and France. The Duke of Savoy had seized on Saluzzo, and would not consent to restore it. After many unavailing negotiations, Henry IV at length attacked the duke

[1] At the end of the edition of the " Mémoires d'Angoulême," by Didot, 1756, i. 131-163, will be found, under the title " Autres Mémoires," a detailed account of the negotiations at Vervins, which is remarkable for accuracy and impartiality: the notices given above are derived from this source; the last from p. 337. See Appendix, No. 75.

by force of arms. The management of this affair having been expressly committed to the Pope at Vervins, he felt that all depended on the restoration of peace in this quarter also; he pressed for it at every opportunity and in every audience; whenever the King sent him assurances of his devotion, he required this peace as a proof thereof, and as a favor that must be granted to himself. The real difficulty consisted in the fact that the interests of Italy in general seemed to suffer injury by the restitution of Saluzzo; the Italians could not willingly see the French regain possession of a province in Italy. It was that Minorite Calatagirona—so far as I can discover—by whom it was first proposed as an expedient, that Saluzzo should be left to the duke, but that France should be indemnified by the cession of Bresse, and some adjoining districts of Savoy.[2] The merit of carrying this proposal into actual effect is due to Cardinal Aldobrandino, by whom it was accomplished at Lyons, in the year 1600. The French, also, were grateful to him for this conclusion, because Lyons thus acquired an extension of her boundaries, which had been long desired.[3]

Under these fortunate circumstances, Clement VIII sometimes thought of directing the combined forces of the whole Catholic world, now united, under his auspices, against its old hereditary enemy. The Moorish war had again burst forth in Hungary; but even then it was thought that a continual increase of weakness had become perceptible in the Ottoman empire; the personal inefficiency of the sultans, the influence of the seraglio, and the perpetual insurrections, more especially in Asia, made it probable that something effectual might now be done against Turkey. The Pope, at least, did not fail on his part. Even so early as the year 1599 the sum he had expended on this war amounted to 1,500,000 scudi, and we soon afterward find a papal army of 12,000 men on the Danube. But how much more important were the consequences that might be expected, if the powers of the West could once be united on a large scale for an Eastern expedition—above all, if Henry IV would resolve to combine his forces with those of Austria. The Pope neglected nothing that might encourage him to this; and Henry did, in fact, write to the Venetians, immediately after

[2] "Ossat to Villeroy," March 25, 1599.
[3] Bentivoglio gives us these transactions circumstantially, in the most important section of his "Memorie" (c. 2-c. 6).

the peace of Vervins, to the effect that he hoped shortly to embark in Venice, like the French of old times, for an expedition against Constantinople. He repeated his promise at the conclusion of the peace with Savoy; [4] but it is certain that its execution required to be preceded by a much more cordial understanding than could possibly have been attained, so soon after collisions of so much violence.[5]

But, on the other hand, the opposition and rivalry still subsisting between the two principal powers were more than once advantageous to the Papal See in its own affairs. Pope Clement had, indeed, once more occasion to avail himself of them for the interests of the States of the Church.

Amid so many brilliant undertakings, and so successful a progress in external affairs, Clement failed not to exercise a rigorous and very monarchical authority in his own court and States.

The new arrangement given by Sixtus V to the college of cardinals seemed calculated to secure it, for the first time, a due and legitimate influence on public affairs. But forms do not of necessity include the substance, and the direct contrary took place. The course of business was impeded by legal technicalities, and the immobility to which a deliberative assembly is condemned, principally because of the conflict of opinion arising on every question, rendered it impossible that Clement should confide important affairs to the congregations. At the first he continued to consult them—although even then he frequently deviated from their decisions; afterward, he communicated matters only when on the point of conclusion. The consistories were soon used rather for the publication of ordinances than for consultation; and the Pope at length employed them for subordinate affairs or mere formalities only.[6]

The new direction which Clement had given to the policy of the Roman Court, indubitably rendered this mode of proceeding, to a certain extent, needful; but he was also partly

---

[4] "Lettre du Roi," in the appendix to the second volume of Ossat's "Letters," p. 11.

[5] See Appendix, No. 75.

[6] Delfino: "The consistories now serve for no other purpose than to receive communications of appointments to benefices, and to publish the resolutions of all kinds taken by the Pope. The congregations, from that of the Inquisition down (which has, however, preserved itself in some little decorum, and meets weekly); even those of the monastic orders, and of bishops, are for appearance only; for if they pass resolutions in one manner, the Pope executes affairs in another; and that in the most important matters, such as sending aid to princes, despatching legates, or appointing governors."

induced to adopt it by his personal inclination for absolute sovereignty.[7] The country was governed in a similar spirit. The Pope decreed new taxes without asking counsel of any one. The revenues of the communes were placed under special supervision; the barons were subjected to the most rigid application of the laws; and no regard was now paid either to high birth or privileges.

So long as the Pope conducted all affairs in person, everything proceeded well; or at least the cardinals, though they did not perhaps suffer all their thoughts to appear, contented themselves with the expression of admiration and submission.

But as the pontiff advanced in years, the possession and exercise of this monarchical power fell gradually into the hands of his nephew, Pietro Aldobrandino: he was a son of that Pietro Aldobrandino who had distinguished himself among the brothers by his practical talent for the law. He seemed to promise little at first sight—was of mean appearance, and marked by the small-pox; he suffered from asthma, was incessantly coughing, and in youth he had not made any great progress, even in his studies. But no sooner did his uncle take him into the management of business, than he displayed an address and versatility of talent that no one had ever expected from him; not only did he know how to accommodate himself to the character of the Pope—to complete it, or supply its deficiencies, if we may so speak—tempering its asperities, and rendering the weaknesses that gradually appeared in it less apparent and less injurious [8]—but he also gained the confidence of foreign ambassadors, whom he satisfied so completely that they unanimously desired to see affairs in his management. Pietro was at first to have shared his vocations with his cousin Cinthio, who was indeed not without talent, more especially for literature, but he quickly dispossessed this associate. In the year 1603, we find Cardinal Pietro all-powerful in the court; "all business and negotiation," says a report of that year, "all favors and promotions, depend on him. Prelates, nobles, courtiers, and ambassadors crowd his palace. It may be averted that all things pass through his ear, and depend or are determined by his good

[7] See Appendix, No. 71.
[8] "Relatione al Cl. Este:" "Where the Pope exasperates, Aldobrandino pacifies; where he destroys, the nephew restores; where Clement thinks only of justice, his kinsman intercedes for mercy." See Appendix, Nos. 69 and 70.

pleasure; that every purpose is announced by his mouth, and that all execution is committed to his hands." [9]

Such a power—so unlimited, so all-pervading, and which was besides in nowise legitimate—aroused of necessity, and in defiance of the adherents it might attract, a secret, profound, and general opposition. It was on a trifling occasion that this unexpectedly displayed itself.

A man who had been arrested for debt found means to throw off his fetters at the critical moment and sprang into the Farnese palace, before which his captors were leading him.

The popes had long refused to hear mention of the right by which certain distinguished families claimed to grant an asylum in their houses to criminals. Cardinal Farnese, although connected with the Pope by the marriage into his family of a lady belonging to the house of Aldobrandino, now asserted this right once more. He caused the sbirri, who were about to seek their prisoner in the palace, to be driven out by force, and replied to the governor, who interposed his authority, that it was not the custom of his house to give up the accused. Cardinal Aldobrandino, desiring to avoid a public discussion, presented himself in person to make an amicable arrangement, but Farnese gave him a repulsive answer, reminding him that after the death of the Pope, which might be expected soon to happen, a Farnese would be of more importance than an Aldobrandino.

He gained courage for this insolence of demeanor principally from his connection with the Spaniards. The renunciation of Saluzzo by Henry IV, which in Rome had been considered a little pusillanimous, had given rise to the conclusion that he did not intend to occupy himself with Italian affairs. The importance of Spain had become restored in a great measure by this inference, and since the Aldobrandini displayed so decided a disposition toward France, their opponents attached themselves to Spain; the Spanish ambassador, Viglienna gave his entire approval to the conduct of

[9] " Orbis in urbe." But with him, also, secret influences were in action. This same account tells us: " He has many servants, but he who absorbs all favor is the Cavalier Clemente Senrˤsio, gentleman of the chamber, who had risen to that station from a very obscure condition, and who, for the greater increase of his own authority, has contrived to promote his brother to be secretary of the Consulta: thus they engross all things between them; the one the cardinal's favor, the other the supply of provisions to the offices, and for the more important expeditions." See Appendix, Nos. 69 and 70.

Farnese in the affair of the debtor, to which we have just alluded.[10]

Having the support of a foreign power, and the protection of a great family, could anything more be required to bring the discontent of the Roman nobility to a public outburst? Cavaliers and nobles flocked to the Farnese palace; some of the cardinals joined them openly, others favored them in secret.[1] Everyone exclaimed that the Pope and the Church must be released from the captivity they were subjected to by Cardinal Aldobrandino. As the Pope summoned a body of troops to Rome, the Spanish ambassador advised the confederates—to whom he even promised remuneration—to call in on their part certain armed bands which had just then made their appearance on the Neapolitan frontier; there was but little wanting to cause the outbreak of an open feud, after the manner of past ages, in the very midst of Rome.

But Cardinal Farnese would not permit things to go so far. He thought it enough to have proved his power, his independence, and the possibility of a resistance, and determined to withdraw to Castro, which was one of his family domains. This resolve he executed in grand style. Having secured one of the gates, he posted troops at it, and left the city with a train of ten carriages and three hundred horsemen : by this proceeding he gained all he desired; his insubordination was perfectly effectual; a formal negotiation was commenced; the whole affair was made to seem the fault of the governor, and a reconciliation was effected between that functionary and the house of Farnese. The cardinal then returned, with a magnificence of display equal to that of his departure; all the streets and windows were filled with spectators—every roof was covered. The Farnese had never been so splendidly received, even when they held the government, nor had they ever before been greeted by such loud acclamations.[2]

[10] Contarini, " Historia Veneta," tom. iii. lib. xiii. MS. Among all the authors of that time, he is the most circumstantial and the most trustworthy as regards these transactions: Viglienna sent orders to all the barons and Roman knights who were attached to the crown, that for the service of the King, they should instantly proceed to the house of Cardinal Farnese.

[1] A great sanction was given to these proceedings by the arrival of the Cardinals Sfondrato and Santiquatro, who, in a matter touching Spain, thought but little of the duty of cardinals to the Pope; and to those who declared themselves openly, many were added who adhered to them secretly, among them Cl. Conti; . . . but the populace, the nameless crowd, always eager for change, favored the cardinal, and crowding the streets and squares, they applauded the part he had taken.

[2] He set off for Rome as though go-

But if Cardinal Aldobrandino suffered this to occur, it must not be attributed altogether to weakness, or a forced compliance. The Farnese were, after all, closely connected with the papal house; he would, besides, have gained nothing by showing himself implacable: the first essential was to remove the cause of the mischief, and this was to be found in the existing political relations; no change of system could be obtained from the Spaniards, they would not even recall their untoward ambassador. The only mode in which Aldobrandino could help himself was by inducing Henry IV to take a more lively interest in the affairs of Italy.

In December, 1604, three French cardinals, all distinguished men, arrived in Rome together, and this, we are told, by his opponents, " was as refreshing to Aldobrandino as a cool and gentle breeze on a sultry day." It then became once more possible to form a French party in Rome; the strangers were received with joy; the cardinal's sister, Signora Olympia, declared to these new-comers a thousand times that her house would confide itself unconditionally to the protection of France. Baronius affirmed that his researches in history had convinced him that the Papal See was indebted to no people so much as to the French; at sight of Henry's portrait, he burst forth into cries of joy. He labored to discover whether, after the loss of Saluzzo, some other pass of the Alps might not remain in the hands of the French; and this Baronius was not merely an historian—he was also confessor to the Pope, and saw him every day. The pontiff and Aldobrandino were, it is true, more guarded, and did not express themselves so freely, but since those most nearly connected with them displayed so little reserve, the effect produced seemed to be much the same; and as besides, Henry IV now resolved to confer pensions, he soon had a party presenting a counterpoise to that of Spain.

But the views of Aldobrandino extended much further: he often placed before the Venetian ambassador and the cardinals, the necessity of setting bounds to the presumption of the Spaniards. Was it to be endured that they should command

ing in triumph, amid the shouts of the people that rose to the skies; he was met, as might have been a king, by the ambassador of the Emperor, the Spanish ambassador, Cardinals Sfondrato, Santiquatro, San Cesareo, and Conti, by his brother-in-law, General Georgio, all the cavalry, the papal guard, and a great concourse of barons and cavaliers.

in the house of another, and that in its owner's despite?[3] He knew that it was a perilous thing for a man who must soon return to private life to draw upon himself the displeasure of that power; but regard for his own honor forbade him to permit that the papacy should suffer a diminution of its repute under the rule of his uncle. In effect, he proposed to the Venetians that a league should be formed against Spain by the Italian States, under the protection of France.

He had, besides, already entered into negotiations with the other States. He had no love for Tuscany; he was involved in perpetual disputes with Modena; and Parma was implicated in the proceedings of Cardinal Farnese; but he seemed willing to forget everything in the hope of obtaining revenge on Spain. To that object he devoted himself with passionate eagerness; he spoke of nothing but that, and appeared to think of nothing else. He proceeded to Ancona in the beginning of the year 1605, for the purpose of being nearer to the States with which he proposed to form an alliance; but he had not been able to accomplish anything before his uncle died (on March 5, 1605), and his power then came to an end.

Meanwhile, the mere awakening of the thought, the assiduous renewal of French influence in Rome and Italy, were of themselves matters of great importance: they indicated a bias in the general policy of the Aldobrandini.

We do not, I think, go too far, if we permit ourselves to be thereby reminded of the original position held by this family in Florence. It had always belonged to the French party. In the insurrection of 1527, when the Medici had been driven from the city, and the French invited, Messer Salvestro took a very active part; for this he had to pay the penalty when his enemies, the Spaniards and the Medici, regained possession, and was compelled to leave his country. Could Pope Clement forget this? Could he ever have felt inclined toward the Spaniards and the Medici? He was by nature reserved and retiring; he but rarely unfolded his thoughts even to those in whom he most confided; but when this happened, he would give as an axiom—" Inquire of thy forefathers, and they will show thee thy path." [4] It is certain that he once entertained

[3] " Du Perron au Roi, 25 Janv. 1605," " Ambass." i. 509.
[4] Delfino: " The little inclination that the Pope has toward the Spaniards, both from his own nature and from inheritance."

the idea of reforming, as he expressed it, the state of Florence. His inclination toward France was manifest; he found the papacy in the closest alliance with Spain, but he led it to the very point of an alliance with France against Spain. If the restoration of a national power in France was demanded by the interests of the Church, it was also a matter of inclination with the Pope—a personal satisfaction. But Clement was discreet, far-sighted, and provident; he attempted nothing but what might be safely carried through. Instead of reforming Florence, he reformed, as was remarked by a Venetian, his own thoughts, perceiving that his project was not to be accomplished without universal danger.[5] To call the French arms into Italy was never his intention; it was sufficient for him to restore the balance of power, to free himself from the despotism of Spain, to place the policy of the Church on a broader basis, and to effect this by peaceful means, gradually, without disturbance or outcry, but so much the more securely.

Section XI.—Election and First Measures of Paul V

Even in the next conclave, the French influence made itself obvious. Aldobrandino gave in his adhesion to it, and, thus united, they were invincible. A cardinal whom the Spanish King had excluded by name, a Medici and near relative to the Queen of France, was raised to the papal dignity by their influence. The letters in which Du Perron announced this unexpected event to Henry IV are full of exultation. The accession was celebrated in France with public festivities.[1] But their triumph was of short duration. Leo XI, as this Pope was named, survived his election only twenty-six days. It is affirmed that the sense of his dignity, and the idea he entertained of the difficulties surrounding his office, completely extinguished the powers of a life already much weakened by age.

[5] Venier: " Seeing the preparations and resolutions of your signory, and also of the grand duke, and that our republic had declared itself by sending an ambassador to his holiness expressly for this business; knowing also that a great flame would be kindled in Italy, with danger of perilous conflagration to the Church; in place of attempting to reform the state of Florence, he has reformed his own thoughts."

[1] " Histoire de la Vie de Messire Philippe de Mornay, Seigneur du Plessis," p. 305: " This Pope of the house of Medici, called Leo XI, whom it had cost the King 300,000 crowns to make Pope, on whose favor he counted largely, and at whose election cannons were fired, and feux-de-joie made (for the first time in France for such a cause), lived but a few days, and left the King nothing but the reproaches of the Spaniards for gifts so ill-employed, and the fear, lest the next succession should, as really happened, prove more favorable to Spain."

The tumults of an election contest were now renewed, but with increased violence, since Aldobrandino was no longer in so firm an alliance with the French.   Montalto opposed him powerfully, and a conflict ensued, as at previous elections, between the creatures of the last pontiff and those of his predecessor. Each of the two parties conducted the candidate of its choice, surrounded by his adherents, to one or the other of the chapels, and there proposed him in opposition to his antagonist.   Attempts were made to elect a pope, first from one party and then another.   Baronius, though resisting with all his force, was on one occasion dragged into the Pauline chapel, but the opposition displayed increased strength at each successive attempt, and neither party found it possible to carry any one of its candidates. The choice of a pontiff, like many other promotions, was gradually made to depend on who had the fewest enemies, rather than on who possessed superiority of merit.

Aldobrandino at length cast his eyes on a man among those elevated by his uncle, who had found means to conciliate general favor, and to avoid all dangerous enmities : this was Cardinal Borghese; for him he succeeded in securing the favor of the French, by whom an approach to reconciliation between Montalto and Aldobrandino had already been effected. Montalto, therefore, gave his vote to Borghese, who was elected (assuming the name of Paul V) before the Spaniards had heard that he was proposed.[2]   This election took place on May 16, 1605.

We find, then, that on this occasion, as on many preceding, the nephew of the last Pope determined the election of the new one.   The Borghese family was, besides, in a similar position to that of Aldobrandino.   As the latter had quitted Florence to avoid submission to the rule of the Medici, so had the former left Sienna for the same cause.   There hence appeared a further probability that the new government would be a direct continuation of the preceding.

But immediately after his election, Paul V evinced a peculiarly rugged disposition.

He had risen from the condition of an advocate, through all

[2] The truth may, nevertheless, be that Montalto and Aldobrandino had come to an agreement, of themselves, as to Borghese, since the Conclave di Paolo V. p. 370, says of these cardinals: " After having proposed many, they elected Borghese, the friend of Montalto and the confidential adherent of Aldobrandino."

the degrees of ecclesiastical dignity.[3] He had been vice-legate at Bologna, auditor of the Camera, vicar of the Pope, and inquisitor. He had lived in close retirement, buried in his books and law-papers, and had taken no part in political affairs; thence it was that he had made his way without awakening personal enmities. No party considered him its opponent; neither Aldobrandino nor Montalto, neither the French nor the Spaniards. This, then, was the quality which had secured him the tiara.

But he considered that event in a totally different light. His elevation to the papacy, without any effort on his own part, without the employment of any arts or devices, appeared to him the direct interposition of the Holy Spirit. He felt raised above himself by this conviction. The change in his carriage and demeanor, nay, even in his countenance and the tone of his voice, was matter of astonishment, even to the Court of Rome, which was yet well accustomed to metamorphoses of every sort. But the new pontiff felt himself at the same time enchained and pledged to most important duties. With inflexibility similar to that with which he had observed the letter of the law in his previous offices, he now prepared to administer the supreme dignity.[4]

Other popes had been accustomed to signalize their elevation to the throne by acts of mercy; Paul V, on the contrary, began his reign by passing a sentence, the remembrance of which excites horror even to the present day.

A poor author, a Cremonese by birth, named Piccinardi, impelled by some unexplained disgust, had employed himself in his solitude in composing a Life of Clement VIII, wherein he compared that Pope with the Emperor Tiberius—small as was the similarity to be found between these rulers. He had not only refrained from printing this strange work, but had kept it quite to himself, and had scarcely permitted its existence to be known. A woman, who had formerly resided in his house, gave information of the book. Paul V expressed himself at first very mildly on the subject, and the author seemed to have little cause for anxiety, the rather as many important

[3] "Relatione di IV. Ambasciatori mandati a Roma, 15 Genn. 1605," m. V. i. e. 1606: " His father Camillo, not choosing longer to remain at Sienna, since the city had lost her liberty, departed, and went to Rome. He had a good spirit and an acute mind; thus he succeeded well in the profession of an advocate. . . . The Pope does not wish to be called a Siennese, but a Roman."
[4] See Appendix, No. 76.

persons, and even ambassadors, had interceded for him. How greatly then were all astonished, when Piccinardi was one day beheaded on the bridge of St. Angelo! Whatever might be said by way of exculpation, it is certain that he had committed the crime of high treason *(beleidigten Majestät),* for which this punishment is awarded by the law. From a pope like Paul no mercy was to be expected; even the poor and trifling possessions of the unhappy man were confiscated.[5]

At court this pontiff instantly renewed the regulations of the Council of Trent with respect to residence; he declared it to be a deadly sin for a bishop to remain absent from his diocese and still enjoy its revenues; from this rule he did not except the cardinals, nor would he admit the holding an office in the administration as an excuse for non-residence. Many retired to their sees accordingly, others begged for some delay;[6] but there were some who would not consent to leave Rome, and yet did not wish to be accused of neglecting their duties; these, therefore, sent in the resignation of their bishoprics.

But the most serious evil of Paul's early reign was the circumstance that he had derived from his studies in canon law the most exorbitant ideas concerning the importance of the papacy. The doctrines that the Pope is the sole vicegerent of Jesus Christ, that the power of the keys is intrusted to his discretion, and that he is to be reverenced in humility by all nations and princes, he desired to maintain in their most extended significance.[7] He affirmed that he had been raised to that seat, not by men, but by the Divine Spirit, and with the duty imposed on him of guarding every immunity of the Church and all the prerogatives of God; that he was bound in conscience to put forth all his strength for the deliverance of the Church from usurpation and violence: he would rather risk his life to fulfil these duties than be called to account for the neglect of them when he should appear before the throne of God.

[5] The ambassadors alluded to in the preceding note relate this occurrence, adding the remark: "It is conjectured that this pontiff will prove to be most inflexible and rigorous, and in matters of justice, most inexorable." See Appendix, Nos. 76 and 78.

[6] "Du Perron à Villeroy, 17 May, 1606:" "The Pope having lately intimated his pleasure that all the cardinals who held bishoprics should go to them or should resign them, unless, indeed, they place coadjutors, I have thought, etc."

[7] "Relatione di IV. Ambasciatori:" "The present Pope, knowing his spiritual greatness, and the implicit deference and obedience that is due to and should be paid him by all Christian nations, not excepting any monarch, however great."

With judicial severity he assumed the claims of the Church
to be identical with her rights, and regarded it as a point of
conscience to revive and carry them out in their utmost rigor.

Section XII.—Disputes with Venice

From the time when the papal power had reinstated its
authority in opposition to the efforts of Protestantism, and had
given new life to those ideas which form the chief basis of the
hierarchy, its canonical rights had likewise been all enforced
with regard to the internal administration of Catholic States.

While the Church subdued her opponents, her authority also
received extension, as it related to her own adherents.

When the bishops had been compelled to more rigid obedience, the monastic orders closely attached to the Curia, and
all reforms completed in such a manner as should cause them
at the same time to promote the supreme power of the pontiff,
regular nunciaturas established their seats in all the capitals
of Europe. These offices united with the authority of an embassy from an influential power, certain judicial rights, which
secured them an essential influence over the most important
relations of private life as well as of the State.

Even where the Church had re-established itself in concert
with the State—where both united had opposed themselves to
the advancement of Protestant opinions—this circumstance soon
gave rise to misunderstandings.

In those days, as in our own, the Roman Court was especially careful to maintain all its rights and claims in Italy; and
from this cause we find the Italian States engaged in perpetual
disputes with the ecclesiastical government. The old dissensions between the Church and these States had never been set
at rest, neither in general by some decisive principle, nor yet,
in particular cases, by treaty and agreement. The popes themselves differed in their views of these matters. Pius V insisted most pertinaciously on all his claims, as did Gregory IV;
at least, during the first half of his pontificate. Sixtus V
was much more indulgent as regarded individual cases. The
States and their envoys did their best to escape from all occasions of difficulty with the least possible prejudice to themselves, and to seize on every circumstance capable of being

turned to their own advantage; nor did this method altogether fail of success. The inclinations of different popes were liable to change and pass away; the interests of States were permanent, and remained; or in any case the questions to be resolved were thus rendered less the subjects of the canon law and of judicial interpretation, than of policy and of reciprocal demands and concessions.

The mode in which Pope Paul V viewed his claims was, however, essentially juridical; he held the canonical regulations of the decretals to be the laws of God himself. If his predecessors had made concessions or overlooked failures, he ascribed this, not to the inherent necessity of the case, but to their personal negligence, and he believed himself called to the atonement of these faults. We consequently find him, soon after his accession, involved in bitter contentions with all his Italian neighbors.

In Naples, the Regent Ponte, president of the royal council, had condemned an ecclesiastical notary to the galleys, for having refused to lay the evidence, in a case respecting a marriage, before the civil court, and a bookseller who had circulated the work of Baronius against the Sicilian monarchy, in contravention of the royal ordinance, had received a similar sentence from the same person. A remonstrance (monitorium) from Clement VIII, against these proceedings, had been disregarded; Pope Paul V pronounced a sentence of excommunication without the delay of a moment.[1]

The Duke of Savoy had bestowed certain benefices, the right of nominating to which was claimed by the Roman Court; Genoa had prohibited societies assembling at the Jesuit colleges, because they had sought to control the elections to public offices; Lucca had made a general rule to the effect, that no decree whatever, proceeding from the papal officers, should be executed without the previous assent of the native magistracy; and, finally, Venice had caused certain ecclesiastics, who had been guilty of heinous crimes, to be arraigned before the civil tribunals. It was precisely the universality of this opposition to the spiritual power that roused the official zeal and anger of the Pope. In every case he interposed his authority with imperative commands and heavy menaces; nay, at this very

[1] "Les Ambassades du Cardinal du Perron," ii. 683-736.

moment he even extended still further the former claims of ecclesiastical supremacy. Among other things, he affirmed what had never before been heard of—that it did not belong to the temporal power to forbid the intercourse of its subjects with Protestants; this was not the business of the State, but of the Church, and belonged exclusively to the ecclesiastical jurisdiction.

The greater part of the Italian States considered these measures as extravagances, that, after more extended experience, would disappear of themselves. None wished to be the first to break with the pontiff. The Grand Duke of Tuscany declared that he had affairs on hand, by which the Pope must needs be driven into a fury, but that he was trying to keep them back for a time; that Paul V was a man who judged the world from a town of the Ecclesiastical States, where everything was arranged according to the letter of the law,[2] but that all this must soon be changed; the Spaniards would find themselves entangled, and they must be set free voluntarily, or would certainly rend the net: it was advisable that some such example should be waited for. The other States thought much in the same manner, and in the first instance they submitted. Genoa repealed her edict; the Duke of Savoy permitted the benefices in dispute to be made over to a nephew of the Pope; and the Spaniards themselves allowed their regent to request absolution, and receive it before numerous witnesses.

The Venetians alone, usually so prudent and accommodating, disdained to adopt this policy.

It is, however, certain that Venice had more serious cause of irritation than all the rest; and her case presented an example of how offensive the encroachments of the Roman Court might become, more especially toward a neighboring State.[3]

This vicinity proved in itself extremely inconvenient, particularly after the Church had taken possession of Ferrara. The disputes respecting boundaries, which the republic had sometimes to settle with the dukes, were maintained with great increase of violence by the Court of Rome. The Venetians were disturbed in the works they were prosecuting, at heavy cost,

---

[2] " Relatione di IV. Ambasciatori:" " The grand duke remembered that the Pope was not used to reign as a great prince; he had governed in some city of the Church, where all was done in priestly fashion and with ecclesiastical rigor, but he was not capable of ruling as supreme chief."

[3] See Appendix, No. 78.

for regulating the waters of the Po; and in their rights of possession as regarded the fisheries; they could proceed in their operations only when their works were protected by armed vessels, and were driven to seize on certain of the papal subjects, by way of reprisals for the confiscation of their fishingboats by the Legate of Ferrara.

Meanwhile Paul V also laid claim to the rights of sovereignty over Ceneda, which the Venetians had exercised for centuries without dispute, and attempted to remove to Rome the appeals from the episcopal court, which held jurisdiction there. On this subject the exasperation was violent on both sides: the papal nuncio proceeded to excommunications, when the Venetian Senate instantly took measures to secure that no civil injury should result to those affected by them.[4]

Equally bitter were the dissensions respecting the tithes of the clergy; the Venetians affirmed that they had hitherto collected them without consulting the Pope, nor would they now acknowledge the papal sanction to be required for the levying of that impost. But it was a much more serious grievance that the Roman Court daily increased the exemptions from the tax. The cardinals, who held extremely rich benefices, the Knights of Malta, and the monasteries, were exempt from half the amount, while the mendicant orders, with all persons who were occupied abroad in the service of the Church, or could be included under any title in the Pope's household; and finally, even those to whom the Roman Court had assigned pensions payable out of the Venetian benefices, were declared exempt from the whole. It followed that the rich were not obliged to pay anything, so that the whole burden fell on the poor, who could not pay. The revenues of the Venetian clergy were computed to be 11,000,000 ducats, but the tithes did not actually yield more than 12,000 ducats.[5]

In addition to all this came innumerable subjects of dispute

[4] While the dispute proceeded, it appeared, that some refused to hold intercourse with those who had been censured, officers of the republic who had opposed the removal of appeals to Rome, on which the Senate, considering this likely to be injurious, first published a decree against all who should offend such persons, and afterward granted them annuities for life, to each according to his station.

[5] From a declaration that was presented at Rome: While the severity of the magistrates has been exaggerated, it is found that only 12,000 ducats have hitherto been raised, which are not worth such outcries; the fortune of the republic, by the grace of God, not being such as to make even a larger sum of importance. Some arrangements were then made to correct this evil, but Contarini says: " Little good was produced, because the breach was already made, and the abuse was so firmly established, that removing it would have been more than difficult."

affecting individuals rather than the State. Of these I will adduce one instance only.

The prosperous condition enjoyed by the Venetian press during the early part of the sixteenth century is well known. The republic was proud of this honorable branch of trade, but the regulations of the Curia brought it gradually to total ruin. There was no end to the prohibition of books in Rome: first, those of the Protestants; then all writings reflecting on the morals of the clergy or the immunities of the Church; every book departing, in however slight a degree, from the Roman tenets, and the entire works of any author who had once incurred censure. The trade could now be carried on in books of indisputable orthodoxy only; it was indeed somewhat revived, in a commercial point of view, by the richly decorated missals and breviaries, for which the renewal of Catholic opinions and tastes occasioned a very fair demand. But even this portion of the trade was now diminished; alterations and improvements in these books were undertaken in Rome, where alone they were, in their new form, permitted to be published.[6] The Venetians remarked, with that angry disgust always excited when the public authority is perverted to the subservience of private interests, that some of the officials appointed by the congregation of the Index, for the control of matters relating to the press, took share in the profits of the Roman printing establishments.

Under these circumstances, the relations between Rome and Venice were marked by a painful restraint or by evidences of utter hatred.

It is manifest that all this must have contributed largely to produce that opposition, both political and religious, by which Henry IV was so greatly assisted in 1589. This resistance was confirmed and fostered by the victory of Henry, and by the entire development of European affairs. The dissensions with the Pope himself conduced still further toward the gradual investment of those who represented these opinions with the conduct of public affairs. There were none who seemed better fitted to guard the interests of the republic against the ecclesiastical power. Leonardo Donato, the leader of the party op-

[6] They had now got an idea in Rome, that they would themselves print the missals and other books, depriving others of the power of doing so.

posed to Rome, was accordingly raised to the rank of doge in January, 1606. All those friends by whose aid he had succeeded in the conflicts of internal parties he now admitted to a share in the management of public affairs.

While a pope appeared, by whom the disputed claims of his authority were overstrained with reckless zeal, the Venetian Government passed into the hands of men, with whom opposition to the dominion of Rome had grown up with all their convictions, and had become a personal feeling; by this they had risen to power, and they upheld the principle with all the more energy, because it served them at the same time as a means of repression and defence against their opponents within the republic.

It resulted as an inevitable consequence from the nature of both these powers, that the collisions between them should daily become more hostile and more widely effective.

The Pope insisted not only on the surrender of the ecclesiastical malefactors, he demanded also the repeal of two laws, renewed by the Venetians a short time previously, and which forbade the alienation of real property in favor of the clergy, while they made the building of new churches contingent on the approval of the secular authorities. He declared that he would not tolerate ordinances so directly opposed to the decrees of councils, the constitutions of his predecessors, and all the maxims of the canon law. The Venetians would not yield a hair's breadth; they said that these were fundamental laws of their State, handed down to them by their forefathers, who had deserved so well of Christendom, and that in the eyes of the republic they were inviolable.

The disputants did not long confine themselves to the immediate subject of contention; both parties instantly brought forward other grievances. The Church considered itself wronged by the entire constitution of Venice—a republic which forbade all recourse to Rome; which excluded, under the title of papalists, all those who by holding clerical offices were connected with the Curia, from the council of ecclesiastical affairs, and which even laid the burden of taxes on the clergy. The Venetians, on the other hand, maintained, that even these restrictions were utterly inadequate; they demanded that their ecclesiastical benefices should be conferred on natives of Venice only;

that their Inquisition should be directed exclusively by themselves; that every bull should be submitted to the approval of the State; that all ecclesiastical assemblies should be presided over by a layman, and that all sending of money to Rome should be prohibited.

Nor did they stop even here; from the questions immediately in debate, they proceeded to general principles.

The Jesuits had long since deduced from their doctrine of the power of the Pope, the most important consequences in support of clerical rights, and these they now failed not to repeat with their accustomed energy and promptitude.

The spirit, says Bellarmine, guides and controls the flesh, and not the contrary; neither must the secular power exalt itself over the spiritual, to guide, to command, or to punish; this would be a rebellion, a heathenish tyranny.[7] The priesthood has its princes who govern it, not in spiritual things only, but in temporal matters also. It could not possibly acknowledge any particular temporal superior. No man can serve two masters. It is for the priest to judge the emperor, not the emperor the priest; it would be absurd for the sheep to pretend to judge the shepherd.[8] Neither must the prince attempt to derive any revenue from ecclesiastical property. He may draw his tribute from the laity; the priesthood affords him the far more important aids of prayer and sacrifice. The clergyman is exempt from all burdens, whether on person or property: he belongs to the family of Christ. If these exemptions are not founded on any express command of holy Scripture, they are certainly based on consequences to be drawn from it, and on analogy. To the priests of the New Testament belong precisely the same rights that were conferred on the Levites in the Old Testament.[9]

[7] Response of Cardinal Bellarmine to a letter without the name of its author (a pamphlet of 1606): " Reason directs, rules, and commands the flesh, castigating it at times by fastings and vigils; but the flesh neither directs, nor rules, nor punishes the reason: thus the spiritual power is superior to the temporal authority, and, therefore, can and ought to direct, rule, command, and punish, when the latter conducts itself ill; but the secular power is not superior to the spiritual, and cannot direct, rule, command, or punish it, except by rendering itself guilty of rebellion and tyranny, as Gentile and heretic princes have sometimes done."

[8] " Bellarminus de Clericis," i. c. 30: " I reply that the prince is indeed the sheep and spiritual son of the Pope; but the priest can in no wise be called the son or sheep of the prince, because priests and all clergy have their spiritual prince, by whom they are governed, not only in spiritual, but also in temporal things."

[9] These maxims are to be found verbatim either in the " Response " quoted in a previous note, or in the book of " Bellarminus de Clericis," especially in lib. i. c. 30.

This was a doctrine which secured to that spiritual republic, claiming so important an influence over the State, a no less complete independence of any reciprocal influence over itself from the State. It was a doctrine for the establishment of which, no labor was spared in Rome; innumerable arguments from Scripture were quoted; decrees of councils were brought forward; imperial and papal constitutions were cited; and it was considered to be altogether beyond dispute. Who was there in Venice that might venture to oppose himself to a Bellarmine, or a Baronius?

The Venetians, nevertheless, were provided, in the person of their Counsellor of State, Paolo Sarpi, with a man whom nature and circumstances had endowed with such qualifications, and conducted to such a position, that he could venture to take up arms against the spiritual power.

Paolo Sarpi was the son of a merchant, who had removed from St. Valentine to Venice; his mother belonged to the house of Morelli; a Venetian family, enjoying the rights of citizenship. The father was a man of slight figure, and dark complexion; he was impetuous in character, and of a quarrelsome temper, and had ruined himself by imprudent speculations; the mother was one of those beautiful blondes, still often seen in Venice, was of majestic form, modest deportment and intelligent mind; it was to her that the son bore resemblance in external appearance.[10]

Ambrosio Morelli, the brother of this lady, was then at the head of a school, which enjoyed high reputation, and was occupied chiefly in the education of the young nobility. It followed as a matter of course, that the nephew of the master should take part in the instruction; Niccolo Contarini and Andrea Morosini were among his school-fellows, and were also his intimate companions; he thus formed the most influential connections on the very threshold of his life.

He did not, however, permit himself to be prevented either by his mother, his uncle, or these companions, from indulging in a propensity to solitude; he was not more than fourteen or fifteen years old when he entered a convent of Servites.

He spoke little and was always serious; he never ate meat,

[10] Sarpi was born Aug. 14, 1552: His father's name was Francesco, his mother's Elizabetta.—Fra Fulgentio, "Vita di Paolo Sarpi." Griselini, "Memorie di Fra Paolo Sarpi," the German edition of Lebret, p. 13.

and till his thirtieth year he drank no wine; he detested all levity in conversation: "There comes the maiden," his companions would say, when he appeared; "let us talk of something else." All his wishes, inclinations, and desires, were directed toward those studies for which he possessed great natural endowments.

He possessed the inestimable gift of quick and accurate perception; he never failed to recognize a person whom he had once seen, and when he entered a garden would perceive and remark everything it contained at a glance: he was furnished, that is to say, with a clear and penetrating power of sight, mentally and physically.[1] He thence applied himself, with particular success, to the natural sciences. His admirers ascribe to him the discovery of the valves in the blood-vessels, and he is said first to have observed the expansion and contraction of the pupil of the eye,[2] the inclination of the magnetic needle, and many other magnetic phenomena; it is certain that he took effective part in the labors of Aquapendente, and still more, both by suggestion and discovery, in those of Porta.[3] To his physical studies he added mathematical calculations, as also the observation of mental and intellectual phenomena. In the library of the Servites at Venice, a copy of Vieta's works is preserved, in which the many errors of that author are corrected by the hand of Fra Paolo; in the same place there was also a small treatise of his on the origin and decline of the opinions of men, which, to judge by the extracts from it given by Foscarini, contained a theory of the intellectual powers which assumed sensation and reflection as their basis, and had a certain resemblance to that of Locke,[4] even though it did not coincide with it so entirely as has been asserted. Fra Paolo wrote only so far as was strictly necessary; he was not endowed by nature with

---

[1] According to Fra Fulgentio (p. 38), he spoke himself of his extreme delicacy of perception, for he not only received impressions from objects, but even from the least traces of them. As a skilful musician, continues Fra Fulgentio, judges an instrument from a single touch, so by making people speak, he judged with admirable precision of their purposes, intentions, etc.

[2] See also Fischer, "Geschichte der Physik," i. 167.

[3] From whom, says Porta of Fra Paolo, we not only do not blush to have learned some things, but we glory in it, for a more learned man than he, or one more subtle in the whole circle of knowledge, we have never known among all that we have chanced to see.—"Magiæ Natur." lib. vii. præf. Griselini, i. §§ 20-24.

[4] We have a particularly striking instance in their explanations of substance. Paolo Sarpi, according to Foscarini and Griselini, infers substance from the multiplicity of ideas, resting on a basis which we cannot perceive, and in this basis, he says, properly consists what we call substance.—Griselini, i. p. 46 of the German translation. Locke's "Human Understanding," b. ii. chap. xxiii.: "Not imagining how the simple ideas can subsist by themselves, we accustom ourselves to suppose some substratum, wherein they do subsist, and from which they do result, which therefore we call substance."

inclination for producing; he read incessantly; appropriated what he read or remarked; and reflected on all. His mind was temperate and comprehensive, methodical and bold, and he trod the paths of inquiry with a free and fearless step.

With these powers, Paolo Sarpi now approached the questions of theology and of ecclesiastical law.

It has been said that he was secretly a Protestant, but his Protestantism could scarcely have extended beyond the first simple propositions of the Confession of Augsburg, if he really held even those. It is certain that Fra Paolo read mass every day through his whole life. It would not be possible to specify the confession to which he was inwardly attached—it was a mode of belief of which we often perceive traces among the men of those times, more particularly those who were devoted to the study of natural science, adhering to none of the established systems of doctrine, dissentient and speculative, but not yet clearly defined, nor entirely made out.

Of this much we are however certain, Fra Paolo bore a decided and implacable hatred toward the secular influence of the papacy, and this was, perhaps, the only passion he ever indulged. It has been attributed to the refusal of a bishopric, for which he had been proposed; and who shall venture positively to deny the effect that a mortifying rejection, excluding a natural ambition from its path, may produce, even on a manly spirit? But in this case the cause lay much deeper; it must be sought in a sentiment, religious and political, that was mingled and bound up with every other conviction of his mind; it had gained strength from study and experience, and was held in common with those friends and contemporaries who had formerly gathered around Andrea Morosini, and were now arrived at the helm of State. Before the keen glance of his penetrating observation, those chimerical arguments with which the Jesuits labored to confirm their assertions, vanished utterly, and the doctrines really founded only on a devotion to the Roman See, arising from a state of society long gone by, appeared in all their nullity.

It was not without labor that Sarpi first brought conviction to the minds of the Venetian jurists. Some held the exemption of the clergy to be an ordinance of the divine law, as propounded by Cardinal Bellarmine; others maintained that it was at least in the power of the Pope to command it; they appealed to those decrees of councils, in which that exemption was proclaimed, and concluded that what had been in the power of a council was much more within the competence of a pope. The first were easily refuted, and, with the others, Fra Paolo's principal argument was that the councils whose authority they cited were convened by temporal sovereigns, and were to be considered as assemblies of the empire, whence a multitude of political enactments had also proceeded.[5] This is an argument on which the doctrines brought forward by Fra Paolo and his friends were chiefly founded.

They started from the principle which had been successfully contended for in France, that the sovereign power is derived immediately from God, and can be subject to no control. The Pope has not even the right to inquire whether the proceedings of a State be sinful or not. For whither would this tend? Was there any that might not be sinful, at least, as regarded its ultimate aim? The Pope would have to examine everything, to interfere in all. The temporal sovereignty would, in fact, be annihilated.

To this sovereignty the clergy is subjected as well as the laity. All power, says the apostle, comes from God. From the obedience due to the established authorities no one is exempt any more than from obedience to God. The prince gives the law; he judges every man, and demands tribute from all; in all things the clergy owe him an obedience equal to that required from the laity.[6]

The Pope also undoubtedly possesses jurisdiction, but one that is exclusively spiritual. Did Christ exercise a temporal jurisdiction? Neither to St. Peter, nor to his successors, could he have transferred what he did not claim for himself.

In no degree therefore can the exemption of the clergy be

---

[5] " Letter from Sarpi to Leschasser," 3 Feb. 1619, in Lebret's " Magazine," i. 479; an observation which is the more important for those times, because Mariana, for example, deduced the most extensive secular privileges for the clergy from those decrees of the Spanish councils; but it must be always observed that even at that time the spiritual and temporal claims were already either mingled together or in dispute. The old Gothic monarchy in Spain had in effect a powerful spiritual element, for old laws are generally founded on a far remote condition of things.

[6] Risposta d'un dottore in theologia ad una lettera scrittagli sopra il breve delle censure: " All persons, therefore, both ecclesiastic and secular, are subject to the temporal sovereign by divine right. Let every soul be subject to the higher powers (omnis anima potestatibus sublimioribus subdita sit); and the reason is clear, for as none is exempted from the obedience due to God, so none is exempted from the obedience due to the prince, because, as the apostle says, all power is from God (omnis potestas a Deo)."

derived from an original divine right;[7] it depends on the will of the sovereign only. The prince has conferred property and jurisdiction on the Church; he is her protector, her general patron. On him, therefore, the nomination of the clergy depends of right; to him also belongs the publication of bulls.

The prince cannot surrender this power, even if he would. It is a trust confided to him; he is bound in conscience to deliver it unimpaired to his successor.

Thus did the claims and theory of the State oppose themselves boldly to the claims and theory of the Church. The tendencies of conflicting powers were expressed in opposite systems. The internal fusion of spiritual and temporal interest in the European states presents a wide domain of human action, wherein both meet and blend. The Church had long demanded this whole domain as its exclusive possession, and now renewed this claim; the State, on the other hand, had also at times asserted a similar claim, but never before, perhaps, had it been so boldly and systematically brought forward as on this occasion. It was impossible that these claims could ever be legally adjusted; and politically, their regulation was possible only by means of mutual concessions. When neither party would make these to the other, it must come to a trial of force. Each side had then to prove how far its strength could reach; if a conflict were commenced for the right to obedience, nothing further remained but to show which had the power to enforce it.

On April 17, 1606, the Pope pronounced sentence of excommunication on the doge, Senate, and government of Venice collectedly, more particularly on the consultors. This he did with all the stern forms of past ages, and with especial reference to the most omnipotent of his predecessors; as, for example, to Innocent III. He allowed the condemned only the shortest intervals for recantation—three of eight days and one of three days, namely. After the lapse of these, all churches of the Venetian territory—those of convents and private chapels not

[7] "Difesa di Giovanni Marsilio a favore della risposta delle otto proposizioni, contra la quale ha scritto l'illmo. e revmo. Sr. Cl. Bellarmino," Venezia, 1606. This explains the meaning of its author, who has expressed himself somewhat obscurely, in the following manner; but the explanation is at least authentic, since it comes from the same side: "The author says two things: first, that the persons of ecclesiastics are not exempt from the secular power, nor yet their property, meaning thereby things to which the said power extends (that is, not to matters purely spiritual); the second is, that the exemption possessed by ecclesiastics is not by divine right, but merely by human law " (p. 62).

excepted—were to be prohibited from performing divine service: they were laid under interdict. It was imposed on the Venetian clergy, as a duty, to publish this letter of interdict before the assembled congregations,[8] and to have it fixed on the church doors. The whole body of the clergy, from the patriarch to the parish priest, were enjoined to execute this command, under pain of rigorous punishments from God and man.

Such was the attack; the defence did not display equal vigor.

It was proposed in the college of Venice to enter a solemn protest, as had been done in earlier times; but this proposal was rejected, on the ground that the sentence of the Pope was in itself null and void, and had not even a show of justice. In a short proclamation, occupying only a quarto page, Leonardo Donato made known to the clergy the resolution of the republic to maintain the sovereign authority, " which acknowledges no other superior in worldly things save God alone." Her faithful clergy would of themselves perceive the nullity of the " censures " issued against them, and would continue the discharge of their functions, the cure of souls and the worship of God, without interruption. No alarm was expressed, no menaces were uttered, the proclamation was a mere expression of confidence and security. It is, however, probable that something more may have been done by verbal communication.[9]

By these proceedings, the question of claim and right became at once a question of strength and of possession. Commanded by their two superiors—the Pope and the republic—to give contradictory proofs of obedience, the Venetian clergy were now called on to decide to which of the two they would render that obedience.

They did not hesitate; they obeyed the republic: not a copy of the brief was fixed up.[10] The delay appointed by the Pope expired; public worship was everywhere conducted as usual. As the secular clergy had decided, so did also the monastic orders.

[8] When the great assemblage of the people should be gathered together for divine service, as had been done in Ferrara with such effective results.—" Letter of censure and of interdict of his holiness, our lord Pope Paul V. against the Venetians," 606.

[9] This proclamation of May 6, 1606, is printed by Rampazetto, the ducal printer (stampator ducale). On the title-page is seen the Evangelist St. Mark with the book of the Gospels and uplifted sword. In the senate, as Priuli tells us, they discussed the many and notorious nullities of the papal brief.

[10] P. Sarpi, " Historia particolare," lib. ii. p. 55, affirms that certain persons who had attempted to fix up the bulls had been arrested by the inhabitants themselves.

The only exception to this was presented by the orders newly instituted, and in which the principle of ecclesiastical restoration was more particularly represented; these were the Jesuits, Theatines, and Capuchins. The Jesuits, in so far as they were themselves concerned, were not altogether decided; they first took counsel of their provincial at Ferrara, and afterward of their general in Rome, who referred the question to the Pope himself. Paul V replied that they must either observe the interdict, or shake the dust from their feet and leave Venice. A hard decision assuredly, since they were distinctly informed that they would never be permitted to return; but the principle of their institution allowed them no choice. Embarking in their boats, they departed from the city, and took shelter in the papal dominions.[1] Their example influenced the other two orders.[2] A middle course was proposed by the Theatines, but the Venetians did not think it advisable; they would suffer no division in their land, and demanded either obedience or departure. The deserted churches were easily provided with other priests, and care was taken that none should perceive a deficiency. The festival of the Corpus Christi next succeeding, was solemnized with extraordinary pomp, and a more than commonly numerous procession.[3]

But it is manifest that the result was a complete schism.

The Pope was amazed; his exaggerated pretensions were confronted by the realities of things with the most unshrinking boldness. Did any means exist by which these might be overcome?

Paul V thought at times of having recourse to arms: even in the congregations, warlike opinions had at one moment the ascendancy. Cardinal Sauli exclaimed that the Venetians should be castigated. Legates were despatched, and troops fitted out; but in effect they dared not venture to attempt force. There would have been cause to apprehend that Venice would call the Protestants to her aid, and thus throw all Italy, nay the Catholic world at large, into the most perilous commotions. They must again betake themselves, as on former occasions,

[1] Juvencius, "Hist. Soc. Jesu," v. ii. p. 93.

[2] If V. Sandi continues to mention the "reformed brethren of St. Francis," that proceeds only from the fact, that the Capuchins were, in effect, reformed Franciscans, and are so called on this occasion by A. Morosini. This error of Sandi has been committed by other writers also.

[3] A. Maurocenus, "Historia Ven." tom. iii. p. 350.

to political measures, for the adjustment of these questions touching the rights of the Church. The arrangement of these measures could not, however, be attempted on this occasion by the parties themselves; the animosities between them were too violent; it was confided to the mediation of the two leading powers—France and Spain. But the private interest of both would, of course, require to be considered in the matter.

There was a party in each of these two kingdoms, to which the outbreak of hostilities would have been welcome. Among the Spaniards, this was formed by the zealous Catholics (who thereby hoped to enchain the Roman See once more to the monarchy), and the governors of the Italian provinces, whose power would be increased by war. The Spanish ambassador to Rome, Viglienna, also wished for war, thinking it would afford him opportunities for advancing his family to high ecclesiastical dignities. In France, on the contrary, it was precisely the most zealous Protestants who desired a rupture. Sully and his adherents would have gladly seen an Italian war, because the Netherlands, just then hard pressed by Spinola, might by that means have gained time to breathe. Each of these parties even proceeded to demonstrations of war. The King of Spain despatched a letter to the Pope, with promises of aid, at least in general terms. In France the Venetian ambassador also received offers from men in high positions; it was his opinion that he could gather an army of 15,000 Frenchmen in a month. This mode of thinking did not, however, obtain the ascendancy. Lerma and Villeroy, the leading ministers of Spain and France, desired to maintain peace. The Spanish statesman placed his glory chiefly in the restoration of peace, and Villeroy belonged to the rigidly Catholic party, and would never have consented that the Pope should be attacked by the French.[4] The princes agreed with their ministers; Henry IV remarked with justice, that if he drew his sword for the republic he should endanger his reputation as a good Catholic. Philip III despatched a new declaration to the Pope—he would assist him, but certainly not

[4] " Relatione di Pietro Priuli ritornato di Francia, 4 Sett. 1608," contains a circumstantial account of the interest taken by the French in these transactions. Villeroy declares this to be a most opportune and proper occasion for gaining the good will of the Pope; the King, assured by his ambassador to the republic, that your serenity (he is addressing the Venetian republic) would not put the negotiations into any other hands than his own, had the intention of employing this opportunity for gaining over the pontiff and binding him to himself.

without security for the return of the cost; and even then, it must be for good and not for evil.[5]

All possibility of war was thus destroyed. The two powers were emulous only of contributing the most effectually to the restoration of peace, so that each might thereby the better extend and secure its own interest. For this purpose Francesco di Castro, the nephew of Lerma, proceeded to Venice on the part of Spain; as did Cardinal Joyeuse on that of France.

I have neither inclination nor means for a detailed account of these negotiations through the whole course of the proceedings; it will besides be sufficient if we obtain a clear perception of their most important characteristics.

The first difficulty was presented by the Pope, who insisted, before all things, that the Venetian laws, which had given him so much offence, should be repealed; and he made the suspension of his ecclesiastical censures to depend on their repeal.

But the Venetians, also, on their part, with a certain republican self-complacency, were accustomed to declare their laws sacred and inviolable. When the papal demand was brought under discussion in January, 1607, although the college wavered, yet at last it was decidedly rejected in the Senate.[6] The French, who had given their word to the Pope, succeeded in bringing the question forward once more in March, when of the four opponents in the college, one at least withdrew his objections. After the arguments on both sides had again been fully stated in the Senate, there was still, it is true, no formal or express

---

[5] Francesco Priuli, "Relatione di Spagna, 26 Ag. 1608": "The constable came to seek me at my house, and told me frequently, that the order for assembling troops was given for no other purpose than to avoid being idle, when all the powers of the world were arming themselves; but that they were by no means provided with money; he recommended peace in Italy, and said the republic would lose nothing by being liberal in obsequious words, to obtain in effect all that it desired. . . . At the time when the Duke of Lerma spoke in exaggerated terms to the English ambassador of the forces to be gathered, they were even then writing to the Pope that his Majesty had, doubtless, promised to aid him, but that this was intended to be for good and not for evil, . . . that the commencement of wars was in the hands of men, but their conclusion was in the power of God alone." See Appendix, No. 81, Section 7.

[6] Ger. Priuli, "Cronica Veneta, 20 Zener. 1606" (1607): "After a long discussion of eight days, and among many fluctuations of opinion, the Senate determined to reply to the ambassadors of France and Spain, that the republic cannot agree to any form of suspension whatever, seeing that this case would be a perpetual precedent; this resolution was proposed by S. Bembo and Al. Zorzi, elders of the council, and by A. Mula and S. Venier, elders of the mainland." Others desired to adopt a more moderate decision; nor is it improbable that they would have carried their point, had not intelligence arrived that there was nothing to fear from the Spanish arms, in consequence of the disturbances in Naples. A positive refusal of the suspension was then determined, by ninety-nine votes to seventy-eight, giving a majority of twenty-one. Yet Bembo himself withdrew his support from that proposal on the 9th of March; and, on the 14th, the more moderate decision was carried, in despite of the opposition made by Zorzi, Mula, and Venier.

repeal of the laws, but a decision was adopted to the effect that " the republic would conduct itself with its accustomed piety." However obscure these words appear, the ambassador and the Pope thought they discovered in them the fulfilment of their wishes. The Pope then suspended his censures.

But there immediately arose another and very unexpected difficulty; the Venetians refused to permit the return of the Jesuits, who had been excluded, after their departure, by a solemn decree.

Could it, however, be supposed that the Pope would suffer his faithful adherents, who had committed no other offence than that of an inviolable attachment to himself, to be left at such heavy disadvantage? He sought by every possible expedient to alter the resolution of the Venetians. The Jesuits had the French also on their side; they had secured the good-will of Henry IV on this occasion likewise by a special embassy, and Joyeuse took particular interest in their case; the Venetians nevertheless remained immovable.[7]

A very extraordinary circumstance was, that the Spaniards declared themselves rather against the order than for it. The Dominican interest was predominant in Spain, and Lerma, who did not favor the Jesuits, considered it unadvisable, as a general principle, that a State should be compelled to permit the return of disobedient subjects. Francesco di Castro at first avoided all mention of the Jesuits, and at length opposed himself directly to the intercession made for them by the French.[8]

This manifestation, although based, in fact, on the actual condition of things, was yet so striking, that the Pope himself was startled by it, and suspecting that a deeper mystery was somewhere concealed in it, he ceased to insist that the Jesuits should be restored.[9]

But how dearly must this resolution have cost him! For the

---

[7] Pietro Priuli, " Relatione di Francia," adds to this: " Solamente l'ufficio dell' ambasciatore ritenne la dispositione che aveva S. Ma. eccitata dall' efficaci instanze che furono fatte da un padre Barisoni Padoano mandato in Francia espressamente dalla sua congregazione col pensiero d'ottener di interessarsi acciocchè fussero di nuovo ricevuti." (See text.)

[8] Francesco Priuli, " Relatione di Spagna ": " The Spaniards hearing that the French insisted on the restoration of the Jesuits, wrote to Rome and to Venice, declaring that they would not enter on that subject, and to the republic, they gave as a reason, their not desiring to negotiate with the aforesaid persons, who had so gravely offended her."

[9] Francesco Priuli: " Venuto l'avviso dell' intiero accomodamento, desisterono dal procurare che si trattasse di loro con la Sta. V., non solo per non aver voluto parlar di loro, ma per essersi attraversati agli gagliardi ufficj di Francesi: che fece dubitare il papa di qualche recondito mistero, e non vi volse insistere con che essi non sapevano che dire." (See text.)

sake of a couple of insignificant laws he had shown himself willing to permit the whole world to be embroiled; yet he now abandoned his most faithful adherents to perpetual exile from a Catholic and Italian territory.[10] On the other hand, the republic consented to deliver up the two priests who had been arrested.

But she still claimed the right of entering an assertion of her legal powers, of which the Pope refused absolutely to hear one word. The expedient finally adopted was very singular.[1] The secretary of the Venetian Senate conducted the prisoners to the palace of the French ambassador, " and delivered them into his hands, out of respect," he said, " for the most Christian King, and with the previous understanding that the right of the republic to judge her own clergy should not thereby be diminished." " So I receive them," replied the ambassador, and led them before the cardinal, who was walking up and down in a gallery (loggia). " These are the prisoners," said he, " who are to be given up to the Pope;" but he did not allude to the reservation. Then the cardinal, without uttering one word, delivered them to the papal commissary, who received them with a sign of the cross.

But how far were the parties from having yet arrived at a clear understanding: a mere external appearance of reconciliation was their principal object.

Even that was, however, not to be attained until the censures had been removed and absolution granted.

The Venetians had, moreover, objections to make against this very absolution; they persisted in maintaining that the censure was in itself null and void; that it had in no way affected them, and that they were consequently in no need of absolution. Joyeuse declared to them, that he could not alter the forms of the Church. Finally they came to an agreement that the absolution should not be conferred with the usual publicity. Joyeuse appeared in the college, and pronounced it there, as it were, privately. The Venetians have always persuaded themselves

[10] Ger. Priuli: "This affair of the Jesuits weighed heavily on the Pope; it grieved him deeply, not indeed for their sakes, but on account of his own reputation."
[1] Joyeuse speaks of this as a condition, he says: " If the censures are removed, the two prisoners shall be delivered up to those who shall receive them in the name of his holiness; and though her serenity (Venice) declares that she resigns them for the gratification of his most Christian Majesty, yet they are to be given up without a word said."

that they escaped altogether without absolution.[2] It is true that absolution was not given with all the formalities, but given it certainly was.[3]

Upon the whole, it is sufficiently obvious that the points in dispute were not arranged so entirely to the advantage of the Venetians as is commonly asserted.

The laws of which the Pope complained were suspended, the priests whose surrender he had required, were given up to him, the absolution itself was received; but all these concessions were made with the most extraordinary limitations. The Venetians proceeded as in an affair of honor. With anxious care for their reputation, they limited every concession by all possible restrictive clauses, and did their utmost to neutralize the effect of each. The Pope, on his part, remained at a disadvantage also, since he had been compelled to resolve on a concession, manifest to all, by no means honorable in its character, and which at once excited the attention of the whole world.

These arrangements being made, the relations between Rome and Venice returned—at least in appearance—to their former course. Paul V exclaimed to the first ambassador from the Venetians, " Let old things be put away—let all now be new." He more than once complained that Venice would not forget what he, on his side, had forgotten; and displayed as much forbearance and mildness as any one of his predecessors.[4]

Yet all that was gained amounted only to this: that new dissensions were avoided; the essential grounds of dispute remained; a true and mutual confidence was not indeed to be easily restored.[5]

Section XIII.—Issue of the Affairs of the Jesuits

The contest between the Jesuits and Dominicans was meanwhile terminated in a similar manner; that is, very imperfectly.

Clement died, as we have seen, before he had pronounced judgment. The question was taken up by Paul V with all the zeal by which the early part of his administration was distin-

[2] Daru, at the close of his 29th book, gives the letter of Joyeuse, which is, beyond all doubt, the only one of importance that he has adduced respecting this affair; but he makes certain objections to it, which appear to me entirely untenable.

[3] See Appendix, No. 79.
[4] " Relatione di Mocenigo," 1612. The Pope declared that, for the interest of Italy, there should always be a good understanding between that see and this republic.
[5] See Appendix, No. 81.

guished. No fewer than seventeen meetings were held in his presence, from September, 1605, to February, 1606. He was equally disposed with his predecessor toward the old system, and to the side of the Dominicans. In October and November, 1606, meetings were even held for the purpose of deciding on the form in which the Jesuit doctrines should be condemned. The Dominicans believed they held the victory already in their hands.[1]

But it was just at this time that the Venetian affairs had been arranged in the manner we have been observing. The Jesuits had given the Roman See a proof of attachment, whereby they greatly surpassed every other order, and for this Venice was making them pay the penalty.

Under these circumstances it would have seemed cruelty in the Roman See to have visited these, its most faithful servants, with a decree of condemnation. When all was prepared for that purpose, the Pope paused; for some time he suffered the affair to rest; at length, on August 29, 1667, he published a declaration, by which " disputatores " and " consultores " were dismissed to their respective homes; the decision was to be made known in due time; meanwhile it was the most earnest desire of his holiness that neither party should asperse or disparage the other.[2]

By this decision the Jesuits, after all, derived an advantage from the losses they had sustained in Venice. It was a great gain for them that their controverted doctrines, though certainly not confirmed, were yet not rejected. They even boasted of victory; and with the public prepossession in favor of their orthodoxy once again secured, they now pursued with unremitting ardor the course of doctrine to which they had before attached themselves.

The only question yet remaining was, whether they would also succeed in perfectly composing their internal disquietudes.

Violent fermentation still prevailed in the order. The changes made in its constitution proved insufficient, and the members of the Spanish opposition persisted in their efforts for securing their principal aim; namely, the removal of Ac-

[1] Serry, " Historia Congregationum de Auxiliis," gives the documents respecting this matter in p. 562, and following pages: " Gratiæ victrici," he says himself, " jam canebatur ' Io triumphe.' "
[2] Coronelli, secretary of the Congregation, in Serry, p. 589: " Tra tanto ha ordinato (S. Sa.) molto seriamente che nel trattare di queste materie nessuno ardisca di qualificare e censurare l'altra parte. (See text.)

quaviva. The procurators of all the provinces at length declared a general congregation necessary, which was a circumstance that never had occurred before. In the year 1607, the members assembled, and effectual changes were to be once more brought under discussion.

We have already more than once alluded to the close alliance into which the Jesuits had entered with Henry IV, and the favor accorded to them by that sovereign. He even took part in the internal disputes of the order, and was entirely on the side of Acquaviva. In a letter written expressly for the purpose, he not only assured the general of his friendly regard, but also gave the congregation to understand his wish that no change in the constitution of the society should be proposed.[3]

Nor did Acquaviva fail to make excellent use of so powerful a protection.

It was principally in the provincial congregations that the opposition he encountered had its seat. He now carried through a law, by virtue of which, no proposition should in the first place be considered as adopted by a provincial assembly, unless supported by two-thirds of the votes; and further, even when thus adopted, such proposition should not be admitted for discussion in the general assembly, unless a majority of the latter had previously assented to it. These regulations were manifestly calculated to produce extraordinary diminution in the authority of the provincial congregations.

Nor was this all; a formal sentence of condemnation was also pronounced on the enemies of the general, and the superiors of provinces received express command to proceed against the so-called disturbers of the peace. Tranquillity was thus gradually restored. The Spanish members resigned themselves to submission, and ceased to contend against the new direction taken by their order. A more pliant generation gradually arose, which was educated under the predominant influences. The general, on his side, endeavored to requite Henry IV, by redoubled devotion, for the favors received at his hands.

[3] " Literæ Christianissimi regis ad congregatos patres," iv. Kal. Dec. 1607, in Juvencius, v. ii. lib. ix. n. 108: " And we exhort you to maintain your institution in its integrity and splendor."

Conclusion

Thus were all these contentions once more allayed, and gave promise of subsiding into peace.

But if we reflect on their progress, and their results as a whole, we perceive that the most essential changes had been thereby produced in the centre and heart of the Catholic Church.

We started from that moment when the papal power, engaged in victorious conflict, was marching forward to the plenitude of authority. In close alliance with the policy of Spain, it conceived the design of impelling all the Catholic powers in one direction, and overwhelming those who had separated from it by one great movement. Had the papacy succeeded in this purpose, it would have exalted the ecclesiastical impulse to unlimited sovereignty; would have bound all Catholic States in one all-embracing unity of ideas, faith, social life, and policy; and would thus have secured to itself a paramount and irresistible influence even over their domestic affairs.

But at this precise moment the most violent dissensions arose within its own bosom.

' In the matter of France, the feeling of nationality arrayed itself against the pretensions of the hierarchy. Even those who held the Catholic faith would not endure to be dependent on the ruling principles of the Church in every particular, nor to be guided on all points by the spiritual sovereign. There were other principles remaining—as of temporal policy, of national independence; all which opposed themselves to the designs of the papacy with invincible energy. Upon the whole, we may affirm that these principles obtained the victory; the Pope was compelled to acknowledge them, and the French Church even effected its restoration by adopting them as its basis.

But it followed, from this circumstance, that France again plunged herself into perpetual hostilities with the Spanish monarchy; that two great powers, naturally prone to rivalry, and always disposed for battle, confronted each other in the centre of the Catholic world—so little was it possible to preserve unity. The circumstances of Italy were indeed of such a character, that these dissensions, and the balance of power resulting from them, produced advantages to the Roman See.

Meanwhile, new theological discords also broke out. However acute and precise the definitions of the Council of Trent might be, they were yet not equal to the prevention of disputes. Within the limits traced by these decisions there was still room for new controversies respecting the faith. The two most influential of the orders opposed each other in the lists. The two great powers even took part to a certain extent in the contest; nor had Rome the courage to pronounce a decision.

In addition to these dissensions, came those regarding the limits of the ecclesiastical and secular jurisdictions; dissensions of local origin, and with a neighbor of no very important power, but conducted in a spirit, and with an effect that raised them into universal importance.[4] Justly is the memory of Paolo Sarpi held in honor through all Catholic States. He it was by whom those ecclesiastical rights, which they enjoy in common, were contended for and won. The Pope did not find himself capable of putting him down.

Conflicts thus marked between ideas and doctrines, between constitutional and absolute power, effectually impeded that ecclesiastical and secular unity which the papacy desired to establish, and even threatened to subvert it entirely.

The course of events made it nevertheless obvious that pacific and conservative ideas were once more the stronger. Internal discords were not to be prevented; but an open struggle was avoided. Peace was restored and maintained between the two great powers. Italian interests had not yet advanced to a full perception of their own strength, nor to an effectual activity in employing it; silence was imposed on the contending orders; the differences between Church and State were not carried to extremity. Venice accepted the proffered mediation.

The policy of the papacy was to assume, as far as possible, a position above that of parties, and to mediate in their dissensions; a purpose which it still possessed sufficient authority to effect.

This policy, without doubt, experienced reaction from that which had in part proceeded from itself, the continued progress, namely, of the great external movement, the advance of Catholic reformation, and the struggle with Protestantism, which was still proceeding without interruption.

To the further development of that struggle we must now return.

[4] " Your serenity, exclaims P. Priuli to his government, on his return from France, may be said to have declared within what limits it shall be permitted to the pontificate to extend its authority, whether spiritual or temporal."—Relatione di Francia, 1608.

THE SPIRIT OF HOPE.

Photo-engraving from the original statue in the foyer of the Grand Opera House, Paris.

M. Bruyer has embodied here, in the art of pure form, a triple conception of his subject that is a sermon in itself. First note the star above the forehead, to lead, guide, and beckon the toiler; then mark the anchor, which holds the voyager in his riding-ground, though storms assail; finally see the wreath held out to crown the final struggle. The artist has embodied poetry and moral inspiration in a manner which demands the highest praise.

BOOK VII

COUNTER REFORMATION

SECOND PERIOD, 1590–1630

I THINK I do not deceive myself, or pass beyond the province of history, in supposing that I here discover, and in seeking to indicate, one of the universal laws of social life. It is unquestionably true that there are at all periods forces of the living mind by which the world is moved profoundly; gradually prepared in the long course of bygone centuries, they arise in the fulness of time, called forth by natures of intrinsic might and vigor from the unfathomed depths of the human spirit. It is of their very essence and being that they should seek to gain possession of the world—to over-match and subdue it. But the more perfect their success, the more extended the circle of their action, so much the more certainly do they come in contact with peculiar and independent forms of social life, which they cannot wholly subdue or absorb into their own being. Hence it happens that, being, as they are, in a state of never-ceasing progress, they experience modifications in themselves. While appropriating what is foreign to their own existence, they also assume a portion of its characteristics; tendencies are then developed within them—crises of existence—that are not unfrequently at variance with their ruling principle; these also must, however, necessarily expand and increase with the general progress; the object to be then secured is that they do not obtain the predominance: for if this were permitted, all unity, and that essential principle on which it reposes, would be utterly destroyed.

We have seen how violently internal contradictions and profound contrasts were in action during the restoration of the papacy; still the ruling idea retained the victory; the higher

247

unity yet preserved its ascendancy, though not perhaps with all its ancient and comprehensive power, and continually pressed forward with unremitting steps, even during periods of internal strife, from which indeed it seemed to derive increased energy for new conquests.

These enterprises now solicit our attention. How far they succeeded; the revolutions that were their consequences, and the opposition they encountered, whether from within or from without, are all questions of the utmost importance to the world in general.

CHAPTER FIRST

PROGRESS OF THE CATHOLIC RESTORATION.—
A.D. 1590-1617

Section I.—Enterprises of Catholicism in Poland and the Neighboring Territories

AN opinion has been expressed that the Protestants, who for some time certainly had, as we have seen, the decided supremacy in Poland, would also have been in a condition to raise a king of their own faith to the throne; but that even they themselves came at length to consider a Catholic more advantageous, because in the person of the Pope he had a still higher power and judge placed over him.

If this were so, they brought a very heavy punishment upon themselves for a decision so adverse to Protestantism.

For it was precisely by the agency of a Catholic king that the Pope was enabled to make war on them.

Of all the foreign ambassadors in Poland, the papal nuncios alone possessed the right of demanding audience of the King without the presence of a senator. We know what these men were; they had prudence and address enough to cultivate and profit by the confidential intercourse thus placed within their reach.

In the beginning of the eightieth year of the sixteenth century, Cardinal Bolognetto was nuncio in Poland. He complained of the severity of the climate; of the cold, to which, as an Italian, he was doubly susceptible; of the close, suffocating air in the small heated rooms, and of the whole mode of life, which was utterly uncongenial to his habits and predilections. He nevertheless accompanied King Stephen from Warsaw to Cracow, from Wilna to Lublin—throughout the kingdom in short; at times in rather melancholy mood, but none the less indefatigable. During the campaigns, he kept up his intercourse with the King, at least by letter, and maintained an uninterrupted connection between the interests of Rome and the royal personage.

We have a circumstantial relation of his official proceedings, and from this we learn the character of his undertakings, and how far he prospered in them.[1]

Above all things, he exhorted the King to appoint Catholics only to the government offices; to permit no other form of worship than that of the Catholic Church in the royal towns, and to re-establish the tithes; measures which were adopted about the same time in other countries, and which promoted or indicated the renovation of Catholicism.

But the nuncio was not wholly successful in the first instance. King Stephen thought he could not go so far; he declared that he was not sufficiently powerful to venture it.

Yet this prince was not only imbued with Catholic convictions, he had besides an innate zeal for the interests of the Church, and in many other particulars his decisions were regulated by the representations of the nuncio.

It was under the immediate patronage of royalty that the Jesuit colleges in Cracow, Grodno, and Pultusk were established. The new calendar was introduced without difficulty, and the ordinances of the Council of Trent were for the most part carried into full effect. But the most important circumstance was, the King's determination that the bishoprics should, for the future, be conferred on Catholics only.[2] Protestants had previously made their way even to those ecclesiastical dignities; but the nuncio was now authorized to summon them before his tribunal, and to depose them; a fact of all the more importance, inasmuch as that a seat and vote in the Senate were attached to the episcopal office. It was this political efficacy of the spiritual institutions that the nuncio most especially sought to turn to account. Above all, he exhorted the bishops to be unanimous, as regarded the measures to be adopted at the diet, and these measures were prescribed by himself. With the most powerful of the Polish ecclesiastics, the Archbishop of Gnesen

[1] Report to the most illustrious and most reverend Cardinal Rusticucci, secretary of our lord Pope Sixtus V, concerning the religious affairs of Poland, and of the measures of Cardinal Bolognetto, during four years that he was nuncio in that province. See Appendix, No. 61.
[2] "The King being resolved that none should hold churches who were not of the true faith of Rome."—Spannocchi.

and the Bishop of Cracow, Bolognetto had formed a close personal intimacy, which was of infinite utility for the promotion
of his views.   Thus he succeeded, not only in awakening new
zeal among the clergy, but also in at once obtaining extensive
influence over temporal affairs.   The English were making
proposals for a commercial treaty with Poland, which promised
to become very advantageous, more particularly for Dantzic.
It was by the nuncio alone that this purpose was defeated, and
principally because the English required a distinct promise
that they should be allowed to trade and live in peace, without
being persecuted on account of their religion.[3]

These things suffice to show, that however moderate King
Stephen might be, it was yet under him that Catholicism first
acquired an essential reinstation in Poland.

And this had all the more importance from the fact that the
most influential party in the country, the Zamoisky faction, to
which by the King's favor, the most important offices were generally intrusted,[4] had also received a deep tinge of Catholicism.
It was this party that on the death of Stephen determined the
conflicts of election in favor of his successor; and the sovereign,
placed by the Zamoisky faction on the Polish throne, was that
Swedish prince whom Catherine Jagellonica had borne in prison,
and who, in the midst of a Protestant country, had ever remained
immovably steadfast in the Catholic faith—either from original
inclination, the influence of his mother, the hope he entertained
of succeeding to the crown of Poland, or, it may be, from these
influences all acting together.

This was Sigismund III, a prince whose modes of thought
were formed in complete accordance with those Catholic impulses by which all Europe was at that period set in motion.

Pope Clement VIII says, in one of his instructions, that while

[3] Spannocchi: " This no sooner came
to the ears of Bolognetto, than he went
to seek his Majesty, and with the most
prevailing reasons, showed him what an
exorbitant evil it would be to make
concessions by public decree to so scan-
dalous a sect, and how it was certainly
not without some hidden deception, and
the hope of important consequences,
that yonder pestilent woman (Elizabeth
of England) desired to have the Anglican sect thus placed at liberty by public decree to exercise its worship in that
kingdom, where it is but too well known
to all the world, that, in matters of religion, all sorts of people may believe
whatsoever they please. By these and
other most efficacious reasons, King
Stephen was so fully persuaded, that he
promised never to make any mention of
religion in any treaty whatsoever with
that queen and her merchants." See
Appendix, No. 61.
[4] Spannocchi: " It is now said that
none are admitted to the senatorial dignity, or to the management of the revenues, but the dependants of this chancellor, to the end that what he and the
King may be pleased to do, shall not
receive impediment from any opposition."

yet a cardinal, and when legate in Poland, he had recommended that prince to bestow all public offices in future on Catholics only. This advice had already been frequently given before, as by Paul IV, by Cardinal Hosius,[5] and again by Cardinal Bolognetto: there were now, for the first time, means for giving this counsel its full effect. What could not be obtained, either from Sigismund Augustus, or from Stephen, was very quickly resolved on by Sigismund III. He established it, in fact, as his principle of action, to confer promotion on none but Catholics, and Pope Clement was fully justified in ascribing the progress of Catholicism in Poland more especially to this regulation.

The most essential attribute of the kingly power in Poland consisted in the right of conferring all dignities and appointments. Every office, whether spiritual or temporal, whether great or small, was in the gift of the King, and their number was said to be nearly 20,000. How important must have been the consequences when Sigismund proceeded to bestow, not ecclesiastical appointments only, but all offices whatever, exclusively on Catholics; when he resolved to accord the beneficence of the State, as the Italians once expressed it, the full right of citizenship, in the higher sense of the word, to his coreligionists only. A man's promotion was all the more certain, the more he could acquire the favor of the bishops and Jesuits; the starost, Ludwig von Mortangen, became Waiwode of Pomerellia, principally because he presented his house in Thorn to the Society of Jesus. As a consequence of this system, disputes arose in the territories of Polish Prussia, between the cities and the nobles, and these soon assumed a religious character: both had originally attached themselves to Protestantism, but the nobles now recanted. The examples of the Kostka, Dzialinsky, and Konopat families, which had risen to power by passing over to Catholicism, produced a great effect on the rest. The schools of the Jesuits were frequented principally by the young nobility, and we soon find that in the towns remaining attached to Protestantism the pupils of the Jesuits had entered into conflict with the sons of the citizens. The new influences were, however, chiefly effectual among the nobles; the College of Pultusk numbered

---

[5] In a letter of the 14th of March, 1568, he begs the King to declare, that in future he would confer no honors, or governments, or public offices whatever, unless it were on such as would openly confess Christ, and abjure all perfidies, whether Lutheran, Calvinistic, or Anabaptist.

400 pupils—all noble.[6]   The impulse originating from and pervading the spirit of the times, the teaching of the Jesuits, the newly awakened zeal of the clerical body, and the favor of the court, all· concurred to determine the Polish nobility toward a return to Catholicism.   But it followed as a matter of course that further steps were soon taken, and those who would not consent to become Catholic were now made to feel the displeasure of the civil power.

In Poland the Catholic clergy set themselves eagerly to revive a claim to the ecclesiastical buildings, on the ground that having been founded by those of Catholic faith, with the co-operation of bishops, and frequently of popes, they were the inalienable property of their Church.   In every place where the Catholic service had been excluded from the parish churches, the bishops instituted legal proceedings founded on that claim.   The tribunals were now filled with zealous Catholics ; the same proceedings were commenced against one town after another, and the same judgments were pronounced.   It availed nothing that the losers appealed to the King, reminding him of that confederation by which both confessions were assured of equal rights and equal protection.   The answer they received was that equal protection consisted precisely in helping each party to obtain its rights, and that the " confederation " comprised no assurance to them of the possession of ecclesiastical buildings.[7]   A few years only had elapsed before the Catholics were in possession of all the parish churches in the towns.   " In the parish churches," exclaims one Polish authority, "the ancient God is worshipped: " throughout the smaller Prussian towns the evangelical service could be now performed in a room of the Town House only.   Of the larger cities, Dantzic alone retained its parish Church.[8]

But during this period of successful progress the Catholics did not confine themselves to contentions with the Protestants ; they turned their attention to the Greek communities also.

On that occasion likewise the King and the Pope combined their influence ; the menace of exclusion from a seat and voice in the Senate would seem to have been particularly efficacious,

[6] Maffei, ii. 140.
[7] The circumstantial letter of the Waiwode of Culm, translated by Lengnich, " Polnisch-preussische   Geschichte," Theil iv. s. 291, gives a clear explication of these motives.   See also Appendix, No. 67.
[8] Lengnich, " Nachricht von der Religionsänderung in Preussen," § 27.

so far as I can discover, with the Greek bishops. It is at all
events certain that in the year 1595 Wladika of Wladimir and
some other bishops of the Greek confession, resolved to unite
themselves to the Roman Church according to the rules laid
down by the Council of Florence. Their emissaries proceeded
to Rome; papal and royal envoys appeared in the province; the
ceremony of reconciliation was performed, and a Jesuit confessor to the King gave it further effect by the animated sermon
he preached on the occasion: here also several churches were
vacated in favor of the Catholics.

This was a remarkable progress to have been made in so few
years. " A short time since," observes a papal nuncio, in the
year 1598, " it might have been feared that heresy would entirely supersede Catholicism in Poland; now, Catholicism is bearing
heresy to its grave."

If we inquire to what causes this change must be principally
attributed, we find that it was above all else to the personal character and modes of thought of the King that they were due.

And these dispositions of Sigismund III, in the peculiar position of that monarch, led immediately to views and purposes of
much more extensive importance.

Section II.—Attempt on Sweden

In the year 1592, Sigismund became King of Sweden, by the
death of John, his father.

But in this kingdom he was by no means possessed of unlimited authority as sovereign, neither was he free from obligations and engagements personal to himself; for in the year 1587,
he had signed an assurance that nothing should be changed in
the ceremonies of the Protestant Church, and that he would
promote no one who was not a Protestant. And now also he
bound himself anew to maintain the privileges of the clergy as
well as of the laity; promised that he would make the religion
of no man a cause for either love or hatred, and would in nowise seek to prejudice or injure the national Church. Notwithstanding these engagements, however, all the hopes of the Catholics were instantly awakened, as were all the fears of the Protestants.

The Catholics had now attained what had always been the

object of their most earnest desires, a king of their own faith in Sweden. Sigismund departed for his hereditary dominions in July, 1593, surrounded by a Catholic retinue, in which even a papal nuncio, Malaspina, was not wanting. His journey through the Prussian provinces was marked by the promotion of Catholic interests. In Dantzic he was met by a papal envoy, Bartholomæus Powsinsky, with a present of 20,000 scudi, " a small contribution," as was declared in Powsinsky's instructions, " toward the expenses that might be occasioned by the restoration of Catholicism."

This " Instruction " is very remarkable. It shows us how confidently that restoration was expected and hoped for in Rome, and how anxiously it was recommended.[1]

" Powsinsky," it states,[2] " a trusted servant of his holiness, and a vassal of his Majesty, has been sent to declare to the King the interest taken by the Pope in the welcome events that had lately occurred to his Majesty, the delivery of his Queen; and the fortunate results of the last Diet; but above all, in the greatest happiness that could befall him, the opportunity, namely, that he now has of reinstating Catholicism in his native land." The Pope did not omit to intimate certain points of view in which this work might be considered.

" It is without doubt," he says, " by God's most special providence that certain bishoprics should be vacant precisely at this moment; among others, even the archiepiscopal seat of Upsala;[3] should the King delay for a moment to depose the Protestant bishops who may still remain in the land, yet he will infallibly, and at once, supply the vacant sees with bishops of the Catholic faith." The envoy was provided with a list of Swedish Catholics who seemed fitted for the purpose. The Pope was convinced that these bishops would then immediately seek to procure Catholic priests and schoolmasters; but he recommends that care should be taken to provide them with the means for doing so.

" It would probably be possible," he thinks, " to establish a Jesuits' college in Stockholm immediately; but if this were not found practicable, the King will without doubt take with him

---

[1] " Instruttione al Sve. Bartholomeo Powsinsky, alla Ma. del re di Polonia e Suetia," MS. Rome.
[2] See Appendix, No. 66.
[3] Understanding that the archbishopric of Upsala was vacant—for divine Providence, the better to facilitate its own service, has not permitted it to be filled up by the late King, during two years that it has been vacant, his Majesty will have especial care to select a Catholic archbishop."

into Poland as many young Swedes as he can find suitable for
the purpose, and have them educated at his court, in the Catholic
faith, by some of the most zealous bishops, or in the Jesuit colleges of Poland."[4]

The principal object here, as in all other places, was to compel
the clergy once more to subordination. The nuncio had meanwhile formed another project. He suggested to the Catholics
yet remaining in Sweden certain grievances for which they
might bring proceedings against the Protestants. The King
would then assume a position above the two parties, and to
every innovation that he might attempt to carry, it might thus
be possible to give the appearance of a legal decision.[5] He
regretted only that Sigismund had not provided himself with
a more imposing force of arms, the better to give effect to his
decrees.

There is indeed no proof that the King at once adopted the
views of the Roman Court. To judge from his own declarations, he intended no more in the first instance than to procure
immunities for the Catholics, without subverting the Protestant
constitution. But would he be capable of restraining the powerful religious impulses by which those around him were mastered, and whose most zealous representatives made a part of
his retinue? Can it be supposed that, having reached that point,
he would have been content to stop there?

The Protestants would not abide the issue. The views and
purposes entertained on the one side called forth an immediate
and almost unconscious opposition from the other.

Instantly after the death of John, the Swedish Councillors
of State, names of high renown both before and since that
period, Gyllenstiern, Bielke, Baner, Sparre, and Oxenstiern,
assembled to acknowledge the zealously Protestant Duke
Charles, one of the sons of Gustavus Vasa, brother of the late
King and uncle of their young sovereign, as governor of the
realm; and agreed, " in the absence of his nephew, to promise
him obedience in all that he should command for the maintenance of the Augsburg Confession in Sweden." With this

---

[4] See Appendix No. 68.
[5] " Ragguaglio dell' andata del re di
Polonia in Suetia" (MS. Rome):
" There were still some remnants of
Catholicism remaining in the kingdom,
and the nuncio, pursuing the plan before adopted by Cardinal Madruzzo, to
strengthen the authority of the Emper-
or, sought to constitute the King judge
between the Catholics and heretics of
Sweden, inducing the former to complain before the King of the insolence
and injurious proceedings of the latter."

purpose a council was held at Upsala, in March, 1593. The Confession of Augsburg was there proclaimed anew; the liturgy of King John was condemned, and all that seemed to recall the usages of Catholicism, even in the earlier ritual, received modification; the exorcism was retained, but in milder expressions only, and merely for the sake of its moral significance.[6] A declaration was drawn up, to the effect that no heresy, whether popish or Calvinistic, would be tolerated in the kingdom.[7] Appointments to public offices were made in the same spirit. Many old defenders of the liturgy now abjured it; but this renunciation did not secure the escape of all; some were dismissed from their offices notwithstanding. The bishoprics, on the vacancy of which such great designs had been founded in Rome, were given to Lutherans; the archbishopric of Upsala to M. Abraham Angermannus, the most zealous opponent of the liturgy, and by an overwhelming majority, the votes of his election amounting to 233; those for the candidate next to him to thirty-eight only. The clergy thus placed the most ardent Lutheran they could find at their head.

Under King John a more temperate state of public feeling had been maintained to the last, a less earnest opposition to the papacy than in other countries; aided by this, Sigismund might easily have effected such a change as the Catholics desired; but these measures had been anticipated by the other side, and Protestantism had fixed itself more firmly in possession than it had ever previously been.

On this occasion even the royal prerogatives of Sigismund were not spared. He was already no longer regarded as altogether King of Sweden, but rather as a foreigner holding claims to the crown; as an apostate, who was menacing religion, and against whom precautions must be taken. The great majority of the nation, unanimous in their Protestant convictions, adhered to Duke Charles.

Arrived in Sweden, the King became fully sensible to the

---

[6] For we must not believe the assertion of Messenius, that it was abolished. The only change was in the words " Faar här uth," which were changed for " Wick här ifra." Duke Charles wished it to be abolished, but was told that the exorcism was to be retained, as a ceremony wherein was an admonition useful to the hearers and spectators at the baptism. To this view Duke Charles assented.—Baaz, " Inventarium," iv. x. 523. The documents will be found in Baaz, and are, in general, tolerably complete.

[7] " The Council enacts, it further says, that no place for public meetings shall be allowed to heretics who may come into the kingdom."

isolation of the position he occupied: he could do nothing, and sought only to evade the demands made upon him.

But while Sigismund remained silent and waited the effects of time, the opposing parties, which had never before so directly confronted each other in that country, came into collision. The evangelical preachers inveighed against the papists; and the Jesuits, who preached in the King's chapel, did not suffer them to remain unanswered. The Catholics of the royal suite took possession of an evangelical church on the occasion of a burial; whereupon the Protestants considered it necessary to abstain for a time from returning to their desecrated sanctuary. Acts of violence were not slow to follow: the soldiers of the guard (*Heiduks*) used force to obtain possession of a pulpit which was closed; the nuncio was accused of having ordered stones to be thrown from his house at some choristers who were singing in the street, and the rancor of the parties was continually increasing in bitterness.

Sigismund at length proceeded with his train to Upsala for the ceremony of his coronation. The Swedes demanded above all things that the decrees of their council should be ratified. The King resisted. He desired nothing more than toleration for Catholicism: he would have been content had they only allowed him the hope of having power to grant it at some future time, but the Swedish Protestants were immovable. It is affirmed that the King's own sister[8] assured them it was his nature to yield only after long and obstinate resistance, but that he would ultimately yield: she exhorted them to keep firm only, and constantly to renew their attacks on him. They demanded peremptorily that the doctrines of the Augsburg Confession should be inculcated everywhere, alone and purely, whether in churches or schools.[9] Duke Charles was at their head. The position which he thus assumed conferred on him a degree of power and independence such as he could in no other manner have hoped to attain. His personal relations with the King became continually more unpleasant and less friendly. The King was almost entirely without arms, as we have said, whereas the duke had raised several thousand men on the domains he held

[8] The " Ragguaglio " calls her " a most obstinate heretic."

[9] Messenius, vii. 19: " They absolutely insisted, that the Confession of Augsburg, as it had prevailed in the reign of the last Gustavus and the early part of John's reign, should for the future be fixed in perpetuity, as well in schools as in churches."

immediately around the city.   The States at length declared to the King in plain terms that they would not render him homage if he refused to comply with their demands.[10]

The unfortunate prince found himself in a painful embarrassment: to grant what was required from him oppressed his conscience; to refuse it would deprive him of a crown.

In this strait he first had recourse to the nuncio, inquiring if he might not venture to yield; but Malaspina could by no means be prevailed on to sanction his doing so.

The King thereupon addressed himself to the Jesuits in his train, and what the nuncio had not dared, they took upon themselves to do.   They declared that in consideration of the necessity and of the manifest danger in which the sovereign found himself, he might grant the heretics their demands without offence to God.   But the King was not satisfied until he had this decision, in a written form, placed in his hands.

Then, and not before, did Sigismund comply with the demands of his subjects.   He confirmed the decrees of Upsala, the exclusive use of the Augsburg Confession, pure and unchanged, without the admixture of any extraneous doctrine, whether in church or school; and he further agreed that no one should be appointed to a public office who was not prepared to defend the Lutheran doctrines.[1]   He also acknowledged the prelates who had obtained their sees in opposition to his will.

But could his Catholic heart feel tranquil under these circumstances?   Could his retinue, devoted to Romanism, remain content with a result that they could not fail utterly to condemn?   It was not in the nature of things that this could be reasonably expected.

And accordingly steps were taken at length for the publication of a protest, such as had before been promulgated in many places on similar occasions.

" The nuncio," says the report of this affair which was sent to Rome, and in the words of which I shall most easily elucidate these occurrences—" the nuncio was zealously busied in seek-

[10] " Supplicatio ordinum:"   " But if the illustrious King should refuse to his subjects the royal approbation of these propositions, our brethren remaining at home forbid us in that case to offer public homage to his royal Majesty."
[1] These words, nevertheless, are so chosen that they leave a possibility of evasion: " None shall be promoted to the public offices of the country, who do not desire the safety of the evangelical religion; those rather shall be preferred to the public offices, who seriously desire to defend the same."—" Generalis confirmatio postulatorum regis Sigismundi," in Baaz, p. 537.

ing to remedy the irregularity that had taken place. He prevailed on the King to draw up a protestation in writing for the security of his conscience, and in this he declared that the concessions he had made were not accorded by his own free will, but that he had been compelled to them solely and entirely by force and against his wish. The nuncio further induced his Majesty to make similar concessions to the Catholics also, that so he might be equally pledged to both parties in Sweden as well as in Poland, a plan that had been adopted in the case of the German Emperor. This the King was content to do.[2]

It was a singular expedient. One protest was not thought enough; and in order to be in some measure freed from an obligation entered into by oath, another oath, of a tendency directly opposite, is taken to another party. Thus an engagement being entered into with both parties, equal rights must of necessity be extended to both.

The Swedes were amazed that the King, after promises so solemn, should extend to the Catholics a protection that was but very slightly veiled. It was undoubtedly the result of this secret engagement. "Even before his departure," continues our authority, with obvious complacency, "the King bestowed offices and dignities on those of the Catholic faith; he caused four governors of towns, although they were heretics, to swear that they would protect the Catholics and their religion. In four places he re-established the exercise of the Catholic religion."

All these measures, though calculated perhaps to pacify the unquiet conscience of a bigoted prince, could not possibly fail to produce the most injurious effects in the course of events.

It was indeed precisely because the Swedish Estates were

[2] "Relatione dello stato spirituale e politico del regno di Suezia, 1598:" "He sent some Polish Senators to inform the Jesuit fathers of the state of his circumstances, and the consequences; then the said fathers declared, that, assuming the need and peril in which his Majesty was placed, he could yield to the heretics what they sought, without offending God; and his Majesty, for his justification, would needs have a writing from the said fathers. Now, the coronation and concessions being completed, the nuncio gave all his thoughts to the discovery of some remedy for the disorder that had occurred; and he contrived that, for the security of his conscience, his Majesty should protest in writing, that he had not yielded those things of his will, but of pure force; and he persuaded the most serene King to grant to the Catholics the same promises that he had granted to the heretics, so that, as in the case of the Emperor, and as for the kingdom of Poland, he should be sworn to both sides (' utrique parti '). His Majesty agreed, and immediately carried the said concessions into effect; for, before his departure, he gave offices and dignities to Catholics, and permitted the exercise of the faith in four places. He also made four governors, whom he left in the kingdom, give him their oath, although they were heretics, that they would see religion and the Catholics protected."

thus kept in continual excitement and irritation, that they threw themselves into so determined an opposition.

The clergy reformed their schools according to the most rigid tenor of the Lutheran doctrines, and appointed a day of solemn thanksgiving for the preservation of the true religion " from the designs and intrigues of the Jesuits." In the year 1595 a resolution was passed in the Diet of Südercöping, that all exercise of the Catholic ritual, wheresoever the King might have established it, was again to be abolished. " We decree unanimously," declare the States, " that all sectaries, opposed to the evangelical religion, who have fixed themselves in the land, shall within six weeks be removed entirely from the kingdom :[3] and this edict was enforced with the utmost rigor." The monastery of Wadstena, which had subsisted during 211 years, and had maintained its ground in the midst of so many convulsions, was now dissolved and destroyed. Angermannus held a visitation of the churches, of which the severity never had been equalled. Whoever neglected to attend the evangelical Church was beaten with rods; the archbishop had several robust young students in his train, by whom this punishment was inflicted under his own superintendence. The altars of the saints were destroyed, their relics were dispersed, and the ceremonies, which in 1593 had been declared indifferent, were in many places entirely abolished in the year 1597.

The relative positions of Sigismund and Charles gave a character of personality to this movement.

Whatever was done, proceeded in direct opposition to the well-known desires, and even to the ordinances, of the King. In everything Duke Charles had a predominant influence. It was in contradiction to the express command of Sigismund that the duke held the Diet, and all attempts of the former to interfere in the affairs of the country were opposed by Charles. He caused a resolution to be passed, by virtue of which the rescripts of the King were effectual only after having been confirmed by the Swedish Government.[4]

Charles was already monarch, and ruler in fact, and the thought had even arisen within him of becoming sovereign in

[3] " Acta ecclesiæ, in conventu Südercöp." in Baaz, 567.
[4] " Attempts of the most illustrious prince and lord Charles, Duke of Sudermania, against the most serene and most potent lord Sigismund III, King of Sweden and Poland; written and published by his royal Majesty's own command." Dant. 1598.

name also. This is intimated by a dream that he had in 1595, as well as by other circumstances. He thought that at a banquet in Finland a covered double dish was set before him; he raised the cover, and on the one side he perceived the insignia of royalty, on the other a death's head. Similar thoughts were prevalent in the nation. A story was repeated throughout the country that in Linköping a crowned eagle had been seen contending with one uncrowned, and that the uncrowned one had remained master of the field.

When things had proceeded so far, when the Protestant principles were enforced with so much rigor, and their champion seemed making a claim to the royal power, a party rose also in favor of the King. Certain nobles, who had sought aid from Sigismund against the duke, were banished, but their adherents remained in the land; the populace were dissatisfied at finding all ceremonies abolished, and attributed such disasters as occurred in the country to that circumstance. In Finland, the governor, Flemming, maintained the standard of the King.

This position of things made it as expedient on the one hand, as it was advisable on the other, that Sigismund should once more essay his fortune. It was perhaps the last moment in which it was possible for him to restore his authority. In the summer of 1598 he set forward for the second time to take possession of his hereditary kingdom.

He was now more rigidly Catholic, if possible, than at his first appearance; the good prince believed that the different misfortunes which had befallen him since his last journey, among others the death of his Queen, had been inflicted on him because he had then made concessions to the heretics. With deep sorrow of heart he revealed these painful convictions to the nuncio, and declared that he would rather die than again concede anything that could stain the purity of his conscience.

But the interests here in question were immediately connected with those of Europe generally. Such was now the progress making by Catholicism that an enterprise undertaken even in this distant portion of the world was also considered principally in the light of a part in the general combination.

In earlier times, and during the wars with England, the Spaniards had occasionally turned their eyes on the Swedish coasts. They had discovered that the possession of a Swedish haven would be of the utmost utility to them, and had commenced a negotiation on the subject. It was now considered certain that Sigismund, on becoming master in his own dominions, would make over to them the port of Elfsborg, in West Gothland. There it would be easy to build a fleet, to keep it in condition for service, and have it manned by Poles and Swedes. How much more readily could war be made on England from this port than from Spain! the English would be compelled to forego their attacks on the Spanish Indies. And even as regarded the maintenance of Sigismund in Sweden, an alliance with the Catholic King could not fail to be advantageous.[5]

But there was yet more. The Catholics extended their views to the establishment of their rule over Finland and the Baltic; from Finland they hoped to make a successful attack on the Russian Empire, and by the possession of the Baltic they trusted to subject the Duchy of Brandenburg to their dominion. The electoral house of Brandenburg had never yet been able to obtain the investiture of that fief, by any negotiation, and the nuncio declared that the King was resolved not to grant it, but had determined, on the contrary, that the duchy should be annexed to the crown; he used every effort to confirm Sigismund in this resolution, principally, as will be obvious, from religious considerations, for never would Brandenburg consent to the re-establishment of Catholicism in Prussia.[6]

If we consider on the one hand the vast extent of views and purposes, thus rendered dependent on Sigismund's success, which was yet by no means improbable, and the great increase of general importance that would accrue to Sweden from the victory of Protestantism on the other, we must acknowledge that this was one of those crises which affect the history of the world.

Zamoisky had recommended the King to advance at the head of a powerful army, and conquer Sweden by force of arms; but Sigismund held the opinion that this could not be needful; he

[5] " Relatione dello stato spirituale e politico." The plan was that at the expense of the Catholic King a garrison should be maintained in the fortress commanding the port, over which garrison his Catholic Majesty should have no authority, but should consign the pay for the garrison to the King of Poland.

[6] " Relatione di Polonia," 1598: " See-ing that the Catholic religion cannot be expected ever to find ingress, if the duchy remain in the house of Brandenburg, his Majesty shows himself resolved to recover the said duchy." King Stephen ought already to have done this; but, finding himself in want of money, while he was also engaged in wars, Brandenburg was not thought of.

would not believe that resistance would be opposed to him in his hereditary dominions, and took with him only about 5,000 men; with these he landed at Calmar, without opposition, and moved forward toward Stockholm. A second division of his troops had previously reached the city and been admitted, while a body of Finlanders marched upon Upland.

Duke Charles also had in the meantime prepared his forces. It was manifest, that his power must have an end, together with the supremacy of the Protestant faith, should Sigismund obtain the victory. While his peasantry of Upland held the Finns in check, the duke himself, with a regular military force, opposed the march of the King, who was advancing on Stege-borg. Charles demanded that the royal army should be with-drawn, and the decision of all questions referred to the Diet; that being done, he also would disband his troops. To this the King would not consent, and the hostile bodies advanced against each other.

They were not considerable in number—insignificant masses —a few thousand men on either side; but the decision was not less important, the results not less enduring, than if large armies had been employed to secure them.

It was on the personal character of the princes that all de-pended. Charles was his own adviser; daring, resolute, a man, in the utmost force of the word, and what was the principal matter, he was in actual possession. Sigismund, dependent on others, yielding, good-natured, no soldier, and now reduced to the unhappy necessity of doing battle for the kingdom that be-longed to him of right, but for which he, the legitimate sov-ereign, must contend with the ruler in possession, and with the existing order of things.

The troops were twice engaged near Stangebro. On the first occasion they met rather by accident than design; the King had the advantage, and is said himself to have put a stop to the slaughter of the Swedes; but in the second encounter, as the Dalecarlians had risen in favor of the duke, and his fleet had arrived, the victory was on his side. No one then put a stop to the carnage of the Poles. Sigismund suffered a total defeat, and was compelled to accede to all that was demanded from him.[7]

[7] " Piacesii Chronicon gestorum in Europa singularium," p. 159. Extracts from the letters of the princes in Geijer, " Schwedische Geschichte," ii. § 305.

He was even brought to consent that the only faithful subjects he had found should be delivered up, to be placed before a Swedish tribunal. In his own case he also promised to submit to the decision of the Diet.

This was, however, only an expedient by which he sought to escape from the difficulties of the moment. Instead of attending the Diet, where he could have taken only the melancholy part of the vanquished, he took ship with the first favorable wind, and returned to Dantzic.

He still flattered himself with the hope that, at some other time, in some more favorable moment, he should yet become master in his hereditary dominions; but in thus departing from them, he resigned them in fact to the modes of thought prevailing there, and to the overwhelming influence of his uncle. That prince did not scruple, after a certain time, to assume the title, with the authority, of king; and he did not then wait until he should be attacked in Sweden, but carried the war into the territories of Poland, where it was conducted with varying fortunes on both sides.[8]

Section III.—Designs on Russia

After the lapse of a short time, however, it appeared probable that Catholicism might be consoled for the failure of the Swedish enterprise, by the more prosperous result of another undertaking.

It is well known that the popes had already more than once conceived hopes of winning Russia—Adrian VI, for example, and Clement VII. The Jesuit Passevin had then tried his fortune with Iwan Wasiljowitsch, and in 1594 Clement VIII had despatched a certain Comuleo to Moscow, with more than usual confidence of success, from the fact that Comuleo was acquainted with the language. All these were, however, but vain efforts. Boris Godunow directly affirmed that " Moscow was now the true orthodox Rome," and caused prayers to be offered up for himself as " the only Christian ruler on earth."

The prospect so unexpectedly presented by the appearance of the false Demetrius was rendered peculiarly welcome by this state of things.

[8] See Appendix, Nos. 66, 67, and 68.

Demetrius may be said to have attached himself even more to the ecclesiastical than the political interests of Poland.

It was to a Catholic confessor that he first discovered himself. Fathers of the Jesuit order were sent to examine him; nor until this had been done, did the papal nuncio Rangone adopt his cause. But, at their first interview, the latter declared to him that he had nothing to hope if he did not abjure the schismatic religion, and embrace the Catholic faith. Demetrius intimated his readiness to comply with little hesitation; he had already given a promise to that effect, and, on the following Sunday, his recantation was performed.[1] He was delighted to find that Sigismund then acknowledged him, and ascribed this with justice to the interposition of the nuncio, to whom he promised that whatever came within the compass of his utmost power should be done for the defence and extension of the Romanist creed.[2]

This was a promise that soon became of the highest importance. His story had not yet obtained the general belief in Poland. How greatly then were all amazed when, immediately after his conversion, the pitiable, wretched fugitive was seen in actual possession of the palace of the czars. The sudden death of his predecessor, which the populace considered to be a judgment from God, may probably have contributed largely to this result.

And here Demetrius now renewed his pledges; he received the nephew of the nuncio with marks of great reverence, and as his Polish consort joined him, soon afterward, with a numerous court, not of knights and ladies only, but still more of monks, Dominicans, Franciscans, and Jesuits,[3] he seemed determined at once to commence the redemption of his word.

But it was principally to these demonstrations that he owed his ruin. That which procured him the support of the Poles deprived him of the friendly dispositions of the Russians. They observed that he did not eat and drink as they did, and that he did not honor the saints. They declared that he was a heathen, and had conducted an unbaptized heathen bride to the

---

[1] Alessandro Cilli, "Historia di Moscovia," p. 11. Cilli was present at the act of recantation. In Karamsin, x. 109, of the translation, there is a passage not rendered so accurately from Cilli as it may seem to be. Karamsin himself did not understand Cilli. The words put into the mouth of Demetrius are not to be found in Cilli.

[2] Cilli: "By renewing at the same time his promise for the extension and defence of the holy Catholic faith, both within his empire and beyond it."

[3] Cilli, p. 66.

throne of Moscow. It was not possible that such a man should be a son of the czars.[4]

They had been induced to acknowledge him by some inexplicable conviction, and by a similar impulse, which had taken still firmer hold on their minds, they felt themselves induced to cast him off.

But here, also, the essential principle and moving cause was religion. In Russia, as in Sweden, a power arose, which, from its very source and nature, was in direct opposition to the tendencies of Catholicism.

Section IV.—Internal Commotions in Poland

Unsuccessful enterprises against a foreign enemy have usually the effect of awakening internal dissensions. Disturbances now took place in Poland, by which it was rendered doubtful whether the King would be able to continue his rule according to the system with which he had commenced. These commotions had the following causes:

King Sigismund did not always preserve a good understanding with those by whose exertions he had obtained his crown. They had called him to the throne from opposition to Austria; and he had allied himself, on the contrary, very closely with that sovereignty. He had twice chosen a consort from the line of Grätz, and at one time incurred the suspicion of desiring to secure the crown to that house.

The high chancellor Zamoisky was already much dissatisfied on that account; but he became still more embittered, when the King, to render himself independent even of his friends and adherents, not unfrequently advanced their opponents to the most important offices, and admitted them into the Senate.[1]

For it was principally by the Senate that Sigismund sought to govern; he filled it with men devoted to his person, and at the same time rendered it exclusively Catholic. The bishops appointed by the King, under the influence of the nuncio, formed

[4] Müller, " Sammlung Russischer Geschichte," v. 373, remarks that letters from the Pope were found on him.

[1] Cilli, " Historia delle Sollevationi di Polonia," 1606-1608, Pistoja, 1627, an author the more worthy of belief, because he was long in the King's service, remarks from the beginning on the authority possessed by Zamoisky: " Zamoisky desired to usurp a portion of the royal authority; " but he mentions also the King's resistance: " His Majesty having power to dispose not only of the dignities of the kingdom, but of the revenues also."

a powerful body in that assembly, and indeed gradually became
the predominant party.

But from this state of things there arose a twofold opposition of the highest importance, both for the political constitution and religious interests of Poland.

To the Senate, as a political body, the provincial deputies
placed themselves in direct opposition, and as the first adhered
to the King, the latter attached themselves to Zamoisky,[2] for
whom they felt unbounded reverence, and who derived from
their devotion an authority nearly equal to that of royalty. It
was a position that for an enterprising magnate must have had
a powerful charm. It was accordingly seized, on the death of
the high chancellor, by Zebrzydowski, palatine of Cracow.

To this party the Protestants now attached themselves, for
it was, in fact, against the bishops that both complained; the
one, on account of their temporal influence, the other, of their
spiritual authority. The Protestants found it intolerable that
in a commonwealth like that of Poland, based on a free agreement, well-earned rights should be continually violated, and
that men of inferior birth should be raised to high dignities,
while those of undoubted nobility were expected to obey them.
In these complaints they were joined by many Catholics.[3]

There can be no question but that this religious impulse gave
an especial virulence to the political dissensions.

After a frequent representation of their grievances, a refusal
of the supplies and the dissolution of the Diet, had all been
found unavailing, the malcontents at length had recourse to
a measure never adopted but in cases of extremity; they summoned the whole body of the nobles to the *rokosz.* The
rokosz was a legal form of insurrection. The nobles thus assembled claimed the right of summoning the King and Senate
before their tribunal: the Protestants obtained the greater
weight in this assembly, from the circumstance of their having
combined with the members of the Greek Church.

Meanwhile the King had also his adherents. The nuncio
kept the bishops well together:[4] the bishops impressed their

[2] Piasecius: " Zamoisky, on whose
authority the deputies greatly depended." From this time the provincial deputies became powerful; one party supported the other.
[3] Cilli: " The heretics, supported by

bad Catholics, made great efforts to obtain the majority in the confederation."
[4] " The nuncio Rangone, by his dexterity and diligence, preserved many of
the principal men firm in their faith."

own views on the Senate; a league was formed in defence of the King and religion, while the favorable moment was prudently seized for terminating the ancient dissensions between the clergy and laity. The King proved himself inflexibly firm in the moment of danger; he thought his cause just, and placed his reliance in God.

And he did, in fact, maintain the ascendancy. In October, 1606, he dissolved the *rokosz,* precisely when a large number of its members were absent. In July, 1607, an appeal was made to arms, and a regular engagement ensued. With the cry of " Jesu Maria," the royal troops attacked the enemy and completely defeated them. Zebrzydowski kept the field for some time, but was compelled to submission in the year 1608, when a general amnesty was proclaimed.

As a consequence of this success it followed that the government could now pursue the measures it had previously resolved on for the furtherance of Catholicism.

All who were not of the Roman communion were excluded from public officers, and the effect produced by this regulation was incessantly praised and rejoiced over in Rome.[5] " A Protestant prince—a prince who should have conferred the dignities of the kingdom in equal proportion on both parties, would fill the whole country with heresies: men are altogether ruled by their private interests, and since the King is so steadfast, the nobles submit to his will."

In royal towns also restrictions were imposed on the Protestant service. " Without open force," says one of the papal instructions, " the inhabitants may yet be compelled to change their religion."[6]

The nuncio was careful to see that the supreme courts of law should be administered exclusively by Catholics, and conducted " according to the words of the holy canonical maxims." Mixed marriages then formed a question of high importance.

[5] " Instruttione a V. Sria. Mre. di Torres:" " The King, although born among heretics, and of a heretic father, is so pious, so devout, and so furnished with holiness of life that even in Rome itself a better could neither have been born nor educated; for, in the course of his reign, he has changed the Senators from heretics, which they were, three only excepted, to Catholics, as they now are, with two or three exceptions." Their principle was, " spiritual things follow the course of temporal affairs." See Appendix, No. 98.

[6] " Instruttione a Mr. Lancelotti:" " You must encourage him [the King] by all means to forbid that in the royal cities dependent on him, there should any religion be exercised excepting the Catholic; nor must he permit them to have their temples or synagogues, for by these gentle means, and without actual violence, people are either converted or driven out of the country." See Appendix, No. 99.

The supreme tribunal would not acknowledge the validity of any, unless they were performed in presence of the parish priest and several witnesses; but the parish priests refused to solemnize mixed marriages, and there could be no wonder that many should conform to the Catholic ritual for the purpose of securing their children from injury. Others were induced to join the Catholics by finding that church patronage, when held by Protestants, was subject to litigation. The State possesses a thousand means for promoting the opinion which it favors. In this case all were employed, so far as was possible, without direct compulsion; the conversions excited but little remark, yet they proceeded steadily and made continual progress.

The earnest zeal and effective ability with which the nuncios administered ecclesiastical affairs had, without doubt, a large share in producing this result. They watched carefully over the bishoprics, and saw that only well-qualified men were appointed to them; they visited the monastic establishments, and would not permit that disobedient and refractory members, of whom in other countries the convents desired to free themselves, should be sent to Poland, as was beginning to be the practice. They gave their attention to the parochial clergy also, and sought to introduce psalmody and schools for children into the parishes; they likewise insisted on the establishment of episcopal seminaries.

Under their direction the Jesuits now labored with remarkable diligence. We find them actively employed in all the provinces, among the docile people of Livonia, in Lithuania, where they had to combat the remains of the old serpent-worship; and among the Greeks, where the Jesuits were often the only Catholic priests; they had occasionally to perform the rite of baptism for youths of eighteen, and sometimes met with very old men who had never received the Lord's Supper. But it was principally in Poland proper that they found the field of their exertions, and where, as one of the society boasts, " hundreds of learned, orthodox, and devout men of the order were zealously employed in rooting out error and implanting Catholic piety, by schools and associations, by preaching and writing."[7]

Here also they excited the accustomed enthusiasm in their

---

[7] " Argentus de rebus Societatis Jesu in regno Poloniæ, 1615." It might, however, have easily conveyed more information.

followers, but it was most unhappily combined with the insolence of an impetuous young nobility. The King abstained from
acts of violence, but the pupils of the Jesuits did not consider
themselves bound to do so.

They not unfrequently celebrated Ascension-day by assault-
ing those of the evangelical persuasion; breaking into their
houses, plundering and destroying their property. Woe to the
Protestant whom they could seize in his house, or whom they
even met in the streets on these occasions.

The evangelical church of Cracow was attacked in the year
1606, and in the following year the churchyard was furiously
stormed, the dead being torn from their graves. In 1611 the
church of the Protestants in Wilna was destroyed, and their
ministers maltreated or murdered. In 1615 a book appeared
in Posen which maintained that the Protestants had no right
to dwell in that city. In the following year the pupils of the
Jesuits destroyed the Bohemian church so completely that they
left no one stone remaining upon another, and the Lutheran
church was burnt. The same things occurred in other places,
and in some instances the Protestants were compelled by continual attacks to give up their churches. Nor did they long confine their assaults to the towns; the students of Cracow proceeded to burn the churches of the neighboring districts. In
Podlachia an aged evangelical minister, named Barkow, was
walking before his carriage leaning on his staff, when a Polish
nobleman approaching from the opposite direction, commanded
his coachman to drive directly over him; before the old man
could move out of the way, he was struck down and died from
the injuries he received.[8]

But with all these efforts Protestantism could not be suppressed. The King was bound by a promise which he had not
the power to retract. The nobles remained free in their own
persons, and did not all pass over immediately to Catholicism.
At times also, after many judgments unfavorable to the Protestants had passed the courts, a favorable decree was rendered,
and a church was restored to them. In the towns of Polish
Prussia the Protestants yet formed the majority; still less were
the Greeks to be put down. The union of 1595 had awakened
more disgust and horror than imitation, and the party of the

[8] " Wengerscii Slavonia Reformata," pp. 224, 232, 236, 244, 247.

dissidents formed by Protestants and Greeks was still of great importance. The richest mercantile cities and the most warlike populations (such as the Cossacks) supported and lent particular efficacy to their demands, and their opposition was all the more powerful, because it was constantly receiving increased assistance from their neighbors, Sweden and Russia, whom it had been found impossible to subdue.

Section V.—Progress of the Counter Reformation in Germany

The principles acted on in Germany were wholly different. There, each prince held it to be his own good right to direct the religion of his territories in accordance with his personal convictions.

The movement that had there commenced proceeded accordingly with but little interference from the imperial authority, and without attracting particular attention.

The ecclesiastical princes more particularly considered it their especial duty to lead back the people of their dominions to Catholicism.

The pupils of the Jesuits were now appearing among them. Johann Adam von Bicken, Elector of Mayence from 1601 to 1604, was educated at the *Collegium Germanicum* in Rome. From the castle of Königstein he once heard the hymns with which the Lutheran congregation of the place was conveying its deceased pastor to his grave. " Let them give their synagogue decent burial," exclaimed the prince. On the following Sunday a Jesuit mounted the pulpit, and from that time a Lutheran preacher was never more seen to enter it. The same things occurred in other places.[1] What Bicken left incomplete was carried zealously forward by his successor Johann Schweikard. He was a man much addicted to the pleasures of the table, but he held the reins of government with a firm hand, and displayed remarkable talent. He succeeded in accomplishing the Counter-Reformation throughout his diocese, not excepting Eichsfeld. He sent a commission to Heiligenstadt, and within two years its members had recovered 200 citizens to Catholicism, many of whom had grown gray in the Protestant faith. There were still some few remaining firm to their creed; these per-

[1] Serarius, "Res Moguntinæ," p. 973.

8

sons he exhorted personally "as their father and pastor, from the depths of a true heart." These were his own words, and he prevailed; thus adjured they also conformed. It was with feelings of extreme satisfaction that he beheld a city return to Catholicism which had been entirely Protestant during forty years.[2]

Ernest and Ferdinand of Cologne, both Bavarian princes, proceeded in like manner, as did the Elector Lothaire, of the house of Metternich of Treves. This prince was distinguished by the soundness of his understanding and by acuteness of intellect. He possessed the talent of surmounting whatever difficulties opposed him, was prompt in the execution of justice, and vigilant in promoting the interests of his country as well as those of his family. He was affable, moreover, and not particularly rigorous, provided always the matter did not affect religion, but no Protestant would he suffer at his court.[3] To these great names must be associated that of Neithard von Thüngen, Bishop of Bamberg. When he took possession of his capital he found the whole Council Protestant with the exception of two members. He had already assisted Bishop Julius in Würzburg, and now resolved to apply the measures of that prince to Bamberg. He published his edict of reformation at Christmas, 1595. This decree commanded the reception of the Lord's Supper according to the Catholic forms, or departure from the diocese; and although it was opposed by the chapter, the nobles, and the landed proprietors, while the most pressing remonstrances were addressed to the bishop by his neighbors, we yet find that in every following year these edicts of reformation were issued, and were for the most part carried into effect.[4] In Lower Germany, Theodore von Fürstenberg, Bishop of Paderborn, proceeded in emulation of the Bishop of Bamberg. In the year 1596 he threw into prison all the priests of his diocese who administered the Lord's Supper in both kinds. He thus inevitably fell into disputes with his nobles, and we find the bishop and the nobility driving off the cattle and horses of each other. Von Fürstenberg at length came to an open feud

[2] Wolf, "Geschichte von Heiligenstadt," § 63. Between 1581 and 1601 497 converts were counted, the greater proportion was in 1598, which gives seventy-three.

[3] Masenius, "Continuatio Broweri," p. 474.
[4] Jäck, "Geschichte von Bamberg," iii. 212, 199, for example, or indeed throughout, for the work is principally relative to the Anti-Reformation.

with the city also; but unhappily a turbulent demagogue here arose, who was not equal to the conspicuous part into which he had obtruded himself, and in the year 1604 Paderborn was reduced to the necessity of again doing homage to the bishop. The Jesuits' college was thereupon magnificently endowed, and soon afterward an edict was published here also which left no alternative to the people but the mass or departure from the diocese. By these measures Bamberg and Paderborn gradually became entirely Catholic.[5]

The rapid and yet lasting change brought about in all these countries is in the highest degree remarkable. Is it to be inferred that Protestantism had never taken firm root in the body of the people, or must the change be ascribed to the method adopted by the Jesuits? It is certain that in zeal and prudence they left nothing to be desired. From every point whereon they obtained footing, their influence was extended in ever-widening circles. They possessed the power of captivating the crowd, so that their churches were always the most eagerly frequented; with the most prominent difficulties they always grappled boldly and at once; was there a Lutheran, confident in his biblical knowledge, and to whose judgment the neighbors paid a certain deference, this was the man whom they used every effort to win, and their practised skill in controversy generally secured them from defeat. They were active in works of benevolence; they healed the sick and labored to reconcile enemies. The converted, those with whom they had prevailed, they bound to them by the most solemn oaths; under their banners the faithful were seen repairing to every place of pilgrimage. Men who but a short time before were zealous Protestants might now be seen forming part of these processions.

The Jesuits had educated not only ecclesiastical, but also temporal princes. At the close of the sixteenth century, their two illustrious pupils, Ferdinand II and Maximilian I, appeared in public life.

It is affirmed that when the young Archduke Ferdinand solemnized the festival of Easter at his capital of Grätz, in the year 1596, he was the only person who received the sacrament according to the Catholic ritual, and that there were but three Catholics in the whole city.[6]

[5] Strunk, "Annales Paderborn," lib. xxii. p. 720.

[6] Hansitz, "Germania Sacra," ii. p. 712: "The number of Luther's ad-

After the death of the Archduke Charles the enterprises in favor of Catholicism had not been pursued with energy—the government during the minority of his successor, displaying no great power. The Protestants had reinstated themselves in the churches of which they had been despoiled, their schools at Grätz had recovered their efficiency by the acquisition of new and able masters, while the nobles had chosen a committee for the more effectual resistance of all attempts that might be made to the disadvantage of Protestantism.

But in defiance of these discouragements, Ferdinand immediately resolved on proceeding to the continuance and ultimate completion of the Counter-Reformation; political and religious motives combined to produce this determination—he declared that he also would be master in his own territories, as well as the Elector of Saxony, or the elector-palatine. When the danger was represented to him of an onslaught from the Turks during a period of internal discord he replied that, until the perfect conversion of the people was effected, the help of God was not to be hoped for. In the year 1597 Ferdinand proceeded by way of Loretto to Rome—to kneel at the feet of Pope Clement VIII. He then made a vow to restore Catholicism in his hereditary dominions, even at the peril of his life; the Pope confirmed him in this resolve, and he at once returned home to commence the work. In September, 1598, his decrees were issued, and by these he commanded all Lutheran preachers to depart from Grätz, within fourteen days.[7]

Grätz was the centre of Protestant doctrine and power. No means were neglected that might dissuade the archduke from his purpose. Neither prayers nor warnings were left untried, nor were even menaces spared—but the young prince, according to the words of an historian of Carniola, was " firm as a block of marble."[8] In October an edict of similar character was published for Carniola, and in December one was issued for Carinthia.

And now the States became exceedingly intractable—even in

herents is so great that only three followers of the faith could be found among almost all the inhabitants of Grätz." The " almost all " (" pœne cunctis ") certainly makes the matter again doubtful.

[7] Khevenhiller, " Annales Ferdinandei," iv. 1718.

[8] Valvassor, " Ehre des Herzogthums Krain," Th. ii. Buch vii. p. 464, doubtless the most valuable relation of this occurrence: " Such a petition, mingled with warnings, found only a block of marble, which their pens could neither penetrate nor soften."

their provincial meetings; for the General Assembly, Ferdinand would no longer permit to be convened. They refused the subsidies, and the troops on the frontier betrayed symptoms of disorder; but the archduke declared he would rather lose all that had been conferred on him by the grace of God than yield one step; the danger menacing from Turkey, whose troops had already taken Canischa, and were daily advancing, compelled the States at length to vote the supplies, although they had not obtained a single concession.

These being secured, the archduke now restrained himself no longer. In October, 1599, the Protestant church of Grätz was closed, and the evangelical service was prohibited under pain of corporal punishment, torture, or death. A commission was formed, which passed through the country, accompanied by an armed force. Styria was first reformed, then Carinthia, and finally Carniola. From place to place the cry rang forth, " The reformation is coming," the churches were torn down, the preachers were exiled or imprisoned, the inhabitants were compelled to adopt the Catholic creed or to leave the country. Many were yet found, who preferred banishment to apostasy; the little town of St. Veit, for example, saw fifty of its burghers abandon their native land,[9] and these exiles were compelled to pay the tenth penny, which in their condition was no small loss.

Such were the cruelties inflicted on the people, and in return for these oppressions the archduke had the satisfaction of counting in the year 1603 an increase of 40,000 communicants.

This was immediately followed by more extensive proceedings, affecting all the Austrian territories.

The Emperor Rudolf had at first dissuaded his young cousin from the measures he contemplated, but seeing them prove successful he proceeded to imitate them. From 1599 to 1601 we find a commission for reforms in active operation throughout Upper Austria, and in 1602–3 these officials were at work in Lower Austria.[10] From Lintz and Steier, preachers and schoolmasters who had grown gray in the service of the gospel were driven forth without mercy; they felt the affliction to be a grievous one. " Now, bent by years," exclaimed the rector of

[9] Hermann, "St. Veit," in the "Karntnerischer Zeitschrift," v. iii. p. 163.   [10] Raupach, " Evangel. Œstreich," i. 215.

Steier, " I am thrust out to poverty and suffering."[1] " We are daily threatened with destruction," writes one of those who remained behind. " Our adversaries lie in wait for us, they mock us and thirst for our blood."[2]

In Bohemia the Protestants hoped they were more effectually protected by the ancient privileges of the Utraquists. In Hungary they trusted to the independence and power of the Estates. But Rudolf now seemed disposed to respect neither the one nor the other; he had been persuaded that the old Utraquists were entirely extinct, and that the Protestants were not entitled to the enjoyment of the privileges that had been accorded to them. In the year 1602 he put forth an edict forbidding the meetings of the Moravian brethren, and commanding that their churches should be closed.[3] All other Protestants felt that they were in danger of similar treatment, nor were they long left in doubt as to what they might expect. Open violence was already resorted to in Hungary. Basta and Belgiojoso, who commanded the imperial forces in that country, took the churches of Caschau and Clausenburg from the Lutherans, and with the aid of these troops the Archbishop of Colocsa sought to force the thirteen towns of Zips to Catholicism. To the complaints of the Hungarians the Emperor replied by the following resolution : His Majesty, who profoundly believes in the holy Roman faith, is desirous of extending it throughout his empire, and especially in Hungary. He hereby confirms and ratifies all decrees that have been issued in favor of that faith from the times of St. Stephen, the apostle of Hungary.[4]

Thus, notwithstanding his advanced age, the cautious Emperor had entirely departed from his accustomed moderation. A similar policy was pursued by the whole body of the Catholic princes, so far as they could possibly make their power extend ; the stream of Catholic opinion was poured ever more widely over the land. Force and argument combined to secure its progress ; the constitution of the empire supplied no means whereby to oppose it. On the contrary, the Catholic adherents felt themselves so powerful that they now began to interfere with

[1] " Jam senio squalens trudor in exilium." Valentia Pruenhueber, " Annales Styrenses," p. 326.
[2] " Hofmarius ad Lyserum," Raupach, iv. 151.
[3] Schmidt, " Neuere Geschichte der Deutschen," iii. 260. An extract from the additions to the apology for the Bohemians of the year 1618, which are often omitted in the later editions.
[4] Art. 22, anno 1604, in Ribiny, " Memorabilia Augustanæ Confessionis," i. p. 321.

the affairs of the empire, and to endanger the still remaining rights of the Protestant communities.[5]

The constitution of the supreme tribunals also received important changes, principally by the interposition of the papal nuncios, more particularly of Cardinal Madruzzi, by whom attention was first drawn to the subject. These alterations presented both opportunity and means for the aggressions anticipated by the Protestants.

Even the imperial court *(Kammergericht)* had assumed a more decided tinge of Catholicism toward the beginning of the seventeenth century, and judgments had been pronounced by it in accordance with the Catholic mode of interpreting the Peace of Augsburg. Those who had suffered from these judgments had adopted the legal remedy of seeking revision, but with the visitations these revisions also were suspended; affairs accumulated, and all remained undecided.[6]

Under these circumstances it was that the Aulic Council *(Reichshrofrath)* rose into activity. This at least gave some hope of termination to an affair, for the defeated party could not take refuge in a legal process which could never be executed; but the Aulic Council was not only more decidedly Catholic than the *Kammergericht*, it was also entirely dependent on the court. " The Aulic Council," says the Florentine envoy Alidosi, " pronounces no final decision, without having first imparted the judgment to the Emperor and his Privy Council, who seldom return the decree without alterations."[7]

But what institutions of universal effect existed in the empire except those of judicial character? To these it was that the unity of the nation was attached. Yet even they were now

[5] " Relatione del Nuntio Ferrero, 1606," enumerates the results that ensued: " During the last few years a vast number of souls have been converted to our holy religion, the churches are restored, many monks have returned to their monasteries, the greater part of the ecclesiastical ceremonies are resumed, the licentiousness of the clergy considerably moderated, and the name of the Roman pontiff received as the acknowledged head of the universal Church."

[6] " Missiv und Erinnerung des Reichskammergerichts am Reichstarg, von 1608: " In the acts of the Diet at Frankfort-on-the-Main, of which I was kindly permitted to take an examination, the Kammergericht declares it to be " known to the country and the empire in what great and notable numbers the revisions of the judgments pronounced by the said Kammergericht have accumulated since the year '86, to such an extent that notice was given to the Imperial College of more than a hundred such, and others might probably be expected daily."

[7] " Relatione del Sig. Rod. Alidosi, 1607-1609: " "It is true that the Aulic Council has this at least of good, that all its decisions, which are to be final, are first transmitted to the Emperor or the Council of State, and they frequently add to or take from or moderate the opinion of the said Council, which being done the decree is returned to the said Council, and in that form is then made public."

subjected to the influence of Catholic opinions and regulated by the convenience of the court. From various quarters complaints had already arisen of partial judgments and arbitrary executions, when the affair of Donauwerth made obvious to the perception of all the great perils by which the country was menaced from this state of things.

A Catholic abbot in a Protestant city, determined to celebrate his processions more publicly and with greater solemnity than usual,[8] and the fact that he was interrupted and insulted by the populace, was considered a sufficient pretext for the Aulic Council to warrant the infliction of a tedious and harassing process on the town itself. Mandates, citations, and commissions followed in long succession, and the town was finally laid under the ban of the empire. The office of carrying this sentence into effect was intrusted to Maximilian of Bavaria, a neighboring prince of rigidly Catholic opinions. Not content with taking possession of Donauwerth, he at once invited the order of Jesuits to settle in the city, permitted none but the Catholic service to be performed, and proceeded in the usual manner to effect a Counter-Reformation.

This affair was regarded by Maximilian himself in the light of its general import. He wrote to the Pope saying that it might be considered as a test by which the decline of the Protestant influence could be judged.

But he deceived himself if he believed that the Protestants would endure these things quietly. They saw clearly what they had to expect, if matters were permitted to proceed in that manner.

The Jesuits had already become so bold as to deny the validity of the Peace of Augsburg; they maintained that it could not have been properly ratified without the consent of the Pope; that in any case it was valid only to the period of the Council of Trent, and must be considered as a sort of *interim* only.

And even those who acknowledged the validity of this treaty were yet of opinion that at least all property confiscated by Prot-

[8] The report, "relating to the execution at Donauwerth," in the acts of the imperial Diet of February 4th, declares (in agreement with the other relations and informations), that all the abbot could claim by ancient custom was the right of walking with banners lowered and furled, without song or bell, and only by a certain narrow lane under the monastery wall, till he was beyond the city and its jurisdiction, and then only was he to lift and unfurl his banners, or to suffer singing or music to begin, when he had got beyond the Donauwerth ground. These restrictions he had now broken through.

estants since its conclusion ought to be restored. To the construction put on the words of the treaty by the Protestants they paid no attention.

But what might not be the result when these views should be adopted by the highest tribunals of the empire, and when judgments, as already began to be the case, were pronounced and carried into effect in accordance with their principles?

When the Diet assembled at Ratisbon in the year 1608 the Protestants would proceed to no deliberation until they should receive a positive confirmation of the Treaty of Augsburg.[9] Even Saxony, which had always before been disposed to the party of the Emperor, now demanded that the processes instituted by the Aulic Council should be done away with, so far as they were contrary to the practice of earlier times; that the judicial system should receive amendment; and not only that the Treaty of Augsburg should be renewed as concluded in 1555, but that the Jesuits, by a pragmatic sanction, should be prohibited from writing against it.

But the Catholics on their side were also very zealous, and were closely united. The Bishop of Ratisbon had previously issued a circular, in which he exhorted his coreligionists to impress upon their envoys the necessity for being unanimous in their defence of the Catholic religion; he admonishes all to " stand together rigid and fast as a wall "; by no means to temporize; there was now nothing to fear, since they had stanch and zealous defenders in august and illustrious princely houses. If then the Catholics showed a disposition to confirm the treaty of Augsburg, they did so with the addition of a clause to the effect " that whatever had been done in contravention of the same should be annulled and restituted "—a clause which comprehended all that the Protestants feared and which they desired to avoid.

With so decided a disagreement on the principal question, it was not to be expected that unanimity of opinion should be obtained on any separate subject of discussion, or that the Emperor should be accorded those subsidies which he was desiring, and greatly needed, for the war against the Turks.

[9] " Protocollum im Correspondenzrath," April 5, 1608, in the acts of the Diet: " The chief consultation of the present Diet has been hitherto suspended, because the States of the evangelical religion desired to have the Peace of Augsburg confirmed, while the Papist party wish to insert the clause that all property confiscated by the Evangelical States since the year '55 should be restored."

This consideration would seem to have made some impression on the Emperor; and the court seems to have resolved at one time on a frank and fair compliance with the Protestant demands.

Such, at least, is the inference to be drawn from a very remarkable report relating to this Diet, and prepared by the papal envoy.[10]

The Emperor did not appear in person—he was represented by the Archduke Ferdinand; neither was the nuncio himself at Ratisbon, but he had sent an Augustine monk thither in his place, Fra Felice Milensio, vicar-general of his order, who labored with extraordinary zeal to maintain the interests of Catholicism.

This Fra Milensio, from whom our report proceeds, declares that the Emperor had in fact determined to publish an edict in conformity with the wishes of the Protestants: he ascribes this resolve to the immediate influence of Satan, and says that it had doubtless been brought about by the agency of the Emperor's chamberlains, of whom one was a Jew and the other a heretic.[1]

Let us hear from himself the report he proceeds to give: "On receiving intelligence of the edict that had arrived, and which was imparted to myself and some others, I repaired to the archduke and inquired if such a decree had really come. The archduke replied that it had. 'And does your imperial highness intend to publish it?' The archduke answered, 'The imperial Privy Council has so commanded, and you perceive yourself, reverend father, the situation in which we are placed.' Hereupon I replied,[2] 'Your imperial Highness will not belie

[10] See Appendix, No. 80.
[1] Account of the imperial Diet held in Ratisbon, 1608, and at which, in place of the most excellent and most reverend Monsre. Antonio Gaetano, Archbishop of Capua and apostolic nuncio, retained in Prague by his imperial Majesty, was resident Father Felice Milensio, chief of Augustinians and vicar-general for the Northern provinces: "It is certain that this was contrived by the devil and promoted by his ministers, of whom were the two chamberlains of Rudolf, the one being a Jew, the other a heretic, and by those of his Council, who were Hussites or worse."
[2] "'Let your most serene highness remember that Catholic piety in which you were born and educated, and for the sake of which, but few years since, fearing no danger, and at the peril of

losing all your dominions, you banished thence all the heretics, with orders, that in a few months they should either declare themselves Catholics, or, selling all they had, should get themselves gone out of the country; remember, too, that in the picture painted in the church of the father Capuchins at Grätz, you are represented with lance in hand, like another St. Michael, having Luther under your feet, and in the act of piercing his throat; and now, you being here in the place of the Emperor, ought not to endure that the goods of the Church should be lost, and that Christ's patrimony should suffer; still less that the diabolical sect of Luther be strengthened by this concession; or, worse than all, that of Calvin, now incorporated with it, and which never received any kind of tolerance

the piety in which you have been educated, and with which but a short time since you ventured, in defiance of so many threatening dangers, to banish all heretics from your dominions. I cannot believe that your imperial Highness will sanction the loss of church property, and the confirmation of the devilish sect of Luther, or that still worse of Calvin, which must all come from this new concession.' The pious prince listened to my words. 'But what is to be done?' he asked. 'I beg your imperial Highness,' I replied, 'to bring this affair before his holiness the Pope, and to take no step in it until we have his reply;' and the archduke did so, for he respected the commands of God more than the decrees of men."

If all this occurred as described, we may readily perceive how important a part this nameless Augustine friar performed in the history of the German Empire. At the decisive moment he contrived to prevent the publication of a concession by which the Protestants would apparently have been contented. In place of this, Ferdinand now promulgated an edict of interposition, which still left an opening for the introduction of the objectionable clause. On April 5, 1608, the Protestants assembled, and united in passing a resolution neither to receive the edict nor to yield obedience to it.[3] But since the other party would also abate no portion of their demands, and since nothing was to be obtained from the Emperor or his representative that might have allayed the fears of the Protestants, they adopted the extreme measure of quitting the Diet. For the first time, that assembly failed to arrive at any conclusion, much less at any agreement—it was a moment in which the unity of the empire was in fact dissolved.

That affairs should remain in this condition was impossible. Any one of the Protestant powers would have been too weak alone to maintain the position that had been taken up; and the pressure of the moment now compelled them to carry into effect an alliance that had long been desired, deliberated upon,

from the Emperor.' This and more I said, and the most pious prince listened. 'I entreat you,' said I, further, 'that you suspend this business till the reply comes from the supreme pontiff;' and this he did, deferring the decrees of men that he might not offend against the decrees of God."

[3] Votum der Pfalz, in "Correspondenzrath": "That the confirmation of the Peace of Augsburg is by no means to be accepted in the form proposed by the letter of interposition; that being entirely useless to those of the evangelical faith, since the decree of the year '66 contains the very clause now in dispute." It did not appear in the decrees of 1557 and 1559. The letter of interposition referred to the year 1556 only, and was rejected because it treated the Emperor as judge in all affairs of religion.

and projected. Immediately after the Diet, a meeting was held at Ahausen, between two princes of the palatinate, the Elector Frederick, and the Count Palatine of Neuburg; two princes of Brandenburg, the margraves Joachim and Christian Ernest; the Duke of Wurtemburg and the Margrave of Baden, by whom a league was formed, known as that of the "Union." They pledged themselves to support and assist each other in every way—even by force of arms; and this with especial reference to the grievances brought forward at the late Diet. They immediately put themselves into a state of military preparation, and each member of the Union undertook to induce such of his neighbors as he could influence, to join the confederacy. Their determination was to obtain for themselves that security which, in the existing state of things, the imperial government did not afford them, and in fact to help themselves.

This was an innovation which involved the most comprehensive results; and the rather as an event of very similar character just then occurred in the Emperor's hereditary dominions.

The Emperor Rudolf was at variance, for several causes, with his brother Matthias; and in their dissensions, the Estates of Austria, oppressed both in their civil and religious liberty, perceived an opportunity for recovering and upholding both; they consequently took part with the archduke.

So early as the year 1606 the archduke, in concert with these States, had concluded a peace with Hungary without consulting the Emperor; they excused themselves on the ground that the Emperor neglected public affairs, and that the condition of things had compelled them to act. But as Rudolf refused to acknowledge this peace, they arose into open rebellion, and that in virtue of the compact they had formed.[4] The Hungarian and Austrian Estates first concluded an alliance for mutual aid and protection; they next induced the Moravians to join them, principally by means of the influence possessed over them by one of the Lichtenstein family, and all agreed to peril fortune and life for the archduke. This force advanced against the Em-

---

[4] Their compact contained the following clause: "But if on account of or in contravention of the Viennese and Turkish Treaty, enemies or disturbance should interpose, then the most serene archduke, and all the States of the Kingdom of Hungary, with those of the Archduchy of Upper and Lower Austria, shall not fail to support each other with mutual aid and assistance.—Reva ap. Schandtner, "Script. rerum Ung. ii. Kurz, Beiträge zur Geschichte des Landes Oestreich ob der Ens," b. iv. p. 21."

peror, under their self-elected leader, on the very day that saw the dissolution of the Diet at Ratisbon, in May, 1608. Rudolf was compelled to resign himself to the necessity of yielding Hungary, Austria, and Moravia to the possession of his brother.[5]

But Matthias was now manifestly compelled to make concessions to the States, in return for the services he had received from them. During a period of forty-eight years the Emperors had evaded the nomination of a palatine in Hungary; that dignity was now conferred on a Protestant; religious freedom was secured in the most solemn manner, not only to the magnates, but to the cities, and to all conditions of men, even to the soldiers stationed on the frontiers.[6] The Austrians would not consent to do homage until the free exercise of their religion was secured to them, whether in their castles or villages, nay, even in the private houses of the cities.

What the Austrians and Hungarians had gained by direct force, the Bohemians procured by aiding in the Emperor's defence; before he could oppose even a show of resistance to his brother, Rudolf was compelled to grant large concessions, and when Hungary and Austria had obtained so great an extent of freedom by means of Matthias, the Emperor could not refuse the demands of the Bohemians, whatever might be urged to the contrary by the papal nuncio or the Spanish ambassador. He conceded to them the imperial rescript, which not only renewed the privileges conferred by Maximilian II, but also permitted the establishment of a special magistracy for their protection.

The aspect of affairs in Germany and the Emperor's hereditary dominions thus assumed a totally different character. The Union extended itself through Germany, and carefully watched over every aggression of Catholicism, which it instantly and forcibly repelled. In the Austrian provinces the Estates had consolidated their ancient privileges into a firmly grounded constitutional government. The difference between the two conditions of things was not inconsiderable. In the empire, Catholicism had once more extended itself through the territories of the Catholic princes, and it was not until it proceeded beyond due limits, until it interfered with violence in the affairs of the empire and endangered the existence of the free Estates, that resistance was opposed to its progress. In the hereditary do-

[5] See Appendix, No. 77.   [6] The article is given in Ribiny, i. 358.

minions, on the contrary, it encountered invincible opposition, even within the territorial power of the imperial house, from the influence of Protestant landholders. There was nevertheless, upon the whole, a common feeling throughout the land. In Austria it was remarked with much significance, that one sword must be kept in its scabbard by the other.

For the opposite party had also at once assumed an attitude of aggression. On July 11, 1609, an alliance was concluded between Maximilian of Bavaria and seven of the ecclesiastical princes—the Bishop of Würzburg, namely, with those of Constance, Augsburg, Passau, and Ratisbon, the Provost of Ellwangen and the Abbot of Kempten; they formed a league for mutual defence, on the model of the ancient treaty of Landsperg.[7] The Duke of Bavaria obtained a great extent of power by this compact. The three ecclesiastical electors soon afterward associated themselves with this league, but retained a certain freedom of action. The Archduke Ferdinand desired to be received into the same confederacy, Spain declared its approval, the Pope gave a promise to neglect no means for promoting the objects of the compact, and without doubt the pontiff in particular became gradually more and more involved in its designs and interests, principally by means of the Spanish influence.[8]

Two hostile parties thus confronted each other, both armed, each in constant fear of being surprised and attacked, but neither strong enough to bring the questions between them to a decisive issue.

It followed of necessity that in Germany the despatch of all important public business, the solution of every difficulty affecting the common weal, had become utterly impossible. In the year 1611 there should have been proceedings for the election of a king of the Romans, but the electoral princes vainly assembled, they could come to no decision.

Even after the death of Rudolf, in 1612, a long time elapsed before an election could be effected. The three temporal electors insisted, by the capitulary of election, on the establishment of an imperial council, the said council to be composed equally

[7] Maximilian refers to this league in his instructions to his ambassador at Mayence; see Wolf, ii. p. 470.
[8] The documents relating to this subject are not known; until further information can be obtained, we may content ourselves with the assertions of Mocenigo, the Venetian ambassador. See Appendix, No. 81.

from both parties. This demand the three ecclesiastical electors opposed; and it was only when Saxony, which in all these affairs had evinced great devotion to the house of Austria, had passed over to the Catholic side that the election was at length completed.

But that which failed to pass in the Council of Electors was insisted on with all the more violence by the Union of princes in the Diet of 1613, where it was opposed with equal pertinacity by the Catholics. No further deliberation was attempted; the Protestants would no longer subject themselves to the yoke of the greater number.

In Juliers and Cleves, notwithstanding the vacillating weakness which characterized the government of the last native prince, effectual measures had at length been adopted for the restoration of Catholicism; principally by the influence of his wife, a princess of the house of Lorraine. It seemed for a certain time that Protestantism would nevertheless obtain the supremacy, the next heirs being both Protestant; but the force of religious division prevailed here also. Of the two Protestant claimants of the sovereignty, one passed over to the Catholic faith; and the two parties placed themselves in opposition here also. As they acknowledged no supreme arbiter, they proceeded in the year 1614 to acts of open hostility; both seized on all around them, so far as their power could be made to reach; the one, with the help of Spain; the other, with that of the Netherlands; and each reformed, after its own fashion, the districts that had fallen to its share, without further ceremony.

Attempts were indeed made to effect a reconciliation; an electoral diet was proposed, but the elector-palatine would not hear of this, because he had no confidence in his colleague of Saxony: the next project was a general diet of composition; but the Catholic States had innumerable objections to oppose to this plan. Others turned their thoughts toward the Emperor, and recommended him to enforce his authority, by the display of a large armed force. But what could have been expected from Matthias, who belonged to both parties, by the very source and cause of his power, but was so trammelled by the chains he had imposed on himself, that he could not possibly attain to any freedom of action? Loud were the complaints of the Pope against him; he declared him unfit to be invested with so high a dignity, in times of so much difficulty; he caused representations to be made to him, in the strongest terms of remonstrance; insomuch that he was himself amazed at the Emperor's long-suffering endurance. At a later period the Catholics were not so much dissatisfied with Matthias; even the most zealous declared that he had been more useful to their Church than could have been expected. In the affairs of the empire he was, however, utterly powerless. In the year 1617 he made an attempt to dissolve both the confederacies; but the union was immediately revived with increased strength, and the league was re-established with all its pristine vigor.

Section VI.—Papal Nunciature in Switzerland

An equal balance of parties had been maintained for a long period in Switzerland. This was now as conspicuously and firmly established as in earlier times, but it rested on a more pacific basis.

The power of self-government, possessed by each separate territory, had been long secured in Switzerland: religious matters were not even permitted to be brought into discussion among the affairs of the Diet. In the beginning of the seventeenth century the Catholic party no longer cherished a single hope of being able to overpower the Protestants, who were not only richer and more powerful than themselves, but had also men of greater ability among them—men better versed in the details of public business.[1]

The nuncios, who had fixed their seat in Lucerne, did not deceive themselves on that point: it is by them, indeed, that this condition of things is pointed out. But notwithstanding the limitations thus imposed on their circle of action, the position they held among the Catholics was always one of high consideration.

One of the most important duties of their office was that of

[1] The " Informatione mandata dal Sr. Cardl. d'Aquino a Monsr. Feliciano, vescovo di Foligno, per il paese de' Suizzeri e Grisoni " (Informationi Politt. ix.), adds to this: " The Catholic cantons down to these times have shown themselves more warlike than the heretic cantons, although the latter have double their power, whether in men or money; but nowadays the Catholics are so changed and degenerated from those old Switzers that unless by the special grace of God they could have no advantage, humanly speaking, over the heretic adversary; nor could they, without foreign aid, go to war with them, the Protestants having, besides, men of more learning, judgment, and practice in all affairs."

holding the bishops firmly to the exercise of their duties.[2] The bishops of the German nation were disposed to consider themselves princes, but the nuncios reminded them continually that they were exalted in reference to their spiritual calling only— a truth they earnestly impressed on them. There was, in fact, much life and zeal in the Swiss Church; visitations were held, synods appointed, monasteries reformed, and seminaries established. The nuncios labored to maintain a good understanding between the ecclesiastical and temporal authorities, and by mildness and persuasion they succeeded for the most part in attaining their end; they contrived also to prevent the intrusion of Protestant publications, but they were compelled to leave the people in possession of their Bibles and German prayer-books. Confraternities of the Virgin were instituted, and these comprehended both old and young; sermons and the confessional were zealously attended; pilgrimages to miraculous images again acquired popularity, and it even became requisite sometimes to mitigate the severity which zealous devotees here and there inflicted on themselves.[3] The nuncios were unable sufficiently to express their value for the service rendered to them by the Capuchins, more particularly by those of Italy.

As a natural consequence of all this, there next followed conversions. The nuncios received the converts into their own care, supported them, recommended them to the good offices of others, and labored to establish funds from the contributions of the faithful, and under the superintendence of the prelates, for the benefit of those newly converted. Sometimes they succeeded in recovering jurisdictions that had been given up as lost; they then restored the mass to these districts with all speed. The Bishop of Basle and the Abbot of St. Gall displayed extraordinary zeal in labors of this kind.

In all these affairs the nuncios were materially assisted by the circumstance of the King of Spain having formed a party of

---

[2] " Relatione della Nuntiatura de' Suizzeri: " " Experience has taught me that, to make the nunciatures useful, it is desirable that the nuncios should not intrude themselves into all that may be done by the bishops, and which belong to the ordinaries, unless it be to assist, and in case of real necessity; for, by interfering in all things indifferently, the nuncios not only offend the bishops, but frequently cause them to oppose and render vain every effort of the apostolic minister; moreover, it is contrary to the wish of Monsignor and to the canons to put the hand to another man's harvest; the nuncios being sent to aid, and not to subvert, the authority of the ordinaries." See Appendix, No. 82.

[3] To give an example, in the " Literæ Annuæ Societatis Jesu, 1596," p. 187, we read: " The rigorous mode of fasting of some was prohibited by the confessor."

his own in Catholic Switzerland.   The adherents of this Spanish party, as, for example, the Lusi in Unterwalden, the Amli
in Lucerne, the Bühler in Schwyz, and others, were found to
be usually the most devoted assistants of the Roman See.   The
nuncios did not fail to turn these dispositions to the best account,
and to cherish them with the utmost regard.   They were careful to show a high sense of their value; listened patiently to the
longest and most tedious discourses; did not spare titles of respect; and professed themselves to be warm admirers of the
great deeds performed of old by the Swiss nation, and of the
wisdom manifest in their republican institutions.   They found
it especially necessary to keep their friends together by feasts,
given at regularly returning intervals; they were careful on their
own part to repay every invitation and mark of respect shown
to themselves by some present.   Presents were particularly effectual in those districts.   He who was nominated Knight of
the Golden Spur, and who received a gold chain or medal in
addition to the honor, felt himself bound to them forever.   But
they were obliged to beware of promising what they were not
quite sure of performing; if, on the contrary, they were able
to perform more than they had promised, that was accounted
a great merit.   Their domestic arrangements and private life
were expected to be very strictly regulated, and to afford no
opportunity for censure.

From all these causes it resulted that the Catholic interests
in Switzerland also had now generally attained to a very prosperous condition and were making quiet progress.

There was only one district where the differences between
Catholics and Protestants inhabiting the same territory, coin-
ciding with an unsettled state of political relations, might occasion disorders and contests.

This was in the Grisons, where the government was essentially Protestant, while the Italian portion of their territories,
more particularly the Valteline, was steadfastly Catholic.

From this cause arose unceasing irritation.   The government would tolerate no foreign priests in the valley; they had
even prohibited attendance on Jesuit schools beyond the limits
of the canton, and would by no means suffer the Bishop of Como,
to whose diocese the Valteline belonged, to exercise his episcopal office in the district.   The native inhabitants, on the other

hand, beheld Protestants residing in their country with extreme dissatisfaction, and the rather as they claimed to be lords and masters in the land; they attached themselves in secret to the Italians, particularly to the orthodox city of Milan, and their zeal was continually inflamed by the young theologians who were sent to them in succession from the *Collegium Helveticum* of that city, in which alone six places were apportioned to the Valteline.[4]

But this state of things was the more dangerous because France, Spain, and Venice were all laboring with their utmost powers to establish each its own party in the Grisons; these parties not unfrequently came into violent collision, and first one then another drove its opponent from the place. In the year 1607 the Spanish faction took possession of Coire, but was soon afterward replaced by the faction of Venice. The first broke up the League, the latter restored it; the Spanish had the Catholic sympathies with them, the Venetians those of the Protestants, and in accordance with these the whole policy of the canton was determined. Much now depended on the side for which France would declare itself. The French had pensioners all through Switzerland, not in the Catholic cantons only, but in those of the Protestant faith also; and they possessed an influence of long standing in the Grisons. About the year 1612 they adopted the Catholic interests; the nuncio succeeded in gaining over their friends to the side of Rome: the Venetian alliance was even formally renounced.

These were party conflicts that would merit but little attention in themselves, were it not that they acquired a greater importance from the fact that it depended on them to which of the powers the Grison passes should be opened or closed. We shall see that their weight affected the balance, and had some share in determining the general relations of politics and religion.

Section VII.—Regeneration of Catholicism in France

The question that was now more extensively important than any other was the position that would be adopted by France in general as regarded religion.

[4] " Relne. della Nuntiatura: " " The Helvetic college of Milan is of great utility, and is, in particular, the very salvation of the Val Telina; for whatever priests it has are students of that college, and have almost all taken high degrees in theology." See Appendix, No. 82.

The first glance shows clearly that the Protestants still maintained themselves there in great power and influence.

Henry IV had accorded them the Edict of Nantes, which not only confirmed them in the possession of all the churches then in their hands, but even conferred on them a share in the institutions for public instruction, and equality with Catholics, as regarded the chambers of Parliament. They also occupied numerous strong places, and altogether possessed a degree of independence which might well have occasioned a question whether it were not incompatible with the supremacy of the State. About the year 1600, 760 parishes were counted in the possession of the French Protestants, and all well organized. Four thousand of the nobility belonged to that confession; it was believed that 25,000 men could be brought into the field without difficulty, and they held nearly 200 fortified places: this was a power that was certain to command respect, and could by no means be prudently offended.[1]

But close beside this power, and in direct opposition to it, there arose a second, the corporation of the Catholic clergy in France.

The large possessions of the French clergy secured to that body a certain degree of independence, and this was rendered more palpable to themselves, as well as more obvious to others, from their having undertaken to liquidate a portion of the public debt.[2]

For this participation was not so entirely compulsory as to preclude the necessity for a renewal of their obligations from time to time with the forms of a voluntary engagement.

Under Henry IV the assemblies which were held for that purpose assumed a more regular form; they were to be repeated every tenth year, and always in May, when the days are long, and give time for the transaction of much business; they were never to be held in Paris, that all interruptions might be avoided.

[1] Badoer, "Relatione di Francia, 1605."

[2] In the "Mémoires du Clergé de France," tom. ix.—"Recueil des contrats passés par le clergé avec les rois"—the documents relating to this affair will be found from the year 1561. At the Assembly of Poissy in that year, for example, the clergy undertook not only the interest but the actual payment of a considerable part of the public debt. The payment was not indeed accomplished, but the clergy maintained its promise of paying the interest. The debts were principally those due to the Hôtel de Ville, and the city profited by the interest, a fixed annual sum being paid to it by the clergy. We may hence see clearly why Paris, even though it had not been so Catholic as it was, could yet never have permitted the ruin of the clergy, or the destruction of ecclesiastical property, which was its own security for the debt.

Smaller meetings were to assemble every second year for the
auditing of accounts.

It was not in the nature of things that these assemblies, the
larger ones in particular, should confine themselves to their
financial duties.   The fulfilment of these gave them courage for
more extended efforts.   In the years 1595 and 1596, they resolved to renew the provincial councils, to oppose the interference of the civil jurisdiction in matters pertaining to the office
of the clergy, and to permit no simony.   It was of great importance to the force of these resolutions that the King, after some
hesitation, accorded them his approval.[3]   It was usual for the
clergy to make general representations of matters regarding
churches and church discipline; from these the King could not
possibly withhold his attention, and new concessions were invariably to be made before the proceedings closed.   At their
next assembly the clergy commenced by investigating the extent to which the changes thus promised had been carried into
effect.

The position of Henry IV was thus very peculiar: he stood
between two corporations, both possessing a certain independence, both holding their assemblies at stated times, and then assailing him, each from its own side, with conflicting representations, while it was not easy for the King to neglect or oppose
himself to either one or the other.

His wish and purpose generally were, without doubt, to
maintain the balance between them, and not to suffer their becoming involved in new conflicts; but if we ask to which of the
two parties he was the more inclined, and which he most effectually assisted, we shall find that it was obviously the Catholic, although his own elevation was attributable to the Protestants.

The gratitude of Henry was not more conspicuous than his
vindictiveness.   He was more anxious to gain new friends
than to reward or favor the old ones.

Were not the Protestants in fact compelled to extort from
him even that edict (of Nantes)?   He granted it to them only
at a moment when he was closely pressed by the Spanish arms,
and when they had themselves, at the same time, assumed a very

[3] Relation des principales choses qui
one esté résolues dans l'assemblée gen-
érale du clergé tenue à Paris ès années
1595 et 1596, envoyée à toutes les dio-
cèses."—" Mémoires du Clergé," tom.
viii. p. 6.

threatening and warlike attitude.[4]   Accordingly, they used their privileges in a spirit similar to that by which they had acquired them.   Their body constituted a republic, over which the King had but little influence; from time to time they even spoke of choosing some other and foreign protector.

The clergy of the Catholic Church attached themselves, on the contrary, closely to the King; they required no pecuniary aid—they even afforded it, and the independence of that body could never become dangerous, because the King held the appointment to vacant benefices in his own hands.   In so much, then, as the position of the Huguenots manifestly imposed a limitation on the royal authority, the extension of that authority became obviously identified with the progress of Catholicism.[5] As early as the year 1598 the King declared to the clergy that his purpose was to render the Catholic Church once more as prosperous as it had been in the century preceding.   He begged them only to be patient, and to confide in him; Paris was not built in a day.[6]

The rights derived from the Concordat were now exercised in a manner totally different from that of former times; benefices were no longer bestowed on women and children.   When appointing to ecclesiastical offices, the King looked most carefully to the learning, mental qualifications, and moral conduct of those on whom they were conferred.

" In all external affairs," observes a Venetian, " Henry IV shows himself personally devoted to the Roman Catholic religion, and disinclined to its opponents."

It was under the influence of these feelings that he recalled the Jesuits.   He believed that their zeal must of necessity contribute to the restoration of Catholicism, and, as a consequence, to the extension of the kingly authority, as he now conceived it, and desired that it should be.[7]

[4] This is placed beyond doubt by the account given in Benoist, " Histoire de l'Edit de Nantes," i. 185.

[5] Niccolò Contarini: " Though the King temporized with both parties, and his Councillors were of both religions, yet he seemed even more and more to alienate himself from the Huguenots, and to wish their power diminished; the principal reason was that many strong places were put into their hands by the edicts of pacification; full thirty of these were of great consequence, and the King did not feel absolute master in his kingdom without them."

[6] " Mémoires du Clergé," tom. xiv. p. 259.

[7] Contarini: " For the abasement of which [the party of the Huguenots] the King thought he might strike a great blow by recalling the Jesuits, thinking also by that means to destroy many conspiracies at their very roots."   He had replied to the Parliaments, that if they could secure his life from machinations, the exile of the Jesuits should never cease.

Yet all this would have availed but little, had not the internal regeneration of the Catholic Church, already commenced in France, made great and rapid progress at that time: it had, in fact, assumed a new form during the first twenty years of the century. Let us cast a glance at this change, more especially as regards the renewal of monastic discipline, in which it most strikingly displays itself.

The ancient orders, Dominicans, Franciscans, and Benedictines, were all most zealously reformed.

The conventual associations of women emulated these efforts. The penances imposed on themselves by the Feuillantines were so extravagantly severe that fourteen are reported to have once died from them in one week. The Pope himself was compelled to exhort them to mitigate their austerities.[8] In Portroyal, community of possessions, silence, and night vigils were introduced anew, and the mystery of the eucharist was adored there, without intermission, day and night.[9] The nuns of Calvary observed the rule of St. Benedict without the slightest mitigation; by ceaseless prayers at the foot of the cross they sought to perform a kind of expiation for the offences committed by Protestants against the tree of life.[10]

In a somewhat different spirit, Saint Theresa had, at the same time, reformed the order of the Carmelite nuns in Spain; she also enjoined the most rigid seclusion; even the visits of the nearest relations at the grate she sought to restrict, and subjected the confessor himself to inspection. Yet she did not consider austerity as the end, and labored only to produce such a disposition of the soul as might raise it to a closer communion with the Divine Spirit. Saint Theresa was convinced that no seclusion from the world, no privations, no discipline of mind, would suffice to restrain the penitent within the requisite limits, unless other means were added. Labor, the direct occupations of the household—works suited to the hands of women—this she found was the path that preserves the soul of woman from degeneracy. It is by labor that the door is most effectually closed against unprofitable and wandering thoughts. But this labor, as she further prescribed, was not to be costly nor require

[8] Helyot, "Histoire des Ordres Monastiques," v. p. 412.
[9] Felibien, "Histoire de Paris," ii. 1339; a work extremely valuable throughout, as regards the history of this restoration, and which is in many places founded on original authorities.
[10] "La Vie du véritable Père Josef," 1705, pp. 53-73.

great skill, neither was it to be fixed for stated times, nor even to be of a nature in itself to absorb the mind.   Her purpose was to promote the serenity of a soul conscious of being itself exist- ent in God; " a soul that lives constantly," to use her own words, " as if ever standing before the face of God, and which has no suffering but that of not enjoying His presence." She desired to produce what she calls the prayer of love, " wherein the soul for- gets itself, and hears only the voice of the heavenly Master."[1] This was an enthusiasm that was conceived, at least, by Saint Theresa herself, in a manner the most pure, most noble, and most true: it accordingly produced a very powerful impression throughout the whole Catholic world.   Even in France, a conviction became felt that something more than penance was demanded.   An especial delegate, Pierre Berulle, was sent to Spain, who then, though not without difficulty, succeeded in transplanting the order to France, where it afterward took root and bore the fairest fruits.

The institutions of St. François de Sales were also established in this milder spirit.   In all his proceedings, François de Sales desired to maintain a cheerful tranquillity, free from hurry, and from all painful effort.   With the aid of his fellow laborer, Mère Chantel, he founded the order of Visitation, expressly for such persons as were prevented by the delicacy of their bodily frame from entering the more austere communities.   He not only omitted from his rule all direct penances, and dispensed from all the more severe monastic duties, but even admonished his followers to refrain from excess of internal enthusiasm.   He recommended that all should place themselves, without an ex- cessive anxiety of self-investigation, in the sight of God, and not labor to enjoy more of His presence than he shall see fit to grant.   Pride of spirit is sometimes concealed under the aspect of religious ecstasy, and may mislead: it is advisable that all should restrain their walk within the accustomed paths of virtue. For this cause, he prescribes to his nuns the care of the sick as their especial duty: they were to go out always two together— one a superior, the other an associate—and visit the sick poor in

[1] Diego de Yepes, " Vita della glo- riosa vergine S. Teresa di Giesu, fonda- trice de' Carmelitani Scalzi, Roma, 1623," p. 303.   " Constituzioni prin- cipali," § 3, p. 208.   The " Exclama- ciones o meditaciones de S. Teresa con algunos otros tratadillos, Brusselas, 1682," exhibit her enthusiasm in too ex- alted a state for our sympathies.

their own dwellings. It was the opinion of François de Sales, that we should pray by good works—by our labors of love.[2] His order diffused a beneficent influence through the whole of France.

It will be instantly perceived that in this course of things there was an obvious progress from austerity to moderation, from ecstasy to calmness, from secluded asceticism to the performance of social duty.

The Ursuline nuns were also now received in France: this community assumed a fourth vow, that of devoting itself to the instruction of young girls, and this duty the members performed with admirable zeal.

A similar disposition was soon seen to be actively at work among the religious communities of men also, as indeed may be readily imagined.

Jean Baptiste Romillon, who had borne arms against Catholicism up to his twenty-sixth year, but who then became its convert, established, with the aid of a friend attached to similar principles, the order of the Fathers of Christian Doctrine, by whom the foundations of elementary instruction were laid anew throughout France.

We have already mentioned Berulle, one of the distinguished ecclesiastics of France at that time. From early youth he had evinced the most earnest wish to render himself fitted for the service of the Church. To this end he had, as he says, kept daily present to his thoughts " the truest and most profound purpose of his heart," which was " to labor for the attainment of the highest perfection." It may perhaps have been the difficulties he experienced in this work that impressed him with the absolute necessity of an institution for the education of the clergy with reference to the immediate service of the altar. He took Filippo Neri as his model, and founded an establishment of " Priests of the Oratory." He would not suffer vows; he permitted simple engagements only, possessing sufficient liberality of mind to desire that all should be at liberty to withdraw from that service who did not feel the strength of purpose required to fulfil its duties. His institution was very successful;

---

[2] As, for example, we find in Gallitia, " Leben des h. Franz von Sales," ii. 285. But it is in his own works that the character of St. Francis is most clearly and most attractively manifested, more especially in his " Introduction to a Devotional Life."

the mildness of his rule attracted pupils of rank, and Berulle soon found himself at the head of a brilliant band of able and docile young men. Episcopal seminaries and schools of a higher order were intrusted to his care. The clergy proceeding from his institution were animated by a more life-like and active spirit, and the character of pulpit oratory in France was determined by that period of its history.[3]

Nor must we here omit to mention the congregation of St. Maur. While the French Benedictines adhered to those re-forms of their order which had been effected in Lorraine, they added to its various obligations the duty of devoting themselves to the education of the young nobility, and to learning in gen-eral. In their earliest efforts of this kind there appeared among them a man of well-merited celebrity, Nicolas Hugo Ménard. From him it was that their studies received the direction toward ecclesiastical antiquities, to which we are indebted for so many magnificent works.[4]

The order of the Brethren of Mercy, a foundation of that in-defatigable attendant of the sick, Johannes à Deo,[5] a Portuguese, on whom a Spanish bishop conferred that name in a moment of admiration; had been introduced into France by Mary de' Medici. The severity of their rule was increased in that coun-try, but they had all the more followers from that circumstance; and in a short time we find thirty hospitals founded by this brotherhood.

But how vast is the undertaking to remodel the religious char-acter and feelings of a whole kingdom—to lead all into one sole direction of faith and doctrine! Among the inferior classes, the peasantry, and even the clergy of remote parishes, the old abuses might still be found prevailing; but the great missionary of the people—of the populace—Vincent de Paul, appeared in the midst of the universal movement, and by him was established that Congregation of the Mission, whose members, travelling from place to place, diffused the spirit of devotion throughout the land, and penetrated to the most remote and secluded corners of France. Vincent de Paul, himself the son of a peasant, was

---

[3] Tabaraud, " Histoire de Pierre de Berulle," Paris, 1817.
[4] Filipe le Cerf, " Bibliothèque his-torique et critique des Auteurs de la Congrégation de S. Maur," p. 355.

[5] " Approbatio Congregationis Fra-trum Johannis Dei, 1572." Kal. Jan. (Bullar. Cocquel. iv. 111, 190.)

humble, full of zeal, and endowed with good practical sense.[6]
It was by him that the order of Sisters of Mercy was also founded.   In this the gentler sex, while still at an age when they
might claim to realize the most radiant hopes of domestic happiness or worldly distinction, devoted itself to the service of the
sick, frequently of the depraved, without venturing to give more
than a passing expression to those religious feelings by which its
earnest toils are prompted, and whence its pious activity proceeds.

These are labors that are happily ever renewed in Christian
lands, whether for the nurture of infancy, the instruction of
youth, or the inculcation of learning, the teaching of the people
from the pulpit, or the purposes of benevolence in general; but
in no place are they effectual without the combination of manifold qualities and energies with religious enthusiasm.   In other
countries they are usually left to the care of each successive generation, to the promptings of present need; but here an attempt
was made to fix these associations on an immutable basis, to give
an invariable form to the religious impulse from which they
proceed, that all may be consecrated to the immediate service
of the Church, and that future generations may be trained imperceptibly but surely into the same path.

Throughout France the most important consequences were
soon manifest.   Even under Henry IV the Protestants already
perceived themselves to be hemmed in and endangered by an activity so deeply searching and so widely extended as that now
displayed by their opponents.   They had for some time made
no further progress, but they now began to suffer losses; and
even during Henry's life they complained that desertion from
their ranks had commenced.

And yet the policy of Henry still compelled him to accord
them certain marks of favor, and to reject the demands of the
Pope, who desired, among other things, that they should be excluded from all public employments.

But under Mary de' Medici the policy previously pursued was
abandoned; a much closer connection was formed with Spain,
and a decidedly Catholic disposition became predominant, both
in domestic and foreign affairs.   And as in the court, so also
in the assembly of the States, was this supremacy obvious.

[6] Stolberg, " Leben des heiligen Vin-
centius von Paulus, Münster, 1818."
But the good Stolberg should hardly
have described his hero as " a man by
whom France was regenerated " (p. 6,
p. 399).

In the two first meetings of the year 1614 not only was the publication of the Tridentine decrees expressly demanded, but the restoration of Church property in Bearn was also required.

There was at that time much life and zeal in the Protestant Church and institutions also ; and most fortunate it was for them that the strength of their political situation and their force in arms made it impossible that this should be suppressed.   As the government had united with their opponents, so the Protestants found support and aid from those powerful malcontents, who have never been wanting in France, and will ever be numerous in that country.   Thus some time yet elapsed before it was possible to venture on directly attacking them.

CHAPTER SECOND

GENERAL WAR.—VICTORIES OF CATHOLICISM.— A.D. 1617–1623

Section I.—Breaking Out of the War

HOWEVER diversified may have been the circumstances of which we have thus traced the development, they yet all concurred to the production of one great result. On all sides Catholicism had made vigorous advances; but it had also been opposed on all sides by a mighty resistance. In Poland it was not able to crush its opponents, from the fact of their having found an invincible support from the neighboring kingdoms. In Germany a closely compacted opposition had presented itself to the invading creed and to the returning priesthood. The King of Spain was compelled to grant a truce to the united Netherlands, involving little less than a formal recognition of independence. The French Huguenots were armed against all aggression by the fortresses they held, by troops well prepared for war, and by the efficiency of their financial arrangements. In Switzerland the balance of parties had long been firmly established, and even regenerated Catholicism had not sufficient power to disturb it.

We find Europe divided into two worlds, which at every point encompass, restrict, assail, and repel each other.

If we institute a general comparison between these powers, we perceive at once that the Catholic presents the appearance of a much more perfect unity. We know, it is true, that this party was not without internal dissensions, but these were for the time set at rest. Above all, there existed a good and even confidential understanding between France and Spain. There was an occasional manifestation of the old animosities of Venice or Savoy, but they did not produce much effect; even such perilous attempts as the conspiracy against Venice passed over without any great convulsion. After the impressive lessons conveyed to Pope Paul V by the early events of his pontificate, he too displayed much calmness and moderation; he found means to maintain peace between the Catholic powers, and occasionally lent an impulse to the movements of the general policy.   The Protestants, on the contrary, were not only without a common centre, but, since the death of Elizabeth and the accession of James I, they had no great leading power on their side; the last-named sovereign having observed a somewhat equivocal policy from the beginning of his reign.   Lutherans and Calvinists (*Reformirten*) stood opposed to each other with a mutual aversion that necessarily disposed them to opposite measures in politics.   The Calvinists were further much divided among themselves.   Episcopalians and Puritans, Arminians and Gomarists, assailed each other with furious hatred.   In the assembly of the Huguenots, held at Saumur in the year 1611, a division arose which could never afterward be completely healed.

It is certain that the difference existing in this last-mentioned point between Catholics and Protestants must not be attributed to an inferior degree of activity in religious movement on the Catholic side.   We have indeed perceived that the contrary was the fact.   The following cause is more probably the true one. Catholicism had no share in that energy of exclusive dogmatic forms by which Protestantism was governed; there were momentous controverted questions which the former left undetermined; enthusiasm, mysticism, and that deeper feeling or sentiment which scarcely attains to the clearness and distinctness of thought, and which must ever arise from time to time as results of the religious tendency: these Catholicism absorbed into itself; controlled them, subjected them to given rule, and rendered them subservient to its purposes, in the forms of monastic asceticism.   By the Protestants, on the contrary, they were repressed, rejected, and condemned.   Therefore it was that these dispositions, thus left to their own guidance, broke forth into the multiform variety of sects existing among Protestants, and sought their own partial but uncontrolled paths.

It resulted from the same cause that literature in general had acquired a much higher degree of order and regularity on the Catholic side.   We may, indeed, affirm that the modern classical forms first prevailed in Italy, under the auspices of the Church.

In Spain also an approach was made to them, in as far as the genius of the nation permitted; a similar process had already commenced in France, where, at a later period, the classic form received so complete a development, and produced such brilliant results. Malherbe appeared; the first who voluntarily subjected himself to rule, and deliberately rejected all license,[1] and whose opinions, wholly favorable to monarchy and Catholicism, acquired increased effect from the epigrammatic precision and somewhat prosaic, yet, according to French ideas, easy elegance with which he expressed them. Among the Germanic nations, the classical tendency in literature could not, at that time, obtain predominance, even on the Catholic side; it first affected Latin poetry only, and even there it occasionally wears the look of a parody, despite the distinguished talent (displayed elsewhere) of the German Balde, in whose works this manner may be seen. Whatever was written in the German tongue, continued to be the pure expression of nature. Much less could this imitation of the antique find favor among these nations on the Protestant side. Shakespeare had placed the whole purport and spirit of the romantic before the eyes of men, in free, spontaneous, and imperishable forms. Antiquity and history were to him but as the servants of his genius. From the workshop of a German shoemaker there proceeded works—obscure—formless and unfathomable—yet possessing irresistible force of attention, a German depth of feeling, and religious contemplation of the world, such as have not their equal—unfettered productions of nature.

But I will not attempt to describe the contrasts presented by these opposing worlds of intellect—to do this effectually a larger share of attention should have been devoted to the writers of the Protestant side. One portion of the subject I may be permitted to bring into more prominent notice, because this was directly influential on the events before us.

In Catholicism the monarchical tendencies were, at that period, fully predominant. Ideas of popular rights, of legitimate opposition to princes, of the sovereignty of the people, and the legality of regicide, as they had been advocated thirty years pre-

[1] As regards the intellectual character of Malherbe and his manner of writing, new and remarkable additions to the poet's biography, by Racan, may be found in the " Mémoires," or rather " Historiettes of Tallement des Reaux," published by Monmerqué, 1834, i. p. 195.

vious, even by the most zealous Catholics, were no longer suited to the time. There was now no important opposition of any Catholic population against a Protestant sovereign; even James I of England was quietly tolerated, and the above-named theories no longer found application. The result was already obvious: the religious tendency became more closely attached to the dynastic principle, and that alliance was further promoted, if I do not mistake, by the fact that the princes of the Catholic side displayed a certain force and superiority of personal character. This may at least be affirmed of Germany. In that country the aged Bishop Julius of Würzburg was still living—the first prelate who had there attempted a thorough counter-reformation. The Elector Schweikard, of Mayence, held the office of high chancellor; that prince performed his duties with an ability enhanced by his warm and earnest interest in them, and which restored to the office its ancient and effective influence.[2] Both the other Rhenish electors were resolute, active men; by their side stood the manly, sagacious, indefatigable Maximilian of Bavaria, an able administrator, full of enlarged and lofty political designs; and with him the Archduke Ferdinand, invincible from the force of his faith, to which he adhered with all the fervor of a powerful spirit. Almost all were pupils of the Jesuits, who certainly possessed the faculty of awakening high impulses in the minds of their disciples; all were reformers too, in their own manner, and had indeed contributed, by earnest labors and religious enthusiasm, to bring about the state of things then existing around them.

The Protestant princes, on the contrary, were rather the heirs of other men's works than founders of their own; they were already of the second or third generation. It was only in some few of them that there could be perceived intimations—I know not whether of energy and strength of mind, but, without doubt, of ambition and love of movement.

And, in further contradiction to the tendencies of Catholicism, there now appeared among the Protestants an obvious inclination toward republicanism, or rather toward freedom for the aristocracy. In many places, as in France, in Poland,

[2] Montorio, "Relatione di Germania, 1624": "Of grave manners, deeply intent on the affairs of government as well spiritual as temporal, extremely well disposed toward the service of this Holy See, anxious for the progress of religion, one of the first prelates of Germany." See Appendix, No. 109.

and in all the Austrian territories, a powerful nobility, holding
Protestant opinions, was in open conflict with the Catholic ruling authorities. The result that might be attained by such a
force was clearly exemplified by the republic of the Netherlands, which was daily rising into higher prosperity. There
was, without doubt, much discussion at this time in Austria, as
regarded emancipation from the rule of the reigning family,
and the adoption of a government similar to that of Switzerland or the Netherlands. In the success of some such effort
lay the only means for restoring their ancient importance to
the imperial cities of Germany, and they took a lively interest in
them. The internal constitution of the Huguenots was already
republican, and was indeed not unmingled with elements of
democracy. These last were already opposing themselves to a
Protestant sovereign in the persons of the English Puritans.
There still exists a little treatise by an imperial ambassador,
who was in Paris at that time, wherein the attention of the
European princes is very forcibly directed toward the common
danger menacing them from the advance of such a spirit.[3]

The Catholic world of this period was of one mind and faith
—classical and monarchical. The Protestant was divided—
romantic and republican.

In the year 1617 everything already betokened the approach
of a decisive conflict between them. The Catholic party appears to have felt itself the superior; it is at all events not to
be denied that it was the first to take arms.

An edict was published in France on June 15, 1617, which had
been long demanded by the Catholic clergy, but which had hitherto been constantly refused by the court, from consideration
for the power possessed by the Huguenots, and in deference to
their chiefs. By virtue of that decree the property of the
Church in Bearn was to be restored. It was obtained from
Luines; that Minister, although the Protestants at first relied
on his protection,[4] having gradually attached himself to the
Jesuit and papal party. Already confiding in this disposition of

[3] " Advis sur les causes des mouve-
mens de l'Europe, envoyé aux roys et
princes pour la conservation de leurs
royaumes et principautés, fait par Mes-
sir Al. Cunr. baron de Fridembourg,
et présenté au roy très Chrestien par
le Comte de Furstemberg, ambassadeur

de l'Empéreur." Inserted in the " Mercure François," tom. ix. p. 342.
[4] This appears, with other matters,
from a letter of Duplessis Mornay,
dated Saumur, April 26, 1617, " sur ce
coup de majorité," as he calls the murder of the Maréchal d'Ancre.—" La Vie
de Du Plessis," p. 465.

the supreme power, the populace had in various quarters risen against the Protestants; sometimes aroused to the attack by the sound of the tocsin. The parliaments also took part against them.

The Polish Prince Wladislaus once more had recourse to arms, in the confident expectation that he should now obtain possession of the throne of Moscow. An opinion prevailed that designs against Sweden were connected with this attempt, and war was immediately resumed between Poland and Sweden.[5]

But by far the most important results were those preparing in the hereditary dominions of Austria. The archdukes had been reconciled, and were now reunited. With the greatness of mind which that house has frequently displayed in moments of danger, a general resignation had been made to the Archduke Ferdinand of all claims that must devolve on them at the death of the Emperor Matthias, who had no children; that prince was in fact shortly afterward acknowledged as successor to the throne, in Hungary and Bohemia. This was indeed only an adjustment and compromise of personal claims; it nevertheless involved results of important general interest.

From a zealot so determined as Ferdinand, nothing less was to be expected than an immediate attempt to secure the absolute supremacy for his own creed in the Austrian dominions, and, this accomplished, it was to be supposed that he would then labor to turn the collective powers of those territories toward the diffusion of the Catholic faith.

This was a common danger, menacing alike to all Protestants, not only in the hereditary dominions of Ferdinand or in Germany, but in Europe generally.

It was from this cause that opposition immediately arose. The Protestants, who had set themselves in array against the encroachments of Catholicism, were not only prepared for resistance—they had courage enough immediately to convert the defence into attack.

The interests of European Protestantism were concentrated

---

[5] Hiärn, "Esth-Lyf-und Lettländische Geschichte," p. 418: "The Swedes knew that the King of Poland had sent his son with a great force into Russia, that he might surprise the fortresses which had been ceded by the Muscovites to the Swedes, so that, if his attack succeeded, he might then more easily fall upon the Kingdom of Sweden; for he was promised aid in that enterprise both by the Diet of the States held in Poland, and by the house of Austria: thus all his thoughts were turned upon this matter more than upon any other thing."

in the Elector Frederick of the Palatinate; his wife was daughter of the King of England and niece of the King of Denmark; Prince Maurice of Orange was his uncle, and the Duke de Bouillon, chief of the French Huguenots of the less pacific party, was his near relation. Frederick himself stood at the head of the German Union; he was a prince of grave character, and had self-command enough to abstain from the dissolute habits then prevalent at the German Courts. He devoted his best efforts to the sedulous discharge of his duties as a sovereign, and was most diligent in attending the sittings of his Privy Council; he was somewhat melancholy, proud, and full of high thoughts.[6] In his father's time there were tables in the dining-hall for councillors and nobles; these he caused to be removed, and would dine with princes or persons of the highest rank only. The presentiment of a high political vocation was cherished at this court; innumerable connections, involving far-reaching results, were diligently formed, but so long a time had elapsed since any serious attempts had been made that no very clear perception existed as to what might be attained or what the future might present; the most daring and extravagant projects were thus admitted to discussion.

Such was the tone prevailing at the Court of Heidelberg when the Bohemians, urged forward by the consciousness of their religious dangers, broke into dissensions with the house of Austria. These disputes continually increased in violence until the Bohemians resolved to reject Ferdinand, although he had already received their promise, and offered their crown to the Elector-Palatine.

For a moment Frederick hesitated. It was a thing never previously known that one German prince should desire to wrest from another a crown devolving on him by legal right. But all his friends combined to urge him onward—Maurice, who had never cordially agreed to the truce with Spain; the Duke of Bouillon; Christian of Anhalt, whose views extended over the whole arena of European politics, who marked all their springs

[6] " Relatione di Germania, 1617: " " Frederick V, now twenty years old, is of middle height, serious aspect, and melancholy disposition; he has a good constitution, is a man of lofty thoughts, and seldom indulges in gayety. By his marriage with the daughter of the English King, and by other connections and associates, he might be led to aim at high things, if a convenient occasion should present itself; so that this disposition being well known to Colonel Schomberg, formerly his tutor, he profited by it with much address, accommodating himself to the prince's humor, and, while he lived, was more his confidant than any other."

of action, and was persuaded that no one would have either power or courage to gainsay the arrangement when once accomplished—all these, his most confidential advisers, pressed his acceptance; the unbounded prospects opened before him—ambition, religious zeal—all tended to promote his compliance, and in the month of August, 1619, he received the Bohemian crown. Could he have maintained the position thus assumed, how vast must have been the results! The power of the house of Austria in Eastern Europe would have been broken, the progress of Catholicism limited forever.

And in all quarters powerful sympathies were already at work in his favor. A general movement took place among the Huguenots in France. The people of Bearn refused obedience to the royal edict mentioned above; the assembly of Loudun espoused their cause; nothing could have been more desirable to the Queen-mother than to win the support of this opposition, so well prepared for war; Rohan was already on her side, and had promised her that his associates should follow.

Amid the perpetual agitations of the Grisons, the Spanish party had once more been dispossessed, and that of the Protestants was again in the ascendant. The government at Davos received the ambassador from the new King of Bohemia with pleasure, and promised to keep the passes of the country forever closed against the Spaniards.[7]

And we must not fail to remark that, together with all this, the republican tendency immediately arose into view. Not only did the Bohemian Estates maintain, with regard to the King they had chosen, a natural independence, but attempts were made to imitate them in all the hereditary dominions of Austria. The imperial cities of Germany conceived new hopes, and it was in fact from these last that Frederick received the most ample supplies of money for his enterprise.

But it was this very union of motives—this double point of view, taken from religion and policy combined—that now united the Catholic princes also in efforts more than ever earnest and active.

[7] The connection of these events was felt by contemporaries, although this was no more regarded in later times.— " Fürstl. Anhaltische Geh. Canzlei Fortsetzung," p. 67.

Maximilian of Bavaria formed the most intimate alliance with Ferdinand, who had the good-fortune to be chosen at that moment Emperor of Germany; the King of Spain prepared his arms for affording effectual aid, and Pope Paul V allowed himself to be prevailed on to contribute considerable and very welcome pecuniary supplies.

As the winds at times veer suddenly round in the stormy seasons of the year, so did the stream of fortune and success now suddenly flow in an altered direction.

The Catholics succeeded in gaining over one of the most powerful Protestant princes to their side: this was the Elector of Saxony, who, being a Lutheran, felt a cordial hatred for every movement proceeding from Calvinism.

This circumstance alone sufficed to inspire them with a certain hope of victory. A single battle—that of the Weissberg, fought on November 8, 1620—put an end to the power of the Palatine Frederick, and ruined all his designs.

For even the Union did not support its chief with the energy and efficiency required by the occasion. A very probable cause for this may have been that the republican tendencies in action may have seemed perilous to the confederate princes—they had no wish to see the Hollanders on the Rhine, feeling too much afraid of the analogies that might be suggested by their constitution, to the people of Germany. The Catholics achieved an immediate predominance in Southern Germany also. The Upper Palatinate was invaded by the Bavarians—the Lower Palatinate by the Spaniards; and in April, 1621, the Union was dissolved. All who had taken arms for or acted in favor of Frederick were driven from the country or utterly ruined. From a moment of the most imminent peril, the Catholic principle passed immediately to unquestioned omnipotence throughout Upper Germany and in all the Austrian provinces.

In France, also, a decisive movement was meanwhile achieved, after an important advantage gained by the royal power over the court factions opposing it, and the party of the Queen-mother, with whom it is certain that the Huguenots then stood in close connection.[8] The papal nuncio insisted that the favorable moment should be seized on for a general attack on the

[8] Even Benoist says, ii. 291: "The reformed would have waited only the first successes to declare themselves for the same party—that of the Queen."

Protestants; he would not hear a word of delay, believing that in France what was once put off was never effected at all: [9] he forced Luines and the King into his own views. The old factions of Beaumont and Grammont still existed in Bearn, where they had been at constant feud for centuries. Their discords afforded opportunity for the King's unopposed advance into the country, where he disbanded its military force, annulled its constitution, and restored the supremacy of the Catholic Church. It is true that the Protestants in other parts of France now took measures for assisting their brethren in the faith, but in the year 1621 they were defeated in all quarters.

There was at the same time a leader in the Valteline, Giacopo Robustelli, who had gathered about him certain Catholics, exiles from the country, with outlaws from the Milanese and Venetian territories, and who now determined to put an end to the domination of the Grisons, whose Protestant rule was felt to be particularly oppressive in those districts. A Capuchin monk brought the flames of religious fanaticism to excite still further this already bloodthirsty band; and on the night of July 19, 1620, they poured down upon Tirano. At the dawn of day they rang the church bells, and, when the Protestants rushed out of their dwellings on hearing that sound, they were fallen upon—instantly overpowered and massacred, one and all. And as in Tirano, so these bandits proceeded throughout the whole valley. The people of the Grisons vainly descended from their high mountains in the hope of regaining their lost sovereignty; they were defeated at every attempt. In 1621 the Austrians from the Tyrol, and the Spaniards from Milan, pressed into the very centre of the Grisons. "The wild mountains resounded with the shrieks of the murdered, and were fearfully lighted up by the flames of their solitary dwellings." The passes and the whole country were occupied by the invaders.

By this great and vigorous advance, all the hopes of the Catholics were aroused.

The Papal Court represented to the Spanish sovereign that the people of the Netherlands were divided, and now without allies, so that no more favorable occasion could occur for renewing the war against these incorrigible rebels. The Spaniards

[9] Siri, " Memorie recondite," tom. v. p. 148.

were convinced by these arguments. On March 25, 1621,[10] the
Chancellor of Brabant, Peter Peckius, appeared at The Hague,
and instead of proposing a renewal of the truce, which expired
at that time, he proposed the recognition of the legitimate
princes.[1] The States-General declared this suggestion to be
unjust and unexpected, nay, inhuman. Hostilities thereupon
recommenced; and here also the Spaniards had at first the
advantage. They took Juliers from the Netherlands—an acquisition by which their undertakings on the Rhine were successfully closed—they occupied the whole of the left bank, from
Emmeric to Strasburg.

These repeated victories—concurring, as they did in time—
gained on so many different points, and brought about by
means so diversified—are yet, when viewed in the light cast
on them by the general state of Europe, but varied expressions
of one and the same triumph. Let us now consider the point
of most importance to us—the uses, namely, to which these
successors were made subservient.

Section II.—Gregory XV

While engaged in the procession appointed for the celebration of the battle of Weissberg, Paul V was struck by apoplexy.
A second stroke followed shortly afterward from the effects of
which he died—January 28, 1621.

The new election was effected, on the whole, in the manner of those preceding. Paul V had reigned so long that the
whole College of Cardinals had been nearly renewed under his
auspices; thus the greater part of the cardinals were de-
pendents of his nephew, Cardinal Borghese. Accordingly, after
some hesitation he found a man with regard to whom all his
adherents agreed—this was Alessandro Ludovisio, of Bologna,
who was forthwith elected (February 9, 1621), and took the
name of Gregory XV.

He was a small, phlegmatic man, who had previously acquired
repute for his dexterity in negotiation, and for the art he pos-

---

[10] " Instruttione a Mre. Sangro:"
" There, where his Majesty could not
direct his forces at a better time, or
with more inviting opportunity." See
Appendix, No. 97.
[1] Literally, his proposal was for a
union under the cognizance of legitimate lords and princes. Both the proposal and reply are to be found in Leo-
nis ab Aitzema, " Historia Tractatuum
Pacis Belgicæ," pp. 2 and 4.

sessed of proceeding silently, and by imperceptible advances, to the attainment of all his purposes.[1] He was, however, already bent with age at his accession, was exceedingly feeble, and in a bad state of health.

What, then, could be expected in the contest now proceeding, and which affected the whole world, from a pontiff to whom his counsellors and servants could sometimes not venture to communicate important affairs, lest they should give the last shock to his frail existence?[2]

But there stood by the side of the dying pontiff a young man, twenty-five years old only, his nephew, Ludovico Ludovisio, who at once took possession of the papal power, and who displayed a talent and boldness fully commensurate to the demands of the period.

Ludovico Ludovisio was magnificent and brilliant; he did not neglect occasions for amassing wealth, for securing advantageous family alliances, and for advancing and favoring his friends; he desired to enjoy life, but he suffered others to enjoy it also; above all, he permitted nothing to interfere with his regard to the higher interests of the Church. His enemies themselves admitted the truth and extent of his talents for business, his peculiar sagacity, and power of discrimination. From the most embarrassing perplexities, the quick discernment and ready tact of Ludovico found a satisfactory issue: he was endowed with that calm courage and cool presence of mind by which possible contingencies are descried through the dim obscurity of the future, and which enable their possessor to steer his course steadily toward the object desired.[3] Had he not been restrained by the feebleness of his uncle, which made it certain that his power could not have long duration, no considerations of expediency, or the world's opinion, would ever have been suffered to fetter his actions.[4]

[1] " Relatione di IV. Ambasciatori, 1621: " " Of a complexion approaching fairness. His disposition has been ever known as placid and cool—careful to involve himself in no disputes, but proceeding amicably, and advancing to his own ends by force of address." See Appendix, No. 94.

[2] Rainier Zeno, " Relatione di Roma, 1623:" " Adding to his failing age a most feeble constitution, in a little, attenuated, and sickly frame."

[3] Rainier Zeno: " He has a most lively genius, and has proved it by the abundance of expedients that his mind, really formed to command, has supplied in every occurrence of grave difficulty; and, if some of these were unsuited to the measures of sound policy, yet the intrepidity with which he showed himself prompt to seize every means he thought good, little caring for the counsels of those who might have been his teachers, gave reason to think that his nature disdained a private condition."

[4] See Appendix, No. 95, " Vita e Fatti di Ludovico Ludovisio,"

It was a fact of infinite moment, that the nephew, as well as the Pope, was possessed by the idea that the salvation of the world must be sought in the extension of the Catholic faith. Cardinal Ludovisio was a pupil of the Jesuits, and their steady patron. The church of St. Ignatius in Rome was in great part erected at his cost. He attributed the most essential moment to the office of protector of the Capuchins, which he held, and which he affirmed himself to consider the most important patronage in his possession. He was devoted with deep and warm predilection to the most rigid forms and order of Romanist opinions.[5]

But if we would desire to render the spirit of the new government particularly clear to our perceptions, we need only remember that it was Gregory XV in whose pontificate the Propaganda was established, and under whom the founders of the Jesuits, Ignatius and Xavier, were advanced to the Calendar of Saints.

The origin of the Propaganda is, however, properly to be sought in an edict of Gregory XIII, by which the direction of Eastern missions was confided to a certain number of cardinals, who were commanded to promote the printing of catechisms in the less known tongues.[6] But the institution was not firmly established; it was unprovided with the requisite means, and was by no means comprehensive in its views. At the time we now speak of, there flourished in Rome a great preacher, called Girolamo da Narni, who had gained universal admiration by a life that had procured him the reputation of a saint. In the pulpit he displayed a fulness of thought, a correctness of expression, and a majesty of delivery that delighted all hearers. On coming from one of his sermons, Bellarmine once said that he thought one of St. Augustine's three wishes had just been granted to himself—that, namely, of hearing the preaching of St. Paul. Cardinal Ludovisio also was in close intimacy with Girolamo, and defrayed the cost of printing his sermons. It was by this Capuchin that the idea was now first conceived of extending the above-named institution.[7] At his

[5] Giunti, " Vita e Fatti di Ludovico Ludovisio," MS.

[6] Cocquelines, " Præfatio ad Maffei Annales Gregorii XIII." p. v.

[7] Fr. Hierothei Epitome Historica rerum Franciscanarum, etc., p. 362: " By public persuasions and private counsels," Fra Girolamo had prevailed upon the Pope. Compare Cerri, Etat présent de l'Eglise Romaine, p. 289. There, also, a circumstantial description may be seen of this institution and of the increase of its wealth and capabilities.

suggestion, a Congregation was established in all due form, and by this body regular meetings were to be held for the guidance and conduct of missions in every part of the world. The members were to assemble at least once in every month, in presence of the Pope himself. The first funds were advanced by Gregory; his nephew contributed from his private property; and since this institution was in fact adapted to a want, the pressure of which was then felt, it daily advanced in prosperity and splendor. Who does not know the services performed by the Propaganda for the diffusion of philosophical studies? And not this only—the institution has generally labored (in its earliest years, most successfully, perhaps) to fulfil its vocation in a liberal and noble spirit.

Similar views were prevalent in the canonization of the two Jesuits. "At the time," says the bull, "when new worlds had been discovered, and when Luther had arisen in the Old World to assail the Catholic Church, the soul of Ignatius Loyola was moved to establish a society, which should devote itself especially to the conversion of the heathen, and to the reclaiming of heretics; but, above all other members of that society, Francis Xavier proved himself most worthy to be called the Apostle of the newly discovered nations. For these services, both are now received into the catalogue of saints. Churches and altars, where man presents his sacrifice to God, shall now be consecrated to them." [8]

And now, proceeding in the spirit revealed in these documents and represented by these acts, the new government took instant measures for completing the victories achieved by the Catholic arms, by laboring to secure their being followed by conversions to the Catholic faith, and for justifying as well as confirming the conquests of Catholicism, by the re-establishment of religion. "All our thoughts," says one of the earliest instructions of Gregory XV, "must be directed toward the means of deriving the utmost possible advantage from the fortunate revulsion of affairs, and the victorious condition of things;" a purpose that was completed with the most brilliant success.

[8] Bullarium, Cocquelines, v. 131, 137.

UNIVERSAL EXTENSION OF CATHOLICISM

Section III.—Bohemia and the Hereditary Dominions of Austria

THE attention of the papal power was first directed to the rising fortunes of the Catholic faith in the provinces of Austria.

The subsidies hitherto paid to the Emperor were doubled by Gregory XV, who further promised him an additional gift of no inconsiderable amount [1]—although, as he said, he scarcely reserved to himself sufficient to live on; he exhorted him, at the same time, to lose not a moment in following up his victory, by earnest efforts for the restoration of the Catholic religion.[2] It was only by this restoration that he could fittingly return thanks to God for the victory. He assumes, as a first principle, that by their rebellion the nations had entailed on themselves the necessity of a vigorous control, and must be compelled by force to depart from their ungodly proceedings.

The nuncio despatched to the Emperor by Gregory XV was that Carlo Caraffa so well known to German history. Two reports from this nuncio still exist,[3] the one printed, the other in manuscript; from these we are enabled to ascertain with certainty the kind of measures adopted by Caraffa for the attainment of the objects thus pressed on his attention.

In Bohemia, where his exertions were first made, his earliest care was to secure the banishment of Protestant preachers and schoolmasters, "who were guilty of treasons and offences against the divine and human majesty."

He found this no easy task; the members of the imperial government in Prague considered it as yet too dangerous. It

---

[1] From 20,000 gulden he raised the subsidy to 20,000 scudi: the gift was 200,000 scudi. He would have liked to have regiments maintained with this money, and wished them to be placed under the papal authority.

[2] "Instruttione al Vescovo d'Aversi," April 12, 1621: "This is no time for delays or for covert attempts." Bucquoi, in particular, was considered at Rome to be much too deliberate: "Prompt measures would be the remedy for so many evils, if they could be hoped for from Count Bucquoi, who is otherwise a valiant captain."

[3] See Appendix, No. 96.

was not until December 13, 1621—when Mansfeld had been driven out of the Upper Palatine, when all peril had ceased, and when some regiments, enrolled at the nuncio's request, had entered Prague—that these measures were ventured on; but even then they spared the two Lutheran preachers, from deference to the Elector of Saxony. The nuncio, representing a principle that acknowledges no respect of persons, would not hear of this; he complained that the whole nation clung to these men; that a Catholic priest could find nothing to do, and was unable to procure a subsistence.[4] In October, 1622, he at length prevailed, and the Lutheran preachers also were banished. It appeared, for a moment, that the fears of the government councillors would be justified; the Elector of Saxony issued a threatening letter, and on the most important questions displayed extremely hostile purposes. The Emperor himself once told the nuncio that matters had been decided much too hastily, and it would have been better to wait a more favorable opportunity.[5] The means for maintaining Ferdinand steadfast to his purpose were, nevertheless, well known and used. The old Bishop of Würzburg represented to him that "a glorious emperor ought not to shrink before dangers, and it would be much better for him to fall into the power of men than into the hands of the living God." The Emperor yielded, and Caraffa had the further triumph of seeing the Elector of Saxony submit to the banishment of the preachers, and desist from his opposition.

In this manner the way was prepared. To the places of the Protestant preachers succeeded Dominican, Augustine, and Carmelite friars, for as yet there was a sensible dearth of secular clergy; a whole colony of Franciscans arrived from Gnesen. The Jesuits did not suffer themselves to be vainly wished for; when directions from the Propaganda appeared, requiring

[4] Caraffa, "Ragguaglio MS:" "The Catholic parish priests were driven to despair at seeing themselves deprived of all emolument by the Lutherans." But the printed "Commentarii" present a more ostensible cause of dissatisfaction: "Quamdiu illi hærebant, tamdiu adhuc sperabant sectarii S. majestatem concessurum aliquando liberam facultatem," p. 130. "As long as they persisted [in retaining their places], so long the sectarians hoped that his Majesty would grant them free powers [of worship]." See Appendix No. 108.

[5] Caraffa, "Ragguaglio:" "His Majesty showed some uneasiness, and proceeded to tell me that there had been too much haste, and that it would have been better to drive out those preachers at some more convenient time, as after the convention of Ratisbon. To which I replied that his Majesty had perhaps erred rather by slowness than haste; for, if Saxony had come to the convention, which they will not admit that he intended, everyone knows that he would have required from his Majesty permission for the Lutheran worship, after his notions, to be continued in Prague as it had before been." See Appendix, No. 108, § 3.

them to undertake the duties of parish priests, it was found that they had already done so.[6]

And now the only question that could remain was, whether it might not be permitted that the national Utraquist ritual should be at least partially retained in the forms assigned to it by the Council of Basle. The government council and the governor himself, Prince Lichtenstein, were in favor of its being retained.[7] They permitted the Lord's Supper to be solemnized once more with both the elements on Holy Thursday, in the year 1622; and a voice was already uplifted among the people, inviting that this ancient usage of their fathers should not be interrupted, and that their privilege should not be wrested from them. But by no argument could the nuncio be prevailed on to consent: he was inflexibly determined to maintain all the views of the Curia, knowing well that the Emperor would at length be brought to approve his decision. And he did in fact succeed in obtaining from him a declaration that his temporal government had not the right to interfere in religious affairs. Mass was hereupon everywhere performed in the Roman ritual exclusively in Latin, with sprinkling of holy-water and invocation of saints. The sacrament under both forms was no longer to be thought of; those who ventured to defend that celebration most boldly were thrown into prison; and finally, the symbol of Utraquism, the great chalice with the sword, at that time still to be seen at the Thein church, and which it was thought would keep alive old recollections, was taken down. On July 6th, which had previously always been held sacred in memory of John Huss, the churches were kept carefully closed.

To this rigorous enforcement of Romanist dogmas and usages, the government lent the aid of political measures. A large part of the landed property of the country was thrown by confiscation into the hands of Catholics, and the acquisition of land by Protestants was rendered almost impossible.[8] The council was changed in all the royal cities; no member would have been tolerated whose Catholicism was in the slightest de-

[6] Cordara, " Historia Societatis Jesu," tom. vi. lib. vii. p. 38.

[7] According to the opinions hitherto prevailing, in Senkenberg, for example, " Fortsetzung der Häberlinschen Reichshistorie," bd. xxv. p. 156, note k, we should believe the contrary of Lichtenstein; this would, nevertheless, be wrong, as is manifest from Caraffa. The nuncio, on the contrary, received support from Plateis.

[8] With regulations to the effect that they could not be inscribed on the registers of the kingdom: a measure of inexpressible advantage to the Reformation during all that period.

gree suspected; the rebels were pardoned on the instant of their conversion; but the refractory—those who could not be persuaded, and refused to yield to the admonitions of the clergy —had soldiers quartered in their houses, "to the end," as the nuncio declares in express terms, "that their vexations might enlighten their understanding." [9]

The effect produced by that combined application of force and exhortation was unexpected, even to the nuncio. He was amazed at the numbers attending the churches in Prague, frequently not less on Sunday mornings than from two to three thousand persons, and at their humble, devout, and to all outward appearance, Catholic deportment. He accounts for this by supposing that Catholic recollections had never been wholly extinguished in the country, as might be seen from the fact that even the consort of King Frederick had not been permitted to remove the great cross from the bridge: the real cause unquestionably was that Protestant convictions never had in fact penetrated the masses of the population. The conversions proceeded unremittingly; in the year 1624, the Jesuits alone profess to have recovered 16,000 souls to the Catholic Church. [10] In Tabor, where Protestantism seemed to have exclusive possession, fifty families passed over to the Catholic Church at Easter, 1622; and all the remaining part of the population at Easter of the following year. In course of time Bohemia became entirely Catholic.

And as matters had gone in Bohemia so did they now proceed in Moravia; the end was indeed attained with more facility in the latter country, where Cardinal Dietrichstein, being at the same time Bishop of Olmütz and Governor of the province, brought both the spiritual and temporal powers to bear with all their forces combined on the point to be gained. There was, however, one difficulty peculiar to that country to be overcome. The nobles would not permit themselves to be deprived of the Moravian Brethren, whose services, whether domestic or agricultural, were invaluable, and whose settlements were the most prosperous districts in the country. [1] They found advo-

[9] To the end that their troubles should give them feeling and understanding, the same thing is also repeated in the printed work, " Cognitumque fuit solam vexationem posse Bohemis intellectum præbere."

[10] Caraffa: " A Catholic priest of great ability was placed there, and afterward missions of the Jesuit fathers were sent thither."
[1] " Ragguaglio di Caraffa: " " These being considered men of industry and

cates even in the Emperor's Privy Council; the nuncio and the principle he represented were nevertheless victorious in this case also: nearly 50,000 of the Moravians were expatriated.

In the district of Glatz, the Protestant banners had once more been led to victory by the young Count Thura, but the Poles advanced in aid of the imperialists; the country was then overmatched, the town also was captured, and the Catholic worship restored with the usual severities. Not less than sixty preachers were driven from the land; they were followed by no inconsiderable portion of their people, whose property instantly was confiscated. The mass of the population returned to Catholicism.[2] Under these circumstances, the often-repeated and as often unsuccessful attempt to restore the Catholic faith in Austria proper was once more renewed, and was at length followed by decided success.[3] First, the preachers that had been accused of rebellion were banished, and then all Protestant preachers whatever. Furnished with a small sum for their journey, the unfortunate people slowly proceeded up the Danube, followed by the taunting cry of "Where now is your strong tower?" The Emperor declared explicitly to the Estates of the country that he "reserved to himself and his posterity the absolute and undivided power of disposing all things that regarded religion." In October, 1624, a commission appeared, by which a certain time was appointed, and within this period all were required to profess themselves of the Catholic faith or to depart from the land. To the nobles only was a

integrity, were employed in the care of estates, houses, wine-cellars, and mills, besides which they were excellent workmen in various handicrafts, and, becoming rich, they contributed a large part of their gains to the nobles of the places where they dwelt; although, for some time previously, they had begun to get corrupted, ambition and avarice creeping in among them, with some degree of luxury in their habits of life. These people have continually increased in Moravia; because, in addition to those whom they win over to join them in the province and places round, they maintain a correspondence with all parts of Germany, whence there flock to this brotherhood all those who despair of gaining a living for themselves; there come to them, besides, great numbers from Suabia and the Grisons, poor creatures who suffer themselves to be allured by that name of "fraternity," and by the certainty of always having bread, which they doubt of being able to gain at home and by their own labor; so that, at times, these Moravians have amounted to 100,000."
[2] Kögler's "Chronik von Glatz," i. 3, 92.
[3] This had been the first thought of the Emperor, even before the battle of Prague, and when Maximilian first entered the territory of Upper Austria. He enforced on the latter the necessity of displacing the preachers without delay, "that the pipers might be sent away and the dance ended." His letter is in Breier's "Continuation of Wolf's Maximilian," iv. 414. In the year 1624 the Jesuits got the University of Vienna completely into their hands: "The Emperor incorporated the society with the university, making the Jesuit body one with it, and granting them the fullest power to teach the polite letters, the Latin, Greek, and Hebrew tongues, philosophy, and theology." "Monitum ad Statut. Acad. Vindob. recentiora," Kollar "Annal." ii. p. 282.

certain degree of indulgence shown, and that but for a short time.

In Hungary these violent proceedings were not possible, though that country was also conquered. A change was nevertheless brought about here also, by the force of events, the favor of government, and above all by the exertions of the Archbishop Pazmany. This prelate was gifted with extraordinary talent as a writer of the mother-tongue: his book, entitled " Kalauz," [4] full of spirit and learning, was found by his countrymen to be irresistible. He was endowed with the gift of eloquence also, and is said to have persuaded no less than fifty families to abjure Protestantism by his own personal exhortations: names such as Zrinyi, Forgacz, Erdödy, Balassa, Jakusith, Homonay, and Adam Thurzo are found among them; Count Adam Zrinyi alone expelled twenty Protestant pastors, and placed Catholic priests in their stead. Under these influences the political affairs of Hungary also took an altered direction. At the Diet of 1625 the Catholic and Austrian party had the majority. One of the converted nobles, an Esterhazy, whom the court desired to see appointed, was nominated palatine.

But we must here at once remark the difference existing between Hungary and other parts of the Austrian dominions. The conversions in Hungary were very much more voluntary than they had been in other portions of the empire. The magnates resigned no one of their rights by conforming to Catholicism; they may rather be said to have acquired increased privileges. In the Austrian Bohemian territories, on the contrary, the entire force of the Estates, their energy, and their independence, had all been thrown into the forms of Protestantism. Their conversion was compulsory, if not in each individual case, yet certainly as a whole; with the reinstatement of Catholicism, the unlimited and absolute power of the government was established there also.

[4] Hodoegus, " Igazságra vezérlö Kalauz.," Presb. 1613, 1623.

Section IV.—The Empire—Transfer of the Electorate

We know that the progress of Catholic restoration in Germany was much more decided than in the hereditary dominions of Austria. The recent events had, nevertheless, an immeasurable effect even there.

The Counter-Reformation at once received an increased impetus, and found a new field of action.

When Maximilian had taken possession of the Upper Palatinate, he permitted no time to be lost before changing its religion. He divided the country into twenty stations, in which fifty Jesuits immediately commenced their labors. The churches were transferred to them by force. The exercise of the Protestant worship was universally prohibited, and in proportion as it became probable that the country would continue annexed to Bavaria, did the disposition of the inhabitants increase toward the Catholic religion.[1]

Even the Lower Palatinate was now regarded by the conquerors as entirely their own. Maximilian even presented the library of Heidelberg to the Pope.[2]

Nay, the conquest had not yet been attempted, to say a word in passing on this subject, when the Pope requested that gift from the duke by means of his nuncio at Cologne, Montorio; and Maximilian promised it with his usual alacrity. At the first intelligence of the capture of Heidelberg, the nuncio availed himself of the right thus obtained. He had been told that the manuscripts, more particularly, were of inestimable value, and forwarded an especial request to Tilly that they might be protected from injury at the plunder of the city.[3] The Pope then commissioned Doctor Leone Allacci, scriptor of the Vatican, to proceed at once to Germany and take the books into his possession. Gregory XV considered this affair as a matter of very high consequence: he declared it to be one of the most fortunate events of his pontificate, and one that must needs be highly beneficial to the sciences as well as to the advantage of the Church and honor of the Holy See. It would also be very glorious to the Bavarian name, he affirmed, that

[1] Kropff, " Historia Societatis Jesu in Germania superiori," tom. iv. p. 271.
[2] See Appendix, No. 101.

[3] Relatione di Mgr. Montorio ritornato nunzio di Colonia, 1624. The passage is given in the Appendix, No. 109.

so precious a booty should be preserved as an eternal remembrance in the world's great theatre—Rome.[4]

Here also the duke displayed his indefatigable zeal for reform. He greatly exceeded even the Spaniards, who were yet most certainly not indifferent to Catholicism.[5] The nuncio was enraptured at the sight of mass performed and conversions taking place in Heidelberg, "whence the rule and guide of Calvinism, the notorious catechism, had proceeded."

The Elector Schweikard was, meanwhile, reforming the Bergstrasse, of which he had taken possession. The Margrave Wilhelm was pursuing a similar course in Upper Baden, as he had expressly promised the nuncio, Caraffa, to do [6] in the event of its being adjudged to him, as it now was after long litigation, although his origin, far from being equal to so high a claim, was scarcely legitimate.

Even in countries not immediately affected by the political events of the period, the former efforts for the restoration of Catholicism were continued with renewed zeal. In Bamberg,[7] in Fulda, on the Eichsfeld, and in Paderborn, where Catholics had been twice appointed in succession to the episcopal see, these efforts were most successful; but more particularly so in the see of Münster, where Meppen, Vechta, Halteren, and many other districts, were rendered wholly Catholic in the year 1624. Archbishop Ferdinand established missions in nearly all the towns, and founded a Jesuits' college in Coesfeld,[8] "for the revival and recovery of the most ancient Catholic religion, by many treated with indifference." Even up to Halberstadt and Magdeburg we find Jesuit missionaries. In Altona they seated themselves for a certain time to learn the lan-

[4] "That so precious a spoil and so noble a trophy should be preserved as a perpetual memorial in this theatre of the world."—"Instruttione al Dottore Leon Allatio per andare in Germania per la libreria del Palatino." In the Appendix we will examine its authenticity; see No. 101.
[5] Montorio: "Even in the countries occupied by the Spaniards they do not proceed to the conversion of the people with the fervor shown by the Duke of Bavaria in those he occupies."
[6] Caraffa, "Germania restaurata," p. 129.
[7] Particularly by John George Fuchs von Dornheim, by whom twenty-three knights' parishes were regained to Catholicism.—Jäck, "Geschichte von Bamberg," ii. 120.
[8] A letter from one of his assistants, Joh. Drachter, dean of Dülmen, has a peculiarly strange sound: "I have been unwilling to refer to your illustrious lordship any great number of these brainless sheep, and have labored, up to the present time, rather myself to drive the whole flock in their panic and perplexity toward the right fold, into which Balthasar Bilderbeck and Caspar Karl have already made a leap with closed feet, and have jumped in." Compare the documents in Niesert generally, "Münstersche Urkundensammlung," i. p. 402.

guage, intending then to proceed from that place to Denmark and Norway.

We see with how violent a course the doctrines of Catholicism were poured from Upper into Lower Germany, from the South to the North. Meanwhile attempts were made to obtain a new position for still more effectually interposing in the general affairs of the empire.

Ferdinand II had promised Maximilian of Bavaria, on the conclusion of their alliance, that in the event of success he would make over the palatine electorate to the duke.[9]

The principal consideration by which the Catholic party were influenced on this occasion, and the light in which they viewed this transfer, cannot possibly be questioned. The majority possessed by that party in the council of princes had been hitherto counterbalanced by the equality of votes which the Protestants held in the electoral college; by the transfer of the Palatinate, this restraint would be done away with forever.[10]

The Papal Court had from time immemorial been closely allied with the Duchy of Bavaria, and on this occasion Pope Gregory made the interests of Maximilian most completely his own.

He caused the King of Spain to be earnestly exhorted by the very first nuncio whom he sent into that country, to do his best for the destruction of the count-palatine, and thus contribute toward the transference of the Palatinate to the house of Bavaria, reminding him that this transfer must secure the imperial crown to the Catholics forever.[1] The Spaniards were not easily persuaded to enter into these views. They were engaged in the most important negotiations with the King of England, and scrupled to offend him in the person of his son-in-law, the Count-Palatine Frederick, to whom the electorate so indisputably belonged. But so much the more zealous was Pope Gregory. He was not satisfied with the services of the

[9] Letter of the Emperor to Baltasar di Zuniga, October 15, 1621, printed by Sattler, "Würtemburg Geschichte," vi. p. 162.

[10] "Instruttione a Mgr. Sacchetti, nuntio in Spagna," describes the restoration of the Palatinate to its rightful owner as "an irreparable diminution of the credit of the late achievements, and loss to the Catholic Church; if the Pope should accede to this resolution, it would be to the unspeakable injury of the Catholic religion and the empire, which has longed for so many a year to have the fourth election also in the interest of the blood of Austria, without being able to devise any possibility of bringing it about."

[1] "Instruttione a Monsr. Sangro:" he is enjoined to instigate and encourage his Majesty, that he by no means permit the Palatine ever to rise again; so that the electorate being in Catholic hands, the empire may be for ever secured to the Catholics. See Appendix, No. 97.

nuncio only, and in the year 1622 we find a Capuchin of great address—a certain Brother Hyacinth, who was greatly confided in by Maximilian—despatched with a special mission from the Papal Court to that of Spain.[2] The subject was then entered on with extreme reluctance, and all that could be gained from the King was a remark that he would rather see the electorate in the house of Bavaria than in his own. But this sufficed to Brother Hyacinth. With this declaration he hastened to Vienna, for the purpose of using it, to remove whatever scruples the Emperor might entertain in regard to the opinion of Spain. He was there assisted by the wonted influence of the nuncio, Caraffa; nay, the Pope himself came to his aid by a special letter. "Behold," exclaimed the pontiff to the Emperor in that letter, "the gates of heaven are opened; the heavenly hosts urge thee on to win so great a glory; they will fight for thee in thy camp." The Emperor was besides influenced by a very singular consideration, and one by which he is strikingly characterized. He had long thought of this transfer, and had expressed his ideas on the subject in a letter that had fallen into the hands of the Protestants, and been published by them. The Emperor felt himself to be in a measure bound by this circumstance: he thought it essential to the maintenance of his imperial dignity that he should adhere to the purpose he had formed, once its existence had become known. Suffice it to say, he determined to proceed to the transfer at the next electoral Diet.[3]

The only question now remaining was whether the princes of the empire would also agree to this arrangement. The decision mainly depended on Schweikard, of Mayence; and that cautious prince, at least according to the nuncio Montorio, was in the first instance adverse to the measure. He is said to have declared that the war would be renewed in consequence, and rage with more violence than before; that moreover, if a change must of necessity take place, the Count-Palatine of Neuberg had the more obvious right and could not possibly be passed over. The nuncio does not inform us by what means he at length persuaded the prince. "In the four or five days"—these are his words—"that I passed with him at Aschaffenburg, I obtained from him the decision desired."

[2] Khevenhiller, ix. p. 1766.   [3] Caraffa, "Germania restaurata," p. 120.

All we can perceive in this matter is that the most strenuous assistance was promised on the Pope's part, should the war break out anew.

It is certain that this acquiescence of the Electoral Prince of Mayence was decisive of the matter. His two Rhenish colleagues adopted his opinion. Brandenburg and Saxony continued to oppose the measure; for though Saxony was persuaded in like manner by the Archbishop of Mayence, this was not till a later period,[4] and the Spanish ambassador now declared himself adverse to it in express terms.[5] Yet, in despite of this opposition, the Emperor proceeded steadily forward; on February 25, 1623, he transferred the electorate to his victorious ally. It is true that in the first instance it was declared to be a personal possession only, and that the rights of the palatine heirs and agnates were reserved to them unimpaired for the future.

The advantage gained was, meanwhile, incalculable, even with this condition. Above all, the Romanists had secured the preponderance in the supreme Council of the empire, whose assent now gave a legal sanction to every new resolution in favor of Catholicism.

Maximilian clearly saw the extent of his obligation to Pope Gregory in this affair. "Your holiness," he writes to him, " has not only forwarded the matter, but by your admonitions, your authority, and your zealous exertions, you have directly accomplished it. It is to the favor and the vigilance of your holiness that it must absolutely and entirely be attributed."

" Thy letter, O son," replied Gregory XV, " has filled our breast with a stream of delight, grateful as heavenly manna. At length may the daughter of Zion shake the ashes from her head, and clothe herself in the garments of festivity." [6]

[4] Montorio calls Schweikard " the sole cause of the change in Saxony's opinion, whereby he was brought to agree with the Emperor in the matter of the transfer." See Appendix, No. 109.

[5] See Oñate's declaration and the vehement letter of Ludovisio against restoring the electorate to a blaspheming Calvinist, in Khevenhiller, x. 67, 68.

[6] Giunti, " Vita di Ludovisio Ludovisi," ascribes the merit principally to the nephew: " Many letters were written by his holiness and the cardinal, even with their own hands, full of ardor, and most proper to persuade the Emperor; and, besides that, Mgr. Verospi, auditor of the Rota, was sent about that matter, and after him, Father Giacinto of Casale, a Capuchin." By these persons the Emperor was told that the vicar of Christ, on the part of our Lord himself, implored and conjured him, even with tears, and promised him, in return for his assent, eternal felicity and the security of his salvation. See Appendix, No. 95.

Section V.—France

And now, at this same moment, the great change in Protestant affairs commenced in France.

If we inquire to what cause the severe losses suffered by the Protestant faith in the year 1621 are to be attributed, we find them principally due to the dissensions existing in the party, and to the apostasy of the nobles. It may very possibly have happened that this last was occasioned by the republican tendencies at that time made manifest in the Protestant body, and which, referring to municipal rights as well as to theological opinions, were unfavorable to the influence of the nobility. The nobles may have found it more advantageous to attach themselves to the King and court than to suffer themselves to be governed by preachers and burgomasters. Certain it is that as early as the year 1621 the fortresses held by Protestants were delivered up by their governors as if in emulation one of another; each seemed to think only of how he should secure the best conditions and highest reward for himself. These things were repeated in the year 1622. La Force and Chatillon received the batons of marshals on deserting their brethren in the faith; the aged Lesdiguières became a Catholic,[1] and even commanded a division against the Protestants. This example induced many others to abjure their belief. Under these circumstances the peace concluded in 1622 could be obtained only on the most unfavorable terms; nay, there was not even ground for hope that its conditions, hard as they were, would be fulfilled.[2] At an earlier period, and when the Protestants were powerful, the King had often disregarded and violated his treaties with them; was it probable that he would observe them more scrupulously now when they had lost their power? Accordingly, all that the peace was to secure the Protestants from suffering, was inflicted on them, in despite of its provisions and promises. The Protestant worship was in many places directly impeded. The reformed were forbidden to sing their psalms in the streets

[1] See "Mémoires de Deageant," p. 190 and many other places, for valuable remarks in respect to this conversion.
[2] "Liste des gentilhommes de la religion réduits au roi," in Malingre, "Histoire des derniers troubles arrivés en France," p. 789. Even Rohan came to terms; but these, as given in the "Mercure de France," vii. p. 845, are, unhappily, not authentic.

or in their shops. Their rights in the universities were restricted.[3] Fort Louis, which, according to the treaty of peace,
should have been razed to the ground, was on the contrary
maintained; an attempt was made to transfer the choice of
magistrates for Protestant cities to the King;[4] and on April
17, 1622, a decree was issued appointing a commissary who
should be present in all assemblies of Protestants. After these
great inroads on their ancient privileges had once been endured,
the government proceeded to interfere in matters purely ecclesiastical; the Huguenots were prevented by the commissaries
from adopting the decrees of the Synod of Dort.

They no longer possessed a shadow of independence. They
could no more oppose any steadfast or effectual resistance.
Conversions proceeded throughout the whole of their territories.

All Poitou and Languedoc were filled with the missions of
the Capuchins.[5] The Jesuits, who had formed new establishments in Aix, Lyons, Pau, and many other places, made the
most extraordinary progress both in the cities and through the
country. Their Fraternities of the Virgin attracted universal
notice, and gained the utmost respect and approbation by the
cares they had bestowed on the wounded during the last war.[6]

The Franciscans also distinguished themselves; as, for example, Father Villele, of Bordeaux, of whom things well-
nigh incredible are related. After having brought the whole
city of Foix over to his own creed, he is said to have converted a man more than a hundred years old, and the same who
had received the first Protestant preacher from the hands of
Calvin, and had conducted him into Foix. The Protestant
church was torn down, and the triumphant fathers caused the
expelled preacher to be followed by a trumpeter from town to
town.[7]

The work of conversion, in short, proceeded with irresistible
force; high and low were alike subjected to the prevailing
influence; even the learned relinquished their creed. On these
last a particular effect was produced by the argument demon-
strating that the ancient Church, even before the Council of
Nice, had permitted the invocation of saints, had offered prayers

[3] Benoist, ii. 419.
[4] Rohan, " Mém." i. 3.
[5] " Instruttione all' Arcivescovo di
Damiata," MS. See Appendix, No. 106.

[6] Cordara, " Historia Societatis Jesu,"
vii. 95, 118. See Appendix, No. 93.
[7] " Relatione Catholique," inserted in
the " Mercure François," viii. 489.

for the souls of the departed, had established a hierarchy, and was in many other respects in perfect accordance with Catholic usages.

We have still the reports of certain bishops remaining, from which we gather the relative numbers of each confession as fixed under these circumstances. In the diocese of Poitiers, half the inhabitants of some towns were Protestant; as for example, those of Lusignan and St. Maixant. In others, as Chauvigny and Norti, a third; in Loudun a fourth; in Poitiers itself a twentieth only, and a still smaller proportion in the rural districts.[8] In all matters relating to conversions the bishops were in direct correspondence with the Papal See; they made reports of what had been done, and expressed their wishes as related to future proceedings. The nuncio was then directed to present the requests or suggestions of these prelates to the King, supporting them with all his influence. The bishops frequently entered into very minute details. The Bishop of Vienne, for example, has found that the missionaries are especially impeded and restrained by a certain preacher in St. Marcellin, who has proved himself unconquerable, and the nuncio is required to press the necessity for his removal on the court. The Bishop of St. Malo claims the help of the nuncio, bewailing that at a certain castle of his diocese they will endure no introduction of the Catholic worship. The Bishop of Xaintes requests him to forward a clever converter who is pointed out by name. And on the part of the nuncio the bishops are sometimes enjoined to specify the causes of such impediments as they meet with, and to state explicitly what they think might be done for their removal, to the end that the nuncio may represent the matter effectually to the King.[9]

The most intimate union was maintained between all the

---

[8] " Relatione del Vescovo di Poitiers," 1623, MS.

[9] " Instruttione all' Arcivescovo di Damiata." A single instance may suffice: " From the report of the Bishop of Candon it appears that he has established a mission of Jesuits in his district of Neaco, where there are many heretics; but they must labor in vain, unless the King send effectual orders from the temporal power; it were well you wrote to that bishop, desiring him to state the things he desires his Majesty to do, for this he does not specify in his report. From the Bishop of St. Malo we hear that, in a castle and hamlet belonging to the Marquis of Moussaye, Calvinism only is allowed to be preached; wherefore it would be good to remind his Majesty of removing the preachers, that the bishop's missionaries may labor to some purpose; the castle and hamlet are not named, and you might write to the bishop respecting this. The Bishop of Montpellier suffered from a scarcity of spiritual laborers, and as the people listen willingly to the Capuchins it would be well to procure a mission of those fathers." See Appendix, No. 106.

ecclesiastical authorities and the Propaganda, which, as we
have remarked, was perhaps most efficiently active during its
earliest years; and these were again in continual communication
with the pontiff himself; earnest zeal and a vigorous activity
following in the train of military successes; a decided sympathy on the part of the court, who sees its own political
interests promoted by the religious changes. All these
things account for the fact that this was the period when the
destruction of the Protestant faith in France was decidedly
accomplished.

Section VI.—The United Netherlands

Nor were these advances of Catholicism confined to such
countries as had Catholic governments; they became obvious
at the same point of time under Protestant rulers also.

We are sufficiently amazed, when we read in Bentivoglio,
that even in those very cities of the Netherlands, where the
King of Spain had been so long and so magnanimously with-
stood, chiefly from religious motives; the greater part of the
principal families had again become Catholic.[1] But our astonishment is increased when we learn, from a very circumstantial report of the year 1622, the great progress of Catholicism under circumstances altogether unfavorable. The priests
were persecuted and expelled; yet their numbers increased.
In the year 1592 the first Jesuit arrived in the Netherlands; in
the year 1622 the order had twenty-two members in that country. New laborers were constantly proceeding from the colleges
of Cologne and Louvain; and in the year 1622 there were 220
secular priests employed in the provinces; that number not by
any means sufficing to the necessities of the time. According
to the report in question, the number of Catholics in the diocese of Utrecht amounted to 150,000; in the diocese of Haarlem, to which Amsterdam belonged, it was 100,000; Leuw-
arden had 15,000; Gröningen, 20,000; and Deventer, 60,000
Catholics.

The apostolic vicar, who was at that time despatched by the
Papal See to Deventer, administered confirmation to 12,000

[1] " Relatione delle provincie ubbi-
dienti," parte ii. c. ii., where the state
of religion in Holland is the subject of
discussion.

persons, in three towns and a few villages. The numbers may, perhaps, be much exaggerated in this report; but we see clearly that in that pre-eminently Protestant country there was a very large proportion of Catholic elements. Even those bishops that Philip II had attempted to establish there had from that time been acknowledged by the Catholics.[2] And this was a condition of things by which the Spaniards were very probably incited and encouraged to renew the war.

Section VII.—Relations of Catholicism with England

More peaceful prospects had meanwhile presented themselves in England. The son of Mary Stuart united the crowns of Great Britain in his own person, and now displayed a more decided disposition to a closer approximation with the Catholic powers.

Even before James I had ascended the English throne, Clement VIII caused it to be intimated to him that " he prayed for him, as the son of so virtuous a mother; that he desired for him all kinds of prosperity, temporal and spiritual, and trusted yet to see him a Catholic." His accession to the throne of England was celebrated at Rome with solemn prayers and processions.

To these advances James could not have dared to make any corresponding return, had he been even disposed to do so; but he suffered Parry, his ambassador in France, to form confidential relations with Bubalis, the papal nuncio at that court. The nuncio displayed a letter from Cardinal Aldobrandino, the Pope's nephew, wherein the latter exhorts the English Catholics to obey King James, as their natural lord and sovereign; nay, they were admonished even to pray for him. This was replied to, on the part of Parry, by an instruction from James I, in which that monarch promised to suffer peaceable Catholics to live quietly and without the imposition of any burdens.[1]

The mass was in fact now again performed openly in the

[2] " Compendium status in quo nunc est religio Catholica in Holandia et confœderatis Belgii provinciis, 2 Dec. 1622: " " Notwithstanding these things, praised be God, the number of Catholics daily increases, the dissensions of the heretics, among themselves, most especially aiding."

[1] A brief report of the matters treated of between his holiness and the King of England.

North of England; and the Puritans complained that 50,000 Englishmen had in a very short time been allured to join the Catholics. To this James is reported to have replied, " that they might, on their part, convert an equal number of Spaniards and Italians."

These favorable results may have induced the Catholics to place their hopes too high; thus, when the King persisted in adhering to the side of their opponents, when the former acts of Parliament were again carried into effect and new persecution ensued, their exasperation became intense in proportion to their disappointment, until at length it found a fearful expression in the Gunpowder Plot.

From that time there was no longer any possibility of toleration on the part of the King. The most rigorous laws were instantly enacted and enforced; domiciliary visits were inflicted, with fines and imprisonment. The priests, and above all the Jesuits, were banished and persecuted. It was thought needful to restrain enemies so daring with the most extreme severity.

But in private conversation the King was found to be much more placable. To a prince of the house of Lorraine, from whom he once received a visit, not without the knowledge of Pope Paul V, James declared in direct terms that after all there was but very slight difference between the two confessions; that it was true he thought his own the best, and held it, not from policy of state, but from conviction; yet that he was perfectly willing to hear what others thought, and since it would be altogether too difficult to convene a council, he would very gladly see a convention of learned men, for the purpose of attempting a reconciliation. He added that if the Pope would make but one step in advance, he on his part would make four to meet him. He also acknowledged the authority of the fathers. Augustine had more weight in his opinion than Luther; and he valued St. Bernard more than Calvin. Nay, he saw in the Church of Rome, even as she now was, the true Church—the mother of all others; he thought only that she required a purification. One thing he would confess to him, a friend and cousin, though he would not say so much to a papal nuncio, namely, that he too beheld in the Pope the head of the Church—the supreme bishop.[2] It was, therefore, doing him great injustice to describe him as a heretic or schismatic. A heretic he certainly was not, since he believed what the Pope believed; only that the latter believed some few things more than he could accede to: neither was he a schismatic, since he considered the Pope to be the head of the Church.

Holding opinions such as these, and entertaining together with them a very consistent aversion to the puritanical side of Protestantism, it would have been infinitely more agreeable to the King to have entered on a friendly undertaking with the Catholics, than to be compelled into keeping them down by force, and with continual danger to himself.

For they were still very numerous and powerful in England. In defiance of grievous reverses and defeats, or rather as a direct consequence of them, Ireland was in a state of perpetual commotion; it was of the utmost importance to the King that he should be relieved from this incessant opposition.[3]

We must not fail to remark that both the English and Irish Catholics attached themselves to Spain. The Spanish ambassadors in London, men of great address, very prudent, and withal extremely magnificent in their mode of life, had secured an extraordinary number of adherents. Their chapel was always full; the Holy Week was solemnized there with much splendor. They extended their protection to their co religionists in great numbers, and came to be considered, according to the report of a Venetian, almost as legates of the Apostolic See.

I think we shall not greatly err in supposing that this state of things may have largely contributed to inspire King James with the idea of marrying his heir to a Spanish princess. He hoped by this means to assure himself of the Catholics, and to conciliate to his own house the attachment they now evinced toward that of Spain. Foreign relations presented an additional motive for this proceeding, since it might be fairly expected that

[2] " Che riconosce la chiesa Romana, etiandio quella d'adesso, per la vera chiesa e madre di tutte, ma ch'ella aveva bisogno di esser purgata, e di più ch' egli sapeva che V. Sta. è capo di essa chiesa e primo vescovo." (See text.) These are expressions that can by no means be reconciled with the principles of the English Church, but they are attributed to this prince from other quarters also.—" Relatione del Sr. di Breval al Papa."
[3] " Relatione di D. Lazzari, 1621," attributes the King's proceedings to his timidity: " For I have seen manifest proof that fear is in him more powerful than anger;" and again: " From the knowledge I have of him [the King], I consider him altogether indifferent to every kind of religion." See Appendix, No. 100.

the house of Austria, when so nearly connected with himself, would manifest more favorable dispositions toward his son-in-law, the Elector-Palatine.

But the question next arising was whether this marriage could be carried into effect. There was an obstacle presented by the difference of religion that in those times was indeed most difficult to overcome.

The world of reality, the rigid order of things, will forever be accompanied by an element of fantasy, which finds expression in poetry and romantic narrations, and these in their turn react on the mind of youth, and thus influence the events of life. The negotiations that were proceeding, being delayed from day to day, and from month to month, the Prince of Wales, with his confidential friend and companion, Buckingham, conceived the romantic idea of setting off himself to fetch his bride.[4] The Spanish ambassador, Gondemar, seems not to have been altogether free from participation in this enterprise. He had told the prince that his presence would put an end to all difficulties.

How greatly surprised was the English ambassador in Madrid, Lord Digby, who had been conducting the negotiations, when, being one day called from his chamber to speak with two cavaliers who desired admission, he found in these cavaliers the son and the favorite of his King.

And now endeavors were indeed made, and that with the utmost diligence, to remove the great obstacle presented by the religious difference.

For this the consent of the Pope was required, and James I did not recoil from entering into direct negotiation on the subject with Paul V; but that pontiff had refused to make the slightest concession, unless on condition that the King should grant complete liberty in religion to all the Catholics in his country. The impression made by the prince's journey on Gregory XV was on the contrary so powerful that he felt instantly disposed to content himself with much less important concessions. In a letter to the prince he expressed the

[4] Papers relative to the Spanish match in the "Hardwicke Papers," i. p. 399. They contain a correspondence between James I and the two travellers, by which great interest is excited for the persons engaged in it. The defects of James seem at least to be those of a kindly nature. His first letter begins thus: "My sweet boys and dear ventrous knights, worthy to be put in a new romanso." "My sweet boys" is the King's usual address. They write to him as their "Dear dad and gossip."

hope "that the ancient seed of Christian piety, which had of old time borne fruit in English kings, would now once more revive in him; certainly he could in no case, desiring as he did to marry a Catholic maiden, resolve on oppressing the Catholic Church." The prince replied that he would never take hostile measures against the Roman Church, but would rather seek to bring things to such a state "that as we all," as he expressed it, "acknowledge one triune God and one crucified Christ, so we may all unite in one faith and one church." [5] We perceive the great advances made by either side. Olivarez declared himself to have entreated the Pope most pressingly for the dispensation, assuring him that the King of England " would refuse nothing to the prince his son, that came within the power of his kingdom." [6] The English Catholics also urgently pressed the Pope, representing to him that a refusal of the dispensation would drawn down fresh persecutions on them.

The parties then proceeded to arrange the points in regard to which James of England was to give his promise.

Not only was the infanta with her suite to be allowed the exercise of their religious rites in a chapel of the royal residence, but the first education of all the children of this marriage was to be directed by her; no penal law was to have any application to them, nor was their right of succession to the throne to be rendered doubtful, even were they to remain Catholic.[7] The King promised in general " not to disturb the private exercise of the Catholic religion; not to require from the Catholics any oath inconsistent with their faith, and to take measures for securing that the laws against Catholics should be repealed by the Parliament.

In August, 1623, King James engaged solemnly, and by oath, to maintain these articles: there now seemed no doubt remaining, nor anything to prevent the completion of the marriage.

[5] Frequently printed. I follow the copy in Clarendon and the " Hardwicke Papers," said to be taken from the original.

[6] In his first joy he even said, according to the relation of Buckingham March 20th, " that if the Pope would not give a dispensation for a wife, they would give the infanta to thy son Baby as his wench."

[7] The most important article, and the source of much mischief; the words are as follow (" Merc Franç." ix. Appendix ii. 18): " That the laws made against Catholics in Great Britain shall not touch the children proceeding from this marriage, and they shall enjoy their free right of succession in the kingdoms and dominions of Great Britain."

This event was celebrated in Spain with festivities; the court received congratulations; formal intimation was given to the ambassadors, and the ladies of the infanta and her confessor were instructed to utter no word that could affect the marriage unfavorably.

King James reminded his son that in his joy at this happy alliance he must not forget his cousin, who had been robbed of his inheritance; nor his sister, whose life was passed in tears; and the affairs of the palatine were very zealously taken in hand. A proposal was made for including the imperial line, and that of the Palatinate, in the contemplated connection, by giving a daughter of the Emperor to a son of the proscribed Elector; and to avoid offending Bavaria, the erection of an eighth electorate was suggested. The Emperor immediately opened negotiations on this subject with Maximilian of Bavaria, who was not at that time averse to the proposal, but demanded that the palatine electorate transferred to him should remain in his possession, and that the eighth electorate to be erected should be given to the palatine. This did not greatly affect the interests of the Catholics. They were to enjoy religious freedom in the restored Palatinate, and in the electoral colleges they would still have held the majority of votes.[8]

Thus did that power, which in the preceding reign had formed the chief bulwark of Protestantism, now enter into the most friendly relations with those ancient enemies, toward whom it appeared to have vowed an implacable hatred, the Pope and Spain. The treatment of Catholics in England already began to evince a change, the domiciliary visits and other persecutions ceased; there were certain oaths which they were no longer required to take; Catholic chapels reappeared, to the vexation of the Protestants, and the zealous Puritans, who condemned the marriage, were punished. King James doubted not that, before the return of winter, he should embrace his son and the young bride as well as his favorite; all his letters express the most earnest longing for this happiness.

The advantages that would have resulted from the execution of the articles described above are manifest; but from the marriage itself, very different consequences might have been

8 Khevenhiller, x. 114.

expected, results of which it was impossible to foresee the extent. What could not be attained by force—the possession of a direct influence over the administration of the State in England—seemed now about to be acquired in a manner the most peaceful and natural.

Section VIII.—Missions

Having gained this point in our consideration of the remarkable progress made by Catholicism in Europe, we may now also profitably direct our attention to those more distant regions of the world, in which, by the force of kindred impulses, it also made the most important advances.

Motives of a religious character were mingled even in the first idea by which the Spaniards and Portuguese were incited to attempt their various discoveries and conquests. By these motives they were constantly accompanied and animated; they were, from the first, made clearly manifest throughout their newly founded empires, both in the East and the West.

In the beginning of the seventeenth century we find the proud fabric of the Catholic Church completely erected in South America. It possessed five archbishoprics, twenty-seven bishoprics, 400 monasteries, with parish churches and *Doctrinas* [1] innumerable. Magnificent cathedrals had been reared, the most gorgeous of all, perhaps, being that of Los Angeles. The Jesuits taught grammar and the liberal arts; they had also a theological seminary attached to their college of San Ildefonso, in Mexico. In the universities of Mexico and Lima all the branches of theology were studied. It was remarked that the Americans of European descent were distinguished by an extraordinary acuteness; but, as they complain themselves, they were too widely distant from the countenance of royal favor to receive rewards commensurate to their deserts. Christianity was meanwhile in course of gradual and regular diffusion throughout South America, the mendicant orders being more particularly active. The conquests had become changed into a seat of missions, and the missions were rapidly proclaiming civilization. The monastic orders taught the natives to sow and reap, plant trees and build houses, while teaching them

[1] Herrera, " Descripcion de las Indias," p. 80.

to read and sing, and were regarded by the people thus benefited, with all the more earnest veneration. When the priest visited his flock, he was received with music and the ringing of bells, flowers were scattered on his path, and the women held up their children toward him, entreating his blessing. The Indians evinced extraordinary pleasure in the externals of divine worship, they were never weary of attending mass, singing vespers, and joining in the choral service. They displayed considerable talent for music, and took an innocent delight in decorating their churches; for they seem to have been most readily impressed by whatever was most simple and innocently fanciful.[2] In their dreams they beheld the joys of paradise; to the sick the queen of heaven appeared in all her splendor, young attendants surrounded her and ministered refreshment to the fainting sufferer; or she presented herself alone, and taught her worshipper a song of her crucified Son, " whose head was bowed down, even as droops the yellow ears of corn."

It was under these forms that Catholicism obtained its conquests in this country. The monks have but one cause of complaint, namely, that the bad examples of the Spaniards and the violence of their proceedings corrupted the natives and impeded the progress of conversion.

A similar process was at the same time in action through East India, so far as the rule of the Portuguese extended. Catholicism obtained a central position of great value in Goa. Thousands were converted every year; even as early as 1565 300,000 of these newly made Christians were computed to be in and around Goa, in the mountains of Cochin, and at Cape Comorin.[3] But the state of things generally was yet entirely different. The arms, as well as doctrines of the Christians, were here opposed by a far-extending, peculiarly constituted, and wholly unsubdued world. Religions of immemorial antiquity, the forms of whose worship enchained both the senses and spirit, were in-

[2] " Compendio y descripcion de las Indias occidentales," MS.: " They show great charity toward the needy, and are especially devoted to the priests, whom they revere and respect as the ministers of Christ. The greater part of them so readily embrace the practices of our holy faith that they are prevented only by the bad example we give them, from having great saints among them, as was manifest to me when I was in those countries." The " Literæ Annuæ Provinciæ Paraquariæ, missæ a Nicolao Duran, Antv. 1636," are extremely remarkable, because the missionaries always contrived to keep the Spaniards from entering that province.
[3] Maffei, " Commentarius de rebus Indicis," p. 21.

timately associated with the manners and modes of thinking of the people.

But there were tendencies in Catholicism which were in their nature well calculated to vanquish even a world thus constituted.

The conviction of this fact was the exciting and unfailing impulse to all the labors of Francis Xavier, who reached East India in the year 1542. He traversed the country in its whole length and breadth, he prayed at the tomb of the Apostle Thomas at Meliapur, and preached to the people of Travancore from a tree. In the Moluccas he taught spiritual songs, which were then repeated by the boys in the market-places and sung by the fishermen in their barks. But he was not born to complete the work he had begun; his cry was ever, " Amplius, amplius," and a kind of passion for travelling shared largely in his zeal for making proselytes. He had already reached Japan, and was on the point of exploring the home and origin of the peculiar opinions he had encountered in those regions—the Empire of China, namely—when he died.[4]

It is perfectly consistent with the nature of men that the example of Francis Xavier and the difficulties of the enterprise should rather excite to imitation than alarm and deter from the attempt. The most active and varied exertions were thus made throughout the East in the earlier periods of the seventeenth century.

In the year 1606 we find Father Nobili in Madaura; he was surprised that Christianity had made so little progress in so long a time, and thinks this fact to be explained only by the circumstance that the Portuguese had addressed themselves to the pariahs, which had caused Christ to be considered merely as a god of the pariahs. He proceeded in a totally different manner. Persuaded that an effectual course of conversion must begin with the upper classes, he declared on his arrival that he was of the highest order of nobles (he was prepared with testimonies to that effect), and connected himself with the Brahmins. He adopted their dress and modes of life, undertook their penances, learned Sanscrit, and proceeded altogether in accordance with their ideas.[5] There was an opinion prevalent among them that

[4] Maffei, " Historiarum Indicarum," lib. xiii. et xiv.
[5] Juvencius, " Historiæ Societatis Jesu," pars v. tom. ii. lib. xviii. s. 9, n. 49: " He knew all the institutions and ceremonies of the Brahmins; he

four roads to truth had formerly existed in India, but that one
of them had been lost. Nobili affirmed that he had come to restore to them this lost but most direct and spiritual road to im-
mortality. In the year 1609 he had already converted seventy
Brahmins. He was scrupulously careful to avoid offending
their prejudices; he tolerated their distinctions of castes, but
giving them a different signification, and even separated the different castes from each other in the churches. The expressions
in which the Christian doctrines had previously been taught
were changed by Nobili for others more refined, more elegant,
and of a higher literary dignity. He proceeded in all things
with so much address that he soon saw himself surrounded by
a host of converts. Although his modes of action gave extreme
offence at first, yet they seemed to be the only means calculated
to promote the object in view, and in the year 1621 they were
sanctioned by the expressed approval of Gregory XV.

The labors undertaken at the same time in the Court of the
Emperor Akbar were no less remarkable.

It will be remembered that the ancient Mongolian Khans, the
conquerors of Asia, had long occupied a peculiarly undecided
position among the various religions by which the world was
divided. The Emperor Akbar would seem to have held nearly
similar dispositions. When he summoned the Jesuit fathers to
his presence, he told them that " he had done his best to acquire
a knowledge of all the religions of the world, and now wished
to learn something of the Christian religion also, by the help of
the fathers, whom he reverenced and valued." The first who
made his permanent residence at the Court of Akbar was Geronimo Xavier, nephew of Francis, who settled there in the year
1595; when the insurrections of the Mahometans contributed to
dispose the Emperor toward the Christians. In the year 1599
Christmas was celebrated at Lahore with the utmost solemnity.
The manger and leading facts of the Nativity were represented
for twenty days in succession, and numerous catechumens proceeded to the church, with palms in their hands, to receive the
rite of baptism. The Emperor read a life of Christ, composed

learnt their currently spoken language
called Tamul, which is widely extended; also the Baddagia, used by
princes and the court; and, finally, the
Grandoun or Sanscrit, which is the
language of the learned, and is so surrounded by difficulties that it was never
well known to any European until that
day; even among the Indians themselves, those who know this are
thought to know the most, even
though they know nothing but that."

in Persian, with great pleasure, and a picture of the Virgin, copied from the " Madonna del Popolo," in Rome, was taken by his orders to the palace, that he might show it to the ladies of his family. It is true that the Christians drew more favorable inferences from these things than the conclusion justified; still they really did make great progress. After the death of Akbar, three princes of the blood-royal were solemnly baptized; they rode to church on white elephants, and were received by Father Geronimo with the sound of trumpets, kettledrums, and martial music.[6] This event took place in 1610. Christianity seemed gradually to acquire a position of fixed character, although with certain vicissitudes and the prevalence of varying opinions; their affairs being affected by the greater or less degree of harmony existing in the political relations between the country and the Portuguese. In 1621 a college was founded in Agra and a station was established at Patna. In 1624 there were hopes that the Emperor Jehanguire would himself become a convert.

The Jesuits had made their way into China at the same period. They sought to win over the well-informed, scientific, and reading people of that empire, by the force of their acquirements and by acquainting them with the discoveries and sciences of the West. Ricci obtained his first entrance among them by the fact that he taught mathematics, and by his selecting the most valuable passages from the writings of Confucius, which he committed to memory, and recited before them. He gained access to Pekin, by the present of a clock striking the hours, which he made for the Emperor; but he owed the favor and esteem of that monarch to nothing so much as to a map which he constructed for him, and which greatly surpassed all attempts made by the Chinese in that department of knowledge. A fact is related that will serve as a characteristic of Ricci. When the Emperor ordered ten such maps to be painted on silk, and hung in his apartments, he seized the opportunity thus afforded to do something for the promotion of Christianity also, and filled the margins and vacant spaces of each map with Christian symbols and texts. His instructions, generally, were conveyed in a similar manner; he usually began with mathematics, but he managed to finish with religion. His scientific attainments pro-

[6] Juvencius, 1. i. n. 1-23.

cured respect for his religious doctrines. He not only succeeded in gaining to Christianity those who were immediately his pupils, but many mandarins, whose dress he had assumed, also went over to his creed. A Society of the Virgin was established in Pekin as early as the year 1605. Ricci died in 1610, exhausted, not by excess of labor only, but more still by the many visits, the long feastings, and all the other duties of Chinese society and etiquette. The advice given by Ricci was followed after his death; namely, " to carry on the work without noise or display, and in this tempestuous ocean to keep ever near the shore." Nor was the example he left as regarded the application of science neglected. In the year 1610 an eclipse of the moon occurred; the predictions of the native astronomers and of the Jesuits differed by a whole hour, and when the truth of the Jesuit calculations was proved by the event, they derived great credit from the circumstance.[7] The rectification of the astronomical tables was now confided to them, together with certain mandarins, their pupils; nor was this all: the interests of Christianity were also greatly promoted by these successes. In 1611 the first church in Nankin was consecrated, and in 1616 Christian churches are described as existing in five different provinces of the empire. In the different assaults to which they were not infrequently exposed, it was constantly found of the utmost advantage to them that their pupils had written works which enjoyed the approbation of the learned. They for the most part contrived to avert the threatening storms: their general habit was to conform as much as possible to the customs of the country; and in regard to various points and practices, they were empowered by the Pope himself, in 1619, to make certain concessions to the opinions prevailing around them. There then passed no year that they did not convert thousands, while those who opposed them gradually became extinct. In 1624 Adam Scharll appeared, and the exact description of two eclipses of the moon, which took place in that year, with a work of Lombardo relating to earthquakes, added increased weight to their dignity and consideration.[8]

[7] Jouvency has devoted the whole of his nineteenth book to the undertakings in China, and has added a dissertation (see p. 561)—" Imperii Sinici recens et uberior notitia "—which is still entirely worthy of attention.

[8] " Relatione della Cina, dell' anno 1621: " " The condition of this Church at present appears to me extremely similar to that of a ship which the clouds and winds threaten with a heavy storm; wherefore the mariners,

The course pursued by the Jesuits among the warlike Japanese was entirely different; the country was torn by perpetual factions, and the Jesuits attached themselves from the first to one or the other of the contending parties. In the year 1554 they were so fortunate as to have declared for that which obtained the victory; its favor was consequently secured to them, and by means of this they made extraordinary progress. In the year 1577 300,000 Christians were computed to have received baptism in Japan. Father Valignano, who died in 1606, a man whose advice in regard to East India was always welcome to Philip II, was himself the founder of 300 churches and thirty houses for Jesuits in Japan.

It was, however, by the connection of the Jesuits with Mexico and Spain that the jealousy of the Japanese authorities was awakened; the success that the Jesuits had previously had in the earlier civil wars was besides not repeated; the party to which they had attached themselves in later conflicts had sustained defeat, and after the year 1612 they were subjected to fearful persecutions.

But they maintained their ground with great steadiness. Their proselytes invoked the death of the martyr, and they had established a fraternity of martyrs, the members of which mutually encouraged each other to the endurance of every possible infliction: they distinguished those years as the *Æra Martyrum.* But despite the increasing violence of the persecutions, their historians affirm that even at that dangerous period new converts were continually added to their numbers.[9] They give the exact amount of 239,339 as that of the converts to Christianity among the Japanese from 1603 to 1622.

In all these countries we find the Jesuits evincing the same persevering industry, unbending pertinacity, and pliant conformity to the circumstances around them, by which they have been

shortening sail and lowering the yards, lie to, and wait till the sky becomes clear and the winds cease their commotion; but it very often happens that all the mischief consists in their fears, and that, the fury of the winds abating, the tempest disappears, satisfied with threatening only. Just so has it happened with the ship of this Church. Four years since, a fearful storm rose against it, menacing to submerge it at one blow; the pilots accommodating themselves to the weather, took in the sails of their works and retired somewhat, but so that they could be found by those who needed their aid, to wait till the day should break and the shadows pass away; but since then there has been no other evil than that of fear."

[9] The " Lettere Annue del Giappone dell' anno 1621 " present an example: " The glorious champions who have died this year were 121. The adults who, by means of the fathers of the company, have received holy baptism, are 2,236, without counting those who have been baptized by other fraternities and by Japanese priests."

characterized from their origin; they made progress beyond all that they could have hoped for, and succeeded in conquering, at least partially, the resistance of the national forms of religion that were paramount in the East.

And in addition to all this they had taken care to provide for the union of the oriental Christians with the Roman Church.

Even in India the Jesuits had found that primitive Nestorian community known as the Christians of St. Thomas. But these believers did not hold the Pope of Rome, of whom they knew nothing, for the head of the Church, but acknowledged the Patriarch of Babylon (at Mosul) as their supreme head and shepherd of the universal Church. Measures were therefore immediately taken for bringing them within the pale of the Roman communion; neither force nor persuasion was spared; in the year 1601 the most important persons among them seemed won, and a Jesuit was nominated as their bishop. The Roman ritual was printed in Chaldaic; the errors of Nestorius were anathematized in a diocesan council; a Jesuits' college was founded in Cranganor, and the installation of the new bishop was effected in 1624, with the assent of those who had previously been the most inflexible in their opposition.[10]

It is self-evident that the political superiority of the Spanish and Portuguese powers contributed largely to these results: this influence also made itself felt at the same time and in various forms in Abyssinia.

Many attempts had been made in the latter country at an earlier period, but all were ineffectual. It was in the year 1603, when the Portuguese of Fremona gave essential aid to the Abyssinians in a battle with the Caffres, that themselves and their religion first attained to more respectful consideration. Just then Father Paez arrived, an able Jesuit of great address, who preached in the language of the country and procured access to the court. The victorious monarch desired to form more intimate relations with the King of Spain, principally for the purpose of securing an ally against his enemies in the interior. Paez represented to him that the only means by which this could be accomplished were his abandonment of the schismatic creed he held, and conversion to the Church of Rome. His arguments produced all the more impression from the fact that

---

[10] Cordara, " Historia Soc. Jesu," vi. ix. p. 535.

amid the internal convulsions of the Abyssinians, the Portuguese had in fact evinced the utmost fidelity and bravery. Disputations were appointed, and in these the Jesuits easily defeated the untaught monks. Sela-Christos, the bravest man in the empire, and a brother of the Emperor Seltan-Segued (Socinius), became a convert, and his example was followed by a multitude of his fellow-countrymen. A connection was then readily formed with Pope Paul V and Philip III. Opposition was naturally aroused among the representatives of the established religion, and in Abyssinia, as in Europe, the civil war assumed the character of a religious conflict. The Abuna and his monks were always on the side of the rebels; Sela-Christos, the Portuguese, and the converts on that of the Emperor. Year after year battles were fought with varied consequences; but the Emperor and his party were at length victorious: their triumph was also that of Catholicism and the Jesuits. In the year 1621 Seltan-Segued decided the ancient controversies respecting the two natures in Christ, in accordance with the views of the Roman Church. He prohibited the offering of prayers for the Patriarch of Alexandria; Catholic churches and chapels were erected in all his towns, and even in his gardens.[1] In 1622, after having confessed to Paez, he received the sacrament according to the Catholic ritual. The Papal Court had been long requested to send a Latin patriarch into the country, but had avoided doing this so long as the opinions or power of the Emperor remained doubtful. That sovereign had now vanquished all his enemies, and the submission he displayed could not well be more perfect. On December 19th, therefore, in the year 1622, Gregory XV appointed Doctor Alfonso Mendez, a Portuguese Jesuit whom King Philip had proposed, to be Patriarch of Ethiopia,[2] and when this dignitary at length arrived, the Emperor solemnly tendered his obedience to the Pope of Rome.

Attention had meanwhile been constantly directed to the Greek Christians resident in the Turkish Empire; the popes despatched mission after mission in that behalf. The Roman *professio fidei* had been introduced among the Maronites by certain Jesuits; and in 1614 we find a Nestorian archimandrite in Rome, where he abjured the tenets of Nestorius in the name

[1] Juvencius, p. 705; Cordara, vi. 6, p. 320. Ludolf calls the Emperor Susneus.

[2] Sagripanti, "Discorso della Religione dell' Etiopia," MS., from the Atti Consistoriali.

of large numbers who had previously held those doctrines. A
Jesuit mission was established in Constantinople, and by the
influence of the French ambassador it acquired a certain degree
of credit and stability.   In the year 1621 these fathers succeeded
in procuring the removal, at least for a time, of the Patriarch
Cyrillus Lucaris, who was disposed to the opinions of the Protestants.

How comprehensive! how unbounded was this activity, laboring at one and the same moment among the Andes and through
the Alps; its pioneers were despatched at once to Scandinavia
and to Thibet.   In China and in England we find it warily making its approaches to the favor of the ruling powers.   Yet, on
this illimitable theatre, undivided, ever vigorous and indefatigable; the strong impulse that worked in the centre, inspiriting,
perhaps with a more intense and vivid force of action, every separate laborer, even to the utmost extremity of its borders.

CHAPTER THIRD

Section I.—Conflict of Political Relations—Further Triumphs of Catholicism

IT is rarely by a resistance from without that a power in rapid progress is arrested in its career; reverses are for the most part occasioned by internal dissensions, which, if not the sole cause of decline, yet largely promote and accelerate it.

Had Catholicism remained of one accord, had its adherents proceeded with united forces to their aim, it is difficult to imagine how Northern Germanic Europe, involved as it was to a considerable extent in the interests, and hemmed in on all points by the policy of Catholicism, could eventually have resisted its domination.

But was it not inevitable that having reached this degree of power, the old elements of discord residing within Catholicism itself, and which, though stilled at the surface, had been constantly active at the centre, should now burst forth anew?

The distinctive peculiarity of religious progress at this period was that it depended in all countries on the preponderance of political and military power. The successes of war preceded the progress of missions. It thus followed that the latter were associated with the most important political changes, which last were in themselves of high significance, and could not fail to cause reactions, of which the particular character could not be foreseen.

Of all those changes, the most important certainly was that the German line of the house of Austria, which had hitherto been too much engrossed by the disquietudes received from its hereditary dominions to assume any great share in the politics of Europe generally, now at once attained the independence, importance, and strength of a great European power. The elevation of German Austria produced the effect of awakening

345

Spain, which had reposed in peace since the times of Philip II,
but which now rose with a renewal of its old warlike spirit to
the assertion of its former hopes and claims.   The Spanish and
German sovereigns were already brought into immediate connection, by the transactions in the Grisons.   The Alpine passes
were held by Austria on the German side, and by Spain on that
of Italy.   On those lofty mountains they seemed to offer each
other mutual aid for enterprises embracing all parts of the
world.

It is certain that in this condition of things there was involved
on the one hand a magnificent prospect for Catholicism, to which
both lines had devoted themselves with inviolable attachment;
but on the other, it presented imminent danger of internal dissension.   How much jealousy had been aroused by the Spanish
monarchy under Philip II!   But with much greater force and
combined solidity did the power of that house now uprear itself;
augmented as it was by the extended growth of its German resources.   It followed that all the old antipathies against it
would be called into more than ever vigorous action.

This was first made manifest in Italy.

The small Italian States, incapable of standing by their own
force, were above all others at that time in need of the protection
gained by all from the balance of power, and were proportion-
ately sensitive to whatever endangered its preservation.   To be
thus enclosed between the Spaniards and Germans, while cut off
from all foreign aid by the occupation of the Alpine passes, they
considered a position of great peril.   With but slight regard to
the advantages presented to their common faith by this combination, they had recourse to France, from whom alone they could
hope for aid, for the purpose of destroying it.   Louis XIII had
also become alarmed, lest his influence in Italy should be lost.
Immediately after the Peace of 1622, and even before he had
returned to his capital, he concluded a treaty with Savoy and
Venice, in virtue of which the house of Austria was to be compelled, by the junction of their common forces, to evacuate the
passes and fortresses of the Grisons.[1]

This was an intention apparently affecting one single point
only, but which might readily endanger the whole existing relations of the European powers.

[1] Nani, " Storia Veneta," p. 255.

The probability of such a result was clearly manifest to Gregory XV. The peril by which the peace of the Catholic world, the progress of religious interests, and consequently the renewal of the papal dignity, were threatened from this point were distinctly obvious; and with a zeal equal to that he had displayed for missions and conversions, the pontiff now labored to prevent that outbreak of hostilities, the consequences of which were to his perception so evidently menacing.

The reverence felt for the Papal See, or rather respect for the unity of the Catholic world, had still so much of vital force that both France and Spain declared their readiness to leave the decision of this affair to the Pope. Nay, he was himself requested to take possession of those fortresses which occasioned so much jealous uneasiness, to hold them as a deposit, and to garrison them with his own troops, until the question concerning them had been fully adjusted.[2]

For some short time Pope Gregory hesitated whether he should agree to take this active and without doubt costly share in foreign transactions; but since it was manifest that the peace of the Catholic world depended chiefly on his decision, he finally suffered a few companies to be formed, and sent them into the Grisons, under the command of his brother, the Duke of Fiano. The Spaniards had wished to retain at least Riva and Chiavenna, but they now surrendered even these places to the papal troops.[3] The Archduke Leopold, of the Tyrol, also finally consented to yield into their hands whatever territories and fortresses he could not claim as portions of his hereditary possessions.

By these arrangements the danger which had been the immediate cause of the Italian anxieties appeared to be effectually removed. The chief consideration now was to provide for the safety of Catholic interests in the further arrangements. In this view it was proposed that as the Valtelline was not to fall again into the hands of the Spaniards, neither should it return to the rule of the Grisons; because the restoration of the Catholic religion would be almost inevitably interrupted by the latter arrangement; it was therefore annexed to the three ancient Rhætian confederacies, as a fourth independent State, possessing equal rights. From the same motives, even the connection

[2] "Dispaccio Sillery, 28 Nov, 1622." Corsini, xiii., 21 Genn. 1623, in Siri, "Memorie recondite," tom. v. pp. 435, 442. "Scrittura del deposito della Valtellina," ib. 459.
[3] Siri, "Memorie recondite," v. 519.

of the two Austrian lines was not to be entirely destroyed, that connection appearing to be still required for the progress of Catholicism in Germany. The passes of the Valtelline and the transit through Worms were always to remain open to the Spaniards; but with the understanding that this was for the passage of troops into Germany, not to facilitate their entrance into Italy.[4]

Affairs were at this point—the treaties had not been actually concluded, but all was prepared for conclusion—when Gregory XV died (July 8, 1623). He had lived to enjoy the satisfaction of seeing dissensions that had alarmed him allayed, and of securing that the progress of his Church should remain uninterrupted. There had even been proposals in the course of those negotiations for a new alliance between the Spaniards and French for the purpose of attacking La Rochelle and Holland.

But after the death of Gregory these intentions were far from being realized.

In the first place, the new Pope, Urban VIII, did not yet enjoy that confidence which proceeds from a well-grounded presumption of perfect impartiality; and secondly, the Italians were by no means satisfied with the arrangements above described. But the most important consideration of all was, that the helm of state in France was now directed by men who applied themselves to the opposition of Spain; not at the request of others, or as mere auxiliaries, but from their own unfettered impulse and as the leading principle of French policy. We allude to Vieuville and Richelieu.

But in this resolution there may possibly have been less of free-will and choice than may be supposed. France, as well as the Austrian-Spanish powers, was occupied in extending all her internal forces. By the victory obtained over the Huguenots the royal power had been largely increased, together with the unity and self-confidence of the nation; and as the claims of France kept pace with her strength to enforce them, so all things now combined to produce the adoption of a bolder line of policy than had been hitherto attempted. This natural tendency inevitably called forth the organs suited to its promotion; men

[4] Art. 9 of the " Plan of the Convention."

disposed to carry it out to its consequences and capable of doing so. Richelieu was from the first resolved to make head
against the ascendancy which the house of Austria constantly
asserted, and which she had but recently acquired new powers
to maintain, and even to increase. He determined to engage
in direct conflict with this power for supremacy in Europe.

This was a resolution by which the Catholic world was menaced with a division more perilous than that which had lately
been averted. The two great powers must of necessity be involved in open war. The execution of the Roman treaty above
mentioned was no longer to be hoped for; all attempts of Pope
Urban to hold the French to their promised concessions were
altogether vain: nor were the French content merely to ally
themselves with the Catholic opposition. Although Richelieu
was a cardinal of the Roman Church, he did not scruple to form
an undisguised league with the Protestants.

He first made advances to the English, in the hope of pre-
venting that Spanish marriage from which the house of Austria could not fail to derive so great an extension of its influence.
In this purpose he was seconded by feelings and circumstances
strictly personal; the impatience of James I, who longed for the
return of his son and his favorite with all the tenderness of an
old man who believes himself near death, and a misunderstanding between the two prime ministers—Olivarez and Buckingham. But here also the result was principally determined by
the nature of the thing itself. The affairs of the Palatinate presented invincible difficulties when they came to be negotiated
between Austria, Spain, Bavaria, and the Palatinate.[5] An alliance with France, on the contrary, seeing the new direction
that power was taking, gave promise of a ready solution of the
difficulty by force of arms; and as this alliance not only secured
to the King of England a very considerable dowry, but also
afforded a prospect of reconciling the English Catholics with the
throne; he resolved to take a French princess as a wife for his
son, and conferred on her the same privileges, in regard to her
religion, as he had promised to the Spaniards.

Preparations were accordingly made for the attack. Richelieu had formed a plan more vast and comprehensive than had

[5] From a letter of the Count Palatine,
dated October 30th, it is manifest that
he could not have been induced to accept the terms proposed by anything
short of force.

ever before been known to European policy, but which was eminently characteristic of himself: by a simultaneous attack from all sides, he proposed to crush the power of the Spanish-Austrian house at one blow.

He was himself to fall upon Italy in concert with Savoy and Venice: without the slightest deference to the papal authority, he despatched French troops unexpectedly into the Grisons, and drove the papal garrisons from the fortresses.[6] Together with the English alliance, he had renewed that formerly contracted with Holland, intending that the Dutch should attack South America while the English ravaged the coasts of Spain. By the intervention of King James, the Turks were called into action, and threatened to invade Hungary; but the most important blow was to be struck in Germany. The King of Denmark, who had long been prepared, was at length resolved to lead the forces of Denmark and North Germany to battle, for the rights of his kinsman, the Elector-Palatine. He not only received promise of aid from England, but Richelieu also engaged to contribute a million of livres toward the expenses of the war.[7] Supported by both, Mansfeld was to form a junction with the King, and march on the hereditary dominions of Austria.

Of the two most powerful Catholic sovereignties we thus see the one arming itself in this general assault with the hope of destroying the other.

There cannot be a doubt that this state of things had an immediate tendency to impede the progress of Catholicism. It is true that the French confederacy was of a political nature, but so intimate was the connection between ecclesiastical and political relations that the Protestants could not fail to perceive in this condition of affairs the opportunity for promoting their own cause. Protestantism accordingly recovered breath.

[6] " Relatione di quattro Ambasciatori, 1625:" " The Pope complained that Bethune had never spoken clearly, and that he had never imagined the arms of the League were to act against his fortresses." The policy commonly pursued in France.
[7] Extract from the Instruction of Blainville, in Siri, vi. 62. Mansfeld was to co-operate with him " in the heart of Germany." " Relatione di Caraffa: " " The French have always had the habit, even to this day, of holding correspondence with the enemies of his imperial Majesty, supplying them with aid both in money and troops; in secret certainly, yet not so secretly but that by intercepted letters and other chances their contrivances and correspondence have been discovered; thus even before the King of Denmark was defeated by Tilly, his Majesty always kept a good force in the Lower Palatinate and about Alsace, suspecting that some mischief might come from those parts." See Appendix, No. 112.

A new champion, the King of Denmark, had risen for its defence in Germany, with energies fresh and unimpaired, and supported by the mighty combination of European policy—a victory on his part would have rendered all the successes of the imperial house ineffectual, and must have arrested the progress of the Catholic restoration.

But it is by the attempt that the difficulties inherent in an enterprise are made manifest. However brilliant may have been the talents of Richelieu, he had yet proceeded too rashly in this undertaking; all his desires and inclinations were attracted toward this project; he had placed it before him, whether in full and conscious perception of all its import, or in obscure presentiment, as the great aim of his life; but there arose from it dangers by which he was himself first threatened.

Not only did the German Protestants, the enemies of the house of Austria, take new courage, but those of France also; the antagonists of Richelieu himself gathered fresh hopes from these new combinations in politics. They expected, as they said themselves, that in the worst possible case they should be able to make their peace with the King by means of his present allies.[8] Rohan put his forces in motion on land; Soubise by sea. In May, 1625, the Huguenots were in arms throughout the country.

And at the same moment the cardinal was assailed by enemies, perhaps more formidable still, from the other side. Urban VIII, notwithstanding his inclination to France, had too deep a sense of his own dignity to endure quietly the expulsion of his garrisons from the Grisons.[9] He raised troops, which he despatched into the Milanese, with the express purpose of making an effort, in alliance with the Spaniards, for recovering the lost fortresses. These warlike menaces may very possibly have meant but little; the ecclesiastical effects associated with them were however most important. The complaints of the papal nuncio, that the most Christian King had

[8] " Mémoires de Rohan," part i. p. 146: " Hoping that if he brought things to bear, the allies of the King would more easily induce him to an accommodation."
[9] " Relatione di P. Contarini: " " His holiness [he is speaking of the time immediately following the arrival of the news] was excessively displeased, esteeming this affair to show but little respect to his banners, and he complained of it bitterly and continually."

become the auxiliary of heretical princes, found a ready response in France. The Jesuits came forward with their Ultramontane doctrines, and the strictly Catholic party made Richelieu the object of violent attacks.[10] It is true that he found support against them in the Gallican axioms, and was defended by the Parliaments, yet he dared not long venture to have the Pope for an enemy. The Catholic principle was too closely bound up with the restored monarchy. Who could secure the cardinal from the effects of the impression that might be produced on his sovereign by the admonitions of the clergy?

Thus, even in France itself, Richelieu found himself assailed, and that by the two opposite parties, at the same time. Whatever he might be able to effect against Spain by maintaining his position, it was yet one that he saw to be wholly untenable; he was compelled to hasten out of it with all speed.

And as in the attack he had displayed his genius for widely reaching combinations, and bold, thorough-going designs, so he now exhibited that treacherous address by which he made his allies mere tools, and then abandoned them; a practice which he pursued through his whole life.

He first prevailed on his new confederates to support him against Soubise. He had himself no naval force. With Protestant armaments, drawn from foreign countries; with Dutch and English ships, he overcame his Protestant opponents at home. In September, 1625, he availed himself of their mediation to impose on the Huguenots the acceptance of disadvantageous terms, his allies having no doubt that when once freed from these enemies he would renew the general attack.

But what was their astonishment when, instead of this, intelligence reached them that France had concluded peace with Spain—when, in March, 1626, the peace of Monzon was made known: a papal legate had proceeded for that purpose to both courts. It is true that he does not appear to have had any material influence on the terms of the agreement; but he certainly gave new vitality and force to the Catholic principle. While Richelieu was employing the Protestants for his own purposes, under a show of the strictest confidence, he had entered still more zealously into negotiations with Spain for their destruction. With regard to the Valtelline, he agreed with

[10] " Mémoires du Cardinal Richelieu," Petitot, xxiii. p. 20.

Olivarez that it should return to the rule of the Grisons; but with an independent power of appointing its own public officers, and with undiminished freedom for Romanist worship.[1] Thus the Catholic powers, which had seemed on the point of commencing a conflict for life or death, now stood in a moment reunited.

This result was facilitated by the misunderstanding that arose between France and England, in regard to the execution of the engagement contracted by the treaty of marriage.

It followed of necessity that a pause ensued in all preparations for the enterprise against Spain.

The Italian princes were compelled, however reluctantly, to endure the arrangements which they found to be unalterable. Savoy concluded a truce with Genoa; Venice considered herself fortunate that she had not fallen upon the Milanese, and now quietly disbanded her forces. It was maintained that the vacillating conduct of the French had prevented the relief of Breda, in 1625, so that the loss of that important fortress, which fell into the hands of Spain, was attributed to them. But the great and decisive reverse was that suffered in Germany.

The powers of Lower Germany had gathered around the King of Denmark, under shelter, as was believed, of the general alliance formed against Spain. Mansfeld advanced toward the Elbe. The Emperor, on his part, had armed with earnest diligence to meet him, knowing well how much depended on the issue.

But when the forces came into actual conflict, the general alliance had ceased to exist. The French subsidies were not paid; the English succors came in far too slowly. The imperial troops were more practised in war than their opponents, and the result was that the King of Denmark lost the battle of Lutter, while Mansfeld was driven as a fugitive into the Austrian provinces, through which he had hoped to march as a victor and restorer.

This was a result of which the effects were of necessity commensurate with the universality of their causes.

[1] Dumont, vol. ii. p. 487, s. 2: "That they may not have any other religion henceforward than the Catholic. . . . S. 3: That they may elect, by choice amongst themselves, their own judges, governors, and other magistrates, all Catholics." Then follow certain limitations.

First, as regarded the imperial dominions, we may describe them in a word. The last attempt for the cause of Protestantism ventured on there, in the hope of aid from the general combination above named, was suppressed, and even the nobles, who had previously remained exempt from personal molestation, were now obliged to conform to the Catholic ritual. On the festival of St. Ignatius, 1627, the Emperor declared that, after the lapse of six months, he would no longer tolerate any person in his hereditary kingdom of Bohemia, even though of noble or knightly rank, who did not believe with himself and the apostolical Church, in the only true and saving Catholic faith.[2] Edicts to the same effect were proclaimed in Upper Austria; in the year 1628 they were sent into Carinthia, Carniola, and Styria, and after a certain period into Lower Austria likewise. Even a respite was vainly entreated; the nuncio Caraffa representing that these prayers for delay were put forward only in the hope of a general change of fortune. It was from that time that these districts once more became thoroughly Catholic. How mighty had been the resistance opposed to the imperial house, by the Austrian nobles, eighty years before! And now the sovereign power—orthodox, victorious, and unlimited—rose high above all opposition.

And the effects of the late victory were still more extensive in other parts of Germany. Lower Saxony was invaded and taken into possession. The imperial forces were in action, even up to the Cattegat; they held Brandenburg and Pomerania; Mecklenburg also was in the hands of the imperial generals—all principal seats of Protestantism, and all now subjugated by Catholic armies.

The manner in which Catholicism proposed to profit by this state of things was very soon made obvious. An imperial prince was nominated Bishop of Halberstadt, and the Pope, by virtue of his apostolic power, appointed the same prince to be Archbishop of Magdeburg. There could be no question but that, when the government of a Catholic archduke was established, the rigor with which other ecclesiastical princes had

---

[2] Caraffa, " Relatione," MS.: " The signor cardinal and I, having submitted to his Majesty's consideration, that as the heretic barons and nobles were not reformed, there could be but little good expected from the conversion of their subjects, and that by consequence they would be likely by degrees to infect others, it pleased his Majesty to grant the cardinal and other commissioners power to reform the nobles also."

carried forward the work of restoring Catholicism would be zealously imitated throughout the diocese.

The Anti-Reformation, meanwhile, proceeded with renewed ardor in Upper Germany. The list of edicts proclaimed by the imperial chancery during these years, and to be found in Caraffa, well deserves examination. What a host of admonitions, resolutions, decisions, and recommendations—all to the profit of Catholicism.[3] The youthful Count of Nassau-Siegen, the younger Count-Palatine of Neuburg, and the grand master of the Teutonic order undertook new reformations. In the Upper Palatinate, even the nobility were compelled to adopt the Catholic faith.

The ancient legal processes instituted by ecclesiastical dignitaries against temporal estates, in relation to confiscated church property, now took a different course from that of earlier times. How grievous were the disquietudes inflicted on Würtemberg alone! All the old complainants, the Bishops of Constance and Augsburg, the Abbots of Mönchsreit and Kaisersheim, pressed forward their claims against the ducal house. Its very existence was endangered.[4] The bishops gained their cause against the towns in every instance; the Bishop of Eichstädt against Nuremberg, the chapter of Strasburg against the city of Strasburg; Hall in Suabia (Schwäbisch Hall), Memmingen, Ulm, Lindau, and many other towns, were compelled to restore to the Catholics the churches that had been taken from them.

If the letter of the Treaty of Augsburg was at this time appealed to from all quarters, of how much greater importance was the more general application of its principles, as they were now understood?[5]

"After the battle of Lutter," says Caraffa, "the Emperor seemed to wake as from a long sleep; liberated from a great fear that had hitherto enchained his predecessors and himself, he conceived the idea of bringing back all Germany to the rule prescribed by the Treaty of Augsburg.

In addition to Magdeburg and Halberstadt, Bremen, Verden, Minden, Camin, Havelberg, Schwerin, and almost all the North

---

[3] "Brevis enumeratio aliquorum negotiorum quæ . . . in puncto reformationis in cancellaria imperii tractata sunt ab anno 1620 ad annum 1629," in the Appendix to the "Germania Sacra restaurata," p. 34.

[4] Sattler, "Geschichte von Würtemberg unter den Herzogen," th. vi. p. 226.

[5] Senkenberg, "Fortsetzung der Häberlinschen Reichsgeschichte," bd. xxv. p. 633.

German benefices were restored to Catholicism. This had always been the remote object on which the Pope and the Jesuits, in the most brilliant moments of their prosperity, had fixed their eyes. But that was precisely the cause which made the Emperor anxious respecting such a step. He had no doubt, says Caraffa, of the justice and right of the measure, but only of the possibility of its execution. Yet the zeal of the Jesuits—above all, that of his confessor Lamormain—the favorable dispositions of the four Catholic electors, the unwearied entreaties of the papal nuncio, who informs us himself that it cost him the labor of a month to prevail, at length removed all scruples. As early as August, 1628, the edict for the restitution of church property was drawn up, the terms being those in which it afterward appeared.[6] Previous to being published, it was once more submitted to the Catholic princes for their consideration.

Nor was this all; a plan much more extensive was connected with this design: hopes were entertained of conciliating the Lutheran princes; but this was not to be attempted by theologians. The Emperor himself, or some Catholic prince of the empire, was to undertake it. They were to proceed from the principle that the ideas of Catholicism formed by the people of North Germany were erroneous, and that the difference between the unaltered Confession of Augsburg and the genuine Catholic doctrine was very slight. They hoped to gain over the Elector of Saxony by giving up to him the patronage of the three archbishoprics situated in his dominions.[7] Nor did they despair of exciting the hatred of the Lutherans against the Calvinists, and then making that hatred instrumental to the perfect restoration of Catholicism.

This idea was eagerly seized on at Rome, and worked out into a feasible project. Nor did Urban VIII by any means propose to content himself with the conditions of the Treaty of Augs-

[6] That the edict was prepared at this period is gathered from Caraffa, " Commentar. de Germ. Sacra restaurata," p. 350. He remarks that the edict was drawn up in 1628 and published in 1629; he then proceeds — " God himself assented; for but a few days after that resolution, he rewarded the Emperor by a signal victory." He alludes to the victory of Wolgast, which was gained on August 22d.

[7] Hopes of the conversion of this prince were felt in Rome as early as the year 1624. " Instruttione a Monsr. Caraffa: " " There came again some intelligence of the expected reunion of the Duke of Saxony to the Catholic Church, but the hope very soon vanished. Yet his not being inimical to Catholics, while he is the deadly enemy of the Calvinists, his being most intimate with the Elector of Mayence, and his having agreed to the Electorate of Bavaria, make us still have good hope; and, in regard to this it will not be inexpedient that his holiness should take measures with the said Mayence for this desirable acquisition." See Appendix, No. 110.

burg, which had indeed never received the sanction of a pope.[8]
He was determined to rest satisfied with nothing less than a
complete restitution of all church property, and the return of
all Protestants to Catholicism.

But in that moment of prosperity the pontiff had raised his
thoughts to a design still more vast and daring if possible than
that just described. This was no other than an attack on England; an idea that had reappeared from time to time, as if by
a sort of necessity, among the grand combinations of Catholicism. Urban VIII now hoped to make the good understanding re-established between the two crowns subservient to the
promotion of this favorite design.[9]

He first represented to the French ambassador the great
offence that was offered to France by the total disregard of
England to the promises made at the marriage. Either Louis
XIII ought to compel the English to fulfil their engagements,
or he should wrest the crown from a prince, who, as a heretic
before God, and regardless of his word before men, was altogether unworthy to wear it.[10]

He next addressed himself to the Spanish ambassador,
Oñate; and in this case the Pope declares it to be his opinion
that as a good knight Philip IV was bound to take up the cause
of the Queen of England, so near a connection of his own (she
was his sister-in-law), who was now oppressed on account of
her religion.

When the Pope saw that he might venture to hope for success, he transferred the negotiations to Spado, his nuncio in
Paris.

Among the influential men of France, Cardinal Berulle, who

[8] "To which," says the Pope, in a
letter to the Emperor, of the Treaty of
Passau, "the Apostolic See has never
given its assent."
[9] In Siri, "Memorie," vi. 257, some
account is given of this affair, but it is
very imperfect. The report of it in the
"Mémories de Richelieu," xxiii. 283, is
also very partial. The relation of Nicoletti, which we use here, is much more
circumstantial and authentic.
[10] In Nicoletti, the Pope says: "The
King of France has been offended
by him, first, in his State, by the help
given by England to the Huguenot
rebels; in his life, by the instigations

and felony of Sciales, who had induced
the Duke of Orleans to plot against his
Majesty, for which crime he afterward
suffered death; in his reputation, by
the many breaches of promise he had
committed; finally, in his own blood,
because of the injuries inflicted on the
Queen of England, his sister; but what
is more than all this, he is offended in
his soul, the Englishman planning evil
to the salvation of that of the Queen,
together with that of the most Christian King himself, and that of all who
had been too forward in effecting that
unhappy marriage."

had conducted the negotiations for the marriage, was the person who entered most earnestly into this project. He calculated how the trading vessels of England might be captured on the French coast, and how the English fleets might be burnt in their own harbors. On the Spanish part, Olivarez adopted the plan without much hesitation. He might indeed have been rendered cautious by former instances of perfidy, and another high officer of State, Cardinal Bedmar, opposed the measure on that ground; but the idea was too vast and comprehensive to be rejected by Olivarez, who in all things loved the great and magnificent.

The negotiation was conducted with the utmost secrecy; even the French ambassador in Rome, to whom the first overtures had been made, was not acquainted with the progress of the affair.

Richelieu drew up the articles of the treaty; they were amended by Olivarez, and to the form thus given them, Richelieu assented. On April 20, 1627, they were ratified. The French engaged to make instant preparation of their forces and to put their harbors in a state of defence. The Spaniards were ready to commence the attack before the close of that year, and it was arranged that the French should join them with all their forces in the following spring.[1]

The accounts remaining to us do not make it very clearly appear how the booty was to be divided between France and Spain; but we collect from them sufficient to show that regard was paid on this occasion also to the interests of the Pope. Cardinal Berulle revealed to the nuncio, in the most profound confidence, that in the event of success, Ireland was to become the portion of the Papal See, and might be governed by the pontiff through the medium of a viceroy. This communication was received by the nuncio with extreme satisfaction, but he recommended his holiness to allow no word to transpire on the

[1] " Lettere del Nunzio, 9 Aprile, 1627: " " The courier aforesaid returned to Paris from Spain, with advices that the Catholic King agreed to make the first movement, as he had been desired to do by France; provided the French would abide by both the two proposals that had been previously made as alternatives; namely, that the most Christian King should pledge himself to move in the May or June following, and should, at this time, supply the Catholic armament with some galleys and other vessels. The same courier also brought intelligence, that the count-duke had broken off the negotiations proceeding in Spain with the King of England, who had offered the Catholic King a suspension of arms for three years, or any longer period, as well in the name of the King of Denmark as in that of Holland: a similar treaty was also broken off by order of the Catholic King in Flanders."

subject, lest it might appear that his suggestions had been actuated by worldly views.

Neither had the interests of Germany and Italy been forgotten in these calculations.

There still appeared a possibility of destroying the superiority of the naval power of England and Holland, by a general combination. The formation of an armed combination was suggested, and under the protection of this force a direct communication was to be established between the Baltic, Flanders, the French coasts, Spain, and Italy, without the participation of the two maritime powers. The Emperor made proposals with this view to the Hanse Towns. The infanta at Brussels desired that a port in the Baltic should be ceded to the Spaniards.[2] Negotiations were entered into with the Grand Duke of Tuscany, who by this means might have drawn the Spanish and Portuguese trade to Leghorn.[3]

It is true, that matters were not carried so far. Controlled by the complexity of the interests involved, the event took a very different course; but yet such as eventually to produce results entirely favorable to the cause of Catholicism.

While plans of such imposing magnitude were in process of arrangement for an attack on England, it came to pass that the projectors were themselves assailed by a force from England.

In July, 1627, Buckingham appeared with a noble fleet off the coasts of France; he landed on the island of Rhé and took possession of it, with the exception of the citadel of St. Martin, to which he instantly laid siege. He called on the Huguenots to arouse themselves once more in defence of their liberties and religious independence, which certainly were exposed to more imminent dangers from day to day.

English historians have usually attributed this expedition to an extraordinary passion of Buckingham for the Queen of France, Anne of Austria. Be the truth as it may with regard to that inclination, there is certainly a very different cause for this enterprise (but without doubt the real one) to be found

2 Pope Urban says this in an instruction to Ginetti, in Siri, " Mercurio," ii. 984.
3 " Scrittura sopra la compagnia militante," MS. in the Archivio Mediceo, contains a discussion as to the practicability of this plan: " It is believed that the people of the Hanse Towns would enter the military companies to please the Emperor, and that the Tuscans could not well refuse to do so, when called on by such great monarchs."

in the great course of events. Was Buckingham to wait in England for the proposed attack? It was doubtless better policy to anticipate the onslaught and to carry the war into France.[4] A more favorable moment for the purpose could scarcely be desired; Louis XIII was dangerously ill, and Richelieu engaged in a contest with powerful factions. After some hesitation, the Huguenots did in fact again take arms; their brave and practised leaders appeared in the field once more.

To have produced effectual results, however, Buckingham should have conducted the war with more energy and been better supported. Charles I acknowledges, in all his letters, that this was not sufficiently done. As the affair was arranged, the assailants were soon proved to be no longer equal to Cardinal Richelieu, whose genius developed its resources with redoubled power in occasions of difficulty, and who had never given more decided proofs of steadfast resolution and unwearied persistence. Buckingham saved himself by a retreat. His expedition, which might have placed the French Government in extreme peril, had in reality no other result than that of causing the whole strength of France, directed by the cardinal, to be poured with renewed violence on the Huguenots.

The central point of the Huguenot power was without doubt in La Rochelle. At an earlier period, and when residing in the neighborhood of the city, at his bishopric of Luçon, Richelieu had frequently reflected on the possibility of reducing that fortress; he now found himself called upon to direct such an enterprise, and he resolved to accomplish it, be the cost what it might.

It was a peculiar circumstance that nothing afforded him so effectual an assistance as the fanaticism of an English Puritan.

Buckingham had, at length, resumed his arms for the relief of La Rochelle. His honor was pledged to effect this; his position in England and the world depended on it; and he would, unquestionably, have strained all his powers for its ac-

---

[4] It may be asked whether Buckingham had not heard something of that mysterious treaty. It is extremely probable that he had done so, for how rarely is a secret so completely kept that no portion of it transpires. It is certain that the Venetian ambassador, Zorzo Zorzi, who arrived in France while these designs were in preparation, heard of them instantly: "It was added that the two crowns were forming treaties, and plotting to assault England, with equal forces and arrangements, in concert." It is highly improbable that nothing of this should be mentioned in England, with which country the Venetians were in close connection; they had even been suspected of advising the expedition against the island of Rhé.—"Relatione di Francia, 1628."

complishment. This was the moment chosen by a fanatic, impelled by desire for vengeance and by a mistaken zeal for religion, and Buckingham was assassinated.

In a crisis of great moment, it is necessary that powerful men should make the enterprise their own personal concern. The siege of La Rochelle was as a duel between the two ministers. Richelieu alone now survived. No one was found in England to take Buckingham's place, or heartily to adopt the defence of his honor. The English fleet appeared in the roads, but without doing anything effectual. It was said that Richelieu knew there would be nothing attempted by it. He persisted with inflexible firmness in the siege, and in October, 1628, La Rochelle surrendered.

When the principal fortress had thus fallen, the neighboring places despaired of holding out: their only care now was to obtain tolerable terms.[5]

And thus, from all these political complexities, which at first seemed to promise so much aid to the Protestant cause, there proceeded, at last, a further triumph for Catholicism, and a mighty promotion of its interests. The Northeast of Germany and Southwest of France, both of which had so long resisted, were alike subdued. There now seemed nothing more required but to secure the perpetual submission of the conquered enemy, by restrictive laws and institutions of permanent efficiency.

The help afforded by Denmark to the Germans, and by England to the French, had been rather injurious than advantageous to those assisted; it had served to bring upon them an irresistible enemy, and these powers were now themselves endangered or attacked. The imperial forces penetrated even into Jutland, and in the year 1628, negotiations for a combined assault upon England proceeded with the most earnest activity between France and Spain.

---

[5] Zorzo Zorzi, "Relatione di Francia, 1629": "The conquest of La Rochelle, completed under the eyes of the English fleet, which professed to relieve the besieged, and throw succors into the town; the expedition against Rohan, who was the chief and soul of that faction; the progress made against the Huguenots in Languedoc, with the recovery of full fifty places, have shaken the hearts and exhausted the powers of that party; so that, having lost their internal force, and being disappointed of foreign aid, they have remitted themselves wholly to the will and clemency of the King." He remarks that the Spaniards certainly came to take part in the siege of La Rochelle, though late, and with only fourteen ships: still they did come. He attributes this accession to their "certainty of the termination," and their wish "to participate in the honors."

CHAPTER FOURTH

MANTUAN WAR — THIRTY YEARS' WAR — REVO-LUTION IN THE STATE OF AFFAIRS

THE course of human affairs, the progress of a develop-ment once begun, presents, at the first glance, an aspect of undeviating persistency.

But on examining more closely, we not infrequently per-ceive that the primitive cause on which the fabric of events reposes is but frail and yielding; merely some personal in-clination, perhaps, whether of attachment or aversion, and which may be shaken without any great difficulty.

If we inquire by what agency the new and important ad-vantages we have enumerated were obtained for the Catholic restoration, we shall find that it was not so much the martial forces of Tilly and Wallenstein, or the military superiority of Richelieu over the Huguenots, as the friendly understanding renewed between France and Spain, without which neither the generals nor the nations could have accomplished anything of moment.

The power of a self-sustained resistance had been lost to the Protestant cause from the year 1626, and it was only by the dissensions of the Catholic powers that its adherents were en-couraged to attempt further opposition; the reconciliation of the governments was, therefore, the precursor of their ruin.

But none could fail to perceive the facility with which these friendly relations might be disturbed.

Within the limits of Catholicism, were two distinct and an-tagonist impulses, each arising equally by an inevitable necessity; the one was religious, the other political.

The first demanded unity of purpose, the extension of the faith, and a perfect disregard of all other considerations—the latter continually impelled the great powers to a conflict for pre-eminent authority.

It could not be affirmed that the balance of power in Europe had as yet been disturbed by the course of events. In those times the balance depended on the hostility of interests existing between France and Austrian Spain: but France, also, had greatly augmented her strength in the course of the recent occurrences.

Political action is, however, prompted and governed, no less by what is perceived on looking forward into the future, than by the pressure and embarrassment of the present. The natural course of things now seemed inevitably conducting to a state of universal insecurity.

North Germany, the earliest home of Protestantism, was overwhelmed by the forces of Wallenstein; and this state of things seemed to present the possibility of restoring the imperial supremacy throughout the empire, where, one short period in the life of Charles V excepted, it had for ages been a shadow only, to real power and essential importance. Should the Catholic restoration proceed on the path it had entered, this result must of necessity ensue.

France, on the other hand, could expect no advantage equivalent to this. When once the Huguenots were completely mastered, France had nothing more to gain. But it was principally among the Italians that disquietudes were awakened; they considered the revival of a mighty imperial authority, asserting so many claims in Italy, and connected so immediately with the detested power of Spain, to be not only dangerous but intolerable.

The question once more recurred, whether Catholic efforts toward universal predominance were to be continued without regard to these considerations, or whether political views would gain the ascendancy, and raise impediments to these efforts.

While the torrent of Catholic restoration was sweeping in full force over France and Germany, a movement was made in Italy, by the result of which this question was ultimately decided.

Section I.—Mantuan Succession

At the close of the year 1627 the Duke of Mantua, Vincenzo II, of the house of Gonzaga, died without leaving children. His next of kin *(agnat)* was Carlo Gonzaga, Duke de Nevers.

Considered in itself only, this succession presented no difficulty, since no doubt could prevail as to the rights of the next of kin; but it involved a political change of the utmost importance.

Charles de Nevers was born in France, and was of necessity to be regarded as a Frenchman. It was believed that the Spaniards would not permit a Frenchman to acquire a sovereignty in Upper Italy, which they had been laboring from time immemorial, and with especial jealousy, to secure from the influence of France.

But if, after the lapse of so long a time, we seek to ascertain the pure truth of this matter, we shall perceive that no intention of excluding the Duke de Nevers was at first entertained, either at the Spanish Court or that of Austria. He was, indeed, related to the imperial house, the Empress being a Mantuan princess, and always greatly disposed to favor him. " There was nothing injurious to his interests required from him in the beginning," says Khevenhiller, who was employed in Mantuan affairs; " it was rather considered how he might best be induced to devote himself to the imperial house." [1] Olivarez, also, has expressly asserted the same thing; he relates, that when intelligence arrived of Don Vincenzo's serious illness, it was resolved at once to send a courier to the Duke de Nevers, to offer him the protection of Spain for his taking peaceable possession of Mantua and Montferrat.[2] It is very possible that conditions might have been imposed on him, and that securities might have been demanded, but there was no thought of wrenching from him his inheritance.

The manner in which this natural course of things was opposed is remarkable.

[1] " Annales Ferdinandei," xi. p. 30.
[2] Francesco degli Albizzi, negotiato di Monsr. Cesare Monte. His Majesty, says Olivarez, " hearing of the grave indisposition of Duke Vincenzo, ordered that a courier should be sent into France to the said Nevers, promising him his protection, that he might peaceably obtain possession of Mantua and Montferrat; but scarcely were the orders given, when by another courier, arrived from Italy, he heard of the death of Vincenzo, the marriage of Rethel without the consent or knowledge of the King, etc."

It was not expected in Italy that the Spaniards would proceed so equitably in this matter: however frequently they had affirmed their intentions of permitting Nevers to assume his rights without opposition, the Italians had never believed them.[3] The Spanish rulers in Italy had brought upon themselves the suspicion of resolving to attain unlimited power, even though the means for doing so were unlawful. No one could now be convinced that they would not seek to confer the duchy on some member of the house of Gonzaga more devoted to themselves.

We must, nevertheless, admit that the wish of the Italians to see Mantua in possession of a prince naturally allied to France and independent of Spain had a considerable share in causing this opinion. They would not believe that Spain would accede to a thing desired by them chiefly as being so adverse to the Spanish interest. They even persuaded the rightful line of succession to think as they did; so that Gonzaga thought it best to place himself in possession by whatever means presented themselves.

The case may be said to have resembled that of the animal constitution, wherein some internal disease sought only an occasion—some aggrieved point—for bursting forth.

In the most profound secrecy, and before the death of Vincenzo, the young Gonzaga Nevers, Duke de Rethel, arrived in Mantua. All here had been prearranged by a Mantuan Minister, named Striggio, belonging to the anti-Spanish party. The old duke acknowledged the rights of his cousin without difficulty. There was still remaining a princess of the direct native line, great-granddaughter of Philip II of Spain, through his youngest daughter, who had married into the house of Savoy. With her it seemed extremely desirable that the young duke should contract a marriage. Accidental circumstances delayed the preparations, and it was not till Vincenzo had expired [4] that the lady was taken in the night from the convent where she had been educated, and conducted to the palace, where the marriage was immediately solemnized. The death of Vincenzo

[3] "Nor must credit be given," says Mulla, the Venetian ambassador to Mantua, in 1615, among other things, "to what has been repeatedly intimated by the Marquis of Inoiosa, formerly governor of Milan, that should the occasion arise, the Spaniards would never admit any other to the Duchy of Milan than the Duke of Nevers. But why not? We have only the fact; the governor asserts it, the Italians do not believe it; nevertheless it is doubtless so."

[4] Nani, "Storia Veneta," l. 7, p. 350; Siri, "Memorie recondite," vi. 309, both relate this fact; the last, on the authority of a letter of Sabran to the French Court.

was then first made known. Rethel was saluted Prince of Mantua, and received the accustomed homage. An envoy from Milan was kept at a distance till it was concluded, and then, not without a kind of mockery, was made acquainted with the facts.

Intelligence of these proceedings arrived at the courts of Vienna and Madrid, together with that of the duke's death.

It will be readily admitted that they were well calculated to exasperate and imbitter these mighty sovereigns, whose pleasure it was to assume a character of religious as well as temporal majesty, to have a kinswoman married without their consent, nay, without their knowledge, and with a sort of violence; an important fief taken into possession without the slightest deference to the feudal sovereign! Yet the measures adopted by the two courts were entirely different.

Olivarez, proud as a Spaniard, doubly proud as the Minister of so powerful a King, and always possessed by an extravagant sense of his own importance, was now far from disposed to make any advances to the duke: he resolved to mortify him, at least, according to his own expression, if he did nothing more.[5] It is true that the department of Gonzaga was manifestly hostile: after the proofs he had given of his manner of thinking, could the important city of Montferrat, which was always considered as an outwork of Milan, be safely intrusted to his keeping? The Duke of Guastalla laid claim to Mantua, the Duke of Savoy to Montferrat. The Spaniards now formed alliances with both: an appeal was made to arms. The Duke of Savoy advanced on Montferrat from the one side, and Don Gonzalez de Cordova, Governor of Milan, from the other. The French had already gained admittance into Casale. Don Gonzales now hastened to lay siege to that place. He had the less doubt of reducing it speedily, as he confided in the understanding entered into with him by parties within the walls.

The Emperor did not proceed so hastily. He felt persuaded that God would protect him, because he was proceeding in the path of justice. He disapproved the conduct of the Spaniards,

[5] Nicoletti, "Vita di papa Urbano," from a despatch of the nuncio Pamfilio. "The count-duke declared that, at the very least, he would mortify the Duke of Nevers, for the disrespect shown to the King, by concluding the marriage without first imparting it to him: but to what extent this mortification was to go, the nuncio could make no conjecture, and the less, as the reasons which had induced the Pope to grant the dispensation were bitterly impugned by the count-duke." App. No. 120.

and caused a formal remonstrance to be sent to Don Gonzalez. But he was determined, on the other hand, to exercise his right of supreme adjudication without the least restraint, and pronounced sentence of sequestration against Mantua, until he should have decided to which of the several claimants the inheritance belonged. As the new Duke of Mantua, who had entered on his duchy, would not submit, the most severe mandates were issued against him.[6]

Now although these measures differed in their origin and character, they yet concurred to produce the same effects. Nevers found himself threatened no less by the German line of the Austrian house, with its legal claims, than by the violent measures of the Spanish line: while seeking to elude the danger, he had drawn it down upon his head.

His prospects were indeed very unpromising in the beginning. Although it is true that some of the Italian States considered his case very nearly as their own, and neglected no means that might persuade him to firmness in his resolution of resistance; yet they had not in themselves resources adequate to the affording him effectual assistance.

Richelieu also had promised that he would not suffer his cause to be lost, if he could only maintain his hold till France could come to his aid; but the question was, when that would be.

The affairs of Mantua were approaching their crisis during the siege of La Rochelle, and the moment was one of extreme peril; before the reduction of that fortress, Richelieu could not move a step; he dared not venture again to commence hostilities with Spain, while his doing so might give occasion for another formidable rising of the Huguenots.

[6] The intentions of the imperial court may be gathered from the report of Pallotta, June 10, 1628, given in an extract by Nicoletti. "The nuncio became daily more firmly convinced that there was a very unfriendly feeling entertained against the Duke of Nevers: it was affirmed that he had shown contempt for the King of Spain, and still more for the Emperor, by concluding his marriage without their knowledge, and taking possession of his fief without investiture—nay, even without the imperial permission (indulto); that he was an enemy of the house of Austria, and was in good intelligence with the French, whom he designed to aid in their invasion of Milan. Yet his imperial Majesty was much inclined to peace, and to that end had issued the decree of sequestration, that he might disarm the Spaniards and Savoyards, while the pretensions of Guastalla, Savoy, Lorraine, and Spain, to the States of Mantua and Montferrat, should be under discussion. But the duke had further offended the Emperor by acts of discourtesy to the commissioners, and by not admitting them into Mantua; more than all, however, by his appeal and the protest that the Emperor had lapsed from his rights and sovereignty over the said fiefs."

And there were likewise considerations of a different character, which were forced on his attention by his earlier experience. He must on no account dare to provoke a disagreement with the zealous and rigidly Catholic party in his own country; nor could he venture to dissent from the views of the Pope, or pursue a line of policy that might displease his holiness.

And now once more important general interests were depending on the Pope. His position, the nature of his office, all required him to use his utmost efforts for the preservation of peace in the Catholic world. As an Italian prince he possessed an unquestionable influence over his neighbors. His proceedings were to be decisive, as we have seen, even of the measures of France. All depended on the question whether he would avert the bursting forth of the menacing discord, or would himself become a party in the contest.

In the earlier political complexities of his pontificate Urban VIII had found his line of policy marked out—its course prescribed. On this occasion his own modes of thinking first came more completely into view, and this occurred at a moment when they were essentially to affect the great interests of the world.

Section II.—Urban VIII

Among other foreigners who attained to considerable wealth during the sixteenth century by the trade of Ancona, which was at that time in a tolerably prosperous condition, was the Florentine house of Barberini, which distinguished itself by its talents for commerce and by consequent success. A scion of that house, Maffeo, born at Florence in the year 1568, was taken, on the early death of his father, to Rome, where he had an uncle then residing who had risen to a certain position in the Curia. Maffeo also attached himself to the service of the Curia; and in this career, though aided by the opulence of his family, he yet owed his promotion chiefly to the extraordinary talents he displayed. In every degree to which he attained, his colleagues in office perceived in him a decided superiority; but it was principally by his success in a nunciature to the Court of France, the friendship and confidence of which he completely secured, that he was encouraged to entertain more lofty views of his own destiny. On the death of Gregory XV the French party immediately proposed him for the pontificate. The aspect of the conclave on that occasion was to a certain extent different from that of the one preceding it, inasmuch as that the last Pope had reigned for a short time only. Although he had appointed a considerable number of cardinals, yet those nominated by his predecessor were equally numerous; thus the nephew of the last Pope and that of the last but one, met each other in the conclave with a nearly equal force of adherents. Maffeo Barberino is said to have given each party to understand that he was an opponent of the other, and it is affirmed that he thus gained the support of both—each, too, upholding him from hatred to the other. But a still more efficient cause of his success doubtless was that he had always proved himself a zealous defender of the jurisdictional rights of the Roman Curia, and had thus rendered the majority of the cardinals favorable to his own interests. Be this as it may, helped on by his own merits and by the support of others, Maffeo Barberino secured his election, and rose to the pontifical dignity at the vigorous age of fifty-five.

The court very soon discovered a wide difference between the new Pope and his immediate predecessors. Clement VIII was most commonly found occupied with the works of St. Bernard; Paul V with the writings of the holy Justinian of Venice; but on the table of Urban VIII lay the newest poems, or draughts and plans of fortifications.

It will generally be found that the time at which the character of a man receives its decided direction is in those first years of manhood which form the period when he begins to take an independent position in public affairs or in literature. The youth of Paul V, who was born in 1552, and of Gregory XV, born in 1554, belonged to a time when the principles of Catholic restoration were pressing forward with full unbroken vigor, and they were themselves accordingly imbued with these principles. The first influentially active portion of Urban's life, born 1568, coincided, on the contrary, with that period when the papal principality was opposed to Spain—when the re-establishment of France as a Catholic power was one of the reigning topics of the day; and accordingly we find that his inclinations followed by preference the direction then chosen.

Urban VIII considered himself more particularly as a temporal prince.

He had formed the opinion that the States of the Church should be secured by fortifications, and should render themselves formidable by their own arms. When the marble monuments of his predecessors were pointed out to him, he declared that those erected by himself should be of iron. He built Castelfranco on the Bolognese frontier, and this place was also called Fort Urbano; although its military utility was so far from being obvious that the people of Bologna suspected it to be raised against them rather than for their defence. In the year 1625 he began to strengthen the castle of St. Angelo in Rome, by the addition of breastworks, and immediately stored the fortress with provisions and munitions of war, as though the enemy had been before the gates. He built the high wall that encloses the papal gardens on Monte Cavallo, without regard to the destruction thus occasioned to a magnificent relic of antiquity, situate in the Colonna gardens. He established a manufactory of arms at Tivoli.[7] The rooms beneath the Vatican library were used as an arsenal, the public ways were thronged with soldiers, and the seat of the supreme spiritual power of Christendom— the peaceful circuit of the Eternal City—was filled with the uproar of a camp. The pontiff considered a free port also as indispensable to a well-organized State, and Città Vecchia was put into a state rendered proper to that purpose at great cost; but the result was more in accordance with the condition of things than with the views of the Pope. In his new port the Barbary corsairs sold the booty of which they had plundered Christian ships. Such was the purpose to which the labors of the supreme pastor of Christendom became subservient.

As regarded all these arrangements Pope Urban acted with absolute and uncontrolled power. He surpassed his predecessors, at least in the early years of his pontificate, in the unlimited exercise of his authority.

[7] A. Contarini, " Relne. di 1635 " : " With regard to arms, the popes were previously altogether unprovided, confiding more in the attachment of princes secured by benefits, than in warlike defences; now the note is changed, and the present Pope in particular is very earnest in the matter. He has brought a certain Ripa, of Brescia, a subject of your Serenity, to Tivoli, who has from time to time gone to entice a number of workmen from the Gardon country. This Ripa here makes a large quantity of arms, causing the rough iron to be brought from the Brescian territory, and he is also raising some portion of ores found in Umbria: of all these things my letters have given due notice at the proper time, but I rather think they have been passed over without much attention.   The Pope has prepared an arsenal for these arms under the library of the Vatican, where muskets, pikes, carbines, and pistols are stored in good order; there are sufficient to arm 20,-000 foot-soldiers and 5,000 horse, besides a good number that have been sent from this same factory of Tivoli to Ferrara and Castelfranco during the late events." App. No. 115.

If it was proposed to him to take the advice of the college he would reply that he alone knew more and understood better than all the cardinals put together. Consistories were very seldom called, and even when they were assembled, few had courage to express their opinions freely. The congregations met in the usual manner, but no questions of importance were laid before them, and the decisions they arrived at were but little regarded.[8] Even for the administration of the State, Urban formed no proper *Consulta*, as had been customary with his predecessors. His nephew, Francesco Barberino, was perfectly justified in refusing, as he did, during the first ten years of Urban's pontificate, to accept the responsibility of any measure, whatever might be its nature.

The foreign ambassadors considered themselves most unfortunate in their attempts to transact business with this Pope— they could make no way with him. In giving audience he talked himself more than any other person;[9] he lectured and harangued, continuing with one applicant the conversation he had commenced with another. All were expected to listen to him, admire him, and address him with the most profound reverence, even when his replies were adverse to them. Other pontiffs often refused the requests presented to them, but for some given cause—some principle, either of religion or policy. In Urban, caprice was often perceived to be the only motive for refusal, no one would conjecture whether he ought to expect a yes or a no. The quick-sighted Venetians found out that he loved to contradict; that he was inclined, by an almost involuntary disposition, constantly to give the contrary decision to that proposed to him. In order to gain their point, therefore, they adopted the expedient of starting objections to their own wishes; and in seeking for arguments to oppose these, he fell of himself upon propositions to which all the persuasion in the

[8] "The congregations," says Aluise Contarini, "are occasionally used, that is to cover some blunder." App. No. 115.
[9] Pietro Contarini, "Relne. di 1627": "He abounds in talk on all matters, and reasons to a great extent on every subject, putting forward whatever he knows or conceives in every matter of business, and this to such a degree that his audiences are given with double frequency, and are longer than those of his predecessors. The same thing occurs in the congregations whenever he is present, to the great disadvantage of all who have to treat with him; for since he takes up the greater part of the time, there is little left for others. I heard a cardinal say that he was going, not to receive audience, but to give it to the Pope, since he was certain that his holiness would talk more than listen; and it has often happened that those who have gone to him about their affairs have left without having been able to say anything of their business, for if he once took up the discourse they had no longer opportunity for uttering one word." See Appendix, No. 111.

world would not otherwise have obtained his assent. This is a character of mind which sometimes exhibits itself in a certain manner among men of subordinate station also, and was not unfrequently observed in those times among Spaniards and Italians. It would seem to consider a public office as a tribute due to its merit and personal importance; and men thus constituted are far more powerfully influenced in the administration of their duties, by their own feelings and impulses, than by the exigences of the case. They are not greatly dissimilar to an author, who, occupied by the consciousness of his talents, does not so much devote his thoughts to the subject before him as give free course to the fancies of his caprice.

And Urban himself really belonged to this class of authors; the poems of his composition still remaining to us show considerable talent and wit; but how strangely are sacred subjects handled in them! The psalms and axioms, alike of the Old and New Testaments, are compelled to accommodate themselves to Horatian measures. The song of praise of the aged Simeon is presented in two Sapphic strophes! It is manifest that no characteristic of the text can remain: the matter is forced to adapt itself to a form in direct contradiction with its character, and adopted only because preferred by the author.

But these talents, the brilliant appearance they cast about the person of the Pope, nay, even the robust health that he enjoyed, all contributed to increase that self-complacency with which his lofty position had of itself inspired him.[10]

I do not know any pope in whom this self-consciousness attained to so high a degree. An objection derived from ancient papal constitutions was once opposed to some design of his; he replied that the spoken word of a living pope was worth more than the maxims of a hundred dead ones.

The resolution adopted by the Roman people of never raising a statue to any pope during his life was abrogated by Urban, with the declaration that "such a resolution could not apply to a pope like himself."

The mode in which one of his nuncios had conducted himself under very difficult circumstances having been represented

[10] This was remarked from the beginning. "Relatione dei quattro ambasciatori," 1624: "He loves his own opinions, and thinks highly of his own genius; thus he is rigidly tenacious of his own purposes. . . . He is always earnest about things that promise to enhance the idea entertained of his personal qualities." Appendix, No. 104.

to him with praise, he remarked, that " the nuncio had but proceeded in accordance with his instructions."

To such a man it was, so filled with the idea of being a mighty prince, so well disposed to France, both from his early occupation in that country and the support it had afforded him; so self-willed, energetic, and full of self-importance; to such a man, that the conduct of the supreme spiritual power over Catholic Christendom was committed at this critical moment.

On his decisions, on the line of conduct that he should pursue among the Catholic powers, was now principally to depend the progress or interruption of that universal restoration of Catholicism with which the world was occupied.

But it had very early been remarked that this pontiff betrayed a disinclination toward the interests of Austrian Spain.[1]

Cardinal Borgia complained of his aversion and harshness as early as 1625. " The King of Spain," he said, " could not obtain the slightest concession from him—everything was refused to his Majesty."

The same prelate further maintained that Urban did not willingly terminate the affairs of the Valtelline; he affirmed that the King of Spain had offered to resign the disputed passes, but that the Pope had not taken any notice of the offer.

It is also unquestionable that Urban was in part to blame for the failure of the alliance proposed between the house of Austria and that of Stuart. In completing the dispensation already drawn up by his predecessor, he added to the former conditions a demand that public churches for Catholic worship should be built in every English county; this was a requisition with which the majority of an irritated Protestant population rendered compliance impossible, and which the Pope desisted of himself from pressing in the case of the French marriage. He seemed, indeed, to be unwilling that Spain should acquire that increase of power which must have resulted to her from a connection with England. Negotiations were carried on in profound secrecy by the nuncio, then resident in Brussels, for the

[1] Marquemont, " Lettres," in Aubery, " Mémoires de Richelieu," i. p. 65, observes this from the beginning. It will not be difficult, he says, to manage the Pope; his inclination is for the King and for France, but from prudence he will try to content the other sovereigns. The Pope on his part soon became aware of the aversion of the Spaniards.

marriage of the electoral prince palatine—not with an Austrian, but with a Bavarian princess.[2]

In the complexities of the Mantuan succession, also, Pope Urban VIII took an equally efficient part. The recent marriage of the young princess with Rethel, on which the whole affair depended, could not have been completed without the papal dispensation. The pontiff granted this without having consulted the nearest kinsmen of the lady—Philip of Spain and the Emperor; and it was besides prepared precisely at the moment required.

All these things sufficed to render the dispositions of the Pope clearly manifest: his most earnest wish was that of all the other Italian sovereignties, the seeing a prince entirely independent of Spain take possession of the Mantuan duchy.

He did not even wait until the initiative had been taken by Richelieu. His representations to the imperial court having failed of their effect, the proceedings of Austria being indeed more and more threatening, while the siege of Casale was still persisted in, the Pope turned of his own accord to France.

He caused the most urgent entreaties to be used. " The King," he said, " might send an army into the field even before the reduction of La Rochelle was effected; an expedition for the assistance of Mantua would be quite as pleasing to God as the beleaguering of that chief bulwark of the Huguenots. Let the King only appear at Lyons and declare himself for the freedom of Italy, and the Pope on his part would not delay to bring his forces into action and unite himself with the King."[3]

From this side, therefore, Richelieu had nothing now to fear if he should determine to revive that opposition to Spain which he had failed to establish three years before. But he wished to proceed with perfect security; he was not in so much haste as the Pope, and would not suffer himself to be disturbed in the siege of a place by which his ambition was fettered in its career.

But he was all the more determined when once La Rochelle had fallen. " Monsignore," he said to the papal nuncio, whom

[2] The emissary of the nuncio was a Capuchin, Francesco della Rota-Russdorf, " Negotiations," i. 205, gives a particularly detailed account of these transactions.

[3] Extracts from Bethune's despatches of September 23d and October 8th, 1628, in Siri, " Memorie," vi. p. 478.

he instantly sent for, "now we will not lose another moment; the King will engage in the affairs of Italy with all his power." [4]

Thereupon, that hostility to Spain and Austria which had so often displayed itself, rose up with greater vehemence than ever. The jealousy of Italy once more called forth the ambition of France. The state of things appeared to be so urgent that Louis XIII would not wait for the spring, but left Paris at once, even in the midst of January (1629). He took the road to the Alps, and it was in vain that the Duke of Savoy, who, as we have said, adhered to Spain, opposed his progress. The passes of his dominions, which he had caused to be barricaded, were forced at the first assault; Susa was taken, and in the month of March he was compelled to come to terms: the Spaniards were then constrained to raise the siege of Casale.[5]

Thus the two leading powers of Catholic Christendom once more stood opposed to each other in arms. Richelieu again proceeded to bring his boldest plans to bear against the Spanish and Austrian power.

But if we compare the two periods, we perceive that he now held a far more substantial and tenable position than at the time of his enterprise in regard to the Grisons and the Palatinate. Then, the Huguenots might have seized the moment for renewing the civil war. Nor were they completely subdued even now; but since they had lost La Rochelle they occasioned no further disquietude: defeats and losses pursued them without intermission, so that they could no longer effect even a diversion. And perhaps it was of still more importance that Richelieu now had the Pope on his side. In his earlier undertaking the contest in which he was thereby involved with the policy of Rome, was perilous even to his position in France; his present enterprise, on the contrary, had been suggested by Rome itself for the interests of the papal principality. Richelieu found it advisable on the whole to attach himself as closely as possible to the papacy: in the disputes between the Roman and Gallican doctrines he now adhered to the Roman and abandoned the Gallican tenets.

In this state of things how momentous became the animosity of Urban VIII to the house of Austria!

[4] " Dispaccio Bagni, 2 Nov. 1628."
[5] " Recueil de diverses relations des guerres d'Italie," 1629-31. Bourg en Bresse, 1632.

With the development of religious opinions, and the progress of Catholic restoration, were associated political changes, the principle of which continued to make itself more earnestly and deeply felt, and now placed itself in direct opposition even to that of the Church.

The Pope entered the lists against that very power by which the restoration and progress of Catholicism had been most zealously and most efficiently promoted.

The question now was, what would be the course of this power—above all, that of Ferdinand himself, in whose hands the work of restoration principally rested—when confronted by so mighty and so threatening an opposition?

Section III.—The Power of the Emperor Ferdinand II in the Year 1629

The Emperor proceeded as though nothing had occurred.

Under the circumstances prevailing, it was true that he could promise himself no kind of favor from the Pope. In the most trifling matters, as for example in a question relating to the abbacy of St. Maximian, he found his wishes opposed; nay, with regard to the most devout suggestions, he experienced nothing but refusals—as when he desired, among other things, that St. Stephen and St. Wenceslaus—the one of whom was greatly revered in Hungary, and the other in Bohemia—should be admitted into the Roman calendar. Notwithstanding all these disappointments, he published the edict of restitution in the empire on March 6, 1629. This may be regarded as the final judgment in a great suit which had been pending for more than a century. The Protestants were utterly condemned: judgment was given entirely in favor of the Catholics. "There remains nothing for us," declared the Emperor, "but to uphold the injured party, and to send forth our commissioners that they may demand from their present unauthorized possessors the restitution of all archbishoprics, bishoprics, prelacies, monasteries, and other ecclesiastical property confiscated since the treaty of Passau. Commissions were immediately instituted, one for each circle of the empire; these were at once in full activity, and the most indiscriminate executions began. And might not the Pope at least have been appeased by this, and moved to some show of favor and friendliness? Pope Urban considered it all as the mere fulfilment of a duty. The Emperor begged to have the right of nominating, at least for the first time, to the ecclesiastical benefices recovered by the edict of restitution; but the Pope refused him this, affirming that he dared not violate the concordats, which were observed, he said, even in France.[6] There was a kind of mockery in this mode of refusal, since the French concordat secured to the King that very privilege now desired by the Emperor. Ferdinand wished to receive permission for converting the recovered monasteries into colleges, more particularly for the Jesuits. The Pope replied that the monasteries must be instantly delivered over to the bishops.

Meanwhile the Emperor proceeded on his way without regard to the displeasure of the Pope: he considered himself as the great champion of the Catholic Church.

He caused three armies to take the field at the same time.

The first went to the aid of the Poles against the Swedes, and did, in fact, succeed in restoring the Polish fortunes to a certain extent. That was, however, not its only object. It was proposed by this campaign at the same time to restore Prussia to the empire and the Order (Teutonic), from which it had been wrested.[7]

Another body marched upon the Netherlands to support the Spaniards in that country. It swept across the open plains from Utrecht toward Amsterdam, and but for the accident of a surprise at Wesel, would without doubt have produced important results.

A third force was meanwhile assembled at Memmingen and Lindau, for the purpose of proceeding into Italy and bringing the Mantuan affair to a conclusion with the sword. The Swiss would by no means be persuaded to grant permission of passage, and it was therefore made by force. Luciensteig, Coire, and all the passes of the Grisons, even to the Lake of Como, were occupied at one moment by the Austrian troops, and this army, 35,000 strong, then poured down along the Adda and the Oglio.

---

[6] " Lettera di segreteria di stato al nunzio Pallotta li 28 Aprile, 1629." The Pope appointed Pier Luigi Caraffa, his nuncio in Cologne, to Lower Saxony, with powers for the restitution of ecclesiastical property, and resolved also to give him additional powers, to be used, if required, in disputes between clergy and clergy.

[7] " Mémoires et négotiations de Rusdorf," ii. 724. It was lately declared to Count Schwartzenberg at Vienna in plain words, by the counsellors and Ministers of the Emperor, that his Majesty would subject to himself and the empire whatever his arms should occupy and obtain in Prussia.

RANKE

The Duke of Mantua was once more summoned to submit, and declared in reply that he was under the protection of the King of France, and that negotiations must be referred to him. Meanwhile, as the Germans moved upon Mantua and the Spaniards on Montferrat, the French likewise appeared for the second time. On this occasion, also, they gained some advantages, taking Saluzzo and Pinerolo, but in the main they produced no effectual results; they could not even again compel the Duke of Savoy to their wishes. The Spaniards commenced the siege of Casale; the Germans, after a short truce, invested Mantua:[8] their party had a decided preponderance.

It could not occasion surprise if, in this state of things, recollections of the ancient supremacy of the emperors arose, or that they were now frequently alluded to in Vienna.

" The Italians must be taught that there is still an Emperor; they must be called to a strict account."

Venice had more particularly attracted to itself the hatred of the house of Austria. It was the general opinion in Vienna that when once Mantua had fallen, the territories of Venice, situate on the mainland, would no longer be able to offer resistance to the Austrian power. They could not fail to be reduced in a few months, and his Majesty would then demand restitution of the imperial fiefs. The Spanish ambassador went still further: he compared the power of Spanish Austria with that of Rome, and the power of Venice with that of Carthage; " Aut Roma," he exclaimed, " aut Carthago delenda est."

And the secular rights of the empire, as opposed to those of the Papal See, were here also brought to recollection.

Ferdinand II was desirous of being crowned, and required that the Pope should come as far as Bologna or Ferrara to meet him. The Pope dared neither to promise nor positively to refuse, and sought to help himself through the difficulty by a mental reservation [9] (reservatio mentalis). Question was made respecting the feudal rights of the empire over Urbino and Montefeltro, when the papal nuncio was told with little ceremony, that Wallenstein would obtain further information on the subject when he should descend into Italy. And this was in

[8] The eleventh book of the " Istoria di Pietro Giov. Capriata " describes the events of this siege minutely.

[9] " Although Urban once said to the ambassador Savelli, that in case of need he would go to Bologna or Ferrara, he did not mean that to be understood as referring to what the Prince of Eckenberg had mentioned."

fact the purpose of Wallenstein. He had previously opposed the Italian war, but he now declared that, seeing the Pope and his allies were seeking to destroy the power of Austria, he considered that war necessary.[10] He intimated that it was a hundred years since Rome was last plundered, and that it must be now much richer than it was then.

Nor was France to be spared. The Emperor proposed to regain the three alienated bishoprics by force of arms, his plan being to raise Cossack troops in Poland and to send them into France: the dissensions of Louis XIII with his brother and mother seemed to offer the desired opportunity for this expedition.

The house of Austria thus assumed a position from which it continued its efforts against the Protestants with the utmost boldness; while at the same time it kept a firm hand on the movements of the Catholic opposition, and powerfully restrained even the Pope himself.

Section IV.—Negotiations with Sweden—Electoral Diet at Ratisbon

In earlier times, whenever a contingency of this kind had been merely foreseen, or dreaded for the remote future only, every power in Europe, still retaining independence, at once combined. It had now actually occurred. The Catholic opposition looked around for aid and sought it—not now from mere jealousy, but for defence and as a help in its utmost need— beyond the limits of Catholicism. But to what quarter could it turn? England was fully occupied at home by the disputes between the King and his Parliament; she was besides already engaged in renewed negotiations with Spain. The Netherlands were themselves overwhelmed by the enemy; the German Protestants were either beaten or overawed by the imperial

---

[10] The opinion generally entertained of the Pope in Vienna appears from a letter of Pallotta, dated August 10, 1628. " It has been reported here by evil-minded people, who are those desirous of war, that the State of Milan is in extremity of peril, it being certain that Pope Urban is forming vast designs, and has very hostile intentions toward the house of Austria; that his holiness is therefore as much to be feared as the Venetians or French, his States being so near the Duchy of Milan, and he be- ing in a condition instantly to bring troops into the field. And further, the same malignant people have declared, as a thing decided on, that his holiness will in some manner contrive to have the King of France elected King of the Romans; in confirmation of which they affirm that when his holiness was nuncio in France he promised the Queen that if ever he became Pope, her son, then a child, should be made King of the Romans."

armies. The King of Denmark had been compelled to conclude a disadvantageous peace. There remained none but the King of Sweden.

While the Protestants had been suffering defeat in all quarters, Gustavus Adolphus alone had achieved victories. He had conquered Riga, the whole of Livonia, even to Dünamünde, and, " as much of Lithuania," according to the Poles themselves, " as he had been pleased to take." He had then, in 1626, appeared in Prussia, principally, as he said, to look into the state of the clergy in the bishopric of Ermeland. The two chief seats of restored Catholicism in that country, Frauenburg and Braunsburg, namely, he had taken into his own possession, and had afforded a new and powerful support to the oppressed Protestants of those districts. All eyes were turned on him. " Above all men," writes Rusdorf, in the year 1624, " do I estimate this victorious hero; I revere in him the sole protector of our cause, and the terror of our common enemy. His path of glory, which is raised far above the reach of envy, do I constantly follow with my prayers."[1] It is true that Gustavus Adolphus had sustained some loss in a battle on the plains of Stumm, and had himself been on the point of becoming a prisoner, but the chivalrous bravery with which he had cut his way through all opposition cast added lustre on his name, and, despite this disadvantage, he still kept the field.

Toward this prince the French now turned themselves. They first effected a truce between him and the Poles, and it is very possible that the Emperor's views in regard to Prussia may have contributed to dispose the magnates, if not the King of Poland, to a more peaceful temper.[2] This done, they made a nearer approach to their principal purpose, that of drawing the King of Sweden into Germany; the only precaution they took was to stipulate in the treaty for certain regulations in favor of Catholicism; under these conditions they declared themselves ready to support the King, who was able to bring a considerable army into the field, with corresponding supplies in money. After some delay, Gustavus acceded to their pro-

[1] Rusdorf, " Mémoires," ii. 3: " Ejus gloriam invidiæ metas eluctatam, excelsam infracti animi magnitudinem, et virtutis magis ac magis per merita enitescentis et assurgentis invictum robur cum stupore adoro et supplici voto prosequor." (See text.)
[2] Rusdorf, l. i. 724: " If ever the magnates of Poland wished for peace, they did so, for the most part of them, at this time."

posals. In his instructions, he avoids all mention of religious affairs, and represents the objects of the confederacy to be the restoration of the German Estates to their ancient rights; the removal of the imperial troops, and the security of commerce and the sea.[3] An agreement was drawn up, in which the King promised to tolerate the Catholic religion wherever he should find it established, and in all affairs of religion to guide himself (such were the forms of the expression) according to the laws of the empire. This last stipulation was imperative, on account of the Pope, to whom it was immediately communicated. The completion of this treaty was, indeed, still retarded by certain formalities; but in the summer of 1630 it was regarded as definitively settled.[4] The papal nuncio in France affirmed that Venice had engaged to pay a third part of the subsidies.[5] I have not been able to discover on what grounds this assertion was founded, but that Venice should make this promise was entirely consistent with the situation of things.

But could there be a reasonable hope that Gustavus Adolphus could alone suffice to overcome the force of the allied imperial armies, and could conquer them single handed in the field? This was not believed to be possible; it therefore seemed desirable above all things, that a movement should be excited in Germany itself, which might co-operate with and aid him in his enterprise.

And here, without doubt, the Protestants might safely be counted on; whatever might be the policy adopted by individual princes from personal considerations or fear, yet the general mind was fully mastered by that fermentation which penetrates to the ultimate depths of our social life, and is the precursor of mighty movements. I will but mention one idea of those prevalent at the time. When the edict of restitution had begun to be enforced in various places, and the Jesuits

---

[3] " Tenor mandatorum quæ S. R. Maj. Sueciæ clementer vult, ut consiliarius ejus. . . . Dn. Camerarius observare debeat, Upsaliæ, 18 Dec. 1629."—Mosers patriotisches Archiv. b. vi. p. 133.
[4] Bagni, 18 Giugno, 1630. He gives the article, which is also in the compact of January 6, 1631, with a slight variation, as follows: " If the King make any progress, he shall observe the laws of the empire, as regards matters of religion, in all places either taken by, or surrendered to, him." He also shows us in what sense this was understood:

" Which laws, he adds, are reported to be understood as applying to the Catholic religion and the Confession of Augsburg."—So that the Calvinists would have remained excluded.
[5] Bagni, 16 Luglio, 1630. " There have arrived," the extract proceeds to say, " new letters from Bagni, to the effect that the republic of Venice had joined the confederation of France and Sweden, with an engagement to contribute to the extent of one-third of the subsidy."

already signified their determination to pay no regard even to the treaty of Augsburg, the Protestants gave it to be understood in their turn, that before matters could proceed to that length, the German Empire and nations should be utterly overturned— " rather should all laws and restraints be cast away, and Germany be thrown back to the wild life of its ancient forests."

In aid of all this there came discontent and dissension, which now appeared on the Catholic side.

It would be difficult to describe the commotion that ensued among the clergy on perceiving that the Jesuits proposed to constitute themselves possessors of the recovered monastic property. The Society of Jesus was reported to have declared that there were no Benedictines now remaining, that all had departed from the rule of their founder, and were no more capable of resuming their lost possessions. The merits of the Jesuits themselves were then brought into question by the other side, which maintained that they had performed no conversions: what seemed conversion was, as they affirmed, a mere effect of force.[6] Thus, even before the restitution of ecclesiastical property had taken place, it had already excited discord and contention for the right to its possession between the orders, and for the right to the collation between the Emperor and the Pope.

But these ecclesiastical differences were accompanied by others of a secular character, and of far more extensive importance. The imperial troops were found to be an insupportable burden to the country, their passage through a district exhausted the land and its inhabitants equally; as the peasant and the burgher were maltreated by the soldier, so were the princes by the general. Wallenstein allowed himself to use the most arrogant language. The oldest allies of the Emperor,

[6] From the violent controversial writings, the attacks, replies, and rejoinders that appeared on this subject, it is impossible to extract the truth of the facts, but we readily gather the points in dispute. " It is perfectly true," says the papal nuncio, in a letter written in cipher, that the Jesuit fathers have sought, and do seek, by favor of the Emperor, which could not well be greater, not only to obtain a preference over all other orders, but even to exclude all others, wherever they have any interest either political or ecclesiastical. I find, nevertheless, that however devoted the Emperor then was to the Jesuits, yet in the year 1629 he was greatly disposed to make entire restitution to the older orders. Pier Luigi Caraffa, nuncio in Cologne, declares this. But at that very moment the Jesuits had already gained their point in Rome, whence an edict was published in July, 1629, to the effect that a portion of the recovered property might be applied to the foundation of schools, endowments, seminaries, and colleges, as well for the Jesuit fathers, who had been the chief promoters of the decree for restitution, as of other religious orders. The Jesuit schools would thus have extended over the whole of North Germany.

the chiefs of the League, and above all Maximilian of Bavaria, were dissatisfied with the present, and anxious about the future.

While affairs were in this position it happened that Ferdinand assembled the Catholic Electors of Ratisbon in the summer of 1630, for the purpose of procuring the election of his son as King of the Romans. It was not possible that such an occasion should pass away without the discussion of all other public affairs.

The Emperor clearly saw that he must concede something, and his intention was to do this in regard to some portion of the German affairs. He showed a disposition to suspend the edict for restoring church property, in so far as it affected the territories of Brandenburg and Electoral Saxony; was desirous of coming to some definitive arrangement in respect to Mecklenburg and the Palatinate, wished to conciliate Sweden, negotiations for that purpose having been already commenced, and meanwhile to concentrate all his force upon Italy, that the Mantuan war might be brought to an end, and the Pope compelled to an acknowledgment of his ecclesiastical claims.[7]

Ferdinand probably thought, that since he had to deal with German princes, he should effect more for his own purposes by concessions in German affairs than by any other means; but the position of things was not so simple.

The spirit of opposition, as embodied in the league of the French and Italians, had made its way among the Catholic electors, and now sought to avail itself of the discontents existing in their minds for the furtherance of its own purposes.

The papal nuncio, Rocci, first appeared in Ratisbon, and how could he fail to employ every means that presented itself for the prevention of Ferdinand's Italian and anti-papal designs?

The Pope had exhorted him, above all things, to maintain

[7] " Dispaccio Pallotta, 2 Ag. 1630," enumerates the following, as among the points that were to be deliberated upon: 1st. Whether the edict for the recovery of ecclesiastical property should be suspended or carried into execution. 2d. Whether, if it were to be executed, there should be a suspension in regard to property situate in the States of the Electors of Saxony and Brandenburg; and he was inclined to suspend it. 3d. As regarded the benefices and other ecclesiastical possessions recovered it was affirmed that the nomination to them was vested in the Emperor. . . . 6th. The restitution of the Duchy of Mecklenburg to its former possessors was discussed, as also that of the Palatinate, at least the Lower Palatinate, to the palatine, to the perpetual prejudice of the Catholic religion, as had been done in regard to Denmark.

a friendly understanding with the Elector of Bavaria, and soon afterward Rocci reports that this friendly understanding is kept up, but with the most profound secrecy.[8] He contrived to procure from the Catholic electors a declaration that they would maintain a close union with himself in all that appertained to ecclesiastical affairs, and would more especially uphold the jurisdiction of the Papal See, and preserve its dignity inviolate.

But to give the matter a decisive turn, Father Joseph, the trusted confederate of Richelieu, came to the aid of Rocci, and the consummate craft of that Capuchin was, perhaps, never more active, more efficient, or, to those initiated, more obvious, than on this occasion. His colleague in Ratisbon, Monsieur de Leon, who gave his name to the embassy, declared of him, that the father had in fact no soul, but in its stead were holes and quicksands, into which everyone must fall who should attempt to have any dealings with him.

By the agency of intermediaries such as these, the French and Italian opposition soon made the German allies of the Emperor completely its own. For the reconciliation of the empire with Sweden, for the pacification of the Protestants, nothing was done; and never would the Pope have consented to the suspension of the edict of restitution. On the other hand, the electors pressed for the restoration of peace in Italy, and demanded the dismissal of the imperial commander-in-chief, who was conducting himself in the fashion of an absolute dictator.

And so irrepressible was the influence exercised, so craftily was it brought to bear on all points, that the mighty Emperor, though at the zenith of his power, yielded to its force without resistance, and without conditions.

While these negotiations were proceeding in Ratisbon, the troops of Ferdinand had conquered Mantua, and he might then have considered himself master of Italy. Yet at that moment he agreed to resign the duchy to Nevers, with no other condition than the empty formality of an entreaty for pardon. But the other demand made on the Emperor was perhaps still more significant. The German princes, France, and the Pope,

---

[8] " Dispaccio Rocci, 9 Sett. 1630: " " And this friendly understanding proved very profitable, because Bavaria labored heartily to prevent the above-mentioned subjects from being discussed in that Convention."

were at once and equally menaced by the general, on whose personal qualities the fortune of the imperial arms depended; that they should detest him, and desire to be freed from his presence, can occasion no surprise; but what followed may well excite astonishment. The Emperor, for the sake of peace, gave him up.

At the moment when he might have mastered Italy, he suffered it to elude his grasp; at the moment when he was attacked in Germany by the most formidable of enemies, the most practised of warriors, he dismissed the commander who alone was in a condition to defend him. Never have policy and negotiation produced more important results.

Section V.—Swedish War—Situation of the Pope

And now it was that the war really began. Gustavus Adolphus commenced it, as must needs be admitted, under the most favorable auspices; for had not the imperial army been brought together by the name of Wallenstein, and was it not wholly devoted and bound to his person? The Emperor even disbanded a part of it, and subjected the contributions levied by the generals, and which had previously been regulated by their own discretion, to the control of the circles of the empire.[9] It is not to be denied that the Emperor, when he dismissed his general, destroyed his army at the same time, and deprived it of its moral force. Torquato Conti, an Italian, who had formerly been in the papal service, had to offer resistance, with troops in this State, to an enemy high in courage and full of zeal. It was in the nature of things that failure should ensue; the imperial army was no longer what it had been, nothing was seen but irresolution, weakness, panic, and defeat. Gustavus Adolphus drove it completely from the field, and established himself in firm possession on the lower Oder.

It was at first believed in Upper Germany that this was of little importance to the rest of the empire. Tilly continued his operations in the meantime with great composure along the Elbe. When he at length gained possession of Magdeburg the Pope considered it a great victory, and the brightest hopes

[9] Adlzreitter, iii. xv. 48: "The Emperor decreed that in future the pay should not depend on the will of the officers, but on the regulations prescribed by the circles."

were founded on this conquest. At the suggestion of Tilly,
a commissary was even appointed " for the purpose of arrang-
ing the affairs of the archbishopric in accordance with the laws
of the Catholic Church."

But it was by this very measure that all the Protestant princes
who had remained undecided were determined to attach themselves to Gustavus Adolphus; and when Tilly sought to prevent this, he did but further involve them in hostilities with the
League, so that it was no longer possible to make distinction
between Leaguers and Imperialists. The battle of Leipzig followed. Tilly was completely routed, and the Protestant forces
poured alike over the territories of the Leaguers and the Imperialists. Würzburg and Bamberg fell into the hands of the
King. The Protestants of the remote North were met on the
Rhine by those ancient defenders of Roman Catholicism, the
troops of Spain, and there, near to Oppenheim, their skulls are
seen mingled. Mayence was taken, all oppressed princes took
part with the Swedish King, and the expelled count-palatine
appeared in his camp.

Thus it followed, as a necessary consequence, that an enterprise, originated or sanctioned by the Catholic opposition
for political purposes, resulted in the advantage of Protestantism. The party before overpowered and beaten down now
saw itself once more victorious. It is true that the King extended his protection to the Catholics generally, as the terms
of his treaty with the allies compelled him to do; but he declared expressly, at the same time, that he was come to rescue
his brethren in faith from the oppressions they were suffering
for conscience' sake.[10] He received to his especial protection
the evangelical ministers living under Catholic governments—
those of Erfurt, for example; in all quarters he caused the
Augsburg Confession to be reinstated, the exiled pastors returned to the Palatinate, and the Lutheran worship made its
way through the empire once more, together with the victorious
army.

Thus strangely perplexed was the policy of Urban VIII. In
so far as Gustavus attacked and overcame the power of Austria, he was the natural ally of the Pope. This was at once

---

[10] Letter from the King to the town of Schweinfurt in Chemnitz, Schwedi-
scher Krieg, Th. i. p. 231.

made manifest in the affairs of Italy; under the influence of his German losses, the Emperor assented, in the year 1631, to conditions regarding the Duchy of Mantua, still more unfavorable to himself than those submitted to him the year before at Ratisbon. Nay, there even existed, if not direct, yet indirect relations between the Papal See and those Protestant powers now once more in battle array, and making victorious advance. " I speak of this from good authority," says Aluise Contarini, who had been first at the French Court, and afterward at that of Rome. " I was present at all the negotiations. The Pope's nuncios always favored Richelieu's undertakings, whether they were meant to secure his own safety, or to bring about the union of Bavaria and the league with France. When the alliance of Richelieu with Holland and the Protestant powers generally was in question, they remained silent, to save themselves from admitting that they approved it. Other popes would perhaps have found this offend their conscience; but the nuncios of Urban VIII obtained, by such means, increased consideration and personal advantages."[1]

Loud and bitter were the complaints of the Emperor. First, the Roman Court had prevailed on him to publish the edict of restitution, and then abandoned him in the war occasioned by it. The election of his son as King of the Romans, had been impeded by the Pope, who had encouraged the Elector of Bavaria, both by word and deed, to pursue a separate line of policy and to ally himself with France. It was in vain to ask Urban for such assistance as earlier popes had so often afforded, either of money or troops; he even refused to utter a condemnation of the alliance of France with heretics, or to declare the present war a war of religion.[2] In the year 1632 we find the imperial ambassadors in Rome insisting with extreme earnestness on the last-mentioned point; they affirmed

[1] Aluise Contarini, Relatione di Roma, 1635. See Appendix, No. 115.
[2] Aluise Contarini: " Gli Alemanni si pretendono delusi dal papa, perchè dopo aver egli reiteratamente persuaso l' imperatore di ripetere dagli eretici i beni ecclesiastici d' Alemagna ch' erano in loro mani, origine di tante guerre, resistesse S. Sta. poi alle reiterate spedizioni di cardli. e d' ambri. nelle assistenze di danaro, nel mandar gente e bandiere con l' esempio de' precessori. nel publicar la guerra di religione, nell' impedire colle scomuniche gli appoggi ai medesimi heretici della Francia: anzi nel medesimo tempo ritardata l' elettione del re de' Romani, confortato il duca di Baviera con la lega cattolica all' unione di Francia, assistendo lo medesimo di danari e di consiglio per sostenersi in corpo separato. [See text.] Il papa si lagna d' esser tenuto eretico et amatore di buoni progressi de' protestanti, come tal volta in effetto non li ebbe discari." The Pope complains that he is considered a heretic, and accused of delighting in the good progress made by Protestants; and in fact, they are sometimes not unwelcome to him.

that the declaration of his holiness might still produce the most important effects, that it was not yet altogether impossible to drive back the King of Sweden, who had not more than 30,000 men.

The pontiff replied with cold pedantry, " With 30,000 men Alexander conquered the world."

He maintained that the war was not one of religion, that it related to matters of state only, and, besides, that the papal treasury was exhausted, and he could do nothing.

The members of the Curia and the inhabitants of Rome were amazed. " Amid the conflagration of Catholic churches and monasteries "—thus it was they expressed themselves—" the Pope stands cold and rigid as ice. The King of Sweden has more zeal for his Lutheranism than the holy father for the only true and saving Catholic faith."

The Spaniards proceeded once more to a protestation: as Olivarez had formerly appeared before Sixtus V, so did Cardinal Borgia now present himself to Urban VIII for the purpose of solemnly protesting against the conduct of his holiness. The scene that followed was even more violent than that of the earlier occasion. While the Pope gave way to ebullitions of rage, the cardinals present took part either with one party or the other, and the ambassador was obliged to content himself with delivering his protest in writing.[3] But the zealously Catholic party were not satisfied with this; the thought immediately arose of summoning a council in opposition to the Pope, and was more particularly promoted by Cardinal Ludovisio, nephew of the preceding pontiff.[4]

But what a fire would have been kindled by this proceeding! The course of events was already taking a direction that left no doubt as to their nature, and which must of necessity determine the papal policy to a different character.

Urban VIII flattered himself for some time that the King of Sweden would form a treaty of neutrality with Bavaria, and would reinstate the ecclesiastical princes who had fled their territories ; but it soon became evident that all attempts to recon-

---

[3] " In which," says Cardinal Cecchini, in his autobiography, " it was concluded that all the injuries inflicted on Christendom by these present troubles would be attributable to the negligence of the Pope." See Appendix, No. 121.

[4] Aluise Contarini speaks of " the ear they lent in Spain to Ludovisio's intimations and attempts to procure a council."

cile interests so directly at variance must of necessity be utterly
vain. The Swedish arms pressed onward to Bavaria; Tilly
fell, Munich was taken, and Duke Bernard advanced toward
the Tyrol.

It was now no longer possible to doubt of what the Pope
and Catholicism had to expect from the Swedes. How completely was the state of things changed in a moment! The
Catholics had been hoping to restore the Protestant endowments of North Germany to Catholicism, and now the King
of Sweden was forming his plans for changing the South German bishoprics that had fallen into his hand into secular principalities; he was already speaking of his Duchy of Franconia,
and seemed to intend establishing his royal court at Augsburg.
Two years before, the Pope had been dreading the arrival of
the Austrians in Italy, and had been threatened with an attack
on Rome; now the Swedes were appearing on the Italian borders: and with the name of the King of the Swedes and Goths,
borne by Gustavus Adolphus, were associated recollections that
were now revived in the minds of both parties.[5]

Section VI.—Restoration of a Balance between the Two Confessions

I will not enter into the details of that struggle which for
sixteen years longer extended over Germany; let it suffice
that we have made ourselves aware of the means by which
the mighty advance of Catholicism, which was on the point of
taking possession of Germany (*unser Vaterland*) forever, was
at once arrested in its course; was opposed, when preparing to
annihilate the Protestant faith at its sources, by a victorious
resistance. It may be remarked generally that Catholicism,
considered as one body, was not able to support its own victories; the head of that Church himself believed it imperative
on him to oppose, from political motives, those very powers by
whom his spiritual authority was most effectually defended and
enlarged. It was by Catholics, acting in concert with the
Pope, that the yet unsubdued powers of Protestantism were
called forth, and that the path was prepared for their progress.

[5] Yet Aluise Contarini assures us that the opinion still prevails that his holiness regrets the death of the King of Sweden, and that he liked better, or, to speak more accurately, that he feared less, to hear of progress on the Protestant side than on that of the Austrians.

Purposes of so vast a magnitude as those formed by Gustavus Adolphus when at the climax of his prosperity could not indeed be carried into execution after the early death of that prince, and for the obvious cause that the successes of Protestantism were by no means to be attributed to its own unaided power. But neither could Catholicism, even when its forces were more closely combined—when Bavaria had again made common cause with the Emperor, and when Urban VIII once more contributed subsidies—find strength that should suffice for the overpowering of the Protestant faith.

This conviction soon gained prevalence, at least in Germany, and was indeed the main cause of the Treaty of Prague. The Emperor suffered his edict of restitution to drop, while the Elector of Saxony and the States in alliance with him resigned all thought of restoring the Protestant faith in the hereditary dominions (*Erblanden*).

It is true that Pope Urban opposed himself to all that should be determined in opposition to the edict of restitution, and in the Emperor's spiritual council he had the Jesuits, and particularly Father Lamormain, on his side: the latter was sufficiently extolled for that reason as " a worthy confessor—a man regardless of all temporal considerations ";[1] but the majority was against him. The Capuchins, Quiroga and Valerian, with the cardinals Dietrichstein and Pazmany, maintained that, provided the Catholic religion were kept pure in the hereditary dominions, liberty of conscience might be safely granted in the empire. The Peace of Prague was proclaimed from every pulpit in Vienna. The Capuchins boasted of their part in this " honorable and holy work " ; they instituted special solemnities for the occasion; it was with difficulty that the nuncio prevented them from singing a Te Deum.[2]

[1] " Lettera del Cardl. Barberino al nuntio Baglione, 17 Marzo, 1635." " This being the action of a noble Christian, and the worthy confessor of a pious Emperor, for he has acted more with regard to heaven than earth."

[2] From the correspondence of Baglioni, which is extracted in the sixth volume of Nicoletti, as, for example, April 14, 1635, we find " Count Oñate one day said that the King of Spain would positively have given no aid to the Emperor, but on condition of peace with Saxony; at which the nuncio, marvelling, replied that the piety of the Catholic King required him to give those aids more abundantly if there were no peace, and ought to be disturbed at peace with heretics, applying itself only to thoughts of universal peace among Catholic princes. Fulli replied that so it would have happened if the war had been for the salvation of souls, and not for the recovery of ecclesiastical wealth; and Father Quiroga added that the Emperor had been cheated by those who had persuaded him to issue the edict of restitution—meaning the Jesuits, who had done all for their own interest; but the nuncio remarking that their persuasion had been from good motives, Father Quiroga became

Now Urban VIII, although in practice he had contributed so largely to the defeat of all the plans formed by Catholicism, yet in theory he would not relinquish any portion of his claims; but all he effected was to place the popedom in a position removed from the living and actual interests of the world. This is rendered clearly manifest by the instructions he gave to his legate Ginetti, when the latter proceeded to Cologne, at the first attempt to negotiate a general peace in the year 1636. The hands of the legate were tied, precisely in regard to all those important points on which everything was absolutely depending. One of the most urgent necessities, for example, was the restoration of the Palatinate; the legate was nevertheless enjoined to oppose the restitution of the Palatinate to a non-Catholic prince.[3] That certain concessions to Protestants in respect of ecclesiastical property were unavoidable was sufficiently obvious, even during the discussions at Prague; this truth became afterward yet more evident, but the legate was none the less exhorted " to especial zeal in guarding against the resignation of any point that might be turned to the advantage of Protestants in the matter of church property." Even the conclusion of peace with Protestant powers the Pope refused to sanction; the ambassador was commanded to withhold his support from any proposal for including the Dutch in the peace, and to oppose every cession to the Swedes (the question at that time was merely one relating to a sea-port), " the divine mercy would certainly find means for removing that nation out of Germany."

The Roman See could no longer entertain a reasonable hope of overpowering the Protestants; yet it is a striking and important fact that its own pertinacity in adhering to claims now become utterly untenable was the true though involuntary cause of making their subjugation forever impossible, and moreover rendered itself incapable of exercising any efficient influence on the relations of its own adherents to those of the Protestant faith.

so much excited that he burst into the most intemperate, nay, exorbitant language, so that the nuncio could scarcely get in a word to reprove and stop him, that he might fall into no further excesses; but Oñate went still further, saying that the Emperor could not avoid the peace with Saxony, because of the necessity he was in, and his inability to withstand so many enemies; and that he was not obliged to resign what belonged to his hereditary dominions, but only certain rights of the empire, which were but small, nor was it advisable that he should go forward at the risk of losing both one and the other."

[3] Siri, " Mercurio," ii. p. 98.

It is true that the Papal Court did not fail to send its ambassadors to the congress assembled for the negotiation of peace: to Ginetti succeeded Macchiavelli, Rosetti, and Chigi. Ginetti was reported to be very penurious, and thus to have decreased his efficiency; Macchiavelli was said to think only of obtaining rank—the qualification for a more important position; Rosetti was not acceptable to the French. It is thus that explanation has been attempted of the insignificance of their influence.[4] The truth is that the thing itself, the position which the Pope had assumed, made all effective interference on the part of the legates impossible. Chigi was able and popular, yet he accomplished nothing. A peace was concluded before his eyes, precisely of the character which the Pope had expressly condemned. The Elector-Palatine and all the exiled princes were restored. It was so far from being possible to think of the demands set forth by the edict of restitution that many Catholic endowments were absolutely secularized and given up to the Protestants. Spain resolved at length to acknowledge the independence of those rebels to Pope and King, the Hollanders. The Swedes retained a considerable portion of the empire. Even the peace which the Emperor concluded with France was such as the Curia could not approve, because it included disputations relating to Metz, Toul, and Verdun, by which the rights of Rome were infringed. The papacy found itself under the melancholy necessity of protesting. The principles which it did not possess the power of making effectual, it was at least resolved to express. But this also had been foreseen. The articles relating to ecclesiastical affairs in the Peace of Westphalia were opened by a declaration that no regard should be paid to the opposition of any person, be he whom he might, and whether of temporal or spiritual condition.[5]

By that peace the great conflict between Protestants and Catholics was at length brought to a decision, though to one very different from that proposed by the edict of restitution. Catholicism still retained immense acquisitions, since the year 1624 was assumed as the normal period, to which the condition of the respective parties was to be referred; but the Protes-

[4] Pallavicini, " Vita di Papa Alessandro VII.," MS. Appendix No. 130.   [5] Osnabrückischer Friedensschluss," art. v. § 1.

tants, on the other hand, obtained that indispensable equality which had so long been withheld. According to this principle all the relations of the empire were regulated.

How entirely vain had it moreover now become even to think of such enterprises as had formerly been ventured on, and had even succeeded!

Nay, further, the results of the contests in Germany reacted immediately on the neighboring countries.

Although the Emperor had succeeded in maintaining the Catholic faith supreme in his hereditary dominions, he was nevertheless compelled to make concessions to the Protestants of Hungary; in the year 1645, he saw himself constrained to restore to them a no inconsiderable number of churches.

And now, after the elevation attained by Sweden to a position of universal importance, was it possible that Poland should ever again think of renewing her old claims to that country? Wladislaus IV did not indeed partake the zeal of his father for conversions, and was a gracious King to the dissidents in opinion.

Even in France the Huguenots received favor from Richelieu, after they had been deprived of their political independence, and still more effectually did he support the principle of Protestantism, by continuing to wage against the predominant Catholic power, the Spanish monarchy—a war for life or death, by which it was shaken even to its foundations. That dissension was the only one which the Pope could have adjusted altogether without scruple. But while all other discords were effectually composed, this remained unappeased, and continued to convulse the bosom of the Catholic world.

Until the Peace of Westphalia, the Dutch had continually taken the most successful part in the war against Spain. This was the golden age of their power, as well as of their wealth; but when laboring to attain to preponderance in the East, they came at once into violent contact with the progress of the Catholic missions.

It was only in England that Catholicism, or at least something analogous to that faith in its outward forms, seemed at times on the point of finding admission. Ambassadors from the English Court were at this time to be found in Rome, and papal agents in England. The Queen, to whom a sort of official recog-

nition was accorded in Rome,[6] possessed an influence over her
husband which seemed likely to extend even to religion; an
approach had already been made in many of the church ceremonies to the usages of Catholicism.   But from all these things
there resulted the very reverse of what might have been expected.   It can scarcely be supposed that Charles I ever dis-
sented in his heart from the tenets of Protestantism; but even
those slight approaches which he permitted himself to make to
the Catholic ritual were decisive of his ruin.   It seemed as if the
violent excitement which had produced such long-continued,
unremitting, and universal conflicts in the Protestant world at
large had become concentrated in the English Puritans.   Vainly
did Ireland struggle to escape from their domination, and to or-
ganize itself in the spirit of Catholicism; the subjection of the
country was but rendered the more complete by these efforts.
In the aristocracy and commons of England a secular power
was formed and matured, the rise of which marked a revival of
Protestantism throughout Europe.

By these events, limits were imposed at once and forever
to the extension of Catholicism, which has now its appointed
and definite bounds: that universal conquest formerly projected
could never more be seriously contemplated.

A direction had indeed been taken in the intellectual development of the world which rendered any such attempt impossible.

The preponderance had been obtained by impulses endan-
gering the higher principle of unity; the religious element was
repressed—political views and motives ruled the world.

For it was not by themselves that the Protestants were delivered.   It was by the schism established in the bosom of Catholicism that they were enabled to recover themselves.   In the year
1631 we find the two great Catholic powers in league with the
Protestants—France confessedly so, Spain at least covertly.   It
is certain that the Spaniards had at that period formed relations
of amity with the French Huguenots.

[6] Nani, " Relatione di Roma, 1640."
" Communication is held with the
Queen of England by the Ministers.
Offices and gifts of courtesy also pass;
nomination of cardinals is likewise conceded to her Majesty as to other sovereigns.—Spada, " Relatione della nun-
ziatura di Francia, 1641." Count Rosetti, resident in that kingdom, attends
carefully to the orders of Cardl. Barberini, the protector, which orders are
full of the earnest zeal of his eminence."
See Appendix, Nos. 117, 118.

But the Protestants were not more perfectly united among themselves than the Catholics. Not only did the Lutherans and the Reformed, or Calvinists, contend with each other—that they had done from time immemorial—but the different sects of Calvinists, although, beyond all doubt, they had a common cause to battle for, yet proceeded to attack each other during this war. The naval power of the French Huguenots was broken solely by the support which their ancient allies and brethren in the faith had been induced to afford to the crown of France.

Even the supreme chief of Catholicism, the Pope of Rome, who had hitherto directed the attacks on the Protestants, finally placed the higher interest of the spiritual authority in abeyance, and took part against those who had labored most zealously for the restoration of the Catholic faith; he proceeded in accordance with the views of a secular sovereignty only, and returned to that line of policy which had been abandoned from the time of Paul III. It will be remembered that Protestantism in the earlier half of the sixteenth century was indebted for its progress to nothing so much as to the political labors of the popes. It was to these, so far as human judgment can decide, that Protestantism now owed its deliverance and confirmed strength.

And this example could not fail to produce an effect on the remaining powers; even German Austria, which had so long preserved itself immovable in its orthodoxy, at length adopted a similar policy; the position assumed by that country, after the Peace of Westphalia, was based on its intimate connection with North Germany, England, and Holland.

If we now attempt to investigate the more remote causes of this phenomenon, we should seek them erroneously in the depression or decay of religious impulses. We must, I think, look elsewhere for the first cause and the significance of the fact.

In the first place, the great spiritual contest had completed its operation on the minds of men.

Christianity in earlier times had been rather a matter of implicit surrender and acquiescence, of simple acceptation, of faith undisturbed by a doubt; it was now become an affair of conviction—of conscious and deliberate adoption. It was a point of high moment that men had to choose between the different confessions—that they could reject, abjure, or pass from one to the other. The individual man became the subject of direct appeal;

his freedom of judgment was called into action. Thence it followed that Christian ideas became more closely intertwined with and penetrated more deeply into every portion of life and thought.

To this must be added another momentous consideration.

It is perfectly true that the prevalence of internal dissension disturbed the unity of the collective faith; but, if we do not deceive ourselves, it is another law of life, that this circumstance prepared the way for a yet higher and more extended development of the human mind.

In the pressure of the universal strife, religion was adopted by the nations, after the different modifications of its dogmatic forms; the system thus chosen had blended with and been fused into the feeling of nationality—had become, as it were, a possession of the community of the State, or of the people. It had been won by force of arms, was maintained amidst a thousand perils, and had become part and parcel of the national life.

Thence it has happened that the States on both sides have formed themselves into great ecclesiastico-political bodies, whose individuality was characterized on the Catholic part by the measure of their devotion to the Roman See, and their toleration or exclusion of non-Catholics; but still more decidedly on the Protestant side, where the departure from the symbolical books appealed to as tests, the mingling of the Lutheran and Calvinistic confessions, with the nearer or more remote approximation to the episcopal constitution, presented the groundworks of so many clear and manifest distinctions. The first question in regard to every country is, what form of religion is predominant there? Christianity appears under manifold aspects. However striking the contrasts presented by these, no one party can dispute with another its possession of that which forms the basis to the faith of all. These various forms are, on the contrary, guaranteed by compacts and treaties of peace, in which all have part, and which form what may be called the fundamental laws of a universal republic. The idea of exalting one or the other confession to supremacy of dominion can never more be entertained. All must now be referred to the question, of how each State, each people, may best be enabled to develop its energies, while proceeding from its own religious and political principles. On this depends the future condition of the world.